Essential Writings of Christian Mysticism
Medieval Mystic Paths to God

by Jacob Boehme and Meister Eckhart

Red and Black Publishers, St Petersburg, Florida

The Signature of all Things, published EP Dutton, New York, 1912
Sermons by Meister Eckhart, Claud Field, Trans, published 1909
The Cloud of Unknowing, Evelyn Underhill, Ed, published 1922

Library of Congress Cataloging-in-Publication Data

Essential writings of Christian mysticism : medieval mystic paths to God / by Jacob Boehme and Meister Eckhart.
   p. cm.
 ISBN 978-1-934941-92-8
 I. Böhme, Jakob, 1575-1624. De signatura rerum. English. II. Eckhart, Meister, d. 1327. Sermons. English. Selections. III. Cloud of unknowing. English.
 BV5082.3.E8813 2010
 248.2'2--dc22
                                                 2010018900

Red and Black Publishers, PO Box 7542, St Petersburg, Florida, 33734
Contact us at: info@RedandBlackPublishers.com
   Printed and manufactured in the United States of America

Contents

Editor's Preface   5
The Signature of All Things, by Jacob Boehme   11
Sermons, by Meister Eckhart   209
Thee Cloud of Unknowing, by Anonymous   235

Editor's Preface

"God became human so that man might become God." — Athanasius of Alexandria

Christian mysticism

The origins of Christian mysticism go back to the very beginnings of Christianity. From the earliest days, devoted seekers have searched for "theosis", or union with God. These mystics pursue the goal of Christ himself — to become a "son of God", reaching unity with the Holy Spirit so that God Himself may be seen directly, face to face. God, the mystics say, dwells in the heart of all Christians. While most view God "through a glass, darkly" (I Corinthians 13:12), the mystics wish to remove the obscuring glass and experience God directly.

In many ways, Christian mysticism is similar to the Asian mystic traditions, such as Zen, Taoism and Buddhism. Indeed, most mystics would declare that these traditions all have the same goal — unity with the Divine — and that each merely uses different symbolisms and paths to reach that goal. As the Chinese Taoists say, "There are many paths to climb a mountain. But once you reach the top, the view is the same for everyone."

Christian mysticism bases itself on several Biblical passages. The most often cited verse is John 3:2—"Beloved, now we are the sons of God, and it doth appear that we shall be; but we know that, when he shall appear, we shall be like him; for we shall see him as he is." Another prominent passage is Galatians 2:20—"I am crucified with Christ; nevertheless I live; yet not I, but Christ liveth in me, and the life which I now live in the flesh, I live by the faith of the Son of God, who loved me, and gave himself for me."

Unlike the Biblical literalist fundamentalists, the mystics view the Bible as poetic and symbolic, as a map that points the way inside one's own soul. Like a Zen koan, these words might appear paradoxical or nonsensical, yet to one who has understanding, they are wonderfully transparent. To all mystics, the direct experience of the Divine cannot be described in words—words may help others find the beginning of the path, but the words cannot be understood completely without experiencing the things they describe. Mysticism is, above all, nonverbal awareness.

And because mysticism is an individual journey, and does not require any outside authority, it often leads to direct conflict with organized religion and church authorities. Rare indeed is the Christian mystic who has not been condemned, excommunicated, or executed by the organized church.

The Christian mystic path has been described as having three steps. The first step is the loss of egoism. To see God, the mystic must learn to stop seeing with his own eyes, and learn to see with God's eyes. This involves the loss of selfish or self-centered desires and outlooks. Through prayer and faith, the mystic expands his love from merely himself to all his surroundings, and thus gives up his own desires, and focuses on the larger picture around him and his place within it. The Bible says we must "put to death the deeds of the flesh by the Holy Spirit" (Romans 8:13).

The second step is sensing the Divine. Through contemplation, illumination, and what can only be described weakly as "visions", the mystic begins to see the workings of God in all his surroundings. God is everywhere, the mystics say, if we are only willing to look. In many cases, this insight comes quite suddenly as the result of some apparently random thing—an experience the Zen refer to as "*satori*".

The third and final step is unity with God. In this transendent state, God and individual are no longer separate, but the individual soul, as with everything else in Creation, becomes just another facet of

God. "God is love", says the Bible, "and he who abides in love abides in God, and God in him" (John 4:16). This "theosis" is the highest goal of Christian mysticism.

Jacob Boehme

"When thou art gone forth wholly from the creation, and art become nothing to all that is nature and creature, then thou art in that eternal one, which is God himself, and then thou shalt perceive and feel the highest virtue of love. Also, that I said whosoever findeth it findeth nothing and all things; that is also true, for he findeth a supernatural, supersensual Abyss, having no ground, where there is no place to dwell in; and he findeth also nothing that is like it, and therefore it may be compared to nothing, for it is deeper than anything, and is as nothing to all things, for it is not comprehensible; and because it is nothing, it is free from all things, and it is that only Good, which a man cannot express or utter what it is. But that I lastly said, he that findeth it, findeth all things, is also true; it hath been the beginning of all things, and it ruleth all things. If thou findest it, thou comest into that ground from whence all things proceed, and wherein they subsist, and thou art in it a king over all the works of God." – Jacob Boehme, *The Way to Christ*

Jacob Boehme was born in Germany in 1575, the son of a peasant farmworker. As a young boy, he was apprenticed to a shoemaker and, at the age of 17, he travelled to Gorlitz and set up his own shop there.

Although unschooled and entirely self-taught, Boehme took up an interest in religion, and began to study the Bible as well as the writings of the Christian mystics Paracelsus and Weigel. In 1600, Boehme had his "*satori*" moment, when he happened to see a beam of sunlight reflecting off a polished pewter dish. In 1612, Boehme wrote a short manuscript about his mystic insights, which he circulated among friends. Although unfinished and never intended for publication, a copy was obtained by a local nobleman, who had it printed under the title *Aurora*. When the local Lutheran pastor read a copy, he condemned it as heresy and threatened to exile Boehme if he did not stop writing such "poison".

The threat was enough to stop Boehme, but only temporarily. By 1924, his first complete work was published, a collection of short essays titled *The Way to Christ*. Once again, the local church reacted, and Boehme was dragged before the Town Council and ordered into exile. He went to stay with a sympathetic nobleman named von Schweinitz, where he wrote a number of books, including *The Signature of All Things*, and soon had a number of followers across Europe, known as Behmanites.

To protect himself from church authorities, many of his writings were couched in obscure astrological and alchemist symbolism, which made them all but impenetrable to outsiders. In Boehme's symbolism, God is depicted as Fire, Christ is depicted as Light, and the Holy Spirit is depicted as "the Living Principle" or "the Divine Life".

Several mystical themes run through Boehme's works. Humans, Boehme pointed out, had originally a unity with God, living with the Divine in a state of grace. It was selfish ego desires, in the form of Satan's rebellion, that broke this unity, and led to the separation of man from God. The goal of both God and Man, then, is to reform that original unity by giving up ego-centered desires.

In Boehme's view, the Creation itself was an attempt by God to become more self-aware, by providing Himself with an opportunity to interact with an entity that was part of God, but also distinct and independent of God. The most profound level of this interaction comes with humans, who are made in the "image of God". By giving free will to humanity, God gave Himself a unique opportunity to learn about Himself by interacting with an entity that was very much like Himself. Because of this, Boehme concludes, all individual humans have the capacity to see and understand God, so that God can better see and understand Himself.

In the birth of Christ, Boehme further concludes, God chose to Himself become a part of his Creation, and takes on all the sufferings and challenges that the rest of Creation labors under. But Christ, who is both human and divine, shows that unity with God is possible for humans, and that this unity leads to the end of suffering. Boehme also points to the example of Mary, who, though human, is chosen by God to become the vehicle of the Divine. God, Boehme concludes, must be reborn inside each of us, as He was within Mary.

In November 1624, Boehme, dying of an intestinal disease, travelled home to Gorlitz, where the church refused to give him the Sacraments until after a long interrogation. He died a few days later.

Meister Eckhart

"The Eye with which I see God is the same with which God sees me." -
- Meister Eckhart, *Sermons*

Eckhart von Hochheim, known as "Meister Eckhart", is probably the most famous of the Christian mystics.

Eckhart was born to a minor noble family in Thuringia in around the year 1260. He joined the Dominican Order and was sent to the University of Paris in 1300. By 1307, he was the Dominican vicar-general for the entire province of Bohemia. In 1311, he was appointed as a teacher at the University of Paris. Most of his *Sermons* were apparently written during that time.

Within a few years, Eckhart had become a teacher at the University of Cologne, and it was here, in 1327, that the Archbishop made charges of heresy against him. The local Dominican authorities exonerated Eckhart, but the charges were then taken all the way to the Pope. Eckhart protested that he did not intend any violations of church doctrine, and he repudiated any parts of his writings which could be viewed as heretical. Before the Pope could make a decision, Eckhart died. After Eckhart's death, the Pope issued a ruling, aimed at Eckhart's surviving followers, which concluded that some of Eckhart's statements were heretical, and some others were suspected of heresy. Eckhart's followers, however, formed a group called the Friends of God, and carefully preserved the Meister's writings and views.

Eckhart's basic message was the mystic view of the underlying unity between God and Man. His *Sermons* were written at a time when there was chaos in the Catholic Church—rival Popes sat in Rome and in Avignon and fought over doctrinal authority, the Inquisition was everywhere, and the Dominican and Franciscan Orders examined each other for heresy. In response, a large number of lay groups, not connected with the church hierarchy, began appearing, in which ordinary people tried to find their way through the theological minefield. It was to these lay groups that Eckhart wrote his *Sermons*. The *Sermons* were written in vernacular German rather than the Latin used by the educated church hierarchy, and they were intended to be practical straightforward messages whereby people could give up their attachment to the world and see the

Godhead within themselves, free from all the current theological and political conflicts and controversies.

Many modern scholars have compared Eckhart's views to those of Buddhism and Taoism.

The Cloud of Unknowing

"And so I urge you, go after experience rather than knowledge. On account of pride, knowledge may often deceive you, but this gentle, loving affection will not deceive you. Knowledge tends to breed conceit, but love builds." – The Book of Privy

The author of *The Cloud of Unknowing* is unknown. The manuscript, written in Middle English, appeared throughout Europe in the second half of the 14th century. Because of literary and thematic similarities, it is believed that the same anonymous author also produced a somewhat later manuscript, titled *The Book of Privy Counseling*, and may also have written a number of shorter *Epistles*.

The Cloud of Unknowing emphasizes a theme which is also present in other mystic works—the insufficiency of words. The mystic experience is above all experiential—the Divine, being beyond human logic and beyond the capacity of intellectual reasoning, cannot be understood logically or rationally, and cannot be adequately expressed with our limited language. "If it could be talked about," say the Taoists, "everyone would already have told his brother." The only way to understand the Divine is to experience it directly. To attain freedom from the illusions of the intellect, one must discard the use of logic, words and rational categorizing, and intuitively grasp reality with your entire being.

The Cloud of Unknowing, then, is a collection of prayers, meditations, and rituals, all of which are designed to quiet the mind and allow the student to experience the Divine directly, without allowing the intellect to interfere. We understand God by seeing Him and experiencing unity with Him, not by reading about Him. The author of *The Cloud of Unknowing* points out the crucial difference between "God" and "A Book About God".

The Signature of All Things
by Jacob Boehme

Chapter I
How That All Whatever Is Spoken Of God Without The Knowledge Of The Signature Is Dumb And Without Understanding; And That In The Mind Of Man The Signature Lies Very Exactly Composed According To The Essence Of All Essences

1. All whatever is spoken, written, or taught of God, without the knowledge of the signature is dumb and void of understanding; for it proceeds only from an historical conjecture, from the mouth of another, wherein the spirit without knowledge is dumb; but if the spirit opens to him the signature, then he understands the speech of another; and further, he understands how the spirit has manifested and revealed itself (out of the essence through the principle) in the sound with the voice. For though I see one to speak, teach, preach, and write of God, and though I hear and read the same, yet this is not sufficient for me to understand him; but if his sound and spirit out of his signature and similitude enter into my own similitude, and imprint his similitude into mine, then I may understand him really and fundamentally, be it either spoken or written, if he has the hammer that can strike my bell.

2. By this we know, that all human properties proceed from one; that they all have but one only root and mother; otherwise one man could not understand another in the sound, for with the sound or speech the form notes and imprints itself into the similitude of another; a like tone or sound catches and moves another, and in the sound the spirit imprints its own similitude, which it has conceived in the essence, and brought to form in the principle.

3. So that in the word may be understood in what the spirit has conceived, either in good or evil; and with this signature he enters into another man's form, and awakens also in the other such a form in the signature; so that both forms mutually assimilate together in one form, and then there is one comprehension, one will, one spirit, and also one understanding.

4. And then secondly we understand, that the signature or form is no spirit, but the receptacle, container, or cabinet of the spirit, wherein it lies; for the signature stands in the essence, and is as a lute that liest still, and is indeed a dumb thing that is neither heard or understood; but if it be played upon, then its form is understood, in what form and tune it stands, and according to what note it is set. Thus likewise the signature of nature in its form is a dumb essence; it is as a prepared instrument of music, upon which the will's spirit plays; what strings he touches, they sound according to their property.

5. In the human mind the signature lies most artificially composed, according to the essence of all essences; and man wants nothing but the wise master that can strike his instrument, which is the true spirit of the high might of eternity; if that be quickened in man, that it stirs and acts in the centre of the mind, then it plays on the instrument of the human form, and even then the form is uttered with the sound in the word: As his instrument was set in the time of his incarnation, so it sounds, and so is his knowledge; the inward manifests itself in the sound of the word, for that is the mind's natural knowledge of itself.

6. Man has indeed all the forms of all the three worlds lying in him; for he is a complete image of God, or of the Being of all beings; only the order is placed in him at his incarnation; for there are three work-masters in him which prepare his form or signature, viz. the threefold fiat, according to the three worlds; and they are in contest about the form, and the form is figured according to the contest; which of the masters holds the predominant rule, and obtains it in the

essence, according to that his instrument is tuned, and the other lie hid, and come behind with their sound, as it plainly shews itself.

7. So soon as man is born into this world, his spirit plays upon his instrument, so that his innate genuine form or signature in good or evil is seen by his words and conversation; for as his instrument sounds, accordingly the senses and thoughts proceed from the essence of the mind, and so the external spirit of the will is carried in its behaviour, as is to be seen both in men and beasts; that there is a great difference in the procreation, that one brother and sister does not as the other.

8. Further we are to know, that though one fiat thus keeps the upper hand, and figures the form according to itself, that yet the other two give their sound, if their instrument be but played upon; as it is seen that many a man, and also many a beast, though it is very much inclined either to good or evil, yet it is moved either to evil or good by a contrary tune, and often lets its inbred signature or figure fall, when the contrary tune is played upon his hidden lute or form: As we see that an evil man is often moved by a good man to repent of and cease from his iniquity, when the good man touches and strikes his hidden instrument with his meek and loving spirit.

9. And thus also it happens to the good man, that when the wicked man strikes his hidden instrument with the spirit of his wrath, that then the form of anger is stirred up also in the good man, and the one is set against the other, that so one might be the cure and healer of the other. For as the vital signature, that is, as the form of life is figured in the time of the fiat at the conception, even so is its natural spirit; for it takes its rise out of the essence of all the three principles, and such a will it acts and manifests out of its property.

10. But now the will may be broken; for when a stronger comes, and raises his inward signature with his introduced sound and will's spirit, then its upper dominion loses the power, right, and authority; which we see in the powerful influence of the sun, how that by its strength it qualifies a bitter and sour fruit, turning it into a sweetness and pleasantness; in like manner how a good man corrupts among evil company, and also how that a good herb cannot sufficiently shew its real genuine virtue in a bad soil; for in the good man the hidden evil instrument is awakened, and in the herb a contrary essence is received from the earth; so that often the good is changed into an evil, and the evil into a good.

11. And now observe, as it stands in the power and predominance of the quality, so it is signed and marked externally in its outward form, signature, or figure; man in his speech, will, and behaviour, also with the form of the members which he has, and must use to that signature, his inward form is noted in the form of his face; and thus also is a beast, an herb, and the trees; everything as it is inwardly in its innate virtue and quality so it is outwardly signed; and though it falls out, that often a thing is changed from evil into good, and from good into evil, yet it has its external character, that the good or evil that is, the change may be known.

12. For man is known herein by his daily practice, also by his course and discourse; for the upper instrument, which is most strongly drawn, is always played upon: Thus also it is with a beast that is wild, but when it is overawed and tamed, and brought to another property, it does not easily shew its first innate form, unless it be stirred up, and then it breaks forth, and appears above all other forms.

13. Thus it is likewise with the herbs of the earth; if an herb be transplanted out of a bad soil into a good, then it soon gets a stronger body, and a more pleasant smell and power, and shews the inward essence externally; and there is nothing that is created or born in nature, but it also manifests its internal form externally, for the internal continually labours or works itself forth to manifestation: As we know it in the power and form of this world, how the one only essence has manifested itself with the external birth in the desire of the similitude, how it has manifested itself in so many forms and shapes, which we see and know in the stars and elements, likewise in the living creatures, and also in the trees and herbs.

14. Therefore the greatest understanding lies in the signature, wherein man (viz. the image of the greatest virtue) may not only learn to know himself, but therein also he may learn to know the essence of all essences; for by the external form of all creatures, by their instigation, inclination and desire, also by their sound, voice, and speech which they utter, the hidden spirit is known; for nature has given to everything its language according to its essence and form, for out of the essence the language or sound arises, and the fiat of that essence forms the quality of the essence in the voice or virtue which it sends forth, to the animals in the sound, and to the essentials in smell, virtue, and form.

15. Everything has its mouth to manifestation; and this is the language of nature, whence everything speaks out of its property, and continually manifests, declares, and sets forth itself for what it is good or profitable; for each thing manifests its mother, which thus gives the essence and the will to the form.

Chapter II
Of The Opposition And Combat In The Essence Of All Essences, Whereby The Ground Of The Antipathy And Sympathy In Nature May Be Seen, And Also The Corruption And Cure Of Each Thing

1. Seeing then there are so many and diverse forms, that the one always produces and affords out of its property a will different in one from another, we herein understand the contrariety and combat in the Being of all beings, how that one does oppose, poison, and kill another, that is, overcome its essence, and the spirit of the essence, and introduces it into another form, whence sickness and pains arise, when one essence destroys another.

2. And then we understand herein the cure, how the one heals another, and brings it to health; and if this were not, there were no nature, but an eternal stillness, and no will; for the contrary will makes the motion, and the original of the seeking, that the opposite sound seeks the rest, and yet in the seeking it only elevates and more enkindles itself.

3. And we are to understand how the cure of each thing consists in the assimilate; for in the assimilate arises the satisfaction of the will, viz. its highest joy; for each thing desires a will of its likeness, and by the contrary will it is discomfited; but if it obtains a will of its likeness, it rejoices in the assimilate, and therein falls into rest, and the enmity is turned into joy.

4. For the eternal nature has produced nothing in its desire, except a likeness out of itself; and if there were not an everlasting mixing, there would be an eternal peace in nature, but so nature would not be revealed and made manifest, in the combat it becomes manifest; so that each thing elevates itself, and would get out of the combat into the still rest, and so it runs to and fro, and thereby only awakens and stirs up the combat.

5. And we find clearly in the light of nature, that there is no better help and remedy for this opposition, and that it has no higher cure

than the liberty, that is, the light of nature, which is the desire of the spirit.

6. And then we find, that the essence cannot be better remedied than with the assimilate; for the essence is a being, and its desire is after being: Now every taste desires only its like, and if it obtains it, then its hunger is satisfied, appeased and eased, and it ceases to hunger, and rejoices in itself, whereby the sickness falls into a rest in itself; for the hunger of the contrariety ceases to work.

7. Seeing now that man's life consists in three principles, viz. in a threefold essence, and has also a threefold spirit out of the property of each essence, viz. first, according to the eternal nature, according to the fire's property; and secondly, according to the property of the eternal light and divine essentiality; and thirdly, according to the property of the outward world: Thereupon we are to consider the property of this threefold spirit, and also of this threefold essence and will; how each spirit with its essence introduces itself into strife and sickness, and what its cure and remedy is.

8. We understand that without nature there is an eternal stillness and rest, viz. the Nothing; and then we understand that an eternal will arises in the nothing, to introduce the nothing into something, that the will might find, feel, and behold itself.

9. For in the nothing the will would not be manifest to itself, wherefore we know that the will seeks itself, and finds itself in itself, and its seeking is a desire, and its finding is the essence of the desire, wherein the will finds itself.

10. It finds nothing except only the property of the hunger, which is itself, which it draws into itself, that is, draws itself into itself, and finds itself in itself; and its attraction into itself makes an overshadowing or darkness in it, which is not in the liberty, viz. in the nothing; for the will of the liberty overshadows itself with the essence of the desire, for the desire makes essence and not the will.

11. Now that the will must be in darkness is its contrariety, and it conceives in itself another will to go out from the darkness again into the liberty, viz. into the nothing, and yet it cannot reach the liberty from without itself, for the desire goes outwards, and causes source and darkness; therefore the will (understand the reconceived will) must enter inwards, and yet there is no separation.

12. For in itself before the desire is the liberty, viz. the nothing, and the will may not be a nothing, for it desires to manifest in the nothing; and yet no manifestation can be effected, except only

through the essence of the desire; and the more the reconceived will desires manifestation, the more strongly and eagerly the desire draws into itself, and makes in itself three forms, viz. the desire, which is astringent, and makes hardness, for it is an enclosing, when coldness arises, and the attraction causes compunction, and stirring in the hardness, an enmity against the attracted hardness; the attraction is the second form, and a cause of motion and life, and stirs itself in the astringency and hardness, which the hardness, viz. the enclosing, cannot endure, and therefore it attracts more eagerly to hold the compunction, and yet the compunction is thereby only the stronger.

13. Thus the compunction willeth upwards, and whirls crossways, and yet cannot effect it, for the hardness, viz. the desire stays and detains it, and therefore it stands like a triangle, and transverted orb, which (seeing it cannot remove from the place) becomes wheeling, whence arises the mixture in the desire, viz. the essence, or multiplicity of the desire; for the turning makes a continual confusion and contrition, whence the anguish, viz. the pain, the third form (or sting of sense) arises.

14. But seeing the desire, viz. the astringency becomes only the more strong thereby (for from the stirring arises the wrath and nature, viz. the motion), the first will to the desire is made wholly austere and a hunger, for it is in a hard compunctive dry essence, and also cannot get rid and quit of it, for itself makes the essence, and likewise possesses it, for thus it finds itself now out of nothing in the something, and the something is yet its contrary will, for it is an unquietness, and the free-will is a stillness.

15. This is now the original of enmity, that nature opposes the free-will, and a thing is at enmity in itself; and here we understand the centre of nature with three forms, in the original, viz. in the first principle, it is Spirit; in the second it is Love, and in the third principle Essence; and these three forms are called in the third principle Sulphur, Mercury, and Sal.

16. Understand it thus: Sul is in the first principle the freewill, or the lubet in the nothing to something, it is in the liberty without nature; Phur is the desire of the free lubet, and makes in itself, in the Phur, viz. in the desire, an essence, and this essence is austere by reason of the attraction, and introduces itself into three forms (as is above mentioned) and so forward into the fourth form, viz. into the fire; in the Phur the original of the eternal and also external nature is understood, for the hardness is a mother of the sharpness of all

essences, and a preserver of all essences; out of the Sul, viz. out of the lubet of the liberty, the dark anguish becomes a shining light; and in the third principle, viz. in the outward kingdom, Sul is the oil of nature, wherein the life burns, and everything grows.

17. But now the Phur, viz. the desire, is not divided from Sul; it is one word, one original also, and one essence, but it severs itself into two properties, viz. into joy and sorrow, light and darkness; for it makes two worlds, viz. a dark fire-world in the austereness, and a light fire-world in the lubet of the liberty; for the lubet of the liberty is the only cause that the fire shines, for the original fire is dark and black, for in the shining of the fire in the original the Deity is understood, and in the dark fire, viz. in the anguish-source, the original of nature is understood, and herein we do further understand the cure.

18. The source is the cure of the free lubet, viz. of the still eternity; for the stillness finds itself alive therein, it brings itself through the anguish-source into life, viz. into the kingdom of joy, namely that the nothing is become an eternal life, and has found itself, which cannot be in the stillness.

19. Secondly, we find that the Sul, viz. the lubet of the liberty, is the curer of the desire, viz. of the anxious nature: for the lustre of the liberty does again (from the enkindled fire out of nature) shine in the dark anguish, and fills or satiates the anguish with the liberty, whereby the wrath extinguishes, and the turning orb stands still, and instead of the turning a sound is caused in the essence.

20. This is now the form of the spiritual life, and of the essential life; Sul is the original of the joyful life, and Phur is the original of the essential life; the lubet is before and without nature, which is the true Sul; and the spirit is made manifest in nature, viz. through the source, and that in a twofold form, viz. according to the lubet of the liberty in a source of joy, and according to the anxious desire's lubet; according to the astringency, compunctive, bitter, and envious from the compunction, and according to the anguish of the wheel wholly murderous and hateful; and each property dwells in itself, and yet they are in one another; herein God's love and anger are understood, they dwell in each other; and the one apprehends not the other, and yet the one is the curer of the other; understand through imagination, for the eternal is magical.

21. The second form in nature, in eternity is the Orb with the compunctive bitter essences: for there arises the essence, understand

with the perturbation; for the nothing is still without motion, but the perturbation makes the nothing active: but in the third principle, viz. in the dominion in the essence, and source of the outward world, the form is called Mercury, which is opposite, odious, and poisonful, and the cause of life and stirring, also the cause of the senses: Where one glance may conceive itself in the infinity, and then also immerse itself into it, where out of one only the abyssal, unsearchable, and infinite multiplicity may arise.

22. This form is the unquietness, and yet the seeker of rest; and with its seeking it causes unquietness, it makes itself its own enemy; its cure is twofold, for its desire is also twofold, viz. according to the lubet of the liberty, according to the stillness and meekness; and then also in the hunger according to the rising of unquietness, and the finding of itself; the root desires only joy with the first will, and yet it cannot obtain it, except through the opposite source, for no joy can arise in the still nothing; it must arise only through motion and elevation that the nothing finds itself.

23. Now that which is found desires to enter again into the will of the still nothing, that it may have peace and rest therein; and the nothing is its cure; and the wrath and poison is the remedy of the seeker and finder, that is their life which they find, an example whereof we have in the poisonous gall, whence in the life arises joy and sorrow, wherein we also understand a twofold will, viz. one to the wrathful fire and anxious painful life to the original of nature, and one to the light-life, viz. to the joy of nature; this takes its original out of the eternal nothing.

24. The first will's cure is the lubet of the liberty, if it obtains that, then it makes triumphant joy in itself; and the wrath in the hungry desire is the curer and helper of the other will, viz. the will of nature; and herein God's love and anger are understood, and also how evil and good are in the centre of each life, and how no joy could arise without sorrow, and how one is the curer of the other.

25. And here we understand the third will (which takes its original out of both these, viz. out of such an essence, viz. out of the mother), viz. the spirit, which has both these properties in it, and is a son of the properties and also a lord of the same; for in him consists the power, he may awaken which he pleases; the properties lie in the essence, and are as a well-constituted life, or as an instrument with many strings, which stand still; and the spirit, viz. the egress is the real life, he may play upon the instrument as he pleases, in evil or

good, according to love or anger; and as he plays, and as the instrument sounds, so is it received of its contra-tenor, viz. of the assimulate.

26. If the tune of love be played, viz. the liberty's desire, then is the sound received of the same liberty and love-lubet; for it is its pleasing relish, and agreeable to its will's desire; one similar lubet takes another.

27. And thus likewise is it to be understood of the enmity and contrary will; if the instrument be struck according to the desire to nature, viz. in the wrath, anger, and bitter falsehood, then the same contrary sound and wrathful desire receives it; for it is of its property, and a satiating of its hunger, wherein we understand the desire of the light, and also of the dark world; a twofold source and property.

28. The desire of the liberty is meek, easy, and pleasant, and it is called good; and the desire to nature makes itself in itself dark, dry, hungry, and wrathful, which is called God's anger, and the dark world, viz. the first principle; and the light world is the second principle.

29. And we are to understand, that it is no divided essence, but one holds the other hidden or closed up in it, and the one is the beginning and cause of the other, also its healing and cure; that which is awaked and stirred up, that gets dominion, and manifests itself externally with its character, and makes a form and signature according to its will in the external after itself. A similitude whereof we see in an enraged man or beast; though the outward man and beast are not in the inward world, yet the outward nature has even the same forms; for it arises originally from the inward, and stands upon the inward root.

30. The third form is the anxiousness which arises in nature from the first and second form, and is the upholder or preserver of the first and second; it is in itself the sharp fiat; and the second form has the Verbum, viz. the property to the word, and it consists in three properties, and makes out of herself with the three the fourth, viz. the fire; in the external birth, viz. in the third principle, it is called Sal, or salt, according to its matter; but in its spirit it has many forms; for it is the fire-root, the great anguish, it arises betwixt and out of the astringency and bitterness in the austere attraction; it is the essentiality of that which is attracted, viz. the corporality, or comprehensibility; from Sulphur it is of a brimstone nature, and from Mercury a blaze or flash; it is in itself painful, viz. a sharpness of

dying, and that from the sharp attraction of the astringency: It has a twofold fire, one cold, another hot; the cold arises from the astringency, from the sharp attraction, and is a dark black fire; and the hot arises from the driving forth the compunction in the anguish in the desire after the liberty, and the liberty is its enkindler, and the raging compunction is the cold's fire's awakener.

31. These three forms are in one another as one, and yet they are but one; but they sever themselves through the original into many forms, and yet they have but one mother, viz. the desiring will to manifestation, which is called the father of nature, and of the Being of all beings.

32. Now we are to consider the hunger of the anxiety, or the salt-spirit, and then also its satiating or fulfilling: The anguish has in it two wills, from the original of the first will out of the liberty to the manifestation of itself; viz. the first will is to nature, and the other reconceived will is the son of the first, which goes out of the manifestation again into itself into the liberty; for it is become an eternal life in nature, and yet possesses not nature essentially, but dwells in itself, and penetrates nature as a transparent shining, and the first will goes outwards, for it is the desire of manifestation; it seeks itself out of itself, and yet amasses the desire in itself; it desires to educe the internal out of itself.

33. Thus it has two properties; with the seeking in itself it makes the centre of nature: For it is like a poison, a will of dreadful aspiring, like a lightning and thunder-clap; for this desire desires only anguish, and to be horrible, to find itself in itself, out of the nothing in the something; and the second form proceeds forth as a flagrat, or produces sound out of itself; for it is not the desire of the first will to continue in the horrible death, but only thus to educe itself out of the nothing, and to find itself.

34. And we understand by the centre in itself, with the aspiring wrathfulness, with the wrathful will to nature, the dark world, and with the egress out of itself to manifestation, the outward world; and with the second will out of the first, which enters again into the liberty, we understand the light world, or the kingdom of joy, or the true Deity.

35. The desire of the dark world is after the manifestation, viz. after the outward world, to attract and draw the same essentiality into it, and thereby to satisfy its wrathful hunger; and the desire of the

outward world is after the essence or life, which arises from the pain and anguish.

36. Its desire in itself is the wonder of eternity, a mystery, or mirror, or what is comprehended of the first will to nature.

37. The outward world's desire is Sulphur, Mercury, and Sal; for such an essence it is in itself, viz. a hunger after itself, and is also its own satisfying; for Sul desires Phur, and Phur desires Mercury, and both these desire Sal; for Sal is their son, which they hatch in their desire, and afterwards becomes their habitation, and also food.

38. Each desire desires only the essentiality of salt according to its property; for salt is diversee; one part is sharpness of cold, and one part sharpness of heat; also one part brimstone; and one part salniter from Mercury.

39. These properties are in one another as one, but they sever themselves, each dwelling in itself; for they are of a different essence, and when one enters into another, then there is enmity, and a flagrat. A similitude whereof we may apprehend in thunder and lightning, which comes to pass when the great Anguish, viz. the mother of all salts, understand the third form of nature, impresses itself; which comes to pass from the aspect of the sun, which stirs up the hot fire's form, so that it is penetrative, as the property of the fire is; and when it reaches the salniter, then it enkindles itself; and the salniter is in itself the great flagrat in Mercury, viz. the flash, or compunction, which enters into the coldness, so also into the cold sharpness of the salt-spirit; this coldness is exceedingly dismayed at the flash of the fire, and in a trice wraps or folds up itself in itself, whence arises the thunder-clap (or the tempestuous flash, which gives a stroke in the flagrat) and the flagrat goes downwards, for it is heavy by reason of the coldness, and the sal-nitrous spirit is light by reason of the fire, which spirit carries the thunder or sound sideways, as is to be heard in tempests and thunder; presently thereupon comes the wind or spirit out of all the four forms one against another, for they are all four enkindled in the penetrating flagrat; whereupon follows hail and rain; the hail folds itself together in the coldness, in the property of the cold salt-spirit; for the wrath attracts to itself, and turns the water to ice, and the water arises from the meekness, viz. from the desire of the light, for it is the essentiality of the meekness; this the cold salt-spirit congeals into drops, and distils it upon the earth, for before the congelation it is only as a mist, or steam, or as a vapour, or damp.

40. Thus we see this ground very exactly and properly in thunder and lightning; for the flash, or lightning, or ethereal blaze, goes always before, for it is the enkindled salniter; thereupon follows the stroke in the flagrat of the coldness; as you see, as soon as the stroke is given the astringent chamber is opened, and a cool wind follows, and oftentimes whirling and wheeling; for the forms of nature are awakened, and are as a turning wheel, and so they carry their spirit the wind.

Chapter III
Of The Grand Mystery Of All Beings

1. Courteous reader, observe the meaning right; we understand not by this description a beginning of the Deity, but we shew you the manifestation of the Deity through nature; for God is without beginning, and has an eternal beginning, and an eternal end, which he is himself, and the nature of the inward world is in the like essence from eternity.

2. We give you to understand this of the divine essence; without nature God is a mystery, understand in the nothing, for without nature is the nothing, which is an eye of eternity, an abyssal eye, that stands or sees in the nothing, for it is the abyss; and this same eye is a will, understand a longing after manifestation, to find the nothing; but now there is nothing before the will, where it might find something, where it might have a place to rest, therefore it enters into itself, and finds itself through nature.

3. And we understand in the mystery without nature in the first will two forms; one to nature, to the manifestation of the wonder-eye; and the second form is produced out of the first, which is a desire after virtue and power, and is the first will's son, its desire of joyfulness. And understand us thus; the desire is egressive, and that which proceeds is the spirit of the will and desire, for it is a moving, and the desire makes a form in the spirit, viz. formings of the infinity of the mystery.

4. And this form or likeness is the eternal wisdom of the Deity; and we understand herein the Trinity of the only Deity, whose ground we must not know, how the first will arises in the abyss from eternity, which is called Father; only we know the eternal birth, and distinguish the Deity, viz. what purely and merely concerns the Deity, or the good, from nature, and shew you the arcanum of the greatest

secret mystery; namely, how the abyss, or the Deity, manifests itself with this eternal generation; for God is a spirit, and as subtle as a thought or will, and nature is his corporeal essence, understand the eternal nature; and the outward nature of this visible comprehensible world is a manifestation or external birth of the inward spirit and essence in evil and good, that is, a representation, resemblance, and typical similitude of the dark fire and light world.

5. And as we have shewn you concerning the original of thunder and lightning with the tempestuous stroke; so likewise the inward nature of the inward world is, and stands in the generation: For the outward birth takes its original from the inward; the inward birth is unapprehensible to the creature, but the outward is apprehensible to it; yet each property apprehends its mother from whence it is brought forth.

6. As the soul comprehends the inward eternal nature, and the spirit of the soul, viz. the precious image according to God, comprehends the birth of the angelical light-world, and the sidereal and elemental spirit comprehends the birth and property of the stars and elements; every eye sees into its mother from whence it was brought forth.

7. Therefore we will set down the generation of all essences out of all mothers and beginnings, how one generation proceeds from another, and how one is the cause of another, and this we will do from the eyesight of all the three mothers.

8. Let none account it impossible, seeing man is a likeness according to and in God, an image of the Being of all beings; and yet it stands not in the power of the creature, but in the might of God; for the sight and science of all essences consist alone in the clearest light.

9. We have made mention before how the external birth, viz. the essence of this world, consists in three things, viz. in Sulphur, Mercury, and Sal: Now we must set down and declare what it is, seeing that all things arise from one original, and then how its inward separation is effected, that out of one beginning many beginnings are produced; this is now to be understood, as is before mentioned, concerning the centre of all essences.

10. For Sulphur in the eternal beginning consists in two forms, and so also in the outward beginning of this world: viz. in the internal the first form, viz. the Sul consists in the eternal liberty; it is the lubet of the eternal abyss, viz. a will or an original to the desire; and the other original is the desire, which is the first motion, viz. an hunger to the

something; and in this same hunger is the eternal beginning to the pregnant nature, and it is called Sulphur, viz. a conception of the liberty, viz. of the good, and a conception or comprehension of the desire, viz. of the austere attraction in the desire.

11. Sul in the internal is God, and Phur is the nature; for it makes a spirit of the nature of brimstone, as is to be seen externally in the property of brimstone; for its substance is a dry constringent matter, and is of a painful anxious fiery property, forcing itself forth; it attracts eagerly and hardly into itself, and parches up as a dry hunger, and its painful property does eagerly and anxiously force itself forth: The cause and original is this, because it stands in two beginnings, viz. in the property of the desire, which is an attraction; and in the property of the light or liberty, which is driving forth, or pressing to the manifestation through the desire of nature.

12. The desire, viz. the attraction makes hardness, and is the cause of the fire, and the lubet is a cause of the lustre or light of the fire: Sul is light, and Phur makes fire, yet it cannot be reduced alone in Sulphur to fire and light, but in Mercury, and at last in Sal, which is the real body, but not of the brimstone, but of the essence and water: And so understand, that in the first desire, which arises in the lubet of the liberty, all things are, and are made substantial and essential, from whence the creation of this world is proceeded; and we find herein the property of the earth, so likewise of all metals and stones, and also of the astrum, and the original of the elements, all out of one only mother, which is the lubet and the desire, from whence all things proceeded and still proceed.

13. For Mercury is generated in Sulphur: It is the severing, viz. of light and darkness from one another, the breaking wheel, and cause of the various division or multiplicity: it separates the dark essentiality from the essentiality of the light, viz. the metals from the gross, astringent, dark, stony, and earthly property; for the property of the desire gives and makes dark essence, and the property of the free lubet makes light essence, viz. metals, and all of the same kind and resemblance.

14. Mercury has in the beginning of his birth three properties, viz. the trembling in the austereness, and anguish from the hard impressing of the astringent hard desire, and the expulsion of the multiplicity, viz. the essential life; for the desire attracts very hard to itself, and the attraction makes the motion, or sting of trembling or horrible compunction, and that which is impressed is the anguish; but

if the liberty be therein comprehended, it refuses it, and there arises the original of enmity, and the severing, that one form separates from another, and a twofold will arises.

15. For the lubet of the liberty does again set its desire into the stillness, viz. into the nothing, and forces again out of the darkness of the desire's austereness into itself, viz. into the liberty, without the wrath of the enmity; and so it has only sharpened itself in the austere impression in Mercury, that it is a moving feeling life, and that its liberty is sharpened so that it becomes a lustre, which is, and causes a kingdom of joy in the liberty; and so understand us, that the spirit's dominion, viz. the spirit and the essence do thus separate.

16. The essence remains in the impression, and becomes material; that is not God, but gold, or any other metal, according to the property of the first conception in the Sulphur, or stone, or earth, out of the desire's own peculiar property, all according to the first sude or seething in Mercury; for no metal can be generated without salniter, which is the flagrat in Mercury; which also becomes material in the astringent impression, and divides itself in the separation, one part into brimstone, another into salniter, and a third into a salt sharpness; whereas yet there cannot be any corporeal essence in all these, but only the spirit of the essence; the essence proceeds wholly out of the death through mortification, which is effected in the great anguish of the impressure, where there is a dying source, which is the mercurial life, where the salnitral flagrat arises as an opening, displaying flash: For the liberty, viz. the property of the eternal lubet, does there separate itself, and yet the attracted essence out of the lubet of the liberty continues all along in the comprehension of the attraction in the astringent austere dark anguish: Now if the wrath enters so vehemently into itself as to raise up the salnitral flagrat, then it apprehends the essentiality of the free lubet in itself, from whence arises the flagrat; for the wrath there apprehends the meekness, which is even as if water were poured into fire, which gives a flagrat; and then the wrath of the great anguish dies, and with the flagrat the joy ascends, and the flagrat is out of mercury, or out of the anguish of death, and becomes also material, but by reason of the liberty it changes itself into white, which is salniter: Now if the fire, viz. the horrible anxious sharpness, does again come into it, then the salniter is dismayed, and gives a repulse; for the first property which was before the death is again enkindled with the brimstone spirit; a

sufficient resemblance of which you have in gunpowder, which is the matter of these properties.

17. Further, we are to know the dying with the enkindling of the fire, all which is done in the flagrat; for it is a flagrat to death, and to life; one part immerses itself into the property of death, viz. into the wrath of the austere desire; and the other part, which is from the lubet or love-essentiality, arises up in the kingdom of joy: But seeing there happens also a mortifying in the free materia (though it is no mortifying, but a redeeming from the wrath, for the materia of the liberty will be free from the wrath), thereupon this materia falls downwards, which is water; and it is not of the property of the wrath, but the wrath holds it captive in itself; but they are separated from one another in the essence and source; the wrath's essence gives earth and stones, and the essence of the liberty is water, which arises with the enkindling of the fire through the mortification out of the meekness of the light.

18. But seeing this water does also separate itself in the salnitral flagrat, and before the salniter was all mutually enwrapt together, thereupon it obtains different properties in the separation, and there is a diversity of water; and this various diversity of properties gives in each property also a bodily or corporeal essence, all according to the first separation of mercury in sulphur, for in the mortification in the salnitral flagrat two things are effected and come forth, viz. a life, and a body of the life; understand an essential, and a lifeless senseless body, whose materia is mortified in the flagrat: Thus there is a diversity of water, and a diversity of the life, and a diversity of the body, or of the materia; as each body is, so is also its essential spirit.

19. Now we must consider this from the first original; as (1) from the lubet of the liberty; and (2) from the desire to nature, or the manifestation of the abyss.

20. First, in the salnitral flagrat there is produced through the anxious mortification a sulphureous water from the anguish, which affords a brimstone, as we plainly see, and all whatever is of the like sort and resemblance.

21. Secondly, there is generated from the astringent, austere, attractive property, which draws in to itself, a salt water; its materia is salt; if it be again impressed through the fire or heat, then it turns into salt; and all whatever is sharp and attractive, be it either in herbs or trees, proceeds from thence; for there is as much diversity of brimstone and salt, as there is variety of taste and fire to be found in

all creatures, herbs, and trees; also all whatever lives and grows has brimstone and salt; for the saltish property attracts, and preserves the body; and the brimstone has in it the oil or light, wherein the free lubet to manifestation consists, whence the growth arises.

22. Thirdly, there is brought forth through the salnitral flagrat out of the property of the bitter compunctive attraction, in the first impression in the spirit, an earthly property of water; its materia is earth; for the same arises from the dark essentiality, where the darkness impresses itself in the first desire, wherein the darkness arises, as is before mentioned: Thus it begets out of its property in the impression a mist, smoky steam, or vapour, which the flagrat in the salniter apprehends, and its essence is dismayed or dies, and falls downwards; this is the materia of the earth, though the earth is not of one only sort, but has in it all whatever became corporeal in the flagrat, all which springs through the death of the earth, according as it was wrapt and driven together in the creation into a lump, as we plainly see.

23. Further, we are to consider of the highest arcanum, viz. of the heavenly essentiality, and then of the precious stones and metals, from whence they all take their rise and original; seeing that all things come out of one mother, which is the lubet and desire of eternity to its own manifestation.

24. Now concerning the incorruptible essence of corporality, the same arises also in the first desire to nature, yet in the impression of the free lubet, and goes all along through all the forms even into the highest sharpness, where it retires again into itself, as a life out of the fire: The eternal fire is magical, and a spirit, and dies not; the liberty is its enkindler, but the eternal nature is its sharpness; this same essence loses the wrath's property in the light; it is in the same fire as a dying, yet there is no dying, but an entrance into another source, viz. out of a painful desire into a love-desire; it yields also spirit and essence from the fire-spirit, and the essence of meekness from the light.

25. For that which dies to the fire, or sinks through death, that is divine essence; and it is effected likewise through the salnitral flagrat of the divine joyfulness, where the property trembles in the joy of meekness, and immerses itself through the death of the fire, which is called God's anger, and quenches it, so that God dwells in a meek light; and the first property to the enkindling of the light is fire, and wrath of the eternal nature, and makes the dark world.

26. The properties of the first mother in the lubet and desire do also divide themselves in the salnitral flagrat of joyfulness into distinct parts, as is to be seen in this outward world; it yields also water, but of a very sovereign essence, and it resembles only a spirit of a pleasant lovely desire: This is the water of which Christ told us that he would "give us to drink," and "whosoever should drink the same, it should spring up in him to a fountain of eternal life."

27. It retains also in the flagrat of the disclosure the fiery property which is called heaven, in which the wonders of the divine kingdom of joy are known and manifest; and in the watery property it retains the pleasant spring, or paradise; for in the fiery property the eternal element arises, and it is the real essence of the divine corporality, wherein consists all whatever may be known in God, as is sufficiently and in order cleared at large in our other writings of the Divine revelation, treating of the Divine wisdom, and of the Divine eternal abyssal birth: And now we will turn us to the essence of the outward world, viz. to the manifestation of the eternal, viz. to metals, herbs, and trees; so also to men and beasts.

28. We see that the metals have another manner of body than the living creatures, or are otherwise than the earth and stones are: Now reason asks, How is the original of everything, seeing that in the beginning all arose out of one mother, and yet the eternity has no temporal beginning? Here we must again consider the mother of the first pregnatrix, where, and how one essence separates itself from another, viz. the inchoative from the eternal, time from eternity, and yet they stand mutually in each other, but are severed into two principles, viz. into the kingdom of God, and of this world; and yet all is God's: But seeing Christ calls the devil "a prince of this world," and we also are able to declare how far, and in what he is a prince, and that this world is not his own, but he is the poorest creature in this world, and also not at all in this world; now therefore look upon the first ground, upon the mother which has thus generated all creatures.

29. So also as to the earth, stones, and all metals, the earth's property, consists in a spiritual Sulphur, Mercury, and Sal, and all whatever has had beginning is arisen in and out of her impression, and inchoatively thereupon it came forth with the first form of the mother, viz. with the astringent attraction, through the fiat into a creatural being, and affords a diversity of essence and spirit, according to the first property of the separation.

30. As first, the high spirits, which were created out of the free lubet in the desire, in the fire's property, viz. out of the centre of all essences, had in them the properties of both the eternal worlds; but those which after their corporising or being made creaturely remained with their desire in the property of the free lubet, and introduced their will out of the fire into the light, they became angels; and the other, which introduced their desire again into the centre (viz. into the austere properties), became devils, viz. outcasts from the free lubet out of the light, as is mentioned in other writings.

31. Therefore the devils have neither the kingdom of God, nor the kingdom of this world in possession; for in the beginning of the creation this world was created out of both the inward properties, whereupon the devil has now only the wrath's part in possession, the other profits him nothing; and thus he is in the world, and also not in the world, for he has but one part thereof in possession, from the other he is cast out.

32. After the creation of the highest spirits, God created this visible world with the stars and elements as an external birth out of the mother of all essences; all which proceeded out of the eternal beginning, and took a temporal beginning: For here we are to consider, that the eternal pregnatrix moved itself, and enkindled its own form or similitude, where then the one became corporeal in the other; but afterwards God created the earth, which we are thus to consider of.

33. The first desire to nature impresses itself, and introduces itself with the impression into three forms, viz. into Sulphur, Mercury, and Sal, and in the impression all become rising and moving, which is not in the still nothing, and so forces itself into the highest anguish, even to the salnitral flagrat, where then is the original of the fire: Thus the source whirls in itself, as a boiling of water upon the fire: for the austere desire is attractive, and the fiery is expulsive, which is a sulphur; and the astringent attraction is a wrathful sting or compunction, viz. a contrition; and yet it is held by the austereness, that it cannot move away, whereupon it is painful, and causes pain, as if it were seething, which yet is only spirit without essence, which comes to pass in Mercury, and is Mercury's own form.

34. And there is the separation of two wills, viz. one remains, and is the very anxious essence, seeing it originally arises from the desire; the other, which arises out of the lubet of the liberty, retires back again into itself into the liberty, and yet there is no parting or dividing

from one another, but thus it goes one with another all along through the enkindling of the fire through the salnitral flagrat, where with the enkindling of the fire the death is effected in the wrath of the fire, where the source dies, and yet there is no death, but a likeness of death; and yet the real, eternal, and temporal death is in that manner, even where the liberty apprehends itself in itself, and the death or flagrat falls down into the liberty as impotent, and freely resigns itself; and the spirit, viz. the source (understand the very sharp, fiery, anxious source), becomes material, and retains only an essential working, like to an impotent desire; and in the enkindling of the fire in the salnitral flagrat each property separates itself in itself, and the whole materia is particularised, viz. to metals, stones, and earth.

35. The highest metal, as gold, arises from the liberty, which is comprised all along in the flagrat in the astringent impression; and it is not free from the materia of the rest, for all is comprised or wrapt up together; but seeing the liberty with the Sul, or light's property, is comprised or comprehended therein also, thereupon Sul is expulsive to the manifestation of itself, as it is the property of the liberty so to be: Hence it comes that metals grow, and not the gross hard stones, which are too hard comprised in the impression out of the wrathful essentiality, and have too little Sul in them.

36. But concerning the precious stones, with their radiant lustre and great virtue, the same have their original in the flash of the fire, where life and death separate; as when one part by reason of the dark essentiality descends, and the other by reason of the liberty ascends, and yet all is brought into essence in the flagrat; so that the same flash or glance becomes also material in the flagrat; and therefore they are hard, and of a blinking glance, like an eye; for so also is the original of the eye or sight in the womb, when the life enkindles; all according to the right of eternity.

37. And therefore they are of so great power, efficacy, and virtue, in that they are so nigh to the Deity, and bear the incorporated names of the divine power in them; as also gold is nigh to the divine essentiality, or heavenly corporality: If man could open or disclose the dead body, and reduce it to a flying moving spirit, which only can be effected through the divine motion, then it should be seen what it could be, which no reason believes or understands without divine sight or vision.

38. Further, we are also to consider of the other metals and minerals, which in like manner do thus take their original; but in the

salnitral flagrat each property is separated; as we see that the property of the fire and light is different, and all from the first impression; where before the impression the lubet and desire of the liberty stand mutually in each other, as a chaos, a complexion of great wonders, where all colours, powers, and virtues are contained in this only Chaos, or wonder-eye; which Chaos is God himself, viz. the Being of all beings, who thus manifests himself in particular beings with the eyes of eternity; each materia is an essence according to the spirit from whence it was generated; and if it be enkindled in the fire, it yields likewise such a light as the spirit is in the essence.

39. And thus also we are to consider of the metals; what kind of spirit each of them has, such a glance and lustre it yields, and also such a body it has.

40. As the mind acts and moves the thoughts and senses from the highest to the lowest, and comprehends and commands by the thoughts from the highest to the lowest; so the eternal mind has manifested itself from the highest majesty, even to the lowest meanest, or outermost thing, viz. to the greatest darkness; and this world, with the sun, stars, and elements, and with every creaturely being, is nothing else but a manifestation of the eternity of the eternal will and mind; and as it was in the beginning, so it still stands in its seething and vegetation, and so it still puts forward to light and darkness, to evil and good. And all things consist in these first three forms, viz. in Sulphur, Mercury, and Sal, as one degree in order after another; for so likewise are the quires of the spirits, as also of the stars, trees, herbs, and of all kinds whatever which have been, and are; so also are the inward heavenly quires with their distinction.

Chapter IV
Of The Birth Of The Stars, And Four Elements In The Metalline And Creaturely Property

1. As it is before mentioned, all things proceed out of one only mother, and separate themselves into two essences, according to the right of eternity, viz. into a mortal and an immortal, into life and death, into spirit and body; the spirit is the life, and the body is the death, viz. a house of the spirit: As the holy Trinity stands in the birth, so also is the external birth: There is likewise essence and spirit in heaven; a figure of which we see in this outward world, where there are four elements, and yet there is but one only element, which

separates itself into four properties, viz. into fire, air, water, and earth, as is above mentioned.

2. For so we are to consider of the creation of this world, that the whole essence of eternity has moved itself in the place of this world, and the whole form was enkindled and stirred, and that in the desire to manifestation; and there the generation divided itself in the flagrat of the enkindled fire into four parts, viz. into fire, water, and earth, and the air is its moving egressive spirit; as is to be considered in Sulphur, which consists in these four things.

3. In like manner also the astrum is thus generated out of the first mother; and all put together is only one body, and it all takes its rise from the inward spirit; as a hand or foot grows forth from the inward centre, and has already its form in the centre, viz. in the first operation, and so only grows into a form as the spirit is.

4. The first mother of all things, viz. the lubet with the desire, does especially introduce itself into seven forms, and yet continues steadfast in three only, but manifests itself in seven forms.

5. The first form is astringent, viz. an austere attraction, which is a cause of coldness and salt, and all corporality.

6. The second form is the compunction, viz. the drawing or motion, and causes the feeling, also pricking, aking, tormenting; the affection of bitterness, enmity and friendliness, joy and sorrow.

7. The third form is the great anguish in the impression, which causes two wills, viz. one to the fire, where the will of the free lubet falls down to the wrath in the fire, and again goes into itself, and makes a lustre in the fire's sharpness.

8. Now the fourth form is the fire itself, viz. the first principle in the life, with which the dark and light world do separate; also in this flagrat all material separations are effected, and the corporality and multiplication begin according to the property of the first eternal mind, viz. according to the essentiality a mortal ens, and according to the free source a living ens.

9. The fifth form is now the second desire, which is effected after the separation, and that according to two properties; viz. one according to the lubet of the liberty out of the light, which is the highest love-desire; and the other according to the fire's lubet, which leads its life of its essence in the love in the light, from whence the joyfulness and every true life arises.

10. The love gives essence; for it is expressive, and yielding, viz. itself; for God gives himself to every essence; and the fire is receptive;

for it needs essence in its wrathful hunger, else it extinguishes; and then the lustre of the light would go out, and the desire of love would cease, for the fire makes the light desiring, viz. of the joyfulness; for if the fire dies, the light waxes dark, and love turns into anguish, as may be conceived of in the devils.

11. The sixth form arises from the turning wheel before the fire, where the multiplication of the essence arises out of the property of Mercurius in the salnitral flagrat; with the enkindling of the fire one form is introduced into another; and if now the love-desire penetrates all the forms, then all the forms grow very desirous the one after the other, for the dear lovely child Venus is in all.

12. Here begin the taste, smell, hearing, seeing, feeling, and speaking; for the light opens another principle of another source, and fills all; and here springs up the life in death, viz. the love in the anger, and the light shines in the darkness; here the bridegroom embraces his bride, and God himself resists his anger, viz. the wrath of nature; and in this form all speeches, understanding, and senses arise, and the true real life of all creatures; so also the life in the vegetables, viz. trees and herbs, in each thing according to its property.

13. The seventh form arises from all the other, and is the body, mansion-house, or food of the other, and it is thus effected; when the other forms taste each other in their mutual penetration in the love-desire, then in each form there is an hunger or desire after the love, viz. after the light; now each hunger or desire is reaching forth after the thing it desires, and eagerly attracts the property of the thing desired; and thus out of two one essence is made, viz. out of the hunger, and that which the hunger desires; for this hunger does not stand in death, it does not any more enclose itself up in death, unless it be too great, and the imagination in the hunger be too great, and the hunger cannot obtain that same thing, then it choaks; as many times a child is so choaked or smothered in the mother's womb, if this form be enkindled in another form to eat of some external thing, whereupon the mother grows so ardent in longing, and if she cannot get it, the child also cannot get it; now it choaks in the hunger, or else a member is spoiled, from whence the hunger arose.

14. The first hunger in the centre before the fire is a spiritual hunger, which makes the dark world; and the hunger of the free lubet makes the light world; both which are only spirit, till they pass both together through the enkindling of the fire, where then they are

mortified to the spirit, and are a likeness of the first spirit, viz. a manifestation of the incomprehensible spirit, which is called God in love and anger, in a twofold source: Thus each stands undivided in itself, viz. God in the time, and the time in God, and the one is not the other, but they come from one eternal original; thus the temporal spirit's hunger gives a temporal body, and the eternal spirit's hunger affords an eternal body, and are both mutually in each other, and yet are distinct.

15. The seven forms make them a body according to their hunger out of their own property; therefore all whatever the spirit has in all properties lies in the body.

16. Further we are to know, that there is a separation made in the creation of this world; for this is to be seen in the sun and stars; so likewise in all creatures; also in metals, stones, and earths; for this same is the manifestation of God.

17. We see in the firmament seven planets, and in the earth seven metals which are fixed, and also seven planets only which are fixed in their property; the rest are minerals, and so of the stars: And as the planetary orb has its predominant stamp or influence, so is also the birth of each thing.

18. As the Deity, viz. the divine light, is the centre of all life; so also in the manifestation of God, viz. in the figure, the sun is the centre of all life; in the highest life the highest things have taken their beginning, and so forward successively one from another to the lowest: In every external thing there are two properties; one from time, the other from eternity; the first property of time is manifest; and the other is hidden, yet it sets forth a likeness after itself in each thing.

19. Whatever has its beginning out of the lubet of the liberty stands with the root in an heavenly property, and with the body in an earthly; but the eternal stands in time, and manifests itself with time.

20. Sulphur is on one part in the internal heavenly, and as to the body earthly, yet puts forth an heavenly likeness according to the eternal out of itself, which is fixed and stedfast; as is to be seen in gold, and is much more to be understood in the human body, if it were not corrupted in the desire in Mercury; for the spiritual or heavenly man consists in Sulphur, and in Mercury the corporeal, viz. the similitude of the divine man ; so also the metalline property in Sulphur is the noblest, most excellent, and highest, for it is the highest spirit.

21. Understand it thus: In the heavenly being there is also a property of a seething, when the liberty is apprehended and enkindled in the highest desire, wherein the joyfulness arises; this is effected in the heavenly Sulphur, where it is made essential in the heavenly Mercury, viz. in the eternal word, which is a spiritual essence.

22. But if the same spirituality longs to manifest itself in a similitude, both according to the property of the spirit, and the essentiality too, according to the Trinity of the Deity, according to the mortal and immortal essence, then that image is represented in the stars and elements; and lastly it is set forth in man, who is a lively image of the whole essence according to the divine and outward world; also the inward and outward worlds are represented with the metals in a mortal image, as a resemblance and similitude of the living heavenly essentiality.

23. The beginning is in Sulphur; for Sul is the lubet of the light, or the liberty, which longs to manifestation, and it cannot otherwise be effected but through fire: In Phur arises the desire, viz. an austere attraction, which makes the dark earthly property, and the austereness of the spirit, viz. the fiery essence: In this austereness arises Saturn, which is the thing impressed; and Mercury is the desire of the hunger, and the rager, raver, and breaker; and Mars is the wrath in the hunger, a cause of anger; these three are the property of Phur, viz. of the free lubet's desire.

24. The free lubet's property begets the essence in the three fore-mentioned forms, viz. in Saturn, Mercury, and Mars; for it gives itself in to each property, and the property in the hunger of Mercury makes it a corporeal form; but if the free lubet turns also to an hunger in the austere desiring, then it makes also three forms according to itself, viz. Jupiter, who is the understanding of the lubet; and Venus, which is the desire of the lubet; and Luna, which is the body of the lubet; and according to the property of the light it makes Sol; all this is spirit; but now in every spirit's hunger there is also an essence, both according to the mortal and immortal ens, a fixed, and unfixed; a figure according to the heavenly, and a figure according to the earthly being, or property.

25. In the saturnine property the desire of the free lubet makes (according to Saturn's own property) lead, and according to the watery property in Saturn, salt; and according to the mortal and

earthly property in Saturn, stones, and earth, and all whatever is of that sort and semblance.

26. But according to the liberty, or according to the free desire's own property (in that it yields up itself to Saturn, viz. to the desire), it makes in Saturn gold, according to the desire of the light, where the spirit and body separate; the spirit of its desire is Sol, and the body is gold, understand, the golden body is in Saturn according to the property of the free desire, and not according to Saturn's property; his property in himself is lead, salt, and earth; but he keeps the golden child shut up in himself as a black raven, not in his gray form, but in a darkish cast: He is a great lord, but his dominion, by reason of the golden child which he has in his bowels, stands not in his own power: He is not father of the child, but Mercury is he which forms the child; but he puts his morning mantle upon it, that he can have no joy with the golden child; he corporises the fair child; for he is its fiat or creator, and hides and covers it close under his mantle: He cannot give it the body from his own property, for it (understand the golden body) is the essence of the free desire in the highest degree of corporality in the fixed death, where yet there is no death, but an enclosing, and in the similitude a representation of the divine heavenly essentiality.

27. Mercurius is the master-workman of this child, which Saturn hides; when he gets it into his hunger, he casts off his black cloak, and rejoices in it; but he is too malignant in his fire-wrath, he devours the child, and turns it wholly to his own property: When he is most sharply hungry in the fire, then Sol must be given him (it is his wife) that his hunger may be appeased; and then when he is satisfied, he labours in the materia of the child with his own hunger or fire, and fills up his sufficed desire out of Sol's property, which he before had eaten, and nourishes the child till it gets upon it all the four elements with the constellation, and he grows exceeding pregnant with the child, and then it belongs or is fit for a strange fire, and yet not strange, an earnest fire; and then the father gives it the soul, viz. the fire-spirit; and its first mother, which Mercury did eat down in its hunger, which was fixed and perfect, gives the soul's-spirit, viz. the light-life: Then the death arises, and the child is born, and becomes afterwards its own, and a child of the liberty, and cares no more for its work-master: It is better than its father, but not better than its mother, in whose seed it lay, before the father wrought in it; it bruises the head of its father's fiery essence, viz. of the serpent, and passes freely

through death in the fire: Dost thou understand nothing here? Then thou art not born to the highest knowledge of the spagirical science.

28. Further, we are to consider of the degrees, what the liberty, viz. the eternal lubet, gives to the hunger of the other forms in Sulphur, in the property of the other planets; the form of the birth is as a turning wheel, which Mercury causes in the Sulphur.

29. The birth of the highest degree turns round (viz. the desire), for this world is round, so also the birth; when the liberty has given its highest lubet (as a golden hunger) to Saturn, and placed Mercury for work-master, then it betakes itself into itself, into its desire, according to the property of meekness; for the first conception to the golden child is effected according to the property of joyfulness; but this out of goodness and meekness resigns itself to Luna; for it is a pleasant demission by reason of the meekness, which Mercury apprehends and works therein also; this body is silver, and comes from the first impression, where the yellow and white separate in the fire, viz. the colours of the virtue; then Luna arises out of the yellow and turns into white, by reason of the divine meekness; and because its original is from Sol's colour, therefore it has a perpetual hunger after Sol, and receives the sun's lustre into it, puts it on and shines with it.

30. Now as the superior is, so is likewise the inferior (namely metals), therefore silver is the next degree to gold; and as gold is generated, so is also silver: Venus clothes it, which Mercury cannot endure, seeing he is the master-worker, and he gives his garment also; but the silver has neither the property of Venus nor Mercury, for it retains the property of its mother, viz. the meekness in the liberty, and is hatched, as the gold by reason of the sun: The moon has an heavenly property, but in reference to its own proper form from the property of the desire, it is of a very earthly property, it is a cabinet and keeper of the earthly and heavenly essence: In like manner as the outward body of man, which before the Fall in Adam was comparable to silver, but when he died in the lubet then the earthly property only lived in him, and therefore he continually hungers after Sol's glance and glory, he would fain take again his splendour with Luna from the sun, but he gets only an earthly lunar lustre, wherein he acts and exercises pride, unless he be born again out of Sol's splendour, that is, out of God's power in the heavenly Mercurius; and so he becomes again the golden silver-child in divine essentiality, only covered and clothed this life-time with the earthly moon, that is, with earthly flesh.

31. Saturn also is the house of silver, he is likewise the cause of the first conception, but he turns his desire only upon the golden child, and leaves the silver its garment, and takes it into his stony earthly property, and lets Mercury hatch it.

32. The desire of the free lubet is fixed and steadfast, as concerning the property of the desire only, which brings its will again from the body into the combat in the senses, and makes Jupiter, that is on the orb upwards under Saturn under the saturnine power; its metal is tin, and it is the third degree; for the lubet of the liberty in the desire proceeds forth into the desire of the austereness, and so it gives itself into the fiat.

33. We must understand it thus; the lubet of the liberty goes forth out of itself, as a plant, and makes one degree after another in order, but Mercury makes the sphere, for he is the work-master: And as the eternal birth is in itself in the heavenly Mercury, viz. in the eternal word in the Father's generation; so likewise with the motion of the Father it came into a creaturely being, and so proceeds in its order, as may be seen in the wheel of the planets; for the order is just so placed as man is in his order.

34. First there is in him the true golden divine man, which is the likeness of God: Next there is in him the man of heavenly essentiality, viz. the inward holy body, generated from the fire and light in the tincture, which is like to the pure silver if it were not corrupted. Thirdly, there is in him the elemental man from the pure element resembling Jupiter. Fourthly, the mercurial, which is the growing or paradisical man. Fifthly, the martial, from the fire, viz. the soulish man, according to the Father's property. Sixthly, the venerine man, according to the outward desire, and the water's property. Seventhly, the solar, according to the sun's property, viz. according to the outward world, as a seer and knower of the wonders of God: And yet it is but the one only man; yet is both in the inward and outward world. Thus likewise is the similitude or form of the seven metals; with one property according to the inward world, and with another visible and palpable property according to the outward world.

35. From Jupiter the sphere turns round, and out of the separation Mercury proceeds forth with a broken metal, according to his spirit's property; externally quicksilver, and internally he is a paradisical working; he is in his spiritual property the distinguisher (or articulator) of the words, voices, and speeches. It is written, "God hath made all things by his word: "The heavenly eternal Mercurius is

his word, which the Father expresses in the enkindling of his light, and the expressed is his wisdom; and the word is the worker, framer, and maker of the formings in the expressed wisdom. Now what the inward Mercurius does internally in God's power, that likewise the outward Mercurius effects in the outward power in the created essence: He is God's instrument, wherewith he works extrinsically to death and to life; in each thing according to its property he builds, and breaks down.

36. According to Saturn's property he builds, and according to his own property he distinguishes and dissipates the hardness in Saturn, viz. the enclosed, and opens it to life: He opens the colours, and makes forms and shapes, and carries in him an heavenly, and also an earthly property; in the earthly he carries out of the first desire to nature, viz. out of Saturn, Mars, viz. the wrathfulness of the impression; for he is his soul, wherein Mercury lives; he gives him the fiery essence, and stands under Jupiter in the order upwards on the sphere; for he carries the fire-spirit in Sulphur into all planets, and forms and gives to each thing its source, and true spirit of life.

37. Mars in the first impression is the great anguish, and causes the love-will of the liberty to separate from him; and that which is separated is called God; and the anguish, or fire-source, is called God's anger, viz. the wrath of the eternal nature: And as internally God's love separates from God's anger, that is, from the wrathful property of the eternal nature, viz. heaven from hell, God from the devil; so also it is effected in the birth of the outward nature.

38. Love proceeds out of the wrath, and is an humility, or submission: Thus likewise it came in the creation into order; therefore Venus stands in the sphere on the line of Mars under the sun, for so is the separation in nature; and so one proceeds forth from another: Its metal is copper, the on final whereof is this, that the love is a desire, and desires only light and joy; for the materia is made out of the desire's property: But if the love-desire shall come to be corporeal in the impression, then it must resign itself to the wrathful fiat, viz. to the desire of Mars in the fire, or in the fiery property; for the saturnine property takes all into its might, and makes it corporeal.

39. Therefore the metal of Venus is so nearly related to gold, by reason of her own property from the liberty, but Mars makes it too wrathful; and because it separates itself out of Mars's fire, it retains a great part of the property of Mars in it.

40. Mars's metal is iron, for he is the wrath in Sulphur, in which the fire enkindles, and arises; his original with the materia is in the austereness of the desire: copper separates itself in the generation out of iron, for it arises from the will of Venus, and they differ as body and soul; for Mars is the fire-soul of Venus, and makes Venus corporeal; otherwise Venus, as to her own property, gives only water in the mortification in the salnitral flagrat; for her fire is only a pleasant shining, smile, or love-fire, as she is alone void of other mixture; and therefore she cannot produce any corporeal essence from her own power and ability, which is hard and tough; she is only the mother to her child without a creaturely soul; Mars is her soul, and Saturn makes her body.

41. The spirit of Sol may tincture Mars and Venus, and change them into the highest metalline perfection, viz. into gold; which cannot so easily be effected in silver, unless it be reduced into the first materia, where Saturn, Mars, and Mercury are together in the Sulphur, and then it can be done: Venus receives its toughness from Saturn, and its redness from Mars as the fire.

42. Now the desire of Venus is only eager, and longing after Sol, as after her first mother, from whence she springs forth in her birth in the first original; for the love comes forth originally from God, and so it is likewise in the external birth in the figure: The desire of Venus goes into Sol, into the sun, and receives in its desire the property of the sun, and shines from Sol; she has a very peculiar shining and lustre above all the planets and stars, which she receives from her mother; and in her mother's power consists her joy, viz. the pleasant twinkling smiling aspect which she has in her; she is in her own property (as she is purely alone without the property of the other planets) a real daughter of the sun (understand in Sulphur, where all is wrapt together), therefore she stands next under the sun, as a child of the sun; not that the sun did generate that star, for he is likewise created with her, but in the Sulphur without the creation, merely in the generation, it is so, both in the heavenly and earthly being, or principle.

43. For God the Father generates the love through his heart; now the sun, by way of similitude, betokens his heart; for it is a figure in the outward world according to the eternal heart of God, which gives strength and virtue to every life and essence.

44. And understand it right; all things proceed from the word and heart of God (which is the divine Sulphur) in the birth of the Holy

Trinity, and manifest themselves in and through the proceeded (or egressed) essence, which is God's wisdom; and they again do eagerly force and press out of the egress, in and towards his heart and power, and vehemently long after it, as Paul saith, all creatures groan and pant with us to be delivered from vanity.

45. So also does the outward essence in the outward birth of metals, planets, stars, and creatures; each thing longs after its centre, viz. after its first mother, whence it proceeded, viz. after the sun in Sulphur, for it is the tincture of all essences: Whatever the first desire with the impression in Saturn makes evil in the wrath of Mars, that the sun turns again into good. As the divine sun tinctures the anger or wrath of God, so that the wrathful property of God's anger is changed into a joyfulness; so likewise the outward sun tinctures the outward Sulphur, viz. Saturn and Mars, that there is a pleasant temperature, viz. a growth, springing, and blooming in all metals and creatures; therefore the sun is the centre, which reason will not believe; understand, in the planetary orb, and in all vegetables and animals.

Chapter V
Of The Sulphurean Death, And How The Dead Body Is Revived, And Replaced Into Its First Glory

1. All life and motion, with understanding, reason, and senses, both in animals and vegetables, consist originally in Sulphur, viz. in nature's desire, and in the lubet's desire of the liberty,

2. In nature's desire arises the death and enclosing, and in the desire of the liberty arises the opening and the life; for the liberty's desire tinctures the desire of the dark nature, so that the wrathful mother foregoes her own right, and freely resigns to the liberty's desire, and so the life grows in death, for there is no life without light; but if the light goes out in the essence of the Sulphur, then it is an eternal death, which no man can revive, unless God moves himself in the lubet-desire in the same death; for death can receive no life into it, unless the first desire, viz. the free lubet's desire, manifests itself in the desire to nature, wherein the enclosing and death are generated.

3. Therefore when man died in the Sulphur, none could have made him alive again, unless the free lubet, viz. the desire to the eternal life did again enter into his Phur, viz. into the birth of the nature of the human property, and moved the enclosed death, viz. the

centre of nature, and gave itself again into the centre, viz. into the soul-like property, and into the soul's essentiality and corporality; and this was so brought to pass.

4. We know that the right Sulphur is a generation of all spirituality and corporality; so far as concerns its first original, where it is heavenly, it is the generation of the essence of all essences: For all, whatever eternity and time is in itself, has, and is able to effect, lies in this birth: But now as to the kingdom of this world it is earthly, viz. a figure of the eternal; for in it the time and creature consist, and all whatever is visible and invisible.

5. Now man, and every life also, as to the kingdom of this world, was created and generated out of the outward Sulphur; man out of the inward and outward Sulphur, and the outward creature only out of the outward; for man is an image and likeness of God, and the other creatures are as a similitude according to the figuration in the internal generation in God's wisdom, viz. in the expressed or procreated heavenly essence, according to both eternal principles.

6. But now man was created good and perfect, according to and out of all the three worlds, as an image of the Deity, in whom God dwelled; and he was even that essence what God is, according to eternity and time in all the three worlds; but he was a creature with a beginning, as to the creature, and died through the lubet as to the heavenly and divine essence: For the inward lubet, which was generated in the centre, viz. in the fire, wherein stood the life in the divine essentiality, that is, that which enkindled the essence of the divine meekness, wherein the joyfulness or the angelical form consists; that (I say) turned itself from the inward lubet of the liberty and eternity into the time, viz. into the external birth, into the planetary property, it departed out of the pure divine element into the four elements: Thus the inward divine essentiality, or inward corporality did no longer retain any leader or life: And this was the death; for the soul's fire proceeding from the Father's property turned itself away from the Son's property, in which alone the divine life consists.

7. Thus the property of the soul remained naked only with its will in the outward Sulphur, and the inward disappeared, and continued steadfast in the eternal unchangeableness, as in an eternal nothing, wherein there was no more any effecting or working efficacy to bring to pass.

8. Thus man with his outward body lived barely and merely to the time; the precious gold of the heavenly corporality, which tinctured the outward body, was disappeared, and so the outward body stood barely and alone in the life of nature's desire, viz. in the soul's fiery property; understand in the form and property of Mars, viz. in the wrath of God, which is the wrath in Sulphur, viz. the property of God's anger and the dark world: But seeing the outward body was created out of the time, therefore the time, viz. the constellation with the four elements, presently obtained the dominion in him; and the divine property, viz. the desire of the Deity (which ruled and tinctured time, so that there was a holy life in the creature out of the time), was vanished; its own peculiar love in the divine desire was turned to water, and it became blind and dead in the will and desire of God; and the soul must help itself with the sun's light.

9. But seeing that time has beginning and end, and the will with the desire has given up itself to the temporal leader, therefore the dominion of time destroys its own contrived spirit, and so the body also dies and passes away; and this is that which God said to Adam, that "he should not eat of the tree, or plant, of the knowledge of good and evil," of both properties, lest he died; as it also came to pass, he died in the Sulphur; the Sul in the kingdom of God, viz. the lubet of the divine liberty, out of which the light of God shines, and in which the divine love, viz. the love-fire burns disappeared and withdrew from him.

10. Now there was no remedy for him, unless God's desire entered again into his dead Sulphur, that is, into his Sul, which was dead, viz. into the dead or mortified essentiality, and again enkindled it with the love-fire; which came to pass in Christ: And there the heavenly body, wherein God's light shines, did again arise. But if this must be effected, then the love-desire must again enter into the desire of the enkindled anger, and quench and overcome the anger with the love; the divine water must enter again into the soul's burning fire, and quench the wrathful death in the astringent fiat, viz. in the desire to nature, that the love-desire, which desires God, might be again enkindled in the soul.

11. For man's happiness consists in this, that he has in him a true desire after God, for out of the desire springs forth the love; that is, when the desire receives the meekness of God into itself, then the desire immerses itself in the meekness, and becomes essential; and this is the heavenly or divine essentiality, or corporality; and therein

the soul's spirit (which lay shut up in the anger, viz. in death) does again arise in the love of God; for the love tinctures the death and darkness, that it is again capable of the divine sunshine.

12. And as this is done in man, so likewise it is in the transmutation of metals: The Sulphur is shut up in Saturn, viz. in the death, and yet there is no death, but a vegetative life; and the outward Mercury is the life thereof. Now if the metalline body shall come to the highest perfection, then it must die unto the external dominator, viz. to the elements, and come again into such a Sulphur as it was, when as yet it had not the four elements on it, but lay only in the element in unity.

13. But now none can reduce it into such a body, but he only who has generated; he that has given it the four elements, he alone can take them away; and he that at first made it corporeal, he must bring it to himself, and transchange it in himself into another body; and this is the Sulphur, which has Mercurius as its chief faber in itself. He must again take it out of dark Saturn's bowels in the fiat, and introduce it into his own, and with his own fire separate the four elements from it, and reduce it into one; as God at the last day will in the enkindling of his own fire separate the essence of the four elements from the pure element, that the eternal corporality in the pure element may arise and spring forth: And as in the death of man the four elements separate from the true man (who is the element of God) and the heavenly body remains only in itself; so it goes in the transmutation of metals.

Process

14. The body lies shut up in a disesteemed form in Saturn, not wholly in Saturn's property, in a dark colour, marked with Mercurius its father, and Sol its mother, clothed with Saturn, and manifest with the life of Mars; but its mother is not outwardly manifest and known on it, unless its faber be enraged with its own iniquity; which yet cannot be, unless an alienate be applied, whereby its propriate is enraged; and then (if his anger be set on a fire or fury) he becomes so very hungry and thirsty, and yet can find no refreshment in itself; then it seizes on its faber who has made it, and fights against its creator, as the earthly wicked man does against God, so long till he devours and consumes himself, as a fiery pestilent poison consumes the body, unless you remedy, stay, and allay its hunger; yet there is none that can still this horrible hunger, but God himself who has

made him; and if he assists not in due time, then the hunger in the wrath consumes the body, and puts it into the eternal darkness.

15. This hunger desires nothing but the mercy of God, that he might be freed from the anguish of hell; but this he cannot obtain of himself, for he is shut up in the anger of God; and his dear mother, which nursed him in the beginning, is also shut up in death: But if God shews his grace, and gives him again of his love, then the anger is dismayed at the love; and this is a flagrat of great joy: For he again tastes the sweetness of his dear mother, and then he knows full well that he has been so vile and wicked, and repents of his iniquity, and will turn and mortify the old Adam, and cast it away from him.

16. So the artist takes him presently away with the old Adam from the strange anger, and lays him in a soft bed; for the old Adam is sick, and will die; and then his own faber in the old Adam is in the love of God, which destroyed the anger, and will make a young child, and rejoices in the child; and the old Adam grows sick, and weak, wholly dark, and swarthish, and dies; and the four elements go out from him with their colours: So the faber gives him even leave to go, and continually labours on the new body, which shall arise from death; and none sees his labour, for he works in the dark.

17. But the artist takes no care about the work, but gives the faber his own food, till he sees that a vegetative life appears in the dark death with a new colour out of the black; and then, when the new man is ready, the artist comes, and brings the soul, and gives it the faber; at which the faber is dismayed that another life comes into him; and he puts the soul into the new body, and it goes inwardly in the anger: Thus the new man arises in great power and glory from death, and bruises the head of the old serpent in the anger of God, and passes through the anger, and the anger can do him no harm at all.

Whoe'er thou art, that to this work art born,
A chosen work thou hast, howe'er the world may scorn.

Chapter VI
How A Water And Oil Are Generated, And Of The Difference Of The Water And Oil, And Of The Vegetable Life And Growth
1. All life, growth, and instigation consist in two things, viz. in the lubet, and then in the desire; the lubet is a free will, and as a nothing

in comparison to nature; but the desire is as a hunger: In the desire arises the moving spirit, viz. the natural, and in the lubet the supernatural, which yet is nature's, but not out of its own property, but out of or from the property of the desire.

2. The desire is the instigation of the essence, viz. an hunger, and the lubet is the hunger's essence, which it takes into itself; for the desire is only an hungry will, and it is the natural spirit in its forms; but the lubet is out of the liberty: For God is without desire as concerning his own essence, inasmuch as he is called God; for he needs nothing. All is his, and he himself is all.

3. But he has a lubet-will, and he himself is the will, to manifest himself in the lubet; yet in the lubet which is free, without affection, no manifestation can be effected, for it is void of desire; it is as if it were nothing in respect of nature, and yet it is all; but not according to the desire, viz. according to nature, but according to the satisfying of nature it is the satisfying of the hungry desire, viz. of nature; it freely and willingly gives itself into the hunger of nature; for it is a spirit without essence and desire, wholly free as a nothing; but the desire makes it essential or materialises in itself, and that according to two properties, viz. one according to the eternal liberty, which is free from the source; and the other according to the desire, which gives a vegetative life, viz. a growing, or a giving forth of itself.

4. The free essence is, and gives an oil, and the desire's property gives a life of the oil; the oil is a light, and the desire's property gives to the light the essence, viz. the fiery property, so that the light shines, as is to be seen in the fire and light, and the free lubet remains yet a free will in itself, but gives its meekness, viz. a free resignation into the desire, that it comes to essence and lustre: Its will is only good, it has no other desire but only to be good, meek, and pleasant; there is also no other possibility therein; for it is as a nothing, wherein no disturbance or source can be, but it is the meekness itself.

5. But seeing it cannot be a nothing, by reason that it is a cause and beginning of the desire, therefore it gives itself freely, as the sunshine freely gives itself into every property; and the desire conceives or takes this free lubet, viz. the lustre or shining of the abyss of eternity into itself, and makes it in itself into essence according to its property; so much property as is in the desire, so much also there is of essence: And we are to consider, that when the free lubet gives in itself into the hunger of the desire, that the desire then makes out of the free lubet's

property a similitude according to the liberty, which is as if it were nothing, and yet is; this is a water and oil.

6. But seeing the desire, that is, the hunger, is filled with the free lubet, it makes its own property in the essence of the liberty also into essence; its essence is water, and the essence of the free lubet is an oil. Thus a twofold property arises in one only spirit, viz. a fiery property according to the property of the desire, and a joyful or lucid property according to the liberty.

7. The fiery gives in its essence, viz. in its water a sharpness from the austere desire, which is saltish, or a salt; and from the fiery anguish a brimstone, from whence in the impression and creation of the world, are made stones, earth, and metals; so also the elements and stars, all according to the forms in the desire; and the oleous property gives its meekness, viz. a love-lubet, wherein the fiery is impressed with the desire, and makes corporality: And the oleous gives itself out in its meekness, and makes the vegetable life, viz. a springing and growing in the fiery impression, whereinto the fire must give its essence and instigation, viz. the vehement compunction in the attraction of the desire, which is the separator in the corporality, viz. the distinguisher, carver, and cause of the essence and multiplicity or variety.

8. Philosophers have called this form Mercurius, from the anxious inciting sphere, which is the cause of all life and motion, and a faber in the oily and watery property.

9. Thus we are to search and find out the great mystery, how there is an oil, brimstone, and salt in everything, and how they arise; for God has made all things out of nothing, and that same nothing is himself, viz. a love-lubet dwelling in itself, wherein there is no affection: But now the love-lubet would not be manifest, if it remained one in the stillness without essence, and there would be no joy or moving therein, but an eternal stillness.

10. But seeing he introduces himself into essence through the desire, his eternal stillness becomes an essence and working power, and that with two properties, viz. in an oil, in which the working power is a good spirit according to the property of the love-lubet, which resists the desire's wrath in the brimstone, salt, and poisonful Mercury, and appeases and heals his poisonful hunger with the pleasant meekness; that which Mercury destroys with the raging sphere of his own property, that the lubet of the love-oil does again heal: And thus there is good and evil in each life, and yet there is no

evil in anything, unless the good, viz. the love-oil famishes in its own lubet, which falls out in the forms of the impression of the hunger of the desire.

11. That is, if the hunger-spirit does in its own forms too much impress itself long, or imagine after itself, and too eagerly hunger after its own manifestation, it cannot take the free lubet, which appeases its hunger, into itself; for nature's property must be sincerely bent and inclined to the free lubet's property, viz. to God's love-ens, and wholly direct its hunger after love; and then the hunger receives the love into itself, and makes the same essential in itself, and is no longer a famished dark hunger, which rages in itself, and raves as a poisonful Mercury; but the hunger becomes a love-desire, which is called God's nature, and the hungry fiery desire is called God's anger; and in the outward nature it is called a fire, but in the inward world's property, where the desire does act with energy in the property of the free lubet, this desire is called the divine desire, wherein the fiery love burns, and from whence the joyfulness proceeds; for the free lubet does therefore give itself into the austere desire, that it may bring forth a fiery love, viz. a joyfulness, which could not be in the still lubet; for where there is a stillness there is no joy, or motion.

12. Now the free lubet, viz. God's property, manifests itself through the fiery property, and the fiery property makes the free lubet's essence, viz. the oil which arises in the impression of the desire into a light or lustre; for the austere desire gives the anxious darting flash, viz. a sulphureous spirit, and the meekness of the oil gives its love into it, and dispels that which was drawn into it, viz. the darkness, and manifests the eternal liberty, viz. the nothing, and this is now the seeing.

13. For when the fire-splendour tastes the sweetness of the light, then the fire's desire reaches after the meekness, and the meekness of the free lubet is as a nothing wholly incomprehensible: Now the hunger of the desire comprehends its own essence and devours it, and makes it to nothing; this is the darkness, which is the hunger's essence, which the fiery hunger devours through the property of the light, or free lubet: As we see, that as soon as the light shines it deprives the darkness of its power; therefore God is a Lord over all beings, for he is the eternal Power and Light: A similitude whereof we see in the sun, that it is lord of the darkness and of all essences, and rules whatever grows, lives, and moves in this world.

14. Further, we are to consider of the manifold salts, how they take their rise in the original, and separate into many properties. In the original of the impression, viz. in the verbum fiat, a twofold salt does arise: The first is spiritual, and gives the sharpness in the essence of the free lubet; it is a severising, or a sharpness of the powers: The other salt is the sharpness of the impression, according to the property of the astringent austerity which is the anguish in the impression, that is, brimstone, and the essential property is water.

15. The water is the senseless mortal property of the salt; and the sulphureous, which is from the anguish, is the property of the quick salt; for it has the sting of motion, viz. the Mercury in it, which makes life's form, and yet the brimstone is not the salt, but it is the anguish in the impression, which also comes to be corporeal.

16. The salt is the sharpness in brimstone as to the astringency; the salt causes the anguish to be corporeal; and so salt dwells in the brimstone, and is the brimstone's sharpness, and preserves the brimstone in the corporeal essence, and also the spirit of the brimstone, that it falls not to dust: The salt impresses the powers of the anguish, and the impressed life is the mercurial life; the same is the life of the anguish, viz. of the brimstone, and separates the materia according to the forms to nature, and the materia of the free lubet into two essences, viz. into a watery and oily, and then into a corporeal.

17. The corporeal is twofold; both according to the darkness and the light: According to the property of the austere desire it makes in the watery property a sand, or stony nature, from whence the stones have their original; understand out of the sulphureous, viz. out of the brimstone's water.

18. The other property, as to the mortification in the salnitral flagrat, is the common running water; the other corporeal water is the metalline body from the free lubet's property in the impressed form; and from the watery property (where the brimstone is in the water) it produces trees, herbs, and all whatever grows in the earthly property, viz. in the mortified or dead substantiality, which yet has a life without sense, viz. a vegetative.

19. The oily property is also twofold according to the impression; viz. one part forces again into the liberty to be free from the wrath of the impression, which is the good spirit, viz. the light in the oil; the other part yields itself into the anguish of the brimstone, and remains in the corporality, and unites and applies itself in each thing,

according to the salt-property of the thing; as in a fiery salt, it is fiery; in a bitter salt, it is bitter; in an astringent, astringent, etc.

20. The first property according to the light is sweet in all things, and the other property of the oil is according to the form, viz. the taste of the thing, let it be either sweet, sour, astringent, sharp, or bitter, or how it will; as it is to be found out and known in herbs: In some it is a bitter poison, and in some again a healing of the poison; but if the poisonful property be broken by Mercury in the oil of meekness, then the love of the light inclines itself also into the oil, for the original of both is from one will, but it is altered in the impression: As the devil, when he was an angel, changed himself into a poisonous devilish property, and Adam out of an heavenly into an earthly property.

21. Whatever grows, lives, and moves in this world, consists in Sulphur, and Mercury is the life in Sulphur, and the salt is the corporeal being of Mercury's hunger, though the body is manifold; according as the property of the brimstone and salt is, according to the same property is also the ingrafted oil, which springs up all along in the power; for the oil makes the power or virtual influence in each thing. In the oil of the impression, viz. in the impressed oil, is the other oil, viz. the spiritual, which gives us light, but it has another principle; it receives no other source into it but the lubet of love; it is divine essentiality: Therefore God's own essence is nigh unto all things, but not essentially in all things; it has another principle, and yet inclines itself to all things; as far as the thing has anything of the divine property in it, it receives virtue from the divine property, be it either a vegetable or animal; for there are herbs and trees, and also creatures to be found, in which something of the divine power is couched, with which in the magical cure the false magic, viz. the corrupt evil oil can be resisted, and changed into a good oil.

22. All sharpness of taste is salt, let it be whatever it will in this world, nothing excepted; and all smell proceeds from the brimstone, and Mercury is the distinguisher in all motion or affection, both in the smell, power, and taste; but I understand by my Mercury the sphere of the birth of all essences, as is before mentioned; not a dead Mercury, but a living one, viz. the strongest, according to the property of the dry poison, etc.

23. Now it behoves the artist and physician to know these things, else he cannot cure any sickness or disease, unless he hits on it by chance, if he knows not wherewith the oil is poisoned in the body, and what kind of hunger Mercury has in the sickness, and after what

he hungers; for if he may obtain the salt according to the property of his hunger (after which he is desirous) with such an oil as he fain would have, then is the sickness over very soon; for he turns his oil again into the property of the love of the light, whereupon the life begins again to shine bright.

24. For every disease in the body is nothing else but a corruption or poisoning of the oil, from which the life's-light burns or shines; for when the light of the life shines or burns clear in the oil, it expels and drives away all poisonful influences and operations, as the day expels the night.

25. For if the oil, out of which the life burns, be infected or inflamed with a poisonful Mercury or salt, let it be done either from the constellation, or salt of meat, viz. from a contrary source, whereby a loathing or nauseous detestation arises in the oil, which the oil would always spew out, which Mercury helps; then Mercury eagerly troubles and perplexes itself in the sulphureous fire more and more, and continually labours to drive forth the abominate, but does only inflame itself in itself in this austere endeavour, and more and more enkindles its inward form, whereupon the oil grows more dark and poisonful, until at last the oil becomes wholly waterish and earthly, and then the light, and also the fire, extinguishes, and Mercury with the sulphureous spirit departs from it, as when a candle is put out; thus Mercury passes out with the sulphureous spirit in death's baneful steam, until he also be famished; for a time he may help himself in the sidereal body, which passes along with it; but when Mercury in the spirit of the great world has consumed and starved its property, then is the temporal life wholly gone; for as soon as the light of the vital oil extinguishes, the elemental body falls down into putrefaction, viz. into the fiat, from whence it came to be; and then this time ends in the creature, which is the death, dying, or departure; and from thence there is no deliverance or return, unless the heavenly divine Mercury does once more move itself in him, which yet cannot be, except there has been a good property of the oil in him, viz. from the divine essentiality: In this property, which is capable of 'the divine essentiality, the light does only enkindle itself again.

26. For the divine essentiality, or this heavenly Mercury, changes the dead oil again into his, and becomes its life; for the outward Mercury, which has ruled the life, returns not again, it has only been for a time a mirror of the eternal, but he is changed into another source; for being suffocated, he passes again into the mystery, from

whence he at first proceeded in the creation of the world, and the body also goes into the same mystery.

27. Thus it remains, and belongs yet to another motion of the Deity, viz. to a separating, where the evil, wherein the death was, shall be separated from the good, and the verbum fiat shall restore and bring forth that which has fallen into it in death.

28. The physician is to know, that in the strongest Mercury, which is most poisonful, the highest tincture lies, but not in Mercury's own property, which must be broken; for his own property, even from the centre, is the anxious poisonful life: But he has another property in him, viz. an oil from the light, whereby he is so strong and potent, which is his food and preservation; if this may be separated from him, it becomes a tincturing and mighty enkindling of all obscured lives, viz. of all diseases and sicknesses; for in this oil lies the joyful life, and it is an hunger after life, viz. that it might enkindle the weak, and lift it up on high.

29. In a toad, viper, or adder, or the like poisonful beasts, worms, or insects, the highest tincture is to be found, if they are reduced into an oily substance, and the wrath of Mercury separated from them; for all life, both external and internal, consists in poison and light, as we understand, that the wrath and anger-fire of God is a cause of the divine joyfulness: The like also we are to know is externally; for all life that is void of the poisonful Mercury is mort, and an abominate, and accounted as dead.

30. Now Mercury is an enkindler of the fire, and every moving life consists in the fire; and though some creatures dwell in the water, yet fire is their life, viz. the poison-gall, wherein Mercury manages the life; but the water in the gall is a poison, wherein an oil is hid, in which the life in Mercury does burn and shine; of which thou hast a similitude: If in a creature there be a strong poisonful Mercury, of a dry quality, that creature is strong, bold, courageous, and potent, which has also a clear oil in it; for the fiery property of the Mercury consumes the waterish, but if its fat be enkindled, it yields a clear light; much more would it be, if the watery property were separated from the oleous.

Chapter VII
How Adam In Paradise, And How Lucifer Was A Fair Angel, And How They Were Corrupted And Spoiled Through Imagination And Pride

Process

1. We will give an occasion of consideration to the earnest searcher and seeker, and if he apprehends our meaning he shall indeed be able to find the noble philosopher's stone, but so that he be chosen thereto by God, and his life also stands in the heavenly Mercury, otherwise we are a mystery to him; and we will represent it to him in similitudes, in the most manifest, and yet mystical manner.

2. When Adam was created in paradise, the heavenly Mercury did then lead him; his life burned in a pure oil, therefore his eyes were heavenly; and his understanding did excel nature, for his light shined in the oil of the divine essentiality; the external waterish property was not manifest in his oil; he was iliastrich, that is, angelical, and became in the Fall cogastrish, that is, the watery nature in the mortal property was manifest in his oil, and penetrated, so that the mercury in him became an anxious poison, which before in his oil was an exaltation of joyfulness.

3. For the salnitral flagrat in the impression in the coldness, viz. according to the saturnine property, was thereby elevated, and got the dominion, as a cold poison, which arises in the impression of death, from whence the darkness was generated in the oil, and Adam died to the divine light; to which the devil persuaded him by the serpent, that is, by the essence and property of the serpent; for the kingdom of wrath, and also the outward kingdom was manifest in the serpent; for it was more subtle than any beast of the field, and this subtlety Eve desired; for the serpent persuaded her that her eyes should be opened, and she should be as God, and know good and evil.

4. Which also was the will of the devil, that he would know evil: And in the enkindling to the knowledge in Mercury he became corrupt and dark; for he entered with the imagination, according to his condition, knowledge, and desire, into the fiery byss; and Adam, according to his knowledge and desire, went into the cold byss into the impression, into the procreated watery property in the salniter, where both kingdoms stand separated: He desired to prove and taste the watery mercury, in which is the mortal poison; and Lucifer desired the fiery Mercury, which gives strength and might; from whence his pride arose, viz. out of the fiery Mercury: But both, viz. Lucifer, and also Adam, lost the oil of the meekness of the divine essentiality.

5. Now we are to consider of the serpent, which deceived Adam with its craft; how it was, and what its subtlety was after which Adam

and Eve did imagine; why they did eat of the forbidden tree which was evil and good, and how they did eat death thereby; and what their salvation and restoration is naturally and properly; what evil and good are, what the property of the eternal life, and then the property of eternal death is; what the cure is, whereby the sickness introduced by Adam, and its death, may be healed, and restored both to the temporal and eternal life.

6. Let the reader attend to the sense and meaning; for we have not the ability to give this into his hands; that only belongs to God; but the gates shall stand open for him, if he will enter in; if not, flattery avails him not.

7. The devil was a fair angel, and the serpent the subtle beast, and man the likeness of the Deity; now all three were corrupted by imagination and pride, and got the curse of God for their false lust or cunning.

8. All whatever is eternal proceeds originally from one ground, as angels and souls; but the serpent is not out of the eternal ground, but out of the beginning, as we have before given you to understand, how with the enkindling of the fire in the salnitral flagrat two kingdoms separate, viz. eternity and time; and how the eternity dwells in the time, but yet only in itself; but yet so nigh to the time, as fire and light which are in one another, and yet make two kingdoms; or as darkness and light dwell in each other, and the one is not the other. The like we are to consider of the inchoative poisonful mercury in the devil, and in man, and in the serpent also; how an oil corrupts, and yet the essence or being of God is not hereby at all corrupted, but enters into itself, viz. into the nothing; and the creaturely mercury, which arises, or is begotten with the beginning of the creature in the creature, goes out of itself, that is, out of the eternal into time, viz. into the beginning of the creature; it desires its own self, that is, the beginning; and will be its own, or of a selfish property, and forsakes the eternity, into which it should be wholly confined, and resigned with its desire, and bring its hunger thereinto; and then its poison-source would not be manifest.

9. For whatever hungers after the eternal nothing, viz. after the quiet meek liberty of God, that is not manifest to itself, but it is manifest in the still liberty, viz. in God; for as the hunger is, such is also the essence in the hunger; each hunger or desire makes itself an essence according to the property of the hunger or desire.

10. Thus the devil makes or causes in himself his darkness; for he went with his desire into himself, into the property of the centre to the desire, and forsook the eternity, viz. the nothing, that is, the lubet of love; so that he enkindled himself in his poisonful mercury, that is, in the forms to life in himself, and became an anxious fire-source in the darkness; as wood that is burnt to a coal, which only glows, and has no more any true light in it, also no oil or water; so it went with him. Now in his own property, viz. in his life's forms, there springs forth nothing but a stinging envious property, where one form hates and annoys the other, and yet they so beget each other.

11. And so was the serpent likewise, yet not by its own aspiring haughtiness; but when God said; Let all sorts of beasts come forth, each according to his property or kind, then came forth beasts out of every property of nature, as it was manifest in the separation, when God moved himself to the creation; for the devil would domineer over the love and meekness of God, and put his desire also into the anger, that is, into the austere might, where the poison-life arises, viz. into the fiat of the wrathful property, out of which form are proceeded vipers, serpents, toads, and other venomous worms; not that the devil has made them, that he cannot; only as the desire was in the impression of the fiat, such also was the creature in the evil and good.

12. For in the impression of the fiat, in the original of the outward Mercury, viz. of the life, which is manifest to itself internally, was the separation, where God and the world separate, viz. God inwardly, the world outwardly, as a similitude of the abyss, or a looking-glass of eternity; even there the inward wrath, from whence God is called an angry zealous God, and a consuming fire, manifested itself externally in figures, as in a similitude of the inward birth in the centre; like as the eternal lubet, which he is himself, stirs up awakens and causes the desire to the nature of the eternal manifestation, and gives in itself into the desire, and turns the wrath of the desire into joyfulness.

13. Thus it is also with the serpent's craft: In the highest Mercury is the highest sharpest proof of all things; the more poisonful a thing is, the more sharply it proves a thing; for the sharpest taste and smell consists in the great poison, viz. in a dying source.

14. And the eternal light is generated out of the Father's sharpness, that it attains the shining, and goes forth with its own source through the sharpness out of the anguish-source again into the liberty, viz. into the nothing, where the light, by reason of the fire's-

source and property, becomes also a desire, which is the desire of the divine love and joyfulness; in which desire Mercurius, the eternal word, or the understanding of eternity, or deity, is rightly considered and named: And this efflux from the fire (understand from the eternal magical spiritual fire) is a procreation, viz. of the word of the power, colours, and virtue: And this desire of the same mercury, or word, does also modelise the power into its own desire, and makes it essential; which is the meekness and the love, which quenches the wrath of the Eternal Father, viz. of the eternal nature's desire with love, and changes it into joyfulness, where the name of God has its original from eternity. This immassed essentiality causes two properties, viz. one oleous, which is heavenly essence, a cause of the shining of the light; and also a powerful property from the motion of the eternal impression, or desire of the Father after the birth of the Son; from whence the divine air (as the power through the shining of the light) proceeds forth out of this love-fire, which is the Spirit of God.

15. In like manner know this, that the eternal love (understand the essence, viz. the heavenly essentiality) has given itself forth into the creation with the verbum fiat, to set the Father's anger, viz. the form of the eternal nature, into the highest joyfulness, and to set forth the likeness of the eternal generation; and where the nature of the wrath was most elevated through the fiat, there also the desire did most incline itself towards the liberty, to be free from the wrath, and to bring it into the kingdom of joy, from whence the great and deep knowledge is arisen, and also the most precious and highest tincture; understand the desire of the wrathful hunger received that into itself after which it hungered, viz. the liberty; for all things were created good in the beginning; also the devil was good while he was an angel; so also the serpent was good in its creation before the curse.

16. But seeing the devil went into the highest fire's desire, God departed from him, as a light that is put out, or extinguished in a candle; and afterwards he lived according to his own desire.

17. But seeing he knew that there was such a tincture in the serpent, and the serpent being created out of the beginning of time, therefore he insinuated with his desire into the serpent, and took possession of the serpent's tincture, and wrought forth his desire through the serpent against man, to introduce him to long after the serpent's property: For the serpent's tincture was from both originals, viz. out of the deadly mercury from the dying in the fire, viz. from the

coldness in the impression; and then also from the wrathful fiery property in the impression. The cold impression is earthly, which arises from the wrath, viz. from the dying in the wrath, in the impression; and the fiery impression arises from the quick poison of mercury, in which property the spirit's life consists.

18. Thus Adam and Eve were infected with the devil's desire through the serpent, viz. through the earthly, deadly property of the serpent; and also through the wrathful poisonful living property of God's wrath according to the devil's own property; and was inflamed in his divine oil, that is, in the heavenly essentiality.

19. Even then the divine light, which shined out of the divine body of the heavenly essentiality, was extinct to him; for the curse seized upon the soul. Now God's cursing is a withdrawing, viz. the divine power, which was in the body, departed into its own principle; and his holy oil (wherein the power of God dwelt, and had made a kingdom of joy, viz. the paradise) became a poison.

20. For the earthly part according to the mortifying of the water, viz. the cogastrish property, was manifest; and forthwith mercury, viz. the coldness in the death's property, got the dominion, whereas before he was as it were swallowed up in the divine power: Thus Adam died unto God, and lived to death; here it was necessary that God should regenerate him; and therefore the serpent was cursed, because it had served, and willingly obeyed the devil.

21. Thus we understand what lies hid in the greatest anguish, viz. in the strongest mercury, viz. an oil, which cures and tinctures all diseases; but the cold poison, viz. the death's source must be done away, and put into a fiery property which is desirous of the light; for God created all things good in the beginning, but through his cursing or withdrawing the evil came in: For when God's love-desire dwelt in the outward world's-source, and penetrated it, as the sun the water, or the fire an iron, then the outward world was a paradise, and the divine essence sprang forth and budded through the earthly, the eternal life through the mortal; but when God cursed it for man's sake, the mortal life was manifest in man, and also in the fruit of which man should eat, which property before was only manifest in the "tree of the knowledge of good and evil," on which Adam and his wife were tempted, whether their desire would enter into the eternity, viz. into God's essence, or into the essence of time, into the living or mortal oil, in which source the soul's spirit would live, that is, burn.

22. Thus by God's curse, or withdrawing, the heavenly body was shut up, and the anger-source set open, and so the heavenly body lies still shut up: But seeing man by the eternal mercury, that is, by the word of divine power, was in one part formed out of eternity into body and soul, none could disclose the poison-death, and destroy the mortal mercury, and change it again into the light's-source, viz. into the source of the divine joyfulness, but only the very divine Mercury, viz. the power and the word of life itself: For the serpent's poisonful earthly property was manifest and stirred up in man; therefore when God's word did pity the corruption of man, and did again embrace him, he said, "The seed of the woman shall bruise the serpent's head," and thou (understand the serpent's poison or fire) shalt sting him in the heel.

23. Herein now lies the philosopher's stone, to know how the seed of the woman bruises the serpent's head, which is done in the spirit and essence temporally and eternally; the sting of the serpent is God's anger-fire, and the woman's seed is God's love-fire, which must be again awakened, and illustrate the anger, and deprive the wrath of its might, and put it into the divine joyfulness, and then the dead soul, which lay immersed in God's curse, does arise: When the poisonful Mercury, which resembles God's anger, is tinctured with love, then the death's anguish in Mercury is changed into the highest joyfulness and desire of love, which does again make a love-essence in itself, viz. an heavenly body out of the earthly: When Mercury is changed into an heavenly source, it desires no longer or more the earthly mortal life; it desires not the four elements, but only the one, wherein the four are contained, as it were swallowed up; as the light holds the darkness swallowed up in itself, and yet the darkness is in it, but not manifest in the light; as God dwells in time, and the time comprehends him not, unless it be translated and wrapped up into eternity, that the divine light does again shine in its source, and then the time is manifest with its wonders in the eternity.

24. In this manner also is the process of the wise men with the precious stone: There is no nearer consideration of the same than to consider and know how the eternal word, viz. the heavenly divine Mercury in the divine power, is become man, and has slain death, and the anger in man, viz. changed the Mercury into the divine joyfulness, whereby the human Mercury, which before lay shut up in God's anger, viz. in the source of death, does with its new enkindled desire, which now is called faith in the Holy Ghost, attract divine essentiality,

viz. Christ's body to itself, and sets itself in divine power and light above the anger of God, and the poison of the serpent, and bruise the head of the anger, viz. the poison of death with the life of divine joyfulness: That is, the anger was master, but in the light it became a servant, which now must be a cause of the joyfulness, as it is most plain, clear, and manifestly made known and shewn to us in the mercurial life.

25. Now observe the process, and meditate on it, ye dear children of wisdom, and then you shall have enough temporally and eternally; do not as Babel does, which amuses and comforts itself with the philosopher's stone, and boasts of it, but keeps only a gross mason's stone shut up in poison and death, instead of the precious philosopher's stone: What is it for Babel to have the stone, when it lies wholly shut up in Babel? It is as if a lord bestowed a country upon me, which indeed was mine, but I could not take possession of it, and remained still a poor man notwithstanding, and yet I boasted of the dominion, and so had the name, and not the power: Even thus it goes with Babel about the precious stone of the new-birth in Christ Jesus.

26. In the sweet name, Jesus Christ, the whole process is contained, what, and how the new-birth is out of death into life, which is very clearly understood in the language of nature: For the name Jesus is the property of the free lubet of eternity, which yields itself into the pregnant centre, viz. into the Father's property, and figures itself in the centre in the Father's property, viz. in the Father's fire, to a word of eternal power.

27. Understand, the Father, viz. the Father's fiery forms, do figure shape this divine voice essentially in itself in the lubet of the liberty; that is, the Father's fiery property makes itself in the divine essence of the eternal love to a mercury of joyfulness; for the Father's property is the fire-source, and the Son's, viz. the eternal lubet's property, is the love-source; and yet also there would be no desire of love, if the Father's fire did not enkindle it, and make it movable, viz. desirous; from the fire arises the desire.

28. The Father of all essences begets this holy desire through his fire-source, which is now his heart of love, which gives in his fire the shining lustre and splendour; even there the wrath in the fire's property dies from eternity to eternity, and is changed into a love-desire.

29. Thus observe it; the free lubet's property is here in the fire's property called Christ, which signifies in the language of nature a

potent champion, depriving the wrath of its power, a shining of the light in the darkness, a transmutation, where the love-lubet rules over the fire-lubet, viz. over the wrath, the light over the darkness: Here the seed of the woman (understand of the free lubet, in which there is no source) bruises the head of the wrath of the eternal nature, viz. of the eternal desire; for the fire's property is rightly called the head, for it is the cause of the eternal life; and the liberty, viz. the free lubet, or the nothing, is rightly called the woman; for in the nothing, viz. in the liberty of all source, consists the birth of the Holy Trinity of the Deity.

30. Now the fire gives life, and the free lubet gives essence into the life, and in the essence is the birth, where the Father, viz. the eternal ground, begets his essence, viz. his heart out of the abyss in himself, that is, out of the abyss in himself into a byss; the Son is the Father's byss: Thus the Father remains in himself, as touching his own property only, the byss of the eternal nature; and the Son remains in the Father, the byss of the power and kingdom of joy; a resemblance whereof you see in the fire and light: And thus the Son tinctures the Father with the liberty, viz. with the nothing; and the Father tinctures (the Son) the nothing, that there is an eternal life therein, and no more a nothing, but a sound or voice of the manifestation of the eternity.

31. Thus, dear philosophers, observe here the ground how you should tincture; seek not the Son without the Father to tincture therewith: It must be one body; the serpent-bruiser lies therein beforehand; for the seed of the woman has not bruised the serpent's head without the humanity, but in the humanity: The source of the divine lubet (understand of the love) manifested itself through a resurrection in the human essence, and became manifest in the human life, and tinctured the wrath of death with the blood of the divine tincture, and there the wrath of death was changed into a source of divine love and joyfulness: Thus the love bruised the head of the anger and the oleous poison in Mercury, and deprived the wrath of its dominion, and sublimed the wrath into the highest joyfulness; even there the anger, and the astringent cold death, were made open shew of in a fiery love: Then it was said, "Death, where is thy sting? Hell, where is thy victory? God be thanked who has given us victory."

32. Now it behoves the wise seeker to consider the whole process with the humanity of Christ from his opening in the womb of his mother Mary, even to his resurrection and ascension; and so he may well find the Feast of Pentecost with the joyful spirit, wherewith he may tincture, cure, and heal whatever is broken and destroyed: We

declare it in the ground of truth, as we have highly known it; for the rose in the time of the lily shall blossom in May when the winter is past, for blindness to the wicked, and for light to the seeing.

33. God be for ever praised, who has granted us eyes to see through the poisonful heart of the basilisk, and see the day of restitution of all whatever Adam lost.

34. Now we will come to the process of Christ, and go with him out of eternity into time, and out of time into eternity, and bring again the wonders of time into eternity, and openly set forth the pearl, for honour unto Christ, and scorn to the devil; he that sleeps is blind, but he that wakes sees what the May brings.

35. Christ said, "Seek, and you shall find; knock, and it shall be opened unto you: "You know that Christ signifies in a parable concerning the wounded Samaritan, that he fell among murtherers, who beat him and wounded him, and pulled off his clothes, and went away, and left him half dead, till the Samaritan came, and took pity on him, dressed him, and poured oil into his wounds, and brought him into the inn: This is a manifest and lively representation of the corruption of man in paradise, and also of the corruption of the earth in the curse of God, when paradise departed from it.

36. Now wilt thou be a magus? Then thou must become the Samaritan, otherwise thou canst not heal the wounded and decayed; for the body which thou must heal is half dead, and sorely wounded; also its right garment is torn off, so that it is very hard for thee to know the man whom thou wilt heal, unless thou hast the eyes and will of the Samaritan, and seekest nothing else thereby but to restore the loss of the wounded.

37. Now consider! The eternal word manifested itself in Adam with divine living essentiality, with the heavenly Mercury, but when the soul's-fire in Adam, by the infection of the devil, poisoned the will's spirit in Adam, and introduced it through the property of the serpent into earthly deadly lust, then the heavenly Mercury of the heavenly essence withdrew, that is, the soul's will departed from it with its desire, and introduced its hunger into the earthly mortal essence, viz. into the property of the cold Mercury, which had made stones and earth. Adam's spirit would prove this Mercury, and have the knowledge in evil and good, and so this Mercury of the four elements immediately drew him into its poison, and effectually wrought in him, and robbed him of the divine property, stung, and wounded him with heat and cold, and made him half dead, and

stripped him of his angelical rayment, viz. the garment in the pure element, where the heavenly source penetrates the four elements, and tinctured them in Adam's body: Then he needed no other garment, for heat and cold were as it were swallowed up in him; as the day holds the night swallowed up in itself, and yet the night dwells in the day, but it is not manifest: Thus it went with man when the property and source of the night seized on him, then it domineered in him; and thus it went also with the earth when God cursed it.

38. Now wilt thou be a magus? Then thou must understand how to change the night again into the day; for the source of the night, viz. of the darkness, is the anguish-source of death; and the source of the day, viz. of the light, is the life, and the lustre in the life; now Christ has again enkindled this shining in the humanity, and quickened man again in himself: Now if thou wilt tincture, then thou must change that which is shut up, and closed in the death of the night again into the day, for the day is the tincture, and yet the day and night lie in each other as one essence.

39. Now says reason, How may I begin to do it? Look upon the process, how God began with the humanity, when he would tincture the same.

40. Christ came into this world in the shut-up human form, and brought into the enclosed fortress of death the tincture of life, viz. the Deity; he came into the world as a pilgrim in our poor form; he became ours, that he might tincture us in himself: But what did he do? Did he live in joy? Did he behave and carry himself as a lord? No; he entered into death, and died, and put away the night's-source in him through us: But how did he do it? He assumed the essence of our soul and body unto the divine essence, and quickened our essence with the divine, that our essence entered again with its will and desire into the divine essence, and then the heavenly fiat was moved again in the humanity; for the humanity inclined itself again into the liberty, viz. into the free lubet of the Deity.

41. This being done, the man Christ was tempted forty days, so Iona as the first Adam was alone in paradise, and was tempted: Then the outward earthly food was taken from him, and the humanity must eat with its desire of God's essence; there was represented unto him all whatever the first Adam had amused himself in, and whereinto he imagined, and wherein he was captivated, as in the death of the night. This the devil, being a prince of this world, now represented unto him in the property of death, as he had represented

it to Adam through the serpent, whereon Adam and his wife did amuse themselves, and entered thereinto with the imagination.

42. Now behold! What did Christ do when he was to undergo the combat of this trial, when the human essence was to enter again with its desire into the Deity, and eat of God's bread, that is, of the divine essentiality? He went to Jordan, and was baptized of John. With what? With the water in Jordan, and with the water in the word of life, viz. the divine essence, which must tincture our mortal essence in the outward humanity of Christ, from whence the divine hunger arose in the human essence, that he desired to eat of God's bread: Therefore the Spirit of God took him and carried him into the wilderness, and there the Father's property in the wrath did oppose him through the prince in the wrath; and there God's bread, and also the bread of God's anger according to the death's desire, was tendered to him; now it was tried, whether the soul, which was generated and created out of the Father's property, would after this tincturation of baptism enter again into the love-desire, viz. into the nothing out of all source.

43. What is hereby intimated to the magus? A mystery is hinted to him: If he will do wonders with Christ, and tincture the corrupt body to the new-birth, he must first be baptized, and then he gets an hunger after God's bread, and this hunger has in it the verbum fiat, viz. the archeus to the new generation, that is, the Mercury: But I do not speak here of a priest's baptism; the artist must understand it magically; God and man must first come together ere thou baptizest, as it came to pass in Christ: The Deity first entered into the humanity, but the humanity could not presently comprehend it, till it was quickened through baptism, and the hunger, viz. the dead Mercury in the human essence, was again stirred up in the heavenly part.

44. And here began again the human eating; viz. the Mercury received again divine property and will; and then the inward Mercury (understand man's property) did eat in the taste of the divine word of God's essence: And the four elemental properties did eat of the night's property so long, till the human Mercury sublimed its life, and changed the four elements into one: And the life tinctured death, which was done on the cross: Then the four elements departed from him; that is, he died to time, viz. to the night, that is, to the four elements, and arose in the pure element, and lived to eternity.

45. The magus must keep and observe this process also with his alchymy. Dost thou ask how? I will not put it into thy mouth by

reason of the wicked, who is not worthy of it: Observe only the baptism, that thou baptizest the dead Mercury, which lies in the heavenly essentiality, enclosed and shut up in impotency with its own baptism, and mark of what essence he is in a thing; but thou must have this divine water, and also the earthly; for the earthly Mercury cannot else receive the divine Being except the divine Mercury receives of its power, whereupon it stirs and hungers: Then the heavenly Mercury seeks, but yet finds not divine essence about it for its food; thereupon it brings its will through the desire of death into itself, viz. into the verbum fiat, which has made and produced it, and sets its hunger upon the same; whereupon the divine essence inclines itself to it, and will become joyfulness in him; even then arises the beginning of the new body out of the divine essentiality, which the desire nourishes and brings up; and when the new life is born, viz. the day, then the four elements die: And then the new body is shut up in the dark death, and on the third day it rises again from death; for the night is swallowed up in the grave, and the morning rises.

46. If thou didst understand this, then hadst thou the pearl: But my intent and purpose is otherwise; I will shew thee Christ along with it, and also this pearl; therefore none shall find it but he that loves Christ.

47. Thou sayest, Tell me the baptism? and I have already told it thee. Every hunger is a desire after its property; now if thou givest again the property of death to the hunger of death, then death encreases; but if thou givest him heavenly property, then death receives it not, for hell is against heaven; therefore thou must give death and the anger of God to death, and in this anger give him heavenly essence, viz. the baptism, and so the baptism will swallow up the death into itself, and then the anger dies in the death through the baptism, but not presently; thou must first keep the process of Christ, and suffer the baptized to preach, that is, appear in his divine form and colours; exceedingly persecute and plague him, and give him no rest; for so the right Mercury becomes working and active; and when he has shewn all his wonders through the old Adam, then thou must cast the old and new man into God's great anger, and slay the old man, ventilate him, and hang him naked on the cross, and again take him thence, and lay him into the putrefaction, viz. into the grave.

48. And then Christ will arise from death, and appear; but only his own know him: He walks about in heavenly form, and sometimes in

his own form which he had here until the Feast of Pentecost, for now here is tried in him the highest perfection, whether he will persist in the angel's form, and eat only of the divine essence; and then comes the Holy Ghost, and proceeds with his power out of the whole corpus, viz. out of the body and soul, which then tinctures the dead and broken being; as it may be seen in the Day of Pentecost, where Saint Peter tinctured three thousand souls at once with his heavenly Mercury, and delivered them out of death.

49. Dear seekers, herein lies the pearl; had you the universal, then you could also tincture as Saint Peter did, but your covetous death withholds you and shuts you up; for you seek only covetousness and temporal honour in the pleasure of the flesh, to generate yourselves in the night's property; therefore the pearl hides itself from you; yet the day shall again appear when the wrathful anger of God is fulfilled, satisfied and appeased in the blood of the saints, and turned to a love-life; and the time is near.

Process

50. Every creature keeps in its generation and propagation to its own kind; the male to the female, and the female to the male: Now God said to Adam and Eve after the Fall, "The seed of the woman shall bruise the serpent's head;" he said not the seed of the man: Herein lies the baptism of nature: The male has the fire-spirit, and the female the water-spirit to the tincture; now the Mercury is a fire-life, and makes himself a body according to his hunger and desire; now the chief of the work is in the beginning to give the fire-hunger a love-virgin out of its kind for its consort, that so his wrathful hunger may be changed into a love, and then they sleep together in their own marriage bed: Now the devil is an enemy of this wedlock, who soon comes with a strange desire, and tempts these married people, but dares not lay an hand of violence on them, but only afflicts and plagues them with a false strange desire; now if they yield their desire to his will, and his desire overcomes them, then they become enemies to one another, and bring forth a false child; for Christ said, "An evil tree bringeth forth evil fruits, and a good tree good fruits."

51. Therefore the artist must beware, and keep himself from such anger, and yet must prepare a cross for this married couple; for he is their foe and friend, that so they both in their marriage bed of love might lift up their desire to God, and so with their desire God's essence may be pregnant in their desire, and then in their copulation

they shall beget such a child, which they understand the mother, viz. the female, shall nourish in their belly, till it be ripe.

52. In the meantime let the mother take heed she bear no love to any other besides her consort, and also not imagine after strange things, else she will imprint a spot or mark on the child; she must continue simply in one love, till the child be perfect as to its body, which comes to pass in the fourth month; yet according as the parents are of one or other property, so strife and contrariety will arise in the essence in the child, when the child is to receive its soul's life.

53. But when the essence is in its wresting combat, the artist must assist the soulish, viz. the fiery property, till the soul's spirit attains its life, then he appears in the woman's form and lustre: Now the artist supposes that he has the child that is born, but there belongs a further time to it, till the soul grows strong, and then it appears and shews itself in its red and white coat.

54. But there is yet a wonderful process behind; when the soul's life is born, then the new soul casts away the vegetable life of the parents (which is propagated and inherited to the body from the parents' vegitta, wherein the body of the child congealed and grew till the time of the soul), and the life of the four elements dies, and the life in the one element arises; the child is hidden in the dark death, and the artist supposes it to be dead, but he must have patience till the child be born.

The Peculiar Process In The Shaping Of The Magical Child

55. The course of Christ upon the earth is a real type how the new child is nourished in the mother's womb after its conception, as is before mentioned, and attains a vegetable life, and grows up to the time of its right soul's and spirit's life; and how the child arises from the parents' essence; and how in the enkindling of its right, viz. of its own life, it casts away the parents' vegitta and working; and how a new plant, viz. a new peculiar operation, does now arise according to the new enkindled spirit's property, whereby the child is more noble than its parents, understand as to its outward life.

56. But perhaps some rude clownish sophister might meet with this treatise, and draw a strange understanding from it, in that I write of a soul in the vegetative life; but let him know that we do not understand the image of God, which was formed into a likeness according to God to be in metals, stones, and herbs; but we understand the magical soul, how the eternity, viz. the Deity, imprints

and pourtrays itself into its likeness, according to the model of its wisdom in all things, and how God fills all in all; we understand the summum bonum, the good treasure which lies hidden in the outward world's essence as a paradise.

57. When Christ in his childhood grew up in human and divine property till he was twelve years old, he went with his mother Mary to the feast at Jerusalem, and went into the Temple among the Scribes, asked them, and hearkened to them, and gave answer to the questions of the teachers; but when his parents returned home, supposing him to be among the company, he remained purposely behind among the doctors, and followed not the intent of his parents, but the divine will, till they came back again, and sought him; and then his mother said to him, "My son, why hast thou dealt so with us? Lo! thy father and I have been seeking thee sorrowing. Then he said unto them, How is it that you have sought me? wist ye not that I must be about my Father's business? And he went home with them, and was subject unto them."

58. In this figure we have the type of the wills of the inward and outward world, how they are in one another, and against one another, and yet are but one: Even as in Christ there were two kingdoms manifest; one which was wrought unto God's will, and broke the outward world's will of its parents, in that Christ tarried behind contrary to the will of his parents, at which they were troubled, which the divine will in Christ knew well enough; and the other kingdom, viz. of his parents' will, broke the divine will, that he went home with them, and was obedient to them according to their will.

59. This figure shews the magus, that he shall find two wills in his purpose, which he thinks to carry on; one will not be obedient and subject unto him, viz. the divine will; and yet if its own peculiar external will shall rightly apply itself thereunto, and only seek the dear child Jesus with Mary, with desire and earnest sorrow, and not earthly pleasure of the flesh, then the divine will will be obedient to him, and go home with him, and be used according to his good pleasure.

60. Secondly, it shews him the twofold working and will in all things; and if he will be a magus, and according to his will turn the will and essence of the good property out of the inward into the outward, then he must be first capable of the inward, viz. of the divine will, otherwise he cannot change the inward will into the outward; as Christ was not obedient to the external will of his mother

till she sought him with grief and sorrow of heart, and turned her will into God's will, and wrestled in his compassion with God's will, as Jacob the whole night, till the Lord blessed him, and God said unto him, Thou hast wrestled with God and man, and hast overcome, or got the victory.

61. Also let the magus know, that he need not go about to implant the right will to perfection from without into his purpose; it is already in all things; only he must introduce a divine desirous will according to the thing's property into that thing which he takes in hand, which wrestles with the divine will as Jacob, and blesses the will introduced to God's will, that the divine will yields itself freely into the hunger, or inclines itself to the desire, and makes the imperfect will (which earnestly presses into his compassion) perfect, and then it is rightly said, Thou hast wrestled with God, and hast overcome; then thy purpose obtains a transformed body, which is heavenly and earthly.

62. Observe it! It is the first beginning to baptism, and so you are fit and prepared to the baptism, and not otherwise, else you baptize only with the water of the outward world; but the true magus baptizes with the outward and inward water: If he has a right divine desire in him, then God's will in his baptism is the first glimmering tinder in Mercury, so that the life enkindles death, viz. the Mercury shut up in death, and he gets divine desire; even then Mercury begins to hunger after divine essence, and does his first miracle, and turns the water into wine, as Christ did after his baptism: This is the first tincturation in the dead corpus in the power of baptism, that the vegitta, or working energetical life, obtains another property, viz. an hunger of love, wherewith she embraces her bridegroom, viz. the fire-source, that he is enkindled in her love, and changes his cold deadly wrath and will into a fiery love-will: Then the mortal water turns into wine (a sharpness of a fire and water-taste), out of which at last comes an oil to another baptism, after the manner and disposition of the artist, viz. according as he intends and begins; after the magus has joined the virgin and young man together, then Christ, viz. the bridegroom, is led with his bride into the desert, and tempted of the devil.

63. Here is the trial whereby the artist is proved by God what he seeks with his baptism; for here is the proof in paradise to try whether the bridegroom be not too bad; for the virgin casts her love upon him, and invites him; if he receives it with desire, and gives his will thereinto, then she gives him her heart and will wholly: This is the

heavenly tincture, which gives itself into the enkindled anger of God (viz. into the curse of the earth when God cursed it), that is, into the Mercury enclosed in death, which is the bridegroom, for the seed of the woman, viz. the heavenly tincture, must bruise the head of the serpent, viz. the poisonful Mercury, in the property of death, and change his poison into wine, and then the virgin receives the seed of the bridegroom, and not before.

64. The desert is the earthly outward body, where Mercury is tempted; when the devil appears to Mercury, and plagues him, and assaults him in his fiery essence, then must the virgin come to help him, and give him her love: Now if the Mercury eats of the virgin-like love, that is, of God's bread, then he may stand before the devil; and at last the angels come to him, and serve him; the illuminated magus will well understand what is meant by the devil.

65. Hereby let the magus in the temptation (seeing the whole marriage stands in the devil's temptation) have a careful eye upon his purpose; and if the angels do not appear in forty days' space, then is his purpose in vain; therefore let him look, that he suffer not too fierce a devil to tempt, and also not too weak, lest Mercury become light, and desire to continue in his own poisonful death's property, and devour the baptism as a wolf, and the old one remains.

66. As soon as he espies the forms of angels, let him bring Christ out of the desert, and let the bridegroom eat again his own food, and dismiss the devil, that he may no longer plague him, and then Christ will do many wonders and signs, at which the artist will wonder and rejoice: Then he has nothing to do, the bride is in the bridegroom, they are already married, he need only make their bed ready, they will warm it well enough themselves; the bridegroom embraces the bride, and the bride the bridegroom; and this is their food and pastime till they beget a child.

67. But if the artist will needs be so diligent as to warm the married couple's bed, then let him have a care he do not anger and enrage them in their love; what he begins he must go on with; only the bridegroom is wonderful: He has continually two wills, viz. an earthly hunger after God's anger, and an hunger after his bride; therefore he must always have his own earthly food given him, but not into his belly, but magically, that so he may satisfy only his own will's-hunger; his food is his mother that begets him, as it is before mentioned.

68. In brief, the whole work which men speak so much and wonderfully of consists in two things, in an heavenly and in an earthly; the heavenly must make the earthly in it to an heavenly: The eternity must make time in it to eternity: The artist seeks paradise; if he finds it, he has the great treasure upon the earth: But one dead man does not raise another; the artist must be living, if he will say to the mountain, Arise, and cast thyself into the sea.

69. When the incarnation of the child begins, then first of all Saturn takes it, and then it is dark and disesteemed, and is contemned and derided, that such a mystery should lie hid in such a mean form; there Christ walks in a poor simple form upon the earth, as a pilgrim, and has not so much room and propriety in Saturn as to lay his head: He goes as a stranger, as if he were not there at home.

70. After this the moon takes it, and then the heavenly and earthly properties are mixed, and the vegetative life arises, and then the artist rejoices; but he is yet in danger.

71. After the moon Jupiter takes it, who makes an understanding in Mercury, viz. a pleasant habitation, and gives him its good will; and in Jupiter his enclosed life, viz. Mercury is quickened, who takes it with its orb, and forces it into the highest anguish: And then Mars apprehends it, and gives the fire-soul to Mercury; and in the flagrat of Mars the highest life enkindles itself, and separates itself into two essences, viz. out of the love into a body, and out of the fire into a spirit; then the life of love in the fiery flagrat sinks downwards, and appears beautiful, but it is Venus, a woman: Then the artist supposes that he has the treasure, but the hungry Mercury devours Venus, and the child turns to a black raven; then Mars afflicts Mercury in himself, till he grows faint, and yields himself to death: Then the four elements depart from him, and the sun receives the child into its property, and sets it forth in a virgin-like body in the pure element; for in the property of Mars the light is enkindled, and the right life is born, and stands in the pure element; no anger nor death can destroy it.

72. It seems strange in the eyes of reason, that God has kept such a process with the restoring of man in Christ, that he appeared in such a poor disesteemed form in the human property, and was reviled, mocked, scorned, scourged, crucified and slain; and that he was buried, and rose again out of the grave, and walked forty days upon the earth before he entered into his invisible kingdom. Reason is so blind, that it understands nothing of the eternal birth, it knows nothing of paradise, how Adam was in paradise, and how he fell, and

what the curse of the earth is: If it understood this, the whole process were manifest to it: As the eternal birth is in itself, so is also the process with the restoration after the Fall, and so likewise is the process of the wise men with their philosopher's stone, there is not the least tittle of difference betwixt them; for all things originally arise out of the eternal birth, and all must have one restoration in one and the same manner.

73. Therefore if the magus will seek paradise in the curse of the earth, and find it, then must he first walk in the person of Christ; God must be manifest in him, understand in the internal man, that he may have the magical sight: He must deal with his purpose as the world did with Christ, and then he may find paradise, wherein is no death.

74. But if he be not in this birth of restoration, and walks not himself in the way wherein Christ walked upon the earth, if he steps not forth into the will and spirit of Christ, then let him give over and leave off his seeking; he finds nothing but death, and the curse of God. I tell him plainly and faithfully, for the pearl of which I write is paradisical, which God does not cast before swine, but gives it to his children for their play and delight.

75. And though much might be mentioned here, that even reason might obtain open eyes, yet it is not to be done; for the wicked would grow worse, and more full of pride; therefore seeing he is not worthy of paradise, and also cannot enter thereinto, no heavenly jewel shall be given him: And therefore God hides it, and permits him to whom he reveals it, to speak of it no otherwise than magically; therefore no one attains it, unless he himself be a magus in Christ, unless paradise be manifest in his internal man; and then he may find, if he be born to it, and chosen by God.

Chapter VIII
Of The Fiery Sulphureous Seething Of The Earth, And How The Growth Is In The Earth; Also Of The Separation Of The Several Kinds Of Creatures: An Open Gate For The Wise Seekers

1. Let the reader but consider what before is written concerning the centre of the generation of all essences, and then he may easily proceed here: All whatever is corporeal, let it be either spirit or body, consists in a sulphureous property; the spirit in such a spiritual property, and the body out of the spirit in such a corporeal property.

2. For all things are risen from the eternal spirit, as a likeness of the eternal; the invisible essence, which is God and the eternity, has in its own desire introduced itself into a visible essence, and manifested itself in a time, so that he is as a life in the time, and the time is in him as it were dead; as a master that makes his work with an instrument, and the instrument is mute to the master, and yet it is the making, the master only guides it; even so are all things confined into limit, measure, and weight, according to the eternal generation; and they run on in their operation and generation according to the right and property of eternity.

3. And God has appointed over this great work only one master and protector, which can alone manage the work, which is his officer, viz. the soul of the great world, wherein all things lie; and he has appointed a type of its likeness as the reason over this officer, which represents to the officer what he is to do and make; and this is the understanding, viz. God's own dominion wherewith he rules the officer: Now the understanding shews to the officer what the property of each thing is, how the separation and degrees proceed from each other; for all things are contained in the sulphureous body, and Mercury is Sulphur's life, and the salt is the impression, that preserves the body from falling to ashes, so that the spirit is known in a palpable essence.

4. The property of Mercury is in Sulphur, as the boiling of a water; Sulphur is the water wherein Mercury seethes, and produces continually two forms out of the water; viz. one oleous, living, from the liberty of the divine power's property; and one mortal from the dissolution in the fire in the salnitral flagrat.

5. The oily is in stones and metals, herbs, trees, beasts, and men; and the mortal property is in the earth, in the water, in the fire and air; likewise the oleous property is in these four forms (viz. in the earth, water, fire, and air) as a spirit or life, and these four properties are as a dead body, in which the oil is a light or life, from whence the desire, viz. the growth, arises as a springing out of the dead property, which is the vegetative life, a springing, budding, and growing out of death.

6. But now the oily property could not be a life, if it were not in the anguish of death; the anguish makes it to pullulate or move, in that its will is to fly from, and press out of the anguish, and forces itself eagerly forwards, from whence the growth arises: Thus must

death be a cause of the life, that the life may be stirring or active, and therefore Mercury is the true moving life.

7. In the mortal property he is evil, and is called the life of death, of hell, and the anger of God; and in the oily property he is good, from the efficacy of the meekness and liberty of God; and he is the officer's faber, whereby the officer distinguishes the degrees in the vegetative life, separating the living being from the mortal, the heavenly essentiality from the dead or earthly, and appoints it into two kingdoms; viz. the good in the oleous property into a heavenly being, viz. into a light, and the mortal part into the darkness.

8. These two kingdoms are in continual combat one with another, and there is an incessant wrestling in them; as water boiling on the fire; each boils in its property, viz. the oily in joy and meekness, and the mortal in the anguish of darkness, and yet one is the cause of the other: The light is the death, and deadly destruction of the darkness, viz. of the anguish; for in the light the anguish has no strength, but it changes it into the exultation of joyfulness, and the cause of joy, else there would be no joy; for the meekness is like a stillness, but the source of anguish sublimes it, and turns into a pleasant laughter: So also the anguish, viz. the darkness, is the death and destruction of the oily property; for if it gets the upper hand in the oleous property, it takes possession of the corpus, and turns the oil into a poisonful source, viz. into a dark spirit, or body wholly earthly, as Adam was when he imagined into the evil.

9. And yet we do not acknowledge that the oleous property takes any poison-source into itself; but Mercury, viz. the fire-life, insinuates itself into the anguish, and poisons the essence of time, which the outward Mercury itself makes in its own desire, that is, he departs from the inward oleous essence, and then the internal being remains immoveable in itself, and the essence and spirit of time do separate from the essence and spirit of eternity, and yet there is no parting or dividing, but both principles remain in one essence; whereas there are two essences, but the one comprehends not the other, as eternity does not comprehend time: For thus also Adam and Eve died; the soul's Mercury departed with its imagination from the essence of eternity into the essence of time, viz. into the anguish-source, and then the essence of eternity lost its leader, which Christ restored again by the divine word, or Mercury; so that the essence of eternity, which in Adam was forsaken by the soul's Mercury, obtained the life again.

10. And thus we know that the essence of eternity lies hid in the anxious Mercury, as in the fortress of death; and our writing and teaching are to chew how a man may bring the poisonful Mercury with its desire so far, as to enter with its desire again into the essence of eternity, viz. into the enclosed, and reassume the essence of eternity for a body, and with the same tincture the essence of time, and reconcile them in one, that the whole corpus of the inward and outward world may be only one, that so there may be only one will in the spirit, viz. a love-hunger; and this hunger does then make to itself only one essence, and then every spirit eats of its own essence or body, so that afterwards no evil will can arise any more therein.

11. Thus we understand, that joy and sorrow, love and enmity, do originally arise through imagination and longing; for in the inclination or earnest desire towards God, viz. the free love, the kingdom of joy arises in the midst of the anguish of death; and if the desire departs out of the free love into the anguish of death, viz. into the source of darkness, then is the desire filled with the source of death, and so Mercury works effectually in the source of death.

12. Thus we declare with a true ground, that there is nothing so bad, but there lies a good therein, but the badness is not capable of the good; also there lies in the most poisonful Mercury, the greatest pearl and jewel; if his poisonful will may be introduced into the same, then he himself manifests the pearl; for he changes himself; as is to be seen in the earth, where Mercury seeks its pearl, and turns it in the ore to gold, and to other metals, according as the Sulphur is in each place.

13. For there is a continual combat in the earth; the eternity travels with longing through time to be free from vanity, and in its longing it gives itself to Mercury, as to its life and faber; and when Mercury obtains it in his hunger, he becomes joyful, and makes this free lubet corporeal in him, and there arises gold and silver, together with other metals and good herbs, all according to the powerful efficacy of each place; As the boiling is in each place, so likewise is the metal, all according to the property of the seven forms of nature; that form which is chief in a place, according to the same property grows a metal, also herbs and trees.

14. Here the physicians must observe, that they learn distinctly to know what kind of property is the strongest in each thing with which they would cure; if they do not know it, they will oftentimes give their patients death: Also they must know, that they are to understand, and very exactly know the property of the patient, which

of the properties among the seven forms of nature is the Mercury in Sulphur; for such a salt he also makes: Now if the physician gives him a contrary salt, Mercury is only thereby the more vehemently enraged, and made more venomous; but if he may obtain his own salt according to his own property (after which he hungers) then he rejoices, and readily quits the poison-source in the fire of Mars. But the right physician has another cure, he first brings his Mercury with which he will cure out of death's anguish into the liberty: He may well cure, the other is dangerous and uncertain; if he happens to cure, it is by chance, and very inconstant, and cannot cure any disease fundamentally; for the outward Mercury is shut up, it can reach no further than into the four elements, into the mortal essence; it is able to do nothing in the sidereal body: But if it be turned and introduced into the love, as is before mentioned, then it touches the very root and ground, and renews it even to the divine power in the second principle.

15. We have an excellent resemblance of this in the blooming earth on the herbs; for in the earth Mercury is earthly and venomous; but when the sun tinctures him., then he reaches after the sun's power, after its light, and brings it into his hungry fiery Mars-desire, into his salt, viz. into his corporeal essence, viz. into Sulphur, which is his mother, and wheels it about with its rotation in the essence, as if he also boiled; and then the liberty, viz. the highest power, reaches after its property, viz. after the solar property, and apprehends Mercury also along with it.

16. Now when Mercury tastes the heavenly Being in itself, it grows exceeding desirous after the power of love, and draws the same into its desire, whereupon it changes itself, and its salt, so also its mother, the Sulphur, into a pleasant source; and now if the liberty be so introduced into a moving life with Mercury, then it is very full of joy, and springs up in its joy, as a light from the fire, and puts forth through the Sulphur-spirit in the salt: Thus is the growing of the root, and from thence the root gets such a pleasant smell and taste; for in the original the salt's sharpness in the first impression from Saturn is a sharpness of death's anguish, and here it is turned to a pleasant power; for all taste in herbs is salt.

17. Thus understand us further about the root in the earth; when the inward power of the liberty in Mercury's property, which now is changed, does thus force itself forth to the manifestation of the Deity, then the sun's power does eagerly press towards the divine power,

and inclines itself with great desire to the highest heavenly tincture, and draws it with its desire to it; viz. out of the earthly body into a solar: Thus the sun draws the power out of the root in the earth, and the joyful Mercury ascends up along with it, and continually draws the sun's power from above into itself, and from beneath it draws its mother viz. the Sulphur, to itself: And here all the seven forms of nature arise in joyfulness in the combat, each will be uppermost; for so it is in the taste, viz. in the generation of nature; and what form in nature gets to be the chiefest, according to the same taste is the salt in Sulphur, and such an herb grows out of the earth, let it be what it will; though now everything springs from its mother, yet all things have so taken their original, and do still take it; for just so is the right of eternity.

18. Now we are to consider of the stalk: When the herb or sprig looks out of the earth, it comes up at first below with a white form, then further more upwards with a brownish colour, and above with a green colour: This is now its signature, shewing what kind of form is internally in the essence, in the source; the white colour of the branch is from the liberty of the love-lubet, and the brown is the earthly property from Saturn's impression, and from the wrath of Mars; and the green, which opens itself above, is Mercury's in the form of Jupiter and Venus.

19. For Jupiter is power, and Venus is love-desire, which hasten towards the sun, as towards their likeness; and the heaven, which is created out of the midst of the water, puts upon them its blue and green-coloured garment according to the stars' might; for the spirit of the stars receives the new child also, and gives him its spirit and body, and rejoices therein: Now the forms are in contest, and Mercury is the faber and separator; Saturn impresses, and Jupiter is the pleasant power in sulphur; Mars is the fire-source, viz. the might in sulphur; Venus is the water, viz. the sweet desire; Mercury is the life, Luna the body, and Sol the heart, viz. the centre to which all forms tend and press.

20. Thus the outward sun presses into the sun in the herb; and the inward sun presses into the outward, and there is a mere pleasing relish and delight of one essence in another; Saturn makes four, Jupiter makes a pleasant taste, Mars makes bitter, by reason of his anxious nature, Venus makes sweet, Mercury distinguishes the taste, Luna takes it into her sack and hatches it; for she is of an earthly and

heavenly property, and she gives it the menstruum wherein the tincture lies.

21. Thus there is an instigation in the taste; each form hastens to the sweet water and the sun; Jupiter is pleasant, and ascends up aloft with the love-desire in the sweet source-water, wherein Mars rages, and thinks himself to be master in the house, seeing that he rules the fire-spirit in sulphur, at which Mercury is dismayed, that Mars does so disquiet him, and Saturn makes the flagrat corporeal according to his austere impression, and these are the knots upon the stalk; and the flagrat is salnitral, according to the third form of nature in the first impression to the spirit-life, viz. in the anguish-form, from whence the sulphur takes its original, and in the flagrat Mercury goes up in the salniter on the sides, and takes Venus also into it, viz. the love-desire, from whence grow twigs and branches on the stalk, trunk, or body, be they either herbs, trees, or shrubs; and each branch or sprig is then like to the whole plant.

22. But the sun continually by little and little deprives Mars of his force, whereupon the salniter extinguishes, and Mars loses his bitter property; then Jupiter and Venus wholly yield themselves to the sun in the moon's cabinet, and the outward sun takes full possession of the inward; understand the inward sun is a Sulphur in Mercury, and is of the divine power's property, from the liberty of God, which imprints itself on all things, and gives life and power to all things. Now when that is done, that Jupiter and Venus have given themselves to the power of the sun, then Jupiter forces no more upwards, but Mars and Mercury do continually more and more wind up the stalk from the earth on high; Jupiter stays still above in the inward and outward sun's power, and there is the pleasant conjunction with time and eternity, there the eternity beholds itself in an image in the time.

23. And paradise springs up or opens, for the Sulphur and the salt in the Sulphur are here transmuted in the paradise, and the paradisical joy puts itself forth in the smell and taste. This is now the head or knob of the blossoms, wherein the corn grows; the lovely smell is in one part paradisical, viz. from the divine power, from the liberty; and on the other part earthly, according to the outward sun, and the outward world.

24. The heavenly property sets forth its signature with fair colours of the leaves on the blossoms; and the earthly represents its signature by the green leaves or sprigs about the blossom; but seeing this

kingdom of the outward world is only a time (in which the curse is), and Adam could not stand in paradise, the paradisical property soon passes away with its signature, and changes itself into the corn which grows in the blossom; therein the property of the inward and outward sun, viz. of the inward and outward power, is couched, each property in its principle; for God has cursed the earth, and therefore let none think that the outward is divine, only the divine power penetrates and tinctures the outward being ; for God said, "The seed of the woman shall bruise the serpent's head:" This is now effected after the curse in all things which approach near the Deity, wherein Mercury is a poison; there God bruises its head with the inward and outward sun, and takes away the poisonful might in the anger.

25. O that you would but learn to understand, dear sirs and brethren, wherewith you are to cure; not with the angry Mercury, which in many an herb is an evil poison-source, but with the inward Mercury: If you would be called doctors and masters, then you ought also to know how you may change the outward Mercury in the Sulphur into love, that he may be delivered from the anguish-source, and brought into a joyfulness, viz. that the earthly being be turned into an heavenly, the death into life; this is your doctorship in the right meaning, and not by the officer of reason only.

26. God has placed man above the officer, and ordained him in the understanding to his own dominion: He has ability to change nature, and to turn the evil into good, provided that first he has changed himself, otherwise he cannot; so long as he is dead in the understanding, so long he is the servant and slave of the officer; but when he is made alive in God, then the officer is his servant.

27. Ye haughty caps, let it be told you; pride, and your own honour, and the earthly lust of the flesh, lies in your way, so that you are not masters in the mysteries, but blind children; you will not lay your hands upon the coals, but you take money from the poor and distressed, and give that to many an one which had been far better he had never bought, for which you must give a severe and strict account.

28. Thus it is likewise with the sulphurean seething in the earth with the metals, the power is stronger in metals than in the herbs, the tincture is more heavenly than earthly, if the artist affords it his help, then it changes itself, viz. the earthly into an heavenly, which notwithstanding comes to pass in many places without the artist's ingenuity; as we see, how Mercury in sulphur apprehends the

heavenly tincture in its boiling, whereby he changes his made essence (which he makes in the sulphur) into gold and silver by the power and efficacy of the tincture, understand, by that part of the heavenly property; for out of the earth, or out of the mortified property in the salniter, no gold can be made, for there is no fixedness therein.

29. Now we are thus to consider of this process of the boiling in the Sulphur in the earth: Where the earth is in any place sulphureous in the saturnine property, wherein the sun bears chief rule, there is such a boiling; the outward sun hungers after the inward, which dwells in its own principle in the centre in sulphur, and sets its desire upon time; for the time, viz. the creature, longs after eternity, viz. after the liberty, to be freed from vanity; as the Scripture says, that "all creatures do earnestly long with us to be freed from vanity."

30. Even here the liberty gives itself into the solar property into the time, and when Mercury tastes it, he becomes joyful, and turns his wheel in the joy; then Saturn impresses the meekness; and Mars, which arises in the mercurial wheel in the impression, gives the fire-soul thereinto, so that there is a driving forth and growth; for the liberty puts itself forth in Mercury's property, and Mercury continually separates Saturn and Mars from it; for he will have a fair and pure child to his joy; he suffers Venus to remain on the child, for she is in property akin to the child: copper is nighest to gold by reason of the materia, it wants only the tincture; Mars holds him too hard in possession; if he may be got out, then it is gold, which the artist does well understand.

31. After Venus Mars is akin to gold; for he has swallowed up Venus in his wrath, and uses her for his body, else in his own peculiar property he has no corporeal essence, for he is only wrath, which consumes: He makes him a body out of the water of Venus, which he devours, and Saturn makes it corporeal to him; therefore he does so defile his iron with rust, and that is his property, viz. to be a devourer of his body; but Venus is pleasant, and makes a growing in him, he devours again whatever Venus's property makes in him; for Venus is the food of Mars in the saturnine property; therefore the artist is to consider what lies in Mars; if he has only the solar tincture, he needs nothing else thereto, that he may but deprive Mars of his force, for Mars has his toughness from Venus.

32. Mars in his own peculiar property is only spalt, and causes hardness. as the fire does; but Saturn is the impressure of all things; Venus needs only the tincture, and then she is perfect; but the artist

must rightly understand where the possibility lies, viz. in Sulphur, where Saturn has the Sulphur in his belly, and Mercury shews its colour, there he is in the will, but cannot, for Saturn holds him too fast imprisoned; but if the artist gives him his helping hand, that he may but advance his wheel, and give him his mother's food, which she has hid in the centre, then he grows strong, and casts Saturn away, and manifests the child: For so it is also in the earth, where Mercury is quick in his mother, viz. in the Sulphur, that he is not withheld, that he may only reach Venus in his hunger for food, the sun will soon shine forth, for she beams forth in Venus's meekness: He dresses or seethes his food with his own fire, he needs no artist thereto; which the artist must well observe, for he has his Mars in himself.

33. Now as the boiling is in the earth, so also it is above the earth; when the fruit grows out of the earth, it is first sharp astringent and bitter, also sour and unpleasant, as the apple upon the tree is so; for Saturn has at first the dominion, he attracts it together, and Mercury forms it, and Mars gives the fire to Mercury, which Saturn receives into his cold property, Venus gives the sap, and Luna takes all into her body, for she is mother, and receives the seed of all the planets into her menstruum, and hatches it; Jupiter gives power thereinto, and Sol is king therein, but at the first Sol is weak; for the materia is too earthly and cold. Now the whole essence in its boiling lies in the body of Sulphur; and in the Sulphur the salnitral flagrat makes a salt in Mars's wheel according to each property; for the Sulphur turns into salt, that is, into taste; and in the same taste there is an oil hid in the centre in the sulphureous property, which oil arises from the free love-lubet, viz. out of eternity, and manifests itself with an external essence in the time, which is the manifestation of God.

34. Now in this same oil is the hunger or love-desire after the essence of time, viz. after the manifestation of the Deity; this desire reaches in the essence of time after its property, viz. after the sun, and the sun's property reaches after the oil in the centre of the fruit, and fervently longs after it, and gives itself freely into the fruit, and sucks the virtue into itself, and gives it forth in its joy into the austere property of the fruit, and meekens and sweetens all with the love, which it receives in the centre in the oil of the liberty: Thus a fruit, which at first is sour and sharp, becomes very pleasant and sweet, that a man may eat it; and even thus is the ripening of all fruits.

35. Now by the signature in the external you may see the inward form; for the forms in the salt, viz. in the power, shew themselves externally.

36. There are commonly four colours, as white, yellow, red, and green: Now according to what colour the fruit (as an apple) is most signed, accordingly is the taste also in the salt; as white with a clear thin skin somewhat inclining to dark gives sweetness, which is of Venus property; if the sweet taste be strong and powerful, then Jupiter is potent therein; but if it be weak and fulsom, then the moon is strong therein; but if it be hard, and of a brownish colour, then Mars is strong therein; but if the white colour be of a grayish-brown, then Saturn is strong therein: Venus makes a white colour, Mars red, and bitter in the taste; Mars makes Venus's colour light, Mercury gives a mixt colour, and opens the green in Mars; Jupiter inclines to blue, Saturn to black, almost gray; the sun makes the yellow colour, and gives the right sweetness in the salt, and casts forth the pleasant smell, which takes its rise from Sulphur; Saturn makes astringent sharp and sour; and each property represents itself externally, as it is internally in the dominion, so also by the form or signature of the leaf, or branches.

37. Every root, as it is in the earth, may be known by the signature for what it is good or profitable, even such a form also has the earth, and it is discerned in the leaves and stalks which planet is lord in the property, much more in the flower; for of what taste the herb and root is, even such an hunger is in it, and such a cure lies therein, for it has such a salt. The physician must know what kind of sickness is risen in the body, and in what salt the loathing is risen in Mercury, that so he may not administer a further loathing and nausea to his patient; for if he gives him the herb, in whose property Mercury has before received a loathing, then he ministers poison to him; so that the poison in the loathing of the body does exceedingly inflame itself in Mercury, unless he burns that herb to ashes, and gives it him; then the poison of the loathing loses its might; for these ashes are a death to the poison of the living Mercury.

38. This we find very effectually in the magic; this also the physician must know, that all sicknesses arise from the loathing in the form of nature: As when one form in the life is superior, if then a contrary thing quite opposite to its property be by force introduced into it, let it be either from the stars, or from the elements, or from the seven forms of life, then it deprives this superior or chiefest form

(which is the leader and ruler of the life) of its strength and power in its salt; then the Mercury of this superior form begins effectually to work, that is, to hunger and loath; and if he gets not his own peculiar property, understand the bodily form, which is chief in the body among the seven properties or forms, then he enkindles himself in his own poison-source according to his vital property, and does so forcibly strive so long, till he becomes fiery, and then he awakes his own Mars, and his own Saturn, which impress him, and consume the flesh of the body in the poison-fire, and wholly consume the oil of light; even then the life's light goes out, and it is past recovery.

39. But if the form of life, wherein Mercury is inflamed in the loathing in the anguish and poison-source, may obtain that property into its hunger, of which the spirit and body is chief, then he obtains his own natural food, of which he lives, and does again rejoice, and puts away the nauseate, and then the nauseate dissipates or dissolves and is spewed out; but the physician must have a care, whether or no that thing which he will administer to his patient be in its property strong also in the same essence, from whence the nauseate is risen in the body.

40. As for example; A jovial man receives a nauseate or loathing from the lunar property; now if the physician knew that he had so gotten his nauseate, and prepared him a jovial cure according to the hunger of his own spirit or mercury, this now would be right; but if the moon's property be strong in the salt which he would administer for the nauseate, then he gives him a nauseate; but if the jovial cure be free from the moon, then the jovial Mercury receives its own food with great desire, and quits the nauseate: And thus it is likewise with diseases which arise in the salniter, viz. from fear or frightening; thereto belongs also such a flagrat as the first was, and then there is a present cure, or such an herb, wherein the salniter lies in such a property as it lies in that man.

41. I know, and it is shewn me, that the sophister will cavil at me, because I write, that the divine power is in the fruit, that God's power does appropriate itself into the generation of nature: But hear, my dear friend, become seeing, I ask thee, How was paradise in this world? Was it also manifest in nature? Was it also in the fruit? Was it in the world, or without the world? Did paradise stand in God's power, or in the elements? Was the power of God manifest in the world, or hidden? Or what is the curse of the earth, and the putting of Adam and Eve out of paradise? Then tell me, Does not God dwell also

in time? Is not God all in all? It is written, "Am not I he who filleth all things?" Also, "Thine is the kingdom, the power, and glory, from eternity to eternity."

42. Here consider thyself, and leave me uncensured: I do not say, that the nature is God, much less the fruit proceeding from the earth; but I say, God gives power to every life, be it good or bad, to each thing according to its desire, for he himself is All; and yet he is not called God according to every being, but according to the light wherewith he dwells in himself and shines with his power through all his beings; He gives in his power to all his beings and works, and each thing receives his power according to its property; one takes darkness, the other light; each hunger desires its property, and yet the whole essence or being is all God's, be it evil or good, for from him and through him are all things, what is not of his love, that is of his anger. Paradise is yet in the world, but man is not therein, unless he be born again of God; then as to that new regeneration he is therein, and not with the Adam of the four elements. O that we would but once learn to know ourselves, and even understand it by the created essence or being.

43. Lo! in Saturn there lies gold shut up in a very disesteemed and contemptible form and manner, which indeed resembles no metal; and though it be cast into the fire and melted, yet a man shall have nothing, but a contemptible matter void of any form of virtue, till the artist takes it in hand, and uses the right process about it, and then it is manifest what was therein.

44. So likewise God dwells in all things, and the thing knows nothing of God; he likewise is not manifest to the thing, and yet it receives power from him, but it receives the power according to its property from him, either from his love, or from his wrath; and from which it receives, so it has its signature externally; and the good is also in it, but as it were wholly shut up or hidden to the iniquity or evil ; an example of which you have in bushes, and other thorny and pricking briars, out of which notwithstanding a fair well-smelling blossom grows; and there lie two properties therein, viz. a pleasant and unpleasant; which overcomes, that shapes forms or marks the fruit.

45. Thus also it is with man; he was created a fair blossom and fruit of paradise, but the devil raised up in him his thorny property by the serpent, understand the centre, the property of the wrathful nature, which in his paradisical source was not manifest in him; but

when his hunger entered into the thorny false property of the serpent, viz. into death, then the property of death, and the false serpent in the devil's desire, pressed into his hunger, and filled soul and body, so that the hunger of the false serpent began effectually to work in him, and death awaked in him, and then paradise hid itself in him: For paradise entered into itself, and the poison of the serpent in death's property dwelt also in itself; here was now the enmity; then said God to him, "The seed of the woman shall bruise the serpent's head, and thou shalt sting the heel with death's poison."

46. Understand the paradisical image which is shut up, and captivated in the wrathful death, in which the word of the Deity, viz. the divine Mercury, ruled and wrought, did disappear; as the gold is disappeared in Saturn, so that nothing is seen but a contemptible matter, till the right artist sets upon it, and again awakens the Mercury in the inclosed gold, and then the dead inclosed body of the gold does again revive in Saturn; for Mercury is its life, who must be introduced into it again, and then the dead body of the gold appears, and overcomes the gross Saturn, wherein it lay shut up, and changes its mean contemptible old body into a fair glorious golden body.

47. Thus likewise it is with man; he lies now shut up after his fall in a gross, deformed, bestial dead image; he is not like an angel, much less like unto paradise; he is as the gross ore in Saturn, wherein the gold is couched and shut up; his paradisical image is in him as if it were not, and it is also not manifest, the outward body is a stinking carcass, while it yet lives in the poison: He is a bad thorny bush, from whence notwithstanding fair rose-buds may bloom forth, and grow out of the thorns, and manifest that which lies hidden, and shut up in the wrathful poisonful Mercury, till the artist who has made him takes him in hand, and brings the living Mercury into his gold or paradisical image disappeared and shut up in death; so that the inclosed image, which was created out of the divine meekness and love-essentiality, may again bud and spring forth in the divine Mercury, viz. in the word of the Deity, which entered into the humanity shut up and closed in the death and curse.

48. And then the divine mercury changes the wrathful Mercury into its property, and Christ is born, who bruises the head of the serpent, viz. of the poison and death in the anger of God, understand the might of wrathful death; and a new man arises in holiness and righteousness, which lives before God, and his divine image appears

and puts forth its lustre as the hidden gold out of the earthly property: And hereby it is clearly signified to the artist chosen of God how he shall seek; no otherwise than as he has sought and found himself in the property of the pure gold; and so likewise is this process, and not a whit otherwise; for man and the earth with its secrets lie shut up in the like or same curse and death, and need one and the same restitution.

49. But we tell the seeker, and sincerely and faithfully warn him as he loves his temporal and eternal welfare, that he do not first set upon this way to try the earth, and restore that which is shut up in death, unless he himself be before born again through the divine mercury out of the curse and death, and has the full knowledge of the divine regeneration, else all that he does is to no purpose, no learning or studying avails; for that which he seeks lies shut in the curse, in death, in the anger of God: If he will make it alive, and bring it into its first life, then that life must be before manifest in him, and then he may say to the mountain, "Get thee hence, and be cast into the sea;" and to the fig-tree, "No fruit grow on thee henceforth;" and it shall come to pass; for if the divine mercury lives, and is manifest in the spirit, then when the spirit of the soul's will imagines into anything, Mercury also goes along with it in the imagination, and enkindles the Mercury fast apprehended in death, viz. the similitude of God, or the manifestation, with which the living God has made himself manifest.

50. I know and see, that the mocker in the devil's vizard will yet bring my writing into a misapprehension, and make me more dark and doubtful, because I write of the inward and outward Mercury, and understand by the inward the word of God, or the divine voice, viz. the manifestation of the eternity of the abyss; and by the outward mercury I understand the officer in nature, viz. the instrument, which the inward, living, powerful word, or divine voice uses, wherewith it forms and works. Now the sophister will falsely interpret it, and say, that I mix them both together, making no difference, and hold nature for God, as Babel has already done to me: But I bid him view my words well, and learn to understand them right; for I speak sometimes from the heavenly Mercury, and see that only, and then presently I name the instrument of the heavenly, therefore let him have regard to the sense: I write not heathenishly, but theosophically, from a higher ground than the outward faber is, and then also from the same.

Chapter IX
Of The Signature, Shewing How The Internal Signs The External

1. The whole outward visible world with all its being is a signature, or figure of the inward spiritual world; whatever is internally, and however its operation is, so likewise it has its character externally; like as the spirit of each creature sets forth and manifests the internal form of its birth by its body, so does the Eternal Being also.

2. The Being of all beings is a wrestling power; for the kingdom of God consists in power, and also the outward world, and it stands especially in seven properties or forms, where the one causes and makes the other, and none of them is the first or last, but it is the eternal band; therefore God has appointed six days for man to work, and the seventh day is the perfection wherein the six do rest; it is the centre to which the desire of the six days tend; therefore God calls it the Sabbath or resting-day, for therein the six forms of the working power rest: It is the divine sound in the power, or the kingdom of joy, wherein all the other forms are manifest; for it is the formed world, or divine corporality, by which all things are generated and come forth to a being.

3. This formed world has manifested itself with the motion of all forms with this visible world, as with a visible likeness, so that the spiritual being might be manifest in a corporeal comprehensive essence; as the desire of the inward forms has made itself external, and the internal being is in the external; the internal holds the external before it as a glass, wherein it beholds itself in the property of the generation of all forms; the external is its signature.

4. Thus everything which is generated out of the internal has its signature; the superior form, which is chief in the spirit of the working in the power, does most especially sign the body, and the other forms hang to it; as it is to be seen in all living creatures, in the shape and form of the body, and in the behaviour and deportment, also in the sound, voice, and speech; and likewise in trees and herbs, in stones and metals; all according as the wrestling is in the power of the spirit, so is the figure of the body represented, and so likewise is its will, so long as it so boils in the life-spirit.

5. But if the artist takes it in hand with the true Mercury, then he may turn the weakest form to be uppermost, and the strongest undermost, and then the spirit obtains another will, according to the most superior form; that which before must be servant becomes now lord and master in the seven forms; as Christ said to the sick, "Arise,

thy faith hath made thee whole," and they arose: And thus likewise it is here, each form hungers after the centre, and the centre is the voice of life, viz. the Mercury, the same is the faber or former of the power; if this voice gives itself into the hunger of the meanest form in the strong combat then it lifts up its property (understand the property of that form), and thus its desire or faith has saved it; for in the desire Mercury lifts up or sublimes itself; and thus it was in Christ's patients.

6. Sickness had taken possession of them, and the poison of death had gotten the upper hand in Mercury; but now the form of life in the centre did set its hunger as a famished and mean property after the liberty to be freed from the abomination; but seeing the Mercury was revived in Christ the divine property, therefore the weak hunger entered into Christ's strong hunger after the salvation of man, and so the weak hunger received the strong in the power; and then the divine voice in Christ said, "Arise, lift up thyself, thy faith" (that is, thy desire which thou hast introduced into me) "hath saved thee."

7. Thus the life prevails over the death, the good over evil; and on the contrary, the evil over the good, as came to pass in Lucifer and Adam, and still daily comes to pass: And thus everything is signed; that form which is chief receives the taste, and also the sound in Mercury, and figures the body after its property; the other forms hang to it as co-helpers, and also give their signature thereto, but very weakly.

8. There are especially seven forms in nature, both in the eternal and external nature; for the external proceed from the eternal: The ancient philosophers have given names to the seven planets according to the seven forms of nature; but they have understood thereby another thing, not only the seven stars, but the sevenfold properties in the generation of all essences: There is not anything in the Being of all beings, but it has the seven properties in it; for they are the wheel of the centre, the cause of Sulphur, in which Mercury makes the boiling in the anguish-source.

9. The seven forms are these; viz. the desire of the impression is called Saturn, into which the free lubet of eternity gives itself; this in the impression is called Jupiter, by reason of its pleasant commendable virtue; for the saturnine power encloses and makes hard, cold, and dark, and causes the Sulphur, viz. the vital spirit, understand the moving vital spirit, viz. the natural; and the free lubet makes the impression to long to be freed from the dark astringent hardness, and it is very rightly called Jupiter, being a desire of the

understanding which opens the darkness, and manifests another will therein.

10. In these two properties is pourtrayed and exactly deciphered God's kingdom, viz. the original, and also the kingdom of God's anger, viz. the dark abyss, which is a cause of the motion in Saturn, viz. in the impression; the impression, viz. Saturn, makes the nothing, viz. the free lubet movable and sensible, and also opposite, for it causes it to be essence; and Jupiter is the sensible power proceeding from the free lubet to manifestation out of the nothing into something, in the impression of Saturn; and they are two properties in the manifestation of God according to love and anger, viz. a model of the eternal form, and are as a wrestling combat, viz. an opposite desire against each other; one makes good, the other evil, and yet it is all good; only if we will speak of the anguish-source, and then also of the joyful source, then we must distinguish, that the cause of each source may be understood.

11. The third form is called Mars, which is the fiery property in the impression of Saturn, where the impression introduces itself into great anguish, viz. into a great hunger; it is the painfulness, or the cause of feeling, also the cause of the fire and consuming, also of enmity and malignity; but in Jupiter, viz. in the free lubet, in the nothing, it causes the fiery love-desire, that the liberty, viz. the nothing, is desirous, and introduces itself into sensibility, viz. into the kingdom of joy: In the darkness it is a devil, viz. God's wrath, and in the light it is an angel of joy, understand such a property; for when this source became dark in Lucifer, he was called a devil, but while he was in the light he was an angel; and thus also it is to be understood in man.

12. The fourth property or form is called Sol, viz. the light of nature, which has its original in the liberty, viz. in the nothing, but without splendour, and gives itself in with the lubet into the desire of the impression of Saturn, even to the wrathful or fiery property of Mars; and there the free lubet, which has sharpened itself in the impression, in the property of Mars, in the consuming anguish, and in the hardness of Saturn, displays, or powerfully puts itself forth in Jupiter, as a sharpness of the liberty, and an original of the nothing, and also of the sense; and the effluence from the heat and anguish of Mars, and from Saturn's hardness is the shining of the light in nature, which gives the understanding in Saturn, Jupiter, and Mars, viz. a spirit, which knows what itself is in its properties, which hinders or

prevails against the wrath, and brings it out of the anguish, out of the property of Mars, into Jupiter's, viz. out of the anguish into a love-desire.

13. In these four forms the spirit's birth consists, viz. the true spirit both in the inward and outward being, viz. the spirit of power in the essence; and the essence or corporality of this spirit is Sulphur.

14. Ye rabbies and masters! that you could but understand, how faithfully that is given and revealed to you, which your predecessors have intended and aimed at, wherein you have been a long time blind, the cause of which is your pride: This God, the most high understanding, sets before you by mean, and heretofore ungrounded instruments, which he himself has grounded, if you would yet once see, and escape the tormenting source.

15. The fifth form is Venus, the beginning of all corporality, viz. of the water, which arises in the desire of Jupiter and Mars, viz. in the love-desire, out of the liberty, and out of nature, viz. out of the impression's desire in Saturn, in Mars, in the great anguish, to be freed from the anguish: And it carries two forms in the desire of its property, viz. a fiery from Mars, and a watery property from Jupiter, understand an heavenly and earthly desire; the heavenly arises from the heavenly impression of the union or free effluence of the Deity in nature to its own manifestation; and the earthly arises from the impression of the darkness in Mars, viz. in the wrathful fire's property; therefore the essence of this desire consists in two things, viz. in the water, from the original of the liberty, and in Sulphur from the original of nature according to the impression.

16. The outward similitude of the heavenly Being is water and oil; understand, according to the sun it is water, and according to Jupiter it is oil, and according to the hard impression of Saturn after the heavenly Being according to Mars, it is copper, and according to Sol gold, and according to the earthly impression, according to the property of the darkness, it is in Sulphur grit, gravel and sand; according to the property of Mars a cause of all stones; for all stones are Sulphur from the powerful predominance of Saturn and Mars in the property of Venus according to the dark impression, understand according to the earthly part.

17. O ye dear wise men! if you did but know what lies in Venus, you would not so sumptuously adorn your roofs: The potentate often loses his life for the servant's sake, and he puts the master upon his roof, therefore he is blind; this his false Venus-desire causes in him,

that he forms it in Saturn and Mars, and brings it forth in Sol; if he formed his Venus-desire in Jupiter, then he might rule over the fiery Mars which lies in Venus, and has put his coat upon Venus in Sulphur.

18. Thus Mars clothes all his servants which love him and Saturn with his garment, that they only find the copper of Venus, and not its gold in the copper; the spirit of the seeker enters into Sol, viz. into pride, and supposes that he has Venus, but he has Saturn, viz. covetousness; if he went forth in the water, viz. in the resigned humility of Venus, the stone of the wise men would be revealed to him.

19. The sixth form is Mercury, viz. the life and separation, or the form in the love, and in the anguish: In Saturn and Mars, on the one part he is earthly according to the hard impression, where his motion and hunger is a pricking, adverse, and (according to the fire) a bitter pain and woe; and according to the water in the earthly Sulphur, viz. in the mortification, a poison-source.

20. And according to the other part, according to the lubet of the liberty, he is the pleasant property of joy in Jupiter and Venus, also of springing and growing; and according to the impression of the heavenly Saturn, and according to Mars in the love-desire, he is the sound in the spirit, understand, the separator of the sound, viz. of the tone; also of all pronunciations of speeches, and all the several cries and notes; all whatever sounds is distinguished by his might; Venus and Saturn carry his lute, and he is the lutanist, he strikes upon Venus and Saturn, and Mars gives him the sound from the fire; and thus Jupiter rejoices in Sol.

21. Here lies the pearl, dear brethren: Mercury makes the understanding in Jupiter, for he separates the thoughts, and makes them act and move; he takes the infinity of the thoughts into his desire, and makes them essential; this he does in Sulphur, and his essence is the manifold power of the smell and taste, and Saturn gives his sharpness thereinto, so that it is salt.

22. But I understand here the virtual salt in the vegetable life: Saturn makes the common salt in the water: He is an heavenly and an earthly labourer, and labours in each form according to the property of the form; as it is written, "With the holy thou art holy, and with the perverse thou art perverse." In the holy angels the heavenly Mercury is holy and divine, and in the devils he is the poison and wrath of the eternal nature according to the dark impression's property, and so on

through all things, as the property of each thing is, so is its Mercury, viz. its life; in the angels he is the hymn of God's praise, and in the devils he is the cursing and awakening of the opposite will of the bitter poisonful enmity.

23. Thus likewise it is to be understood in men and all creatures, in all whatever lives and moves; for the outward Mercury is the outward word in the outward world: He is the outward verbum, and Saturn with the impression is his fiat, which makes his word corporeal; and in the inward kingdom of the divine power he is the eternal word of the Father, whereby he has made all things in the outward principle, understand, with the instrument of the outward Mercury.

24. The outward Mercury is the temporal word, the expressed word; and the inward Mercury is the eternal word, the speaking word; the inward word dwells in the outward, and makes through the outward all outward things; and with the inward, inward things: The inward Mercury is the life of the Deity, and all divine creatures; and the outward Mercury is the life of the outward world, and all external corporality in men and beasts, in vegetables and animals, and makes a peculiar principle, viz. a likeness of the divine world; and this is the manifestation of the divine wisdom.

25. The seventh form is called Luna, the amassed essence: What Mercury has comprised in Sulphur, that is a corporeal or substantial hunger of all forms; the property of all the six forms lies therein, and it is as a corporeal being of all the rest; this property is as a wife of all the other forms; for the other forms do all cast their desire through Sol into Luna; for in Sol they are spiritual, and in Luna corporeal: Therefore the moon assumes to it the sunshine, and shines from the sun; whatever the sun is, and makes in the spirit-life in itself, the same Luna is, and makes corporeal in itself.

26. It is heavenly and earthly, and rules the vegetative life; it has the menstruum, viz. the matrix of Venus in it; all whatever is corporeal does congeal in its property; Saturn is its fiat, and Mercury is its husband, which impregnates it, and Mars is its vegetable soul, and the sun is its centre in the hunger, and yet not wholly in the property; for it receives only the white colour from the sun, not the yellow, or the red, viz. the majestic; therefore in its property lies silver in metals, and in the property of Sol gold; but seeing Sol is a spirit without essence, thereupon Saturn holds the sun's corporeal essence in himself to lodge in; for he is the fiat of the sun; he keeps it shut up

in his dark cabinet, and does only preserve and keep it; for it is not his own essence, till the sun sends him his faber Mercury, to whom he gives it, and to none else.

27. Observe this, ye wise men! It is no fiction or fallacy; let the artist but understand us right; he must bring the jewel shut up in Saturn into the mother of generation, viz. into Sulphur, and take the faber, and divide all forms, and separate the variety of hungers, which the faber himself does, when the artist brings the work into the first mother, viz. into Sulphur: But he must first baptize the froward child with the philosophical baptism, lest he makes a bastard of Sol; and then let him lead him into the desert, and try whether Mercury will eat manna in the desert after the baptism; or whether he will make bread of stones; or whether he will aspire aloft as an haughty spirit, and precipitate himself from the Temple; or whether he will worship Saturn, in whom the devil sits hidden: This the artist must observe; whether Mercury, the wicked poisonful child, receives the baptism; whether he can feed of God's bread or no.

28. If he now does eat, and stands out in the temptation, then will the angels appear to him after forty days, and then let him go out of the desert, and eat his own food; and so the artist is ready and fit for his work; if not, then let him by all means leave it, and as yet account himself unworthy of it.

29. He must have the understanding of the generation of nature; else all his labour and pains are to no purpose, except the grace of the Most High has bestowed upon him some particular, that so he is able to tincture Venus and Mars, which is the shortest and most ready way, if God chews him such an herb wherein the tincture lies.

30. The lunar body of metals lies in the seething of the earth, in Sulphur and Mercury, covered internally with the coat of Venus, and clothed externally with the cloak of Saturn, as we see plainly, and is a degree more external than the solar body: Next after Luna, Jupiter's body is also a degree more external; but Venus is a sly bird, she has also the inward solar body; she takes the coat of Mars upon her, and hides herself in Saturn's cabinet; but she is manifest, and not hidden.

31. Next Venus Mars is likewise a degree more external, and nearer to earthliness; and next Mars Mercury's body is a particula of all the rest; on one part most nigh to the earthly corporality, and on the other part nearest the heavenly; and next Mercury Luna is on the earthly part wholly earthly, and on the heavenly part wholly heavenly; it carries an earthly and heavenly face towards all things; to

the evil it is evil, and to the good it is good; to a pleasant creature it gives its best in the taste, and to a bad creature it gives the curse of the corrupted earth.

32. Now in all this, as the property of each thing is internally, so it has externally its signature, both in animals and vegetables; and this you shall see in an herb, so likewise in trees and beasts, and in men also.

33. If the saturnine property be predominant, and chief in a thing, then it is of a black, greyish colour, hard and spare, sharp, sour, or salt in taste; it gets a long lean body, grey in the eyes, of a dark blue, of a very slender body, but of a hard touch, though the property of Saturn is very seldom alone master in a thing; for he soon awakens Mars with his hard impression, who makes his property bending and crooked, full of knots, and hinders the body from growing high, but is full of branches and rugged, as is to be seen in oak-shrubs, and the like trees.

34. But if Venus be next to Saturn in any place in the sude or seething of the earth, then the sude in the Sulphur of Saturn causes a tall strong body; for it gives its sweetness into Saturn's impression, whereby Saturn becomes strong and lusty, and if Venus be not hindered by Mars, it grows a great, tall, slender tree, herb, beast, or man, or whatever it be.

35. But if Jupiter be next to him in the property of Venus, so that Jupiter is stronger in Saturn than Venus, and Mars under Venus, then it falls out to be a very excellent fair body, full of virtue and power, also of a good taste; its eyes are blue, and somewhat whitish, of a meek property, but very potent: If it falls out that Mercury is between Venus and Jupiter, and Mars undermost, then is this property in Saturn graduated in the highest degree with all power and virtue, in words and works, with great understanding.

36. If it be in herbs, then they are long, of a middle-sized stature or stalk, of a very curious form, fair blossoms, white, or blue; but if the sun also casts the influence of his property into it, then does its colour by reason of the sun incline to yellow; and if Mars hinders not, then is the universal very sovereign in the thing, be it either a man, or other creature, or an herb of the earth: This let the magus well observe, it withstands all malignity, and false influences and assaults from the spirits, whatever they be, so far as a man himself is not false and wicked, and inclines not his desire to the devil, as Adam did, in whom also the universal was wholly complete.

37. With these herbs a man may cure, and heal without any art of the artist; but they are rarely and seldom found, yea not one among many sees them, for they are nigh to paradise: The curse of God hides the eyesight of the wicked, that it does not see, although they should stand before his eyes: Yet in such a conjunction of the planets they are manifest, and may not be hidden; therefore there lies a great secret in many an herb and beast, if the artist knew it, and had the true skill to use it; the whole magia lies therein: But I am bidden to be silent by reason of the wicked, who is not worthy of it, and is justly plagued with the plague with which he plagues other honest people, and tumbles himself in the mire.

38. But if Mars in his property be next Saturn, and Mercury casts an opposite aspect, and the power of Venus be under Mars, and Jupiter under the property of Venus, then out of this property all is corrupted and poisoned; a poisonful herb, tree, beast, or whatever it be; if it falls into the corrupt human property, then it is fitted and prone to evil, but if the moon brings its powerful influence thereinto, then is the false magia ready in the lunar menstruum, and witchcraft is manifest, of which I must here also be silent, and will only shew the signature.

39. In an herb, if the blossom be somewhat reddish, and wreathed, or streaked, and inclined to white by the red, then is the power of Venus there, which makes resistance therein; but if it be only reddish, and of dark wriths or streaks, with a rough peel or skin on the stalk, branch, and leaf, then does the basilisk lodge there.

40. For Mars makes it rugged, and Mercury is poisonful therein, which gives a streaked colour, and Mars the red, and Saturn the dark, which is a pestilence in the lunar menstruum; but to the artist it is an herb against the pestilence, if he takes the poison from Mercury, and gives him Venus and Jupiter for food, then Mars brings forth the vegetable soul in Sol, and turns his wrathful fire into a love-fire, which the artist must know, if he will be called a doctor.

41. This property likewise signs the living creatures both in their voice and visage; it gives a gross, dull sound, somewhat inclining to a shrill voice by reason of Mars, soothing, flattering, and very false, lying, commonly red pimples or streams in the eyes, or blinking, and rolling unsteady eyes: In herbs this property likewise yields a taste very loathsome, from whence in man's life, viz. in Mercury, if it takes it down, a stirring boiling poison arises, which darkens and obscures the life.

42. The physician must have a care of the herbs of this property; they are not to be taken into the body, but they are poisonful, of what name soever they be; for there often happens such a conjunction of the planets, which sometimes so prepares an herb, which is good if it be subject to Saturn and Mars: So likewise it falls out sometimes, that an evil herb, by reason of a good conjunction, if in its beginning it stands in the menstruum, may be freed from the malignity, which is to be known by the signature; therefore the physician, who understands the signature, may best of all gather the herbs himself.

43. But if Mars be next Saturn, and Mercury very weak, and Jupiter also under Mars in the property, and Venus casts an opposite aspect or dissent with its desire, then it is good; for Jupiter and Venus change the wrath of Mars into joy, which produces hot wholesome sovereign herbs, which are to be used in all hot diseases and hurts; the herb is rough, and somewhat prickly the leaves on the branches; so likewise the stalk is fine and thin, according to the nature of Venus, but the virtue and power is of Mars and Jupiter, well mixed and tempered, commonly with brownish blossoms forcing forth in the property, and that because Mars is strong therein with his wrath; but seeing his wrath is changed by Jupiter and Venus into a pleasant property, the wrath becomes a desire of joy.

44. The physician must not give Saturn without Mars in hot diseases, not cold without heat, else he enkindles Mars in the wrath, and stirs up Mercury in the hard impression in the property of death; Mars belongs to the cure of every Mars-like sickness, which is of heat, and pricking pangs: But let the physician know, that he must first correct and qualify Mars, which he intends to administer, with Jupiter and Venus, that the wrath of Mars may be changed into joy, and then he will also change the sickness in the body into joy; cold is quite contrary to it.

45. If the physician administers Saturn only and by itself to a martial disease or hurt, then Mars is dismayed with death, and falls down with his force and strength into death's property; and now seeing he is the fire in the body, the life's fire becomes thereupon deadly in the elemental property; for he soon awakens Mercury in the property of cold: But yet the physician must have a care that he administers not in an hot disease the raw undigested hot Mars, in which Mercury is wholly inflamed and burning; for he enkindles the fire more vehemently in the body; he must first mollify Mars and Mercury, and put them into joy, and then it is right and good.

46. The hotter an herb is, the better it is hereunto; yet its wrathful fire must be changed into love, and then he can also change the wrath in the body into joy; all according as the property of the disease is, that the disease be able to bear it; for to a weak fire in the body, which is tired and languished by reason of the heat, and rather inclines to cold, viz. to the poison of Mercury, where the life is in danger, there belongs a cure with a fine subtle heat, wherein Venus is strong, and Mars very tender and mild by reason of the power of Venus; Jupiter need not be strong there, lest he make Mars and Mercury too strong, so that the weak life, before it is quickened and refreshed, is overwhelmed, and brought into the mercurial poison.

47. An herb in this aforesaid property grows not high, it is somewhat rough in the touch; the rougher it is, the stronger is Mars therein; it is better to be used outwardly to wounds and sores, than inwardly: The fine and subtle part is to be taken into the body, and is expulsive; the more subtle it is, the nigher it is to the life in the body, which the physician may very well know by its salt; for no rough wild property is to be taken into the body, unless the body be inflamed with a sudden poison, where the life also is fresh and strong, then a vehement resistance must be used; yet Mercury and Mars must not be administered in the wrath, but in their strongest power, Mars in the greatest heat, but before changed into joy; and then he also changes Mercury according to himself: Jupiter belongs to the transmutation of wrathful Mars, but he must be first introduced into Sol's property, and then he is rightly fit for it.

48. Every living creature, according to its kind in the foregoing property, is friendly and pleasant, if you deal friendly and gently with it; but if it be dealt roughly with, then Mercury is stirred up in the poison-property, for Mars soon boils up, and gets aloft in the bitter property, and then the anger springs forth; for the ground of all malignity lies therein; but if it be not stirred up, then it is not manifest; as a great sickness which lies in the body, but while the same is hid, and not enkindled, it is not manifest and apparent.

49. But if Mercury be next Saturn in the property, and next him the moon, and Venus and Jupiter beneath, and also weak, then let Mars stand where he will, yet all is earthly; for Mercury is held in the austere impression in the cold property, viz. in death's form, and his Sulphur is earthly; if Mars comes near to it, then it is poisonful also, but if Venus makes an opposition therein, then the poison is resisted,

yet it is but earthly; it gives a greenish colour from the power of Venus.

50. But if Venus be next Saturn in the property, and the moon not opposed by Mars, and Jupiter likewise goes in his own power, then all is pleasant and lovely under that property or constellation ; the herbs are slender, single, and soft in touch, of white blossoms, unless Mercury brings in a mixt colour from the power of the sun, viz. from Mars half red, and from Jupiter bluish, and it is weak in the property, and of little use in physic, yet not hurtful: In the creature it gives a pleasant, courteous, humble life, with no deep reason reach or capacity, but if Mars comes thereunto, the creature is small, or thin, of a white, weak, and effeminate nature.

51. There are three special salts which may be used to cure, which belong to the vegetable life, viz. Jupiter, Mars, and Mercury; these are the working life, in which the sun is the right spirit which makes these salts operative. 1

52. The salt or power of Jupiter is of a pleasant good smell and taste from the inward original of the property of the liberty of the divine essence, and from the external principle or original of the property of the sun and Venus, but yet it is not alone of itself of sufficient power in nature; for the outward nature consists in fire and anguish, viz. in poison, and Jupiter's power is opposed to the fiery poison life, which makes a temperature in the poisonful nature, viz. a desire of meekness out of the enmity.

53. The salt of Mars is fiery, bitter, and austere, and the mercurial salt is anxious and raging, like a poison, inclined both to heat and cold; for it is the life in Sulphur, and unites or assimilates itself, according to each thing's property; for if it comes into Jupiter's salt, it causes joy and great power; but if it comes into Mars's salt, it makes bitter pangs, stitches, achings, and woe; but if it comes into Saturn's earthly salt, it makes swellings, anguish, and death, if it be not hindered by Jupiter and Venus: Venus and Jupiter are opposite to Mars and Mercury, that so they might temper them both; and without the power of Mars and Mercury there would be no life in Jupiter, Venus, and Sol, but only a stillness; "therefore the worst is as profitable as the best," and the one is the cause of the other.

54. But the physician is to heed and mind what he takes in hand, lest he inflame the mercurial poison more and more in his patient, or introduce it into another adverse source: He ought indeed to use the martial and mercurial salt for his cure, but he must first reconcile

Mars and Mercury with Venus and Jupiter, that so both these angry adversaries may resign their will into Jupiter's will, so that Jupiter, Mars, and Mercury may all three obtain one will in the power, and then the cure is right, and the sun of life will again enkindle itself in this union and agreement, and also temper the nauseate of the disease in the contrariety in the salt of the disease, and turn Mercury's poison, and the bitter fire of Mars into a pleasant Jupiter.

55. This is now to be understood only concerning the vegetable soul, viz. concerning the outward man, which lives in the four elements, and concerning the sensible and feeling property.

56. Reason likewise is to be cured with its likeness; for as reason may be brought by words into a sensible sickness and disease, so that reason may vex, fret, and torment itself, and at last fall into an heavy sad sickness and death; so also it may be cured with the application of the same thing with its own assimilate.

57. As for example: An honest man falls into great debts, care, trouble and distress, which does even afflict him nigh to death; but if a good friend comes and pays his debt for him, then is the cure soon effected with its likeness: Even thus it is in all things; from whence the disease is risen, even such a like cure is requisite for the restoring its health; and thus it is likewise in the mental soul.

58. The soul of the poor sinner is poisoned in the anger of God, and the Mercury (understand the eternal Mercury in the eternal nature) is inflamed in the soul's property in the fiery Mars of God's anger, which does now burn in the eternal Saturn, viz. in the horrible impression of darkness, and feels the sting of the poisonful angry Mars; his Venus is imprisoned in the house of misery, his water is dried up, his Jupiter of understanding is brought into the greatest folly, his sun is quenched, and his moon turned to dark night.

59. Now he cannot be cured and remedied any other way, but with the likeness; he must again appease the mental Mercury; he must take Venus, understand the love of God, and introduce it into his poisonful Mercury and Mars, and tincture the Mercury in the soul again with love, and then his sun will again shine in the soul, and his Jupiter will rejoice.

60. Now if thou sayest that thou canst not, and that thou art too strongly captivated; I say also, that I cannot; for it lies not in my willing, running, and toiling, but it lies in the compassion of God; for I cannot by my own strength and ability overcome the wrathful anger of God which is enkindled in me; but seeing his dear heart has freely

given itself again out of love, and in love, into the humanity, viz. into the poisonful enkindled Mercury in the soul, and tinctured the soul, viz. the poison-source of the eternal nature in the eternal Father's nature's property; therefore I will cast my will into his tincture, and I will go with my will out of the enkindled poison-source, out of the evil Mercury in God's anger into his death, and with my corrupted will I will die with him in his death, and become a nothing in him, and then he must be my life.

61. For if my will is a nothing, then he is in me what he pleases, and then I know not myself any more, but him; and if he will that I shall be something, then let him effect it; but if he wills it not, then I am dead in him, and he lives in me as he pleases, and so then if I be a nothing, then I am at the end, in the essence out of which my father Adam was created; for out of nothing God has created all things.

62. The nothing is the highest good, for there is no turba therein, and so nothing can touch or annoy my soul; for I am a nothing to myself, but I am God's, who knows what I am; I know it not, neither shall or ought I to know it.

63. And thus is the cure of my soul's sickness; he that will adventure it with me shall find by experience what God will make of him: As for example; I here write, and I also do not do it; for I, as I, know nothing, and have also not learned or studied it; so then I do it not, but God does it in me as he pleases.

64. I am not known to myself, but I know to him what and how he pleases: Thus I live not to myself, but to him; and thus we are in Christ only one, as a tree in many boughs and branches, and he begets and brings forth the fruit in every branch as he pleases, and thus I have brought his life into mine, so that I am atoned with him in his love; for his will in Christ is entered into the humanity in me, and now my will in me enters into his humanity; and thus his living Mercury, that is, his word, viz. the speaking Mercury, tinctures my wrathful evil Mercury, and transforms it into his. And thus my Mars is become a love-fire of God, and his Mercury speaks through mine, as through his instrument, what he pleases; and thus my Jupiter lives in the divine joy, and I know it not; the true sun shines to me, and I see it not; for I live not to myself, I see not to myself, and I know not to myself: I am a thing, and I know not what; for God knows what I am; and so now I tend and run to and fro as a thing, in which the spirit drives or actuates me as he pleases; and thus I live according to my inward will, which yet is not mine.

65. But yet I find in me another life, which I am, not according to the resignation or self-denial, but according to the creature of this world, viz. according to the similitude of eternity; this life does yet stand in poison and strife, and shall yet be turned to nothing, and then I am wholly perfect: Now in this same life, wherein yet I find my selfhood, is sin and death, and these likewise shall be brought to nothing: In that life, which God is in me, I hate sin and death; and according to that life which yet is in my selfhood, I hate the nothing, viz. the Deity: Thus one life fights against the other, and there is a continual contest in me; but seeing Christ is born again in me, and lives in my nothingness, therefore Christ will, according to his promise made in paradise, bruise the head of the serpent, viz. of my selfhood, and mortify the evil man in myself, so that he himself may truly live in me.

66. But what shall Christ do with the evil man? Shall he cast him away? No. For he is in heaven, and does thereby accomplish and effect his wonders in this world, which stands in the curse: Now each labours in its own vineyard ; the outward man labours in the cursed world, which is evil and good in the wonders of God, viz. in the mirror of glory, which yet shall be revealed in him; and the inward man is not its own, but God's instrument, with whom God makes what he pleases, till the outward with its wonders in the mirror shall also be manifest in God; and even then is God all in all, and he alone in his wisdom and deeds of wonder and nothing else besides; and this is the beginning and the end, eternity and time.

67. Now understand it right; to the outward man there belongs a cure from the outward, viz. from the outward will of God, who has made himself external with this visible world; and for the inward man there is a cure from the inward world, in which God is all in all; only one, not many, one in all, and all in one: But if the inward penetrates the outward, and illustrates it with its sunshine, and the outward receives the sunshine of the inward, then it is tinctured, cured, and healed by the inward, and the inward illustrates it, as the sun shines through the water, or as the fire sets the iron quite through of a light glee; here now needs no other cure.

68. But seeing the devil in the wrath of the eternal nature opposes the soul, as an enemy of the soul, and continually casts his poisonful imagination at the soul to tempt and try it, and the anger or wrath of the eternal nature is manifest in the outward man, which Adam awakened and stirred up; thereupon this wrath is oftentimes stirred

up by the devil and his servants, that it effectually works and burns in the outward body, and even then the inward love-fire goes out in the outward man, as a red-hot iron is quenched in the water; yet not so soon in the internal, but in the external man, unless the outward man continues lying in the mire of sin; so that the soul, which had given itself into the nothing, viz. into the liberty, into the life of God, does enter again with its desire into the outward sinful man, then it loses the inward sun; for it goes again out of the nothing into the something, viz. into the source.

69. Thus the outward body must then have an outward cure; and though the inward man yet lives in God, yet whereas the soul has imagined into the outward wrath, so that the divine tincturation is no longer in the outward man, the outward Mercury, viz. the expressed word, must have a tincturation from the outward expressed love and light, unless the will-spirit of the soul does wholly re-enter into the inward hidden man, and be again transmuted; and then the cure may be again introduced into the outward man, being the thorough-shining love of God in the light, which is exceeding precious.

70. But now this herb is rarely to be found upon the earth; for men eat only of the forbidden tree; therefore the poison of the serpent does so spring up in them in the wrath of the eternal and external nature, so that they must also have an external cure for their serpent's poison in the outward Mercury.

71. It is indeed possible for a man to live without sickness, but he must bring the divine tincturation from the inward man through the outward, which is very difficult to do in the world; for the outward man lives among the thorns of God's wrath, which gall and sting him on every side, and blow up the wrath of God, so that it burns in the outward man, and then the tincturation of God's love may not continue there: It is indeed inhere, but not in the outward enkindled abominations, but it dwells in itself, like as the light dwells in the darkness, and the darkness comprehends it not, also knows nothing of it; but when the light is manifest in the darkness, then is the night changed into day.

72. Thus it is likewise with man; of what light man lives, of that also comes his cure; if he lives in the outward world, then the outward goodness and love, viz. the outward Jupiter and Venus with the sun must be his cure, or he remains in the angry Mars, and in the poisonful Mercury, in the earthly moon captivated in the impression of Saturn, viz. in the earthly Sulphur; which however is made

manifest, and awakened in the outward man by Adam, for whose sake the outward man must die, putrify, and so enter again into the nothing, viz. into the end, or as I might better say and signify it, into the beginning of the creation, into the essence, out of which it went and departed with Adam.

Chapter X
Of The Inward And Outward Cure Of Man

1. Let the lover of God understand us right; we do not go upon an historical heathenish conjecture, nor only upon the light of the outward nature; both suns shine to us. Understand us right, and see how God has cured man when the poison of the serpent and devil held him imprisoned in death, and how he yet still cures the poor soul captivated in God's anger; the like process also must the physician keep in curing the outward body.

2. The divine light and love were extinguished in Adam, because he imagined into the serpent's property, viz. into evil and good, so that the poison of death began effectually to work in Mercury, and the source of anger was inflamed in the eternal Mars, and the dark impression of the eternal nature's property took possession of him: His body became earth in the dark impression in the poison of the enkindled Mercury, and was an enmity against God: he was utterly undone, and there was no remedy for him by any creature, neither in heaven, nor in this world; the wrathful death captivated him in soul and body.

3. Now how did God do to cure him and tincture him again? Did he take a strange thing thereunto? No, he took the likeness, and cured him with that which was corrupted in him, viz. with the divine Mercury, and with the divine Venus, and with the divine Jupiter; understand; in man was the expressed word, which I call the eternal Mercury in man; for it is the true ruling acting life; it was inspired or in-spoken into man's image (which God created out of his essence into an image according to God) as into a creaturely image, which was the soul with the property of all the three worlds, viz. with the world of light and understanding, which is God; and with the fire-world, which is the eternal nature of the Father of all beings; and with the light, love-world, which is heavenly corporality; for in the love-desire is the essence, viz. the corporality.

4. The desire of love is spirit, and is the heart of God, viz. the right divine understanding: In the love-essence Mercury is God's word, and in the fiery nature he is the wrath of God, the original of all mobility and enmity, also of strength and omnipotence; the fiery property makes the light, viz. the liberty, desirous; so that the nothing is a desire, and this desire is the love of God, which Adam extinguished in him: For he imagined after evil and good, that is, after earthliness; the earthliness came forth into a being both out of the wrath, and out of the love-being, and that through God's motion, that the wonders of the abyss and byss might be made manifest, that good and evil might be made known and manifest: And this Adam, being the image of God, should not do, for God had created him to his image: He should have tinctured the fire-world and outward world with the word of love, that so none of them should be manifest in him, like as the day holds the night swallowed up in itself.

5. But by false imagination he has awakened and manifested the dark and poisonful mercurial fire-world in him, so that his bodily essence of the dark impression is fallen to the evil part in the poisonful mercurial property, and the soul is become manifest in the eternal nature in the Father's fire-property, viz. in the poisonful hateful Mercury; according to which God calls him an "angry and zealous God," and "a consuming fire."

6. Now to help and restore this again, viz. the image of God, God must take the right cure, and even the same which man was in his innocence: But how did he effect it? Behold, O man, behold and see, open thy understanding; thou art called.

7. He introduced the holy Mercury in the flame, viz. in the fiery love with the desire of the divine essentiality, or after the divine essentiality again (which desire makes divine corporality in itself) into the expressed word, viz. into the mercurial fire-soul (understand, into the soul's essence in the womb of Mary), and became again that same image of God: He tinctured the poison, viz. the wrath of the Father of all essences, with the love-fire: He took only that same Mercury which he had breathed into Adam for an image, and formed into a creature: He took only that same property, yet not in the fire's property, but in the burning love: He did with the love introduce again the light of the eternal sun into the human property, that he might tincture the wrath of the enkindled Mercury in the human property, and inflame it with love, that the human Jupiter, viz. the divine understanding, might again appear and be manifest.

8. Ye physicians, if you here understand nothing, then you are captivated in the poison of the devil: Behold, I pray, the right cure, with which the enkindled Mercury in man's life is to be remedied; it must be a Mercury again, but first enkindled in Venus and Jupiter; it must have the sun's property, which it attains to by Jupiter and Venus: As God deals with us poor men, so must the outward poisonful sick Mercury be tinctured with such an external cure; not with the dark impression of Saturn, with cold (unless it be first sweetly appeased and qualified with Jupiter and Venus, that the sun does again shine in Saturn), but with meek love; this is his right physic, whereby the death is changed into life; yet this is only a common manual cure, which the vulgar may learn.

9. But it behoves the doctor, if he will be called a doctor, to study the whole process, how God has restored the universal in man; which is fully clear and manifest in the person of Christ, from his entrance into the humanity, even to his ascension, and sending of the Holy Ghost.

10. Let him follow this entire process, and then he may find the universal, provided he be born again of God; but the selfish pleasure, worldly glory, covetousness and pride lie in the way. Dear doctors, I must tell you, the coals are too black, you defile your white hands therewith; the true unfeigned self-denying humility before God and man does not relish with you; therefore you are blind: I do not tell you this, but the spirit of wonders in its manifestation.

11. But we will give direction to the desirous seeker, who would fain see if he knew the way fitly to attain his intent; for the time is at hand, where Moses is called from the sheep to be a shepherd of the Lord, which shall shortly be manifest, notwithstanding all the raging and raving of the devil: Let not the dear and worthy Christendom think, seeing now it seems as if she should go to wrack and ruin, that it is utterly undone; No: the Spirit of the Lord of hosts has out of his love planted a new branch in the human property, which shall root out the thorns of the devil, and make known his child Jesus to all nations, tongues and speeches, and that in the morning of the eternal day.

12. Dear brethren, behold, I pray, the right cure: What did God with us when we lay sick in death? Did he quite cast away the created image, understand the outward part, viz. the outward corrupt man, and make wholly another new man? No: He did it not: For though he introduced divine property into our humanity, yet he did not

therefore cast away our humanity, but brought it into the way or process to the new-birth.

13. What did he? He suffered the outward humanity, viz. the outward water, understand the essentiality of Venus, which was shut up in the wrath of death, to be baptized with the water of the eternal essence, and with the Holy Ghost, that the incentive of the outward essentiality shut up in death might again glow, as a fire that falls into tinder: Afterwards he withdrew his outward food from the outward body, and brought it into the desert, and let it hunger, and then the spark enkindled from the fire of God must imagine into God, and eat manna of divine essentiality forty days, of which Israel was a type in the wilderness of Sinai with their manna: The essence of eternity must overcome the essence of time, therefore it is called a temptation of the devil; for the devil as a prince in the wrath of God did there tempt the outward humanity, and represented all that to it wherein Adam fell, and became disobedient to God.

14. There now it was tried whether the image of God would stand, seeing internally there was God's love-fire, and externally the baptism of the water of eternal life: Here the soul was tempted, whether it would be a king, and an angelical throne instead of the fallen angel, and possess the elected throne of God in the royal office, from which Lucifer was taken, and thrust into the darkness, viz. into the throne of poison and death; but seeing he stood (in that the soul did resign and submit its will alone into God's love-fire, and desired no earthly food, nor the earthly kingdom good and evil for outward dominion) the process to the universal, viz. to the restoration of all that which Adam had lost, did further proceed and go on: He turned water into wine.

15. Ye physicians, observe this, it concerns you in your process, you must also go the same way to work: He healed the sick; so you must likewise make the form in your poisonful Mercury whole and sound by the power of the philosophical baptism: He made the dead alive again, the dumb to speak, the deaf to hear, the blind to see, and cleansed the lepers; all this must go before, that all the forms in Mercury may be pure, sound, and living, which Mercury himself does make after the baptism and temptation; as the living speaking Mercury did this in the person of Christ; the artist cannot do it, only there must be faith; for Christ also testifies, that he could not do many wonders at Capernaum, only heal a few diseased; for the faith of those at Capernaum would not enter into the divine Mercury of Christ.

16. So that we see there, that the person of Christ, viz. the creature, could not work the wonders in its own power, but the Mercury, viz. the living, speaking word in him; for the person did cry and call into God, viz. into the speaking word, and set its desire thereinto; as we may see in the Mount of Olives where he prayed, that he sweat drops of blood; and by Lazarus, when he would raise him up, he said, "Father, hear me; but I know that thou always hearest me; yet because of those that stand by, I say it, that they may believe that thou workest by me."

17. Thus the artist must not arrogate anything to himself, the Mercury does itself, after the philosophical baptism, work these wonders before it manifests the universal; for all the seven forms of nature must be crystallised and purified, if the universal shall be revealed; and each form carries a peculiar process when it is to be brought out of the property of the wrath, and entered into the pure and clear life; and it must transmute itself into the crystalline sea which stands before the throne of the ancient in the Revelation, and change itself into paradise; for the universal is paradisical; and Christ also came for that reason into our humanity, that he might again open or make manifest the universal, viz. the paradise, again in man: The speaking word in Christ wrought wonders through all the seven properties or forms, through the expressed word in the humanity, before the whole universal was manifest in the body of the human property, and the body glorified.

18. Even thus it is in the philosophical work, when the Mercury shut up in death receives into it the baptism of its refreshment in love, then all the seven forms manifest themselves in this property, as it came to pass in the process of Christ in his miracles, but as yet they are not perfect in the operation of the manifestation of their properties.

19. The universal is not yet there, till all seven give their will into one, and forsake their property in the wrath, and depart from it with their will, and take into them the love's property: They must take in the will of the nothing, that their will be a nothing, and then it can subsist in the wrath of the fire, and there is no further turba therein; for so long as the desire of the wrath is in the form, it is adverse and opposite to the second form, and inflames the second form with its wrathful property, that is, it strikes the signature of the second, and awakens it in the wrath, and then the voice or sound of the second

enkindles the first form's property in Mercury, and so no form can attain to any perfection, that it might enter into love.

20. Therefore the artist can effect nothing, unless he gives a meat to the forms, which they all desire, and love to eat, wherein there is no turba: Now the properties cannot eat, seeing their mouth is frozen up in the impression of Saturn; the artist must first open their mouth, and make them alive in their zeal, that all the forms may be hungry, and then if there be manna, they all eat together of it, and so the precious grain of mustard-seed is sown.

21. Now when Mercury does thus awake from the death of the impression of Saturn, and gets manna into the mouth of his property of the poisonful death's source, then arises the flagrat of the kingdom of joy, for it is as a light which is enkindled in the darkness, for the joy or love springs up in the midst of the anger: Now if Mercury apprehends the glimpse or aspect of the love in Mars, then the love dismays the wrath, and it is as a transmutation, but it is not fixed and steadfast; and as soon as this comes to pass, the angelical properties appear in view.

The Process in the Temptation

22. Jesus was led by the Spirit into the wilderness, and the devil came to him, and tempted him. When the soul of Christ did hunger, the devil said to Jesus, Open the centre in the stones, that is, the impressed Mercury, and make thee bread, eat the substance of the soul's property: What, wilt thou eat of nothing, viz. of the speaking word? Eat of the expressed word, viz. of the property of good and evil, and then thou art lord in both; this also was Adam's bit, wherein he did eat death: Then said Christ Jesus, "Man liveth not by bread alone, but by every word which proceedeth from the mouth of God."

23. Mark! Whence had the person of Christ the will, that he would not eat with the soul's hunger of the bread which could have been made of stones, which he could well have performed? Or how had it been, if the hunger of the human property had after the unction of baptism eaten in the temptation of the Mercury in the impression of death, viz. of the Sulphur of the expressed word, in which was the anger, and from whence the love was fled, as it is so in the earthly property?

24. Observe! The will and desire to eat of the speaking word came into the soul's property from the motion of the Deity: When the same

had moved itself in the soulish essence, shut up in death in Mary his mother in her essence or seed, and introduced the aspect of the eye of God in the love into the dead soul's essence, and had manifested the love in death, then one divine property desired the other; and the desire of the bodily hunger to eat of God's bread or essence came from the baptism: When the water of the body, which in the impression of the substance was enclosed in death, did taste the water of eternal life in the Holy Spirit, viz. the Holy Spirit's corporality or essentiality in the baptism, then the incentive of the divine hunger of the ardent desire after God's essence did arise in the flesh, as a divine hunger, a glimmering or shining incentive of divine property.

25. Now the man Christ must hereupon be tempted in body and soul, of which he would eat; on one part the expressed word of love and anger was represented before body and soul, in which the devil would be lord and master, and rule therein omnipotently; and on the other part the speaking word in the love-property was only represented to the soul and body.

26. Here now began the combat which Adam should have undergone in paradise; for on one side God's love-desire, which had manifested itself in the soul, did eagerly attempt the soulish and bodily property, and introduced its desire into the soul's property, that the soul should eat of it, and give the body manna thereof; and on the other side the devil in God's wrathful property did assault in the soul's property, and brought his imagination into the property of the first principle, viz. into the centre of the dark world, which is the soul's fire-life.

27. Here was the contest about the image of God, whether it would live in God's love or anger, in the fire or light; for the property of the soul, as to its fire-life, was the Father's according to the fire-world; and seeing the soul in Adam had quenched the light-world, the light-world was again incorporated with the name Jesus, which came to pass in the conception of Mary.

28. Now it was here tried in the temptation of which property man would live; whether of the Father's in the fire, or of the Son's in the light of love: Here the whole property of Christ's person was tempted: The devil said, as he had also said to Adam, Eat of the evil and good: Hast thou not bread? Then make bread of stones: Why dost thou hunger so long in thy own property? Then said the divine desire, "Man liveth not of bread alone, but of every word of God."

29. Thus the property of the fiery soul resigned itself with its desire into the love, viz. into the speaking word's property, and the fiery desire did eat manna in the love-desire. O ye philosophers! observe it well; when this was done, the love transmuted the fiery property into its love-property; here the Father gave the fire-soul to the Son, understand the fiery property of the expressed Mercury to the speaking Mercury in the light; for Christ also said so afterwards, "Father, the men were thine, and thou hast given them me, and I give unto them eternal life."

30. Here God's love gave the eternal love-life to the corrupted humanity; the love did wholly give itself in unto the fire-wrath, and transmuted the wrath of the soul into a triumphant joyful love; but if the soul's and body's property had obeyed the devil in God's wrath, and made bread of the enclosed Mercury, and eaten thereof, then had the will entered again into its selfhood, and could not have been transmuted.

31. But seeing it entered into resignation, into the speaking word of God, and was willing to be and do whatever that pleased, then the will went from its selfhood, through the wrathful death of God's anger, viz. from the expressed word, which the devil had poisoned with his imagination, quite through the property of the wrath, and sprang forth afresh with a new love-desire in God; here the will was paradise, viz. a divine love budding in death.

32. Thus now the love-will being set in opposition to the poisonful Mercury of the soul's property in the anger of God, then came the devil, and said, Thou art the king, who hast overcome, come and shew thyself in thy miracles and deeds of wonder; and he brought him upon the pinnacle of the Temple, and said, "Fall down, that men may see it; for it is written, He hath given his angels charge over thee, that they should bear thee up in their hands, lest thou dash thy foot against a stone." Here the devil would fain that he should use again the fire's might, viz. the soul's selfhood in its own fiery property, and depart out of the resignation into an arrogation of self in its own fire-will, as he had done, and also Adam, when he went with the desire in his own might into evil and good, and would have his eyes open in evil and good, as Moses writes thereof, that the serpent did persuade them to it.

33. Here came the fine adorned beast again, and tempted the second Adam also; for God gave him leave, seeing he said the fire's

matrix had drawn him, he could not stand: Here now that should be tried; for he was an angel also, as well as the human soul, which he had seduced: But the human property in body and soul in the person of Christ had once cast itself into the resignation out of its selfhood into God's mercy, and stood still in the resignation, viz. in the divine will, and would not cast himself down, or do anything but what God alone did by it, and said to the devil, "It is written, Thou shalt not tempt the Lord thy God;" which is as much as if he had said, A creature of God shall will nor do nothing but what God wills and does by it: There must be no other god besides the only one to rule and will, the creature must go and do as the will-spirit of God leads it; it must be God's instrument, with which he works, and does only what he pleases.

34. In this proof Adam did not stand; for he went from the resignation into an arrogation of self, into an own self-will, and would try evil and good, love and anger, and prove how evil and good tasted. Here, dear man, was the trying state before the tree of temptation in paradise, and that was fulfilled which the first Adam could not, and would not do in divine obedience in resignation.

35. When the devil saw that in this also he had no success, that the humanity would not give way to depart out of the resignation, out of God's will, he carried the humanity upon a high mountain, and shewed it all the riches of the world, all whatever does live and move in the expressed word, all the dominions and might in the outward nature, over which he calls himself a prince, but has only the one part in the wrath of death in possession, and said to it (understand to the human property), "If thou fallest down and worshippest me, I will give thee all this."

36. The humanity should again depart out of resignation into a desire of propriety, and desire to possess something of its own in arrogation of self in the cursed property, evil and good; this had been a dainty dish and delight to the devil; then had he remained king, and his lies had been truth: In this Adam also was corrupted, and entered into selfish propriety, and desired worldly dominion and covetousness (which may be seen in Cain), which is the heart of the poisonful Mercury, viz. its hunger's desire, which makes itself essence according to the property of its hunger, not manna, but earth; as we may see in the wild earth, what he has made in the enkindling, or motion of the Father in his fire's property, in which inflammation (viz. in the poisonful wrath of the expressed Mercury) the devil

thought to be a prince, and is so in the same property in the wicked, and also in the government of the world in the wrath; but God holds him captive with the water and light of the third principle, so that he is not prince in the dominion of the expressed word, but the judge's executioner; he must look where turba magna is enkindled in the wrath, and there he is busy as far as turba magna goes in the wrath, further his courage is cooled.

37. He would give the humanity of Christ this whole dominion to rule in, and above all in the essence of all things, as a mighty god, which notwithstanding he only possesses in the part of the turba in the wrath of God, and has it not in his full dominion: He should but set his desire thereinto, and introduce his will into him, and he would bring his Mercury of the creature into the greatest omnipotence, that he should be a lord over good and evil, and have all things at command, to do therewith as he pleased, for so Adam had fooled it.

38. His Mercury went with the desire into the impression, whence cold and heat arise, and imagined thereinto, and so the property of the cold and hot fire did presently boil up in the Mercury of the creature; and so also the outward heat and cold did soon pierce into the enkindled Mercury of the human property, so that the body now suffers pain from the heat and cold, which property before (when it stood in the free-will of God in the resignation) was not manifest; and thus evil and good did rule and domineer in Adam.

39. For the centre of wrath, viz. the dark world's property, was manifest in him, in a poisonful death's property, as the Mercury in man is yet to this day so poisonful, and of a venomous source; whereas indeed he is changed in the vital light into a solar property, but yet the poison and property of death hangs to it, and it is his root; as we plainly see, that as soon as the ready instrument of his martial fiery property's signature or form is a little struck or played upon, that his evil poisonful fiery property comes forth, and shews itself, and inflames the body, that it even trembles and shakes for the very poison of wrath, and will ever enter into the enkindled poison-source in him who has awakened and enkindled the same, and assimilate in his malice with the malignant fomenter's malice, and wrestle in the poisonful property's right; and then must the body set to its strength as a servant, and accomplish the poison's will, and wrangle and contest with his adversary, and beat him, or be beaten by him; let it be either by hand-blows, or words; it is all in this property and desire of this poisonful Mercury.

40. From hence arises all war and contention, namely, from the dominion of God's anger in the corrupt and enkindled Mercury of the expressed word, which does so act its delight and sport in the poisonful wrath's and dark world's property in man.

41. Therefore the warrior is a servant of God's anger: He is the axe wherewith the angry husbandman cuts up his thorns and briars from off his ground: He is the chief worker and accomplisher of the wrathful anger of God: God's anger according to his fire's property will have it so, and not his love; and he that suffers himself to be made use of thereunto, he serves the anger of God according to the dark and fire-world's desire and property, which in the heavy fall of Adam has manifested itself in the human property, and brought man, viz. the angelical image, into an half-devilish vizard and likeness; in which property and image of his will in the expressed creaturely Mercury or vital word he cannot inherit God's kingdom, but must be born anew in his Mercury and will, with and in Christ, in God's love, viz. in the holy speaking Mercury and word of life, that a new obedient will wholly resigned into God's love may proceed from his creaturely Mercury, which neither wills or acts anything but what the will of the speaking divine Mercury wills, who in his selfhood, and selfish arrogation in his own will, is as dead, that he may be the instrument of the great God, whereby he should act, work, and do how and what he pleases: And then is God all in all in him, his will and deed, and he is a branch in the great tree which draws sap, power, and life from the tree of God, and grows and lives in him, and brings forth his fruit; then is the Mercury of the human life a procreated or expressed fruit, which grows upon the paradise-tree of God, and gives forth its note and sound, and strikes the signature in the speaking word of God, viz. God's harp and lute, in his praise, for which end man is created, not that he should necessarily play upon the instrument of anger and death according to the devil's will.

42. The devil has given himself to be such a lutanist who contrives and helps to act and drive on the play in the wrath, viz. in the darkness: He is the instrument and actor in the wrath of the eternal nature, which has its effects and achievements with him and in him, as its instrument: The like also must the wicked man do, as Saint Paul speaks thereof; "The holy man is unto God a sweet savour unto life, and the wicked a sweet savour unto death." All whatever does live and move must enter into the glory of God; one works in his love, the other in his anger: All is generated and created in the infinite being to

the manifestation of the infinite great God; out of all the properties of evil and good, creatures were brought forth by the will of the speaking word; for the property of the darkness and the fire was as well in the speaking as the property of the light; and therefore there are evil and good creatures.

43. But the angels and men were spoken forth in the image of God's love; they ought not to speak and incline their will into the fire and dark world, and introduce their desire thereinto; also not at all will to be their own, but continue steadfast in the resignation in the speaking will of God, as a form of the speaking will, and bear no inclination to anything, but only to the speaking; in which figure they stand as an image or platform of the expressing, as a spoken word, wherewith the speaking word beholds itself in its own likeness, whereby it there manifests the eternal knowledge of the eternal mind, and sets the Spirit's will into a form, and plays therewith.

44. As a limner that pourtrays his own image, and does thereby behold what he is, and how his form and features are; or as a musician composes a curious lesson or song, and so plays and melodises with his life, and will of life, viz. with the sound of his own life's Mercury, in the tune of the song, or upon some musical instrument, as it is agreeable to his life's Mercury, wherewith his vital Mercury does rejoice and delight itself.

45. Thus likewise God created us to his love-consort to his joy and glory, whereby he exalts his speaking eternal word, or plays in the same with us as with his instrument.

46. Therefore, when this melodious instrument was broken in its sound by the wrathful might of his anger, that is, when man's image would play in its own might both in evil and good, in love and anger, viz. in its own self-will, and would not yield itself to be used to what the speaking word had created it, and departed out of resignation into an arrogation of self, and would play as itself pleased, now good, then bad, then this instrument was against the love of God, in which no voice, breath, or smallest degree of anger is manifest or can be, as in the light of the fire no pain of the fire is manifest.

47. For the will of the human Mercury went out from the will of the divine speaking word into its own self-will: Thus it fell into the centre of the pregnatress of all essences, viz. into the anguish, poison, and death, where God's anger, viz. the speaking in the wrath, took possession of it.

Here now was our distress, we were forlorn,
Opprest in wrathful death, and woeful scorn;
If God had not restored us again,
We should have still been rowling in death's plain.

48. Thus, dear reader, it is clearly set before you wherein Christ was tempted; namely, whether the soul, and the whole man, viz. the image of the speaking word (after that God had introduced the spark of his love again into the human property, and freely given itself again with the love into it), would now again enter into its first place, and be God's melodious instrument in his love, or not; or whether it would be a selfish arrogator in its own will, and do what its own speaking would bring forth in the enkindled Mercury of its life; whether it would suffer God's will to strike the signature upon its instrument, or the anger of God to strike it, as before came to pass viz. in the first Adam.

49. Here it was tried: Therefore said the devil, viz. the organist in God's anger, to Christ, that he should fall down and worship him, and then he would give him all dominion, power, and glory; he should and might do what he pleased, he should live and delight in his own self-will; he should only give the devil his will, and forego resignation, and depart out of God's mercy and love-will: And if this had come to pass, then had the fair instrument been once again broken, and the human melody in God's love and deeds of wonder had ended; but Christ said, "Get thee hence, Satan: It is written, Thou shalt worship the Lord thy God, and serve him only. Then the devil left him, and the angels came and ministered unto him."

The Magical Process

50. Herein (as it is already mentioned at large) the magus must well consider his purpose and intent; not desiring with the covetousness of the devil to possess the earthly kingdom, also not to fly or cast himself down from the Temple, much less to work out his intent from the stones; he must think that he is God's minister and servant, not a selfish lord, of whom becomes a fool: If he will help the poor captive shut up in the anger of God out of the bands of darkness, wherein he is swallowed up in the curse of the earth, and deliver him from the anger of God, then he must think and well observe how God with his entrance viz. into the humanity hath redeemed him; he must very exactly and intimately consider the temptation of Christ, not

blindly grope after it with outward manual art, and think with himself, I have a dead stone before me; it neither knows or feels anything, I must by force set upon it, that I may compel it, and take its jewel, which it has hidden in it.

51. He that does so is a fool, and goes on in his own self-will, and is altogether unfit for the work; let him not meddle with it; we desire faithfully to admonish him, that if he will seek aright, then let him consider the process of Christ, how God has again regenerated the universal shut up in death in the human property.

52. For God did not take man as he lay closed up in death, and cast him into a furnace, and melted him in the wrath, as the false magus does; but he gave his love first into his human essence, and baptized the humanity; afterwards he brought him into the wilderness, and set the devil opposite to him, not into him; he let him first fast and hunger forty days, and gave no outward food to the humanity: He must eat of his life's Mercury, that God might see whether the humanity would bring its desire into God; and when the humanity introduced its desire into the Deity, and received the manna, then he let the devil set upon the humanity, who introduced all his subtlety and desires into the humanity, and tempted him: Dost thou not understand anything here? What shall I say more to thee? If thou art a beast, then I give thee not my pearl; it belongs to God's children.

53. God must become man, man must become God; heaven must become one thing with the earth, the earth must be turned to heaven: If you will make heaven out of the earth, then give the earth the heaven's food, that the earth may obtain the will of heaven, that the will of the wrathful Mercury may give itself in unto the will of the heavenly Mercury.

54. But what wilt thou do? Wilt thou introduce the poisonful Mercury (which has only a death's will in itself) into the temptation, as the false magus does? Will you send one devil to another, and make an angel of him? In deed and in truth I must needs laugh at such folly: If thou wilt keep a corrupt black devil, how dost thou think to turn the earth by the devil to heaven? Is not God the creator of all beings? Thou must eat of God's bread, if thou wilt transmute thy body out of the earthly property into the heavenly.

55. Christ said, "He that eateth not the flesh of the Son of Man hath no part in him: "And he says further, "He that shall drink of the water that I shall give, it shall spring up in him to a fountain of eternal

life." Here lies the pearl of the new-birth: It is not enough to play the sophister; the grain of wheat brings forth no fruit, unless it falls into the earth; all whatever will bring forth fruit must enter into its mother from whence it came first to be.

56. The mother of all beings is Sulphur, Mercury is her life, Mars her sense, Venus her love, Jupiter her understanding, Luna her corporeal essence, Saturn her husband: You must reconcile or lovingly betroth the man with the woman; for the man is angry, yet give him his dear spouse into his arms; but see that the spouse be a virgin, wholly chaste and pure; for "the woman's seed shall break the serpent's head," viz. the man's anger: The virgin must be in real love, without any falsehood or unfaithfulness, a virgin which never touched any man in anger according to his manhood; for the pure Deity does so espouse itself in clear love with the humanity, even as Mary said, "Be it unto me as thou hast spoken, for I am the Lord's handmaid;" and so the humanity assumed the Deity, and also the Deity the humanity.

57. The chaste virgin signifies in the philosophic work the clear Deity, the humanity is Mercury, Sulphur, and Salt, both heavenly and earthly; the heavenly property is disappeared, and as a nothing; the deadly property in the wrath is stirred up, and lives to the anger, and in the properties of the anger; the humanity, both in Adam and in Christ, was tempted. Dost thou ask, wherewith? With the like opposite in the wrath, even with such a devil as had all these properties in him, as a potent prince in all the properties of the anger.

58. The properties in Sulphur were tempted with the likeness of the Sulphur; in the Sulphur, or from the sulphureous property, the temptation did come and arise, and its forms are three, as one in the impression, which the philosophers call Saturn, which the human spirit or will should open in the property of Venus, and therewith satiate or feed its hunger, viz. the fire; the other property was, that he should live in his own awakened and opened Venus out of Saturn's property, and aspire in self-will.

59. The third property was, he should introduce his will through the awakened love-desire again into the centre, viz. into the sulphurean mother, which arises in the impression in the anguish: And this he would not do, but the first Adam did it; and therefore God when he would help him tempted him in the Sulphur, viz. in the first mother to the humanity, and suffered a wrathful devil, which was enkindled in the Sulphur, to tempt him with his enkindled

malignity and malice in the Sulphur: Dost thou not understand this? What then shall I say more to thee?

60. Sulphur is the womb whereinto we must enter, if we would be new born. Nicodemus said well; "How can one being old enter into his mother's womb, and be born again?" But Christ said, "Except you be converted, and become as children, you cannot see the kingdom of heaven." The self-will must enter again into the first mother which brought it forth, viz. into the Sulphur, by the will understand Mercury.

61. But now who will persuade it to do so? For it is become a selfish thing, and must enter again into the mother, and become nothing; this seemed a strange and wonderful thing to Nicodemus, but the Lord said to him, "The wind bloweth where it listeth, and thou hearest the sound thereof, but thou knowest not from whence it cometh, or whither it goeth; even so is every one that is born of God." Behold, who persuaded the will of Christ in his humanity, to enter again with the will into the filiation or adoption, as it were in the mother's womb, and eat nothing forty days, and would also eat nothing, but remained in full steadfast resignation in the mother? Did not the Deity do it, which was entered into the humanity?

62. Thus likewise it goes in the philosophic work, therefore let the artist well observe, and rightly understand us: He must seek the evil stubborn child (which is fled from the mother, and entered into the centre, and would be a selfish thing) in Saturn; for the wrath of God has shut him up with its impression in the chamber of death.

63. Not that he has made him to Saturn, but he holds him shut up in the saturnine death; the same he must again take and bring into the mother's womb, and then send the angel with a message to Mary, and tell her, "She shall bring forth a son, whose name shall be called Jesus: "And if the mother shall yield her consent thereunto, and receive the name Jesus, then the new humanity shall begin in the mother, with the new child in the old apostate captivated in the anger of God, and the name Jesus will first give in itself to the dead child which lay captivated in Saturn, and eagerly draw the will of the evil dead child to itself: This is the fair bride, which shews her crown of pearl to her apostate bridegroom; he should but again receive her, and she would again give him her love. Now if the apostate youth shut up in death does again receive her, then is the artist well prepared, and counted worthy by God to finish his purpose: Now will the bride love the bridegroom, and a virgin bring forth a son, at which all the world will

wonder; the virgin shall embrace the man; but he is a man, and not a woman, and has the virgin's heart.

64. Now he must be tempted, whether or no he will live in virgin-like chastity, and in full resignation of his will to God, for he must be a valiant champion, and destroy the devil's fortress of prey (which he has in his mother) in seven kingdoms; then let the devil set his mother's house on fire with his wrath, and tempt him, he will now well enough defend himself with Christ against the devil.

65. This being done, the young man with his virgin-like heart will wholly give himself up to the mother, when the tempter comes and assaults him, and the mother will wholly swallow him up into herself through the devil's wrath: He gives himself forth wholly out of his own will into the nothing. Now, thinks the artist with himself, I have lost all; for he thinks that he has lost heaven; for he seeks nothing, and does not consider that a virgin has now brought forth: But let him have patience; that which is impossible to the artist, that is possible to nature; after the night it is day; when the tempter has finished all his temptations, then comes the sign or appearance of the angels; then the devil which has tempted him must depart.

66. Let the artist well observe this, and pack away the devil, and suffer the young man with his virgin-like heart to lie in his bed, and eat his former food, for he is now become a physician of his sisters in his mother's house; he will do great wonders in all the seven kingdoms of his mother (which are the seven forms of life) as Christ has done.

67. In Saturn he will raise the dead, understand, he will awaken the dead essence which held him captive in his former prison; for he shall turn or make the earth to heaven: Even as the virgin has raised up his will out of the anger in the love, and made him a wonder-worker; so must he also awaken with his will, which is united to the virgin's heart, the form or signature in his mother's womb, whence she has brought forth him and all her children, and enkindle it with the virgin's and his love-desire: This is effected and done in the Sulphur of Saturn in the young man's own personal property, and in his mother; for before the espousing of the virgin the heavenly essence of the young man lies shut up in death: For when God cursed the earth, then the heavenly paradisical body disappeared, and the impression of Saturn took it in possession, till the restitution, where God shall restore that which is hidden, that paradise does again

spring forth afresh in the expressed word, or that the artist does open the same in a part by God's permission.

68. In the second kingdom of the mother, viz. in Luna, he shall also do wonders; for Jesus fed with five barley loaves five thousand people; this is the working in the essentiality or corporality. He turned water to wine: These and the like do all belong to the lunar property, where the champion with his virgin opens paradise, and feeds the body, where nothing is, where the outward Mercury has not laboured and wrought: Thus the forms in the lunar property open themselves as if they are paradisical, even then the artist thinks I am nigh unto it; but he is yet far off from the end.

69. In the third kingdom of the mother, viz. in Jupiter, Christ did make the babes and ignorant, of a very weak and mean capacity, knowing and understanding, viz. of poor fishermen, carpenters, and the like mechanics, he made apostles, and the most understanding men of all; and also of poor, disrespected, vilified people, as of women, and simple ones, he made faithful, devout, dear, godly children, who apprehended in themselves the universal without any art.

70. Thus likewise it goes in the philosophic work; the essentiality which lies disappeared in death, where the Mercury is wholly earthly, cold, and impotent, does now arise in power, as if the whole being and essence were become a new life, at which the artist wonders, and marvels what it is, or how it happens, and yet does also exceedingly rejoice that he sees the divine power to spring forth before his eyes in a half dead essence, and that in the curse of God: He sees all the four elements, each apart, and sees how the wisdom of God represents itself therein, as an harmony of joy, and sees all colours, and the rainbow upon which Christ sits in judgment in the expressed Mercury.

71. The nature of this splendour arises out of the impression of Saturn; the good Jupiter gives himself forth to be seen in such a manner, as God will change the world, and transform it again into paradise; for this is the understanding in the expressed word, even as Christ has made the foolish, rude, ignorant people truly wise and knowing in divine, real, heavenly jovial understanding and knowledge.

72. In the fourth kingdom of the mother of all beings, which is the mercurial in the wheel of the nature of life, Christ made "the deaf to hear, the dumb to speak, and cleansed the lepers" from the poison of

Mercury: All apoplexies, the French or poisonful pox and sores arise from the saturnine water in Mercury, which water is called phlegma, all which Christ healed in the form or signature of the young man and virgin; for the eternal virginity had espoused itself with the young man, viz. with the humanity.

73. This comes to pass also in the philosophic work: The artist will see how the heaven separates itself from the earth, and how the heaven does again sink into the earth, and changes the earth into a heavenly colour; he will see how Mercury purifies the matter, and how the purified colours will appear in antimony in their property, and how the wonder proceeds.

74. In the fifth kingdom of the mother of all beings, Christ expelled the devils out of the possessed, and healed the deaf in this form and property.

75. This likewise the artist will see in the philosophic work, how Jupiter in Mercury will drive up a black twinkling fiery vapour out of the matter, which sticks on like soot; for it is a hunger of the poison in Mercury, and is very rightly compared to the devil, for it is of his property.

76. In the sixth kingdom of the mother of all beings, viz. in the wheel of life, called Venus, Christ loved his brethren and sisters according to the humanity, and washed his disciples' feet, and loved them even to the deepest exinanition, and gave his life into the wrath's property even to death for them, and manifested himself among them that he was Christ: And when they perceived that the king was come that should deprive self-will of its might and dominion, and destroy the devil's kingdom; then they cried out, and said, "We have no king but Cæsar;" they took him in the dark night into their power, bound him, and brought him before their council, mocked him, whipped him, and beat him, stripped him of clothes, and hung him on the cross.

77. This also the artist will see very powerfully in the philosophic work; for as soon as the dark fiery stream, viz. the material devil goes from the matter, then virgin Venus appears in her virginity very glorious and beautiful; for it betokens Christ's love, who did so humble himself, and manifested his love in our humanity; then the artist thinks that he has the philosophic child, then he has now the fine morsel: But he dances with the Jews, who thought, when they had taken Christ, Now we have him, we will keep him well enough. Thus he also thinks, it is finished, and receives the child; and when he

beholds it in the trial, then he has Venus, a woman, and not the virgin with the tincture of the fire and light, and is deceived by the woman. 1

78. Now observe right, What do the properties, viz. Saturn, Mars, and Mercury, when they see the child, viz. the champion in royal colour, and find that he manages no external dominion and royalty with power and authority as they do, but will only rule with love in their poisonful fire-might? They will not suffer him.

79. For Saturn signifies the worldly dominion, and Mercury the spiritual dominion, viz. the Pharisees, and Mars signifies the devil; these three would not endure Christ among them; for he said that he was a king of love, and the Son of God, and was come to deliver his people from sin: Then thought the devil, sure this rhimes not well, thou wilt lose thy kingdom: And the worldly magistrate thought, Is this a king, and God's Son? Then he will take away our might; this does not at all like us: And the mercurial priests thought; This man is too mean for us, we will have a Messiah who may bring us to worldly dominion, and make us to be high and rich in the world, that we may alone possess the honour of the world; we will not receive him, he is too poor for us; we might so lose the favour and respect of the worldly magistrate, and should be much damaged; we will rather abide in our power, respect, and authority, and abandon this beggarly king with his love-kingdom: In like manner as yet to this day they are so minded, and serve his messengers so whom he sends.

80. Thus likewise it goes in the philosophic work, when Venus manifests herself with love, viz. in her own property in the three wrathful forms, viz. in Saturn, Mars, and Mercury; they can by no means endure it, for it is wholly against their austere, dark, fiery might, but especially against the poison of Mercury, they flash and lighten against Venus, and shoot their rays, viz. the mercurial poisonful rays upon her, as the Pharisees did upon Christ. In the meanwhile, Jupiter and Luna hold with Venus, and give their power to Venus; for Venus does here stand forth in the power of Jupiter; at this the Pharisees laugh, and think with themselves, We are wise enough already, what need we knowledge and understanding? We will have might and honour; and Luna signifies the multitude of laymen who stuck to Christ, while it went well with him; so does Luna in the philosophic work to Venus in her lustre, so long as Saturn, Mercury, and Mars do not meddle with and assault her; but when the power of wrath comes, then Luna changes her will, viz. the colour, and looks, arises, and cries also with the rest the crucifige: This

the artist will see, if he be chosen and accounted worthy of God for the work.

Chapter XI
Of The Process Of Christ In His Suffering, Death, And Resurrection: Of The Wonder Of The Sixth Kingdom In The Mother Of All Beings: How The "Consummatum Est" Was Finished, And How Likewise It Is Symbolically Accomplished In The Philosophic Work

1. This now is thus to be considered; We are to know, that the essence of this world, together with man, consists in two properties, viz. in fire and light, that is, in love and anger: Now the fire is twofold, and the light is also twofold, viz. a cold fire from the impression, and an hot fire from the power of Mercury in Sulphur; and so likewise there is a cold light from the cold fire, and a warming light from the hot fire; the cold light is false, and the hot light is good; not that it is false in its property, only in the impression, in the cold Sulphur; in the sharpness of the wrath it turns to a false desire, viz. to a false love, which is contrary to the meekness; for its desire is Saturn and Mars.

2. It puts forth its sun (understand its lustre of life) in Mars, and the warming light (which also receives its fiery sharpness in the impression in Sulphur from Mars) brings its desire again into the liberty, viz. through the dying in the fire, through the anguish: It wholly and freely gives itself forth in the dying of the fire, and forsakes the property of the wrath.

3. And so it becomes a general joy, and not its own only, even like the sun that gives forth its shining lustre universally: The sunshine is neither hot nor cold; only Mercury in the spirit of the great world makes in Mars and Saturn's property a heat therein; for the sun enkindles their desire, upon which they grow so very hungry, eager, desirous, and operative, that even a fire is found to be in the light, which heat is not of the light's own property, but of the soul of the great world, which does so sharpen the pleasant light in its splendor, that it is unsufferable to the eye.

4. And we are highly to consider and know, that if another fire-desire, which is not like to the outward life in Mercury, would rule in the austere wrath of the outward nature, that then it would be an enmity contrary to the austere, cold, bitter, and fiery dominion and life, and that they would exalt or exasperate their wrath, eagerly

desiring to be rid of it: Even as it so came to pass when the divine love-desire did manifest itself with its great meekness to the false, cold, proud, and austere fire-desire of the Saturnalians, Martialists, and especially of the false Mercurialites: It was a great opposition and enmity to them, that love should rule in the death of poison, and dwell therein, this they could not, nor would not endure; for heaven was come into hell, and would overcome the hell with love, and take away its might; as it is to be seen in the person of Christ; he loved them, and did them all manner of good, and healed their plagues or diseases, but in that he was not arisen from their wrathful might, and that he said he was descended from above, and was God's Son; this was unsavoury to the cold, hot fire's might, that he should rule with love over them.

5. Even thus it goes in the philosophic work; when the wrathful forms of the earthliness, viz. the outward Saturn, Mars, and Mercury, see the heavenly champion with the virgin's property among them, and perceive that he has far another desire than they, then they are angry in themselves; for the love-desire, when it casts a glimpse on the fire-flagrat, awakes their fire-flagrat, and then the wrath proceeds forth from the anxiety into love; from whence arises a death's flagrat in the love; but seeing there can be no death therein, the love condescends in the fire-flagrat, and gives forth or diffuses itself into their desire, and leaves its essence; so that in their desire they reach after its property in the death's flagrat; this is a poison to death, and a pestilence to hell; and in this property death was deprived of its power in the humanity; for Christ, when he shed his heavenly blood in the flagrat of death, and left it in death, the wrath of God was driven to retain the heavenly love-essence in itself: Even there the fire-desire in the enkindled humanity was changed into a love-desire, and out of the anguish of death proceeded a joy and strength of divine power.

6. But I will hereby give the well-wisher fundamentally to understand how it went with Christ, and how in like manner it goes with his philosophic work; both have wholly one process. Christ overcame the wrath of death in the human property, and changed the anger of the Father into love in the human property; the philosopher likewise has even such a will, he wills to turn the wrathful earth to heaven, and change the poisonful Mercury into love; therefore observe us here right; we will not write here parabolically, but wholly clear as the sunshine.

7. God would change the humanity (after it was become earthly, and had awakened the poisonful Mercury in the love-property, which poisonful Mercury had devoured the love, and changed it into itself) again into the divine heavenly property, and make heaven of the human earth, of the four elements only one in one desire, and change the wrath of God in the human property into love.

8. Now his anger was a might of the fire and wrath, and was inflamed in man, and therefore there must be right earnestness to withstand the same, and change it again into love: The love must enter into the anger, and wholly give itself in unto the wrath; it would not be enough that God should remain in heaven, and only look upon the humanity with love; it could not be, that the anger and wrath should thereby yield up its might and strength, and freely give itself unto the love: As the fire is not made better by the light, it still holds its wrath notwithstanding in itself; but when a meek essence (as water) comes into the fire, then the fire goes out.

9. Even so heavenly divine essentiality (understand heavenly water, which the tincture of the fire and light changes into blood) must enter into the wrathful fire of God, and become the fire's food, so that the fire of God might burn from another essence; for water could not have done it; the fire does not burn in the water, but the meek oleous property of the fire and light in the essence of divine meekness in the love-desire, that did effect it.

10. The human fire-life consists in the blood, and therein rules the wrath of God; now another blood, which was born out of God's love-essence, must enter into the angry human blood; they must go both together into the death of the wrath, and the wrath of God must be drowned in the divine blood, and therefore the outward humanity in Christ must die, that it might not any more live in the wrath's property, but that the heavenly blood's Mercury, viz. the speaking word, might alone live in the outward humanity, and solely rule in peculiar divine power in the outward and inward humanity; that the self might cease in the humanity, and God's Spirit might be all in all, and the self only his instrument, whereby he makes what he pleases; that (I say) the self-hood might be solely God's instrument, and wholly in resignation; for God has not created man to be his own lord, but his servant: He will have angels under obedience, and not devils in their own fire-might.

11. Now when his love would give itself into death, and deprive death of its might, then the two worlds, viz. the Father's fire-world,

with the outward visible world, and also the divine love-world with the divine heavenly essentiality, that is, with heavenly flesh and blood, and also with corrupted flesh and blood, were formed into one person. God became man, and made man to God: The seed of the woman, viz. of the heavenly virginity, which disappeared in Adam, and also the corrupted man's seed in the anger, viz. Mary's seed, were formed into one person, which was Christ; and the seed of the woman, viz. of the virgin of God, understand the heavenly essentiality, should bruise the head of the serpent, understand, the wrath of God in the corrupted man; the head is the might of God's anger; the divine man, understand the divine property, should change the earthly into itself, and turn the earth to heaven.

12. Now when the person was born, heaven stood in the earth of man. Now the incarnation could not have done it alone, there must be yet after this another earnestness; for as long as Christ walked on the earth, the humanity which was from Mary's property was not almighty, but the humanity from God was omnipotent, they were set opposite one against the other in two principles, yet not shut up, but both manifest in each other, the love against the anger, and the anger against the love.

13. Here now was the trial of the combat one with another, from whence also proceeded the temptation of Christ; and when the divine world overcame, then the great wonders broke forth through the outward human world; but all this could not accomplish it, there must yet be a greater earnestness, the human property, viz. the expressed word, was yet stirring in the inflameable anger: The human Sulphur must be changed into the heavenly, viz. into the heavenly part; and thereupon the human self, viz. the expressed Mercury was astonished, when upon the Mount of Olives the heavenly world in the love wrestles with the anger in the human world, viz. with the selfhood, so that the person of Christ did sweat bloody sweat; even there the one was dismayed at the other, the love at the horrible death, whereinto it should and must wholly yield and give in itself with the divine essentiality, and be swallowed up by the anger; and the anger was dismayed at its death, in that it must lose its might in the love.

14. Hence the whole person of Christ said, "Father, if it be possible, let this cup pass from me; yet not as I will, but thy will be done." The love-world in Christ said, "Can it not be but that I must drink down the cup of thy anger? Then thy will be done." And the

anger said, "If it be possible, let this cup of love pass from me," that I may revenge myself, and rage in the wrath of man for the sake of his disobedience; as God said to Moses, who stood in the spirit of Christ as a type of Christ before God, "Let me alone that I may devour this disobedient people:" But the name Jesus, which had incorporated itself in paradise with the promise of the woman's seed in the aim of the human and divine covenant, would not suffer him; for the humility of the name Jesus has always interposed against the wrath of the Father, against his fire's property, that his fire might not enkindle the half-poisonful Mercury in man, except only sometimes when Israel walked wholly in the wrath and disobedience; as is to be seen by Corah, Dathan, and Abiram, and by Elias.

15. So it was here on the Mount of Olives, the anger would live in the fire's might in man, and the name Jesus put itself into the anger; and here there was no other remedy, but that the name Jesus in divine love and heavenly essentiality must wholly resign up itself to be devoured by the anger: The Son must be, and was obedient to the angry Father, even to "the death of the cross;" as the Scripture says.

16. The dear love-humility and meekness suffered itself to be "scorned, mocked, spit upon," and judged by the anger; that is, the Jews must execute the justice of God; for by man's self-action sin was committed, and by man's self-action death and sin must be blotted out. Adam had introduced his will into the poison of the outward Mercury; so must Christ, viz. the love, freely give up its will also into the same poisonful Mercury. Adam did eat of the evil tree, Christ must eat of God's anger; and as it went inwardly in the spirit, so likewise outwardly in the flesh; and so also it goes in the philosophic work.

17. Mercury in the philosophic work denotes the Pharisees, he will not endure the love-child: When he sees it, he gives it trembling and anguish, and Venus also stands dismayed at the poison of the angry Mercury; they are in one another as if sweat did drop from them, as the artist shall see.

18. Mars says, I am the lord of fire in the body, Saturn is my strength, and Mercury is my life, I will have none of this love, I will devour it in my wrath; this denotes the devil in the anger of God; and seeing he cannot do it, he raises up Saturn, viz. the impression, which signifies the worldly magistracy, and reaches therewith after Venus, and yet cannot get her into him, for she is to him a poison to death: This Mercury also can much less endure, for the love took away his

dominion; as the high priests thought that Christ would take away their government, because he said that he was God's Son.

19. Thus Mercury is vexed at the child Venus, for Venus has wholly discovered herself, and freely given up herself; they may do now what they please, she will go even into the dragon's mouth, he shall only but open his jaws; and this Mars in Mercury does not understand, but they take the fair child, and shoot their venomous darts against it, and bind it with Saturn's might in their wicked bands, as the artist will sec how they surround the colour of Venus.

20. Mars brings it first to Mercury, seeing he is the life, as before the high priest, who must examine and prove the fair child; but he hates it, he cannot reach into the heart after its love-will, he only judges it externally, because it is not of his property, that it stands forth with such a form as the Mercury himself, and yet has another power, virtue and will.

21. But seeing there is another Mercury which lives in its love in the child Venus, therefore he cannot kill it, but brings it to Saturn, as the Jews brought Christ from Caiaphas to Pilate, who signifies Saturn, who also takes the child: But seeing he is a lord of the impression, viz. of the darkness, therefore he cares not at all for the property of the child, but for the dominion only; he seizes on the child with the dark impression, and strips it of its fair Venus garment; and when Luna with the white splendour of the sun sees this, then she hides herself; as the disciples of Christ fled, and the enraged rude multitude also, who did highly presume to stand by him in the cross and persecution, but in the earnestness they fly; for Luna is inconstant, she has not Sol's heart in the love-flame; and Saturn with his thorny impression puts the Sulphur upon the child, viz. the mother of all beings with the purple-coloured raiment of her own peculiar property, in which the wrath of Mars is contained and harboured.

22. When Mars, viz. the devil's crew, and Mercury also, viz. the self-pride of life, see that Venus has her royal garment on, understand the purple robe of Saturn and Mercury in Sol's colour mingled with fiery Mars, and adorned in Mercury's sulphur-colour in the open blaze as a shining lustre, for so is the materia according to the colour of the venereal property, which the artist must well observe, he then will clearly see as it is mentioned.

23. When Mars, Mercury, and Luna also see this, then they cry Crucifige, away with him, he is a false king in our garment; he is a

man as we are, and will be God, that is, they cast their poisonful desire through the purple garment upon the child, and so the artist will see that the child will appear in his own form, as if it were full of streaks from the poisonful rays of Mercury and Mars, which they lay upon the child through the impression of Saturn; as Pilate whipped Jesus: The artist will see the prickly crown of thorns standing very sharp with its point upon the property of the child; also he will see that Venus does not at all move herself, but stands still, and suffers herself to be so done unto.

24. Further we are to understand, how that Adam had taken on him a cold false love, and therewith so shewed himself before God as if he were in peculiar dominion and will, and moreover God's child, whereas he did but mock God therewith; for so the love-desire appears when it is captivated in the impression of death.

25. Thus must the second Adam Christ take all this upon him, and enter into the same ignominy and scorn, and be clothed with a purple garment as a king of this world, and be mocked therein; for Adam had put on the purple garment of the outward world's self-might in the splendour of the property of self; and here it was made open shew of before the anger of God: And the white garment which Herod put upon Christ to mock him in signifies, and is the cold false love as a cloak of falsehood, wherein man pranks up as if he were an angel, and so puts upon himself Christ's purple mantle with his white robe, and covers himself with Christ's pure snow-white garment, viz. with his suffering and death, and yet holds and harbours the man of falsehood, viz. the false love under a vail.

26. Now Christ must set forth this figure, and it was represented on his body; for he should overcome and stay the man of falsehood which lay in the human property, and so it was fully presented before God. Christ must be termed and reviled for such an one as Adam was; the innocent must take the blame upon him.

27. And thus it goes in the philosophic work, when the curse of God's anger which is in the earth is to be changed into love; for seeing Mercury sets the child of love before Saturn, and Saturn cannot, and may not try it, therefore he puts upon it the purple-coloured garment with stripes underneath, and sends it before Sol's splendor, which glimmers in Mars, and the sun puts upon it its white colour, viz. the lunar, and then the purple colour vanishes, and the child stands in the lunar white simple colour, very despicable without lustre: The sun would fain see this child shew forth its golden colour, for it perceives

there is a solar virtue in the child, therefore it gives it the white colour from the property of the eternal liberty; the child should but give the power of the fire's centre thereunto, viz. the divine might, and then it would be like the sun, and would be a lord over the Sulphur of Mars and Mercury, yet only a lord over the outward world's essence, a governor in the wrath, as Sol is the like.

28. But Christ said to Pilate, "My kingdom is not of this world," and would not answer Herod anything in this white raiment when he put it on him, nor in the purple robe; for the purple robe and the white raiment also were both false, and were put upon him to disgrace and mock him, because Adam had put them on, and proudly pranked up therein with falsehood; Christ might not do any sign therein before Herod, though he desired it. Hereby the shame of man, who was an image of God, and yet had made himself a false king, was represented before God's face; as the poor sinner confesses, and sets forth his abominations before God, when he sets upon abstinence and repentance.

29. Thus Christ represented to his Father the abominations or sins of man in this false garment, and stood before him as an ignominy, and confessed the sins of man to his Father in the stead and place of all men: And when his Father beheld him through his imagination in this garment, he would have none of this robe; therefore Pilate must pull it off from him again, and set him before the Jews in his own form; but they cry, "Away, away with him, he must be put to death;" for so his Father would, that he should give himself up to death in his wrath, and drown the same.

30. And Pilate condemned him to death, for he would not acknowledge him for a king: So it also goes in the philosophic work, Saturn will not receive the child, for it is not of his property; and Mars and Mercury likewise will not have it in its property: But what do they do? The child is among them, they would fain be rid of it, but yet cannot: They grow angry and enraged, as the Jews against Jesus, and take the child into their arms, viz. into their false poisonful angry desire, and will murther it, and quite sting and pierce through the materia of the child with their sharp, fiery, and poisonful rays, viz. with three sharp nails.

31. One whereof is Saturn, viz. the impression of the dark world, denoting the wrath of the dark world. The other is Mars, which signifies the devil, viz. the serpent's property in the anger of God. The

third is Mercury, which signifies the false life, viz. how the wrath of God is enkindled in the expressed word in the human property.

32. These three nails pierce through the property of the child. Thus Venus, viz. the essence of love wholly yields itself to the three murtherers, and wholly foregoes its jovial life as if it died; and the mercurial life of the human property, understand the child's power, falls also to the three murtherers in its mother's house, viz. into the corporeal essence, wherein the young man received his virgin, wherein God became man.

33. Now when the heavenly body, and also the earthly, do thus yield unto these three murtherers, then appears the image of John and Mary by the cross as a type; for the young man's life, and also the virgin's in the young man, has freely surrendered, and given forth itself: And now the two properties, viz. the divine and human, divide themselves in the form of each power, which the artist may see if he has the eyes and understanding thereunto.

34. And here, when Saturn with his impression and dark sharpness, and Mars with his wrath, and Mercury with his poison-life do powerfully enter into the property of Venus, then the wrath forces itself into the love, and the love into the wrath essentially mixed, as assimilating one with the other: Here the wrathful death is dismayed at the love, so that in dying he falls into impotence or a swoon, for it loses the might of the wrath; and the love is, and stands also in the source of the wrath in death's flagrat as impotent or in a swoon, and gives itself forth wholly into the flagrat or stroke of death, and even then the heavenly essence, viz. the heavenly blood flows forth from it into the property of the third principle, viz. of the young man. Here the virgin gives her pearl to the young man for a propriety, and God and man become one.

35. For the virgin's blood out of the divine essentiality does here now drown with its love-essence the young man's blood, viz. the self-hood, and the three murtherers surrender their life in the blood of the virgin, and then the red glee from the fire, and also the white from the life of the champion arise up together, viz. from the wrath the life, and from the love the meekness: and both, viz. the life of the anger, and the life of the love, ascend together as one only life; for in death they become one: The death dies away in the love, and becomes in the love the life of the divine kingdom of joy; for it is not a dying, but a free surrendering of its power, might, and will, a transmutation; the virgin's blood changes the human, dead as to God, into an heavenly

blood, the life of the young man dies, and the life of the Deity remains fixed and steadfast, for it stands in its property in the nothing.

36. And here, thou dear seeker, when thou seest the crimson-coloured blood of the young man arise out of death with the virgin's white blood, then know that thou hast the arcanum of the whole world, and a treasure in this valley of misery, which surpasses the value of gold; take it and esteem it more excellent and sovereign than that which shall again arise from death: If thou beest born of God, then thou wilt understand what I mean.

37. For this is the type of Christ, spewing how Christ has drowned sin, and the enkindled anger of God in the human property; it is not only an offering, for then Moses had accomplished it; it is not a bare verbal forgiveness, as Babel teaches: No. The human will must from all its powers enter into this death, into this blood, viz. into the highest tincture.

38. The purple robe which Christ wore could not do it; the white hypocritical pharisaical priest's coat could also not effect it, no flattery or demure hypocrisy avails here; no comfortings, soothings, or giving God good words are effectual here; the crafty malignant man must be mortified in Christ's blood, he must be drowned in the virgin's blood: The seed of the woman must bruise the head of the serpent; the will must wholly disclaim and depart from its selfish property, and become as an ignorant child, and wholly enter into God's mercy, into the virgin-like blood of Christ, that sin and the poisoned Mercury may be drowned in its Mars, that the white lion may arise; for the lion which now appears in the white colour, in crimson red, is the Mercury of life, viz. the expressed word, viz. the soul, which before was a wrathful devil in its self-hood, ruling and domineering in the anger of God in the three forms of the poison-source, viz. in Saturn, Mars, and Mercury: Now it is the white scarlet-coloured lion from the house of David and Israel, fulfilled in the covenant of promise.

39. N.B.—But that we may give satisfaction to the well-wisher, we will further shew him the whole ground even to the resurrection of Christ: When the Jews had hung Jesus upon the cross, and he had shed his human and heavenly divine blood, and drowned the turba in the human blood, then Jesus said, "Father, forgive them, for they know not what they do."

40. When Jesus had broken death in the humanity, and took away self, he did not then wholly cast away the human property, wherein death and the anger of God were, but then he did first truly assume it;

understand, he even then did truly take the outward kingdom into the inward; for the outward kingdom was begotten as a wonder out of the eternal wisdom in the speaking word, and spoken forth into a form, as a manifestation of the Deity in love and anger, in good and evil: So that Jesus would not that the outward type of the wonders in the likeness of God should perish or quite vanish, but the wrath which had overpowered the love in man should be forgiven, that is, it should be given into the nothing, viz. into the liberty, that it might not be manifest in its own self-property; it must be servant, and only a cause of the fiery love and divine joyfulness; nothing should perish or be lost in man, for God had created him to his image.

41. Thus let the philosopher observe, that when the three murtherers, viz. Saturn, Mars, and Mercury, sink in the crimson-coloured blood of the lion, they do not perish; but they are pardoned, that is, their wrath is changed into a love-desire, viz. out of Venus into Sol; for when the fiery desire enters into the watery desire, then a shining, viz. a glorious splendour, arises from and in the fire; for Venus is white, and the fire-desire is red.

42. Here now it is changed into one colour, which is yellow, that is, white and red both in one colour, which is the majestical lustre ; for when Mercury is changed into the power of joy, then arises the multiplication; he changes his mother, wherein he lay shut up in death, into Sol; he makes the earthly heavenly in one property, as the virgin was: For here the virgin loses her name, for she has given her love and pearl to the champion, who is now called here the white lion, as the Scripture speaks of the lion of the house of Israel and David, who should demolish the devil's kingdom, and destroy hell, that is, break the anger of God, and change it into love.

43. This champion or lion is no man or woman, but he is both; the tincture of the fire and light must come into one, viz. of the essence which is Venus, and of the spirit which is Mars in Mercury; the Father's love and anger must become one thing, and then this one thing is called the kingdom of joy; so long as it is separated, there is in the thing only anguish and torment, and mere desire; but when it burns in one will, it is a joyful proceeding forth from itself: And this egressive property is called the Holy Ghost, viz. the life of the Deity.

44. Therefore know that the virgin's and young man's blood must be both shed together, that the fire-lion might die; which was manifest in the human property, that the love of the virgin might change his

wrath in her dear love-blood into her property, and obtain the soul from the young man; for in Adam the virgin disappeared, for the soul departed out of its love-will out of the resignation into its own, and became disobedient to God.

45. Here the virgin does again take the soul into herself, and gives it her crown of pearl, as to a noble champion, and calls him in his own name the white lion or champion. O ye children of men, observe it, I beseech you; open the gates of the world in your heart; Open them wide that the King of Glory may come in, even the great champion in battle, who hath deprived death of its might, and destroyed the hell in God's anger, and made of the world paradise.

46. O ye wise seekers, how does the Lord open his windows! Why do you sleep in the desire of much increase in your covetousness, which is multiplied in the wrath? Do but enter only into the divine resignation; you may partake of that which the powers of heaven are able to afford: If you do but forsake your selfishness, then the earth shall become heaven to you, says the spirit of wonders; but you shall not obtain it in your wicked ways and covetous doings.

47. And when Jesus through the shedding of his blood had given the wrath of God in man to the love, that the Father had received the love in the human property into the wrath; then the kingdom of the devil in the wrath, and the kingdom of love did immediately part asunder; they were divided: And this figure did hang with Christ on the cross, viz. the wicked mocker at the left hand, who reviled Jesus, and was not capable of his blood-shedding; and the other at the right hand, who was converted from his sins to Jesus, and said, "Lord, remember me when thou comest into thy kingdom;" to whom Jesus answered, "Verily, to-day thou shalt be with me in paradise."

48. Thus we are rightly to consider, that when the wrath of God is drowned in the blood of Christ, so that it changes its might into love, that even then paradise is again open; for when Jesus had tinctured the human blood which was corrupted in sin with the virgin's blood in the love, then the virgin received the manhood, viz. the self-hood, into her virgin's love. This was the paradise, and an habitation of God, with and in man, where God dwells in the humanity, and is all in all in it.

49. Thus it falls out also in the philosophic work, when Mars and Mercury die according to the property of the dark impression of Saturn, then Venus takes them into her love-blood, and Venus gives

her love into the poisonful fire-desire: She wholly gives herself in unto the fire of Mars in Mercury, and she yields herself fully to be their own; but seeing Mars and Mercury become impotent (as to the might of the fire and poison) in the love, the love and anger thereupon change themselves into one essence, into one desire; and here, when the fire, viz. the fire-desire, gives in its desire to the love; then saith the love, "To-day thou shalt be with me out of thy fire-anguish in paradise," viz. in joy, that is, thou shalt be changed in me: And here Venus gets the soul in the philosophic work, so that Mars and Mercury become her soul, and the strife ceases; for the enmity is appeased and quelled: And thus the child subsists in the fire immoveably without any change; for Mars does not at all annoy it, and so likewise Mercury and Saturn hurt it not, for they are in the child at the end of nature, where there is no turba any more.

50. Mercury is pure in Saturn, he has no more poison, whereby to make soil or rust in the water, viz. in the salt of Saturn: And let the philosopher and divine also well observe this, that in paradise there is a perfect life without any shadow of change, also without any false evil desire, and a continual day, where the paradisical man is clear as a transparent glass, in whom the divine sun shines through and through, as gold that is thoroughly bright and pure, without any spot or foulness.

51. "And when Jesus knew that all was finished, he seeth his mother and John his disciple standing by under the cross, and saith unto his mother, Woman, to! this is thy son; and to the disciple, Behold thy mother, and forthwith the disciple took her unto his own home."

52. This is an excellent type, how Christ has forsaken this world, viz. the human self-hood, and is again gone to the Father; for he saw his mother according to this world, and his disciple, viz. his uncle, according to the outward humanity from his mother's side, and yet said to his mother, "Woman, behold, there is thy son," I am no more thy son according to my outward humanity; it is changed into God's Son, and is no longer of the world, but it lives to God; But seeing thou art to be yet in the world, take John, who is not yet changed, to be thy guardian; and thou John take thy mother; and he presently took her to himself.

53. This is the type of the Christian Church upon earth: For we the poor children of Eve are not presently wholly changed according to the outward man; but we must also pass into death, and putrify, that

the wrath also in the flesh may rot and putrify, and the spirit might rest in the death of Christ till the general resurrection and transmutation of the outward man; in which the earth of man shall be transformed into heaven, and the mirror or type of the wonders shall appear therein.

54. Thus he commanded his disciple to take care of his mother: His mother is the Christian Church upon earth, wherein the children of God are begotten according to the spirit, whom he should take care for, and guide and lead them, till the number of the humanity out of the flesh shall be accomplished, and then the spiritual body shall arise, and shall be proved in Christ's death, in his entrance into the anger, where he changed the anger into love; and the kingdom with the source of darkness shall be separated from it.

55. But in this life-time, though the spirit be changed in the divine power, and the spirit be baptized with the virgin's baptism, and puts on the image of Christ internally, viz. Venus's body in the love; yet Adam is not capable of it till he also enters into the transmutation of Christ, which comes to pass in death or in the dying to this mortal life.

56. But in the meanwhile, John, as the teacher of Christ in Christ's stead, must provide for the outward mother according to the outward man, and feed and teach the lambs of Christ with Christ's spirit: And it exactly shews us how the outward man is not God's mother; for Christ separates himself from his outward mother, and gives her to John; he has put on the eternal mother, viz. the Father of the eternal birth, and therefore they do very ill that honour and worship the outward mother of Christ for God's mother.

57. The whole true Christendom is Christ's mother, which bears Christ in her: And John, viz. the servants of Christ are her nurses, which take care for the mother of Christ as John did; he presently received the mother of Christ and provided for her, as her son, and not as her lord; for Christ said to him, "Behold, she is thy mother: "So should all the disciples and teachers of Christ do, and take care of the poor Christendom, as sons, with great humility towards the mother, provide for, and cherish her with diligence and circumspection, and serve her with all discreet modesty, courtesy, and humility; feed and comfort her with the spirit of Christ, not as the priests in Babel do, who ride over her as wealthy, rich, domineering masters, and will be lords over the mother, and only seek honours, and to fatten their bellies in pleasure, and live in strife and contention: These, one with the other, of what name or title soever they be, are not all Johannites,

but they are the poisonful mercurial Pharisees, in whom there is nothing but mere anguish, vexation, pain, and torment, where one property does continually torment, envy, and hate the other, and hold it out for false; and yet they are all only out of one root, and have all only one will, except that one colour does not glister as the other.

58. For Saturn is not as Jupiter; Jupiter is not as Mars; Mars, viz. the fire-spirit, is not as the light of the sun; and the sun is not as Venus with her meek water-source; and Venus is not as Mercury with his sound; for she is meek and still, and Mercury sounds and sets up his note; and Mercury also is not as Luna, which as a simple body does give body to all the rest for manifestation; one is far otherwise than another, and has not one property and will; and yet they are in the centre of the essence, viz. in Luna and Saturn, in the property f the soul and body, all of them one and the same lump. Thus the partial sectarian Mercurialites, and Baal's servants, are divided in these properties; they are the Pharisees which judge and condemn Jesus in his members.

59. They wrangle and contend only about the church, and yet none will take care of the poor forsaken mother of Christ: They are mad in their martial and mercurial contest, and are not Johannites, they enter not in Christ's spirit at the door of Christ into the sheepfold; they are wolves, lions, and bears, yea foxes and fearful hares, who fly from and forsake the mother; their rise and original is out of Babel, where they continually contend, wrangle, grin, and bite one another for the letter. Every one will be lord and master over the letter, and transpose and place it as he pleases, only for the honour, applause, and pleasure of this world: They consider not that the mother is a widow, and that Christ has left and ordained them that they should be such curates for her as John.

60. O thou dear mother of Christendom, let these wolves, bears, and lions go, and shelter themselves where they please, regard no longer these evil beasts; take the John, the disciple of Christ, who teaches the love and humility.

61. O thou dear and worthy mother, art thou not only one? Why dost thou suffer the lions to rend and tear thee in pieces? Christ is thy husband, all these are strangers and hirelings, unless they walk in thy filial love, and humble themselves towards the mother, and provide for her as ministers, else they be all wolves, bears, and tearing lions; though there were many thousands of them, yet one is not at all better

than another, unless he comes forth in the line of John, and takes care of Christ's mother, and provides for the mother with earnestness in Christ's spirit: Which if he has not, he is not then called of Christ to be a guardian or curate to the mother; but he is a Mercurialite, a Pharisee, such as Christ called the seed of serpents, and generation of vipers, who crucify Jesus in his members.

62. And thus the philosopher must consider of, and well observe Christ's mother, whom he recommended to John to take care of: He must likewise be a John, and know that his business is about the mother, and that his work in this world is not wholly heavenly: He will not so manifest paradise, that God will appear, and be manifest face to face in his work: No, he remains in the mother, yet he obtains the universal in the mother; for the mother of Christ obtained it also, for it was said to her, "Thou art the blessed among all women."

63. So likewise the philosopher reaches to the blessing in this valley of misery, that he is able to bless his corrupt body, that is, tincture it and free it from sickness, even to the limit of the highest constellation according to Saturn; and therefore let him take heed of covetousness, for so he introduces the turba.

64. By the type of John and the mother of Christ, he is to know, that the kingdom of God and the kingdom of this world are two in his work, and that God's kingdom lies shut up in the mother, viz. in his work, of which he must take care; and be a minister thereunto, and not a lord of the mother, but an almsgiver, and not a gatherer of treasure and wealth, not a covetous muck-worm; also none shall attain to it, or understand our meaning, that will not be a guardian of the mother: The Most High has laid a bar before the foolish understanding, that it is blind, till it be weary with seeking; I speak in the ground of truth.

65. And when Jesus had commended his mother to John, he again turned his desire into the mother of the human property, and said, "I thirst;" he thirsted after the members of human property, and desired the salvation of mankind, viz. the health of his members, understand of his children, which should be begotten in him; and the Jews gave his humanity gall and vinegar to drink; and when he tasted it, he would not drink it.

66. Here is again the outward type, shewing how it went inwardly: The name Jesus, viz. the love of God which was entered into the humanity, and had espoused itself thereunto, did thirst in the love-desire after the corrupt humanity, and would fain taste the pure

water of the humanity in itself; but the wrathful anger of God, which was enkindled in the human property, gave itself in with the human property to the thirst of the love-desire: And when the love-desire tasted of it, it would not drink it, but sunk down into it as wholly resigned, or freely yielded up, and did unite and very essentially incline itself into the anger of God as a full and perfect obedience, and as fully and freely given over as a peculiar propriety thereinto.

67. This was now the flagrat of the wrath, that the love should so come into it; whereupon the earth trembled, and the rocks clave asunder; for so the death was dismayed at the life: And here the awakened wrath's property did separate itself into the centre, viz. into the first principle, into the fire-root; and now from the centre there proceeded forth the hunger to the new-birth in the human property; of the hunger unto death was made a hunger to life; for the love tinctured the anger, that the fire-desire to the dark impression became a desire of life.

68. Understand it here right; God the Father, who gave his dear heart into the humanity to help mankind, did now thirst after the humanity, viz. after his heart or word of power; and the Deity in the humanity, viz. the heart of the Father, did thirst after the Father; and the love or the essence of the light did thirst after the fire's essence: For the fire's, or soul's essence in Adam was departed out of the love-essentiality (wherein the paradise did consist) into a selfishness, and was become disobedient to God; and thereupon the essence, life, and being of the light and love died in its growing, that is, it withered as to the vegetative life, or heavenly growth, blooming, and sense of the paradisical source, and awaked and arose to the earthly world.

69. Here the Father brought the soul, which was entered into his wrath, and had manifested itself in his anger, again into the love, viz. into the disappeared paradisical image: And here the dark world was dismayed in death's flagrat at the fire-flagrat, which arose up in love in the death as a joyful flagrat; which joy-flagrat entered into the dead bodies of those who had hope in Israel (who did hope upon the Messiah) as a sound of the power of God, and awakened them from death.

70. This flagrat rent in twain the veil in the Temple, viz. the veil of Moses, which hung before the clear face of God, so that man could not see God, and therefore he must serve him with an offering, and type of this final discovery, in which God did manifest himself again in the

humanity: This flagrat broke the type in the offerings and sacrifices, and manifested the clear face of God, and united the human time with eternity.

71. All whatever the Jews did outwardly to Christ, the same was a type of the inward, viz. how it went between God and the humanity, viz. between the eternity and time: The Jews gave Jesus gall and vinegar in his thirst, both these properties are a Mercury in the Sulphur of Saturn, viz. in the impression; this is even the type and full resemblance of the soul's property, as it is in itself alone void of the other love-properties.

72. God gave this property of the soul again into his love, the death into the life, the disappeared love-essence (which the word of God had assumed to itself in the essence and seed of Mary, and quickened to life) into the anger's property, into the soul's essence, viz. into the centre of the fire and dark world; whereupon the soul-like fire and dark world became an exceeding triumphant joyful paradisical life: And here the champion upbraided death and hell, viz. the dark world in the soul, and said, "Death! where is thy sting " now in man?" Hell! where is now thy victory" in the wrath of the poison-source in the expressed word or Mercury? All is now dead: O death, I am to thee a death; Hell! I am to thee a conqueror; thou must serve me for the kingdom of joy: Thou shalt be my servant and minister to the kingdom of joy; thou shalt enkindle the flames of love with thy wrath, and be a cause of the spring in paradise.

73. Thus we give the philosopher to understand our sense and deep ground in nature, who desires to seek and open the disappeared essence of the earth, which lies shut up in death, viz. in the curse of God: The veil of Moses hangs also before him, and a very right earnestness is requisite to rend the veil in twain, that he may be able to see the face of nature, otherwise he is not fitted for it.

74. And as it went in the humanity of Christ, betwixt God's love and anger, and both were transformed into one; so likewise it is in his work of nature, the poisonful Mercury in the Sulphur of Mars and Saturn gives its lunar menstruum, viz. the greatest poison of the dark source into Venus's property; when Venus thirsts after the fire of love, then Mercury gives his poison into the thirst of Venus, and Venus's thirst gives itself wholly to the poison, as if it died; it wholly yields up its desiring life, whereupon arises the great darkness in the philosophic work: For the materia becomes as black as a raven, for Venus has resigned its life, from whence the glance or splendour

arises, as it is to be seen by Christ, that the sun lost its light, and there was a great darkness contrary to the common course of nature.

75. For when the inward sun gave in itself unto the anger, viz. into the darkness of God; then the outward sun, which receives its power and lustre from the inward, as a glass or resemblance of the inward, could not shine; for its root from whence it shines was entered into the darkness in the place of this world, and would turn the darkness in the curse of God into light, viz. it would make the place of this world again paradise.

76. Thus likewise the sun of the outward world, which is a figure of the inward all-essential sun, must stand still with its splendour in the darkness, from the sixth hour unto the ninth, which is even the time of Adam's sleep when he entered with the desire into the centre of the eternal nature, viz. into the birth, where the love and anger part themselves into two centres, and would prove the cold and hot fire, which took him, and did powerfully work in him. Here are three hours according to the ternary, and in the grave three days according to the time, viz. according to the humanity.

77. When Adam was in the image of God, and was neither man nor woman, but both; he stood forty days in paradise without wavering, and when he fell he stood even till the third day, viz. forty hours in the sleep, even till God did make or build the woman out of him. Thus Israel must be tempted forty days on Mount Sinai, whether they would live in the obedience of God under the wonders and mighty acts; and when it could not be, God gave them the law of his covenant as a mirror of that which was promised in the covenant; therefore the temptation of the body was upon them forty years, that the body must eat manna to try whether man could be remedied: And when the body or outward person could not stand, then Joshua brought them through the water with the covenant of the type, where Israel must serve with sacrifices in the covenant in the type of the final accomplishment, till the time of restitution came in: And then the valiant champion in battle stood forty days in the wilderness in the temptation, and stood out the first trial of Adam in paradise; and the three hours of darkness on the cross are the three hours of temptation of Christ, when the devil tempted him: And again the forty hours of Christ in the grave are the forty days of Adam in paradise, and the forty days of Moses upon the Mount; and the forty years in the wilderness, and the forty days after the resurrection before the ascension, are even one and the same: And now when the champion

had stood out Adam's trial, the soul was tempted forty days in the human property, whether it would eat of God's word, and live in full resigned obedience in the will of God, and be a true image, likeness, and similitude of the divine power in the unsearchable eternity, according to the Trinity of the Deity.

78. In the like manner let the philosopher observe, that the essence of time does also stand in such a property, for man was created out of the essence of time into an image, as an extract of all essences, a complete image and likeness according to time and eternity, ruling and standing in the time and in the eternity as an instrument of the great infinite God, with whom, by and with his Spirit, he would make and do what he pleased.

79. Now man is the instrument of God, with or by whom he manifests his hiddenness both in his own human property, viz. in the essence and image of God; and then also through man, as with the instrument in the mother of all beings, as in the grand mystery, viz. in the soul of the great world.

80. Man has power so far as he goes, as an instrument of God in divine obedience, as his Spirit guides and leads him, that he can introduce the earth which stands in the curse of God into the benediction, and make of death's-anguish the highest triumphant joy in the outward pregnant mother; but he himself does it not, only his will labours with the understanding therein, and conjoins the compacta, which belong together, as life and death which stand opposite to one another: These he must join together, and bring them into one by such an art as time and eternity are united by and in the man Christ, and by him all those which give their will thereinto.

81. He will see in his work all whatever God did in the humanity; when he brought it again into the universal, viz. into paradise, he will see how the wrath devours and swallows up the fair Venus into his pricking thorny essence, and how Venus does fully yield in herself; and how the wrath also dies away in Venus, and becomes wholly dark and black as a coal; for death and life lie together both in death, viz. in the obedience of God: They both hold still to him, and suffer the Spirit of God to make of and with them what it pleases, who introduces them again into the eternal will of God to which he at first created them: And thus the essence stands again in the beginning in the order as God created it: It must only stand in its impression, in the verbum fiat, viz. in the divine making, till the day of God's separation, when God will change the time again into the eternity.

82. And when Jesus had drank the cup and tasted the vinegar mixed with gall in the outward man, and inwardly in the love-property, viz. in the virgin, the wrathful anger of God; then said the whole man Christ, "My God, my God, why hast thou forsaken me?" For God's speaking word stood still now in the human property, and the new-born essentiality which was dead in Adam, and was again quickened in Christ, cried with the same, "My God, my God, why hast thou forsaken me?" For the anger of God was by the soul's property entered into the image of the divine essentiality, and had devoured the image of God.

83. Here now the image in the creature of the soul cried, "My God, my God, why hast thou forsaken me?" For the human image which disappeared in Adam, and was again revived in Christ's incarnation, should bruise the head of God's anger in the fire-soul, and change its fire-might into Sol: And now the speaking word of God did here forsake it, and it fell into the soul's wrath, where it felt God's anger; for the speaking word did so bring it through the anger into death, and out of the death again into the solar life, understand into the eternal sun.

84. Like as the candle dies in the fire, and out of that death the light and power proceed, viz. the great painless life; so out of Christ's dying and death the eternal divine sun should and must arise in the human property; but the selfishness of the human property, viz. the soul's own self-will to live in the fire's might must here die and be drowned in the image of love, and the image of love must also resign and give itself in unto the wrath of death, that so all might fall down into death, and arise in God's will and mercy through death in the paradisial source in the resignation, that God's Spirit might be all in all. Hell's eye must see through the love, as the light shines out of the fire, and the fire from the darkness, and the darkness takes its original from the eternal desire.

85. And as Adam changed the likeness of God into the dark death's form, so God did again change the likeness through his fire-wrath out of death into the light; he drew forth the likeness again out of death, as a blossom grows from the harsh earth.

86. Thus it goes likewise in the philosophic work; Venus is forsaken when she receives the three wrathful properties into herself in wrath; their wrath, viz. the death devours her life, whereupon she loses the colour, and yet becomes a death to the three forms in the

wrath, for she drowns death with love. Thus the life is made a death to death, viz. to the wrath, and now they both lie in the will of the eternal nature, viz. in the verbum fiat, which proceeds with them the divine way, in manner as it proceeded forth into essence in the beginning of the creation: For in the beginning paradise, viz. the universal was manifest, and the love shined through the death or anger. Even so it must be again, Venus must become the eye or sight in the wrath, and then of Saturn, Mars, and Mercury there will be a Jupiter: Mars becomes sun, and Saturn moon, and so Mars shines with the sun out of Saturn in Luna from Venus's eye, and all seven are only one: Thus the strife has an end, and all is accomplished till the resurrection of the body.

87. And when Jesus had drank the cup, and said, "My God, why hast thou forsaken me?" then he said, "All is finished," understand the work of man's redemption; and he said further, "Father, into thy hands I commit my spirit, and bowed his head, and gave up the ghost." Here the whole life of Christ resigned itself into the Father's desire, viz. into the will of the eternal nature, and fully gave in the will of his self-hood, viz. his creaturely will again into the centre, viz. into the first mother, from whence the soul-like creature was produced, that is, into the grand mystery of eternity: The self-will must again enter into nature's end, so that the selfishness may wholly die, that God's eternal will and spirit may be and do only all in all in the humanity, and that the creature might afterwards be alone his instrument, wherein he might do and work according to his good pleasure: And thus God the Father has in Christ's death and entrance into our humanity again received our self-hood into his will; and that this might be, he first tinctured the humanity with the Deity, that the humanity might be a pleasant sweet savour and offering to him in his power, for before death lay before it.

88. Here the love destroyed death, and opened the fast seal, that the will might again enter into that which it was before it was the creature; and so we all must follow him upon the path which he has made open for us; none can see God, unless God become first man in him, which is brought to pass in faith's desire, and even then the corrupt will (which is apprehended in the death and anger of God, and which blooms in the earthly essence, and brings forth fruit unto death) be wholly mortified, and fall into the free resignation, into the will and mercy of God: And then the own will is with and in Christ at nature's end in the grand mystery of God, viz. in God's hands. God's

hands are the eternal desire, or the eternal will, which is unchangeable; thus the creaturely self-will dies; it enters wholly into the nothing, that it might no more live to itself, but to God.

89. Thus it falls out also in the philosophic work; when the artist has first seen great wonders, which the creaturely and natural will has wrought in the power of Venus, insomuch that he supposes that he is nigh thereunto; even then nature does first die in his work, and becomes a dark night unto him; the property and power of all the forms must give forth themselves from their centre, and fall upon nature's end; all do freely yield over themselves as one dead essence, and there is no longer any effectual working therein, all is divided in the crown into the thousandth number, and then it is again in the mystery as nature's end as it was before it came into the creaturely being; understand, the essential desire, viz. the expressed Mercury, must again come unto the end of its selfishness, and resign itself into the speaking word.

90. The corporal essence remains in the centre of the four elements till the judgment of God, which now at death stands in the centre of Sol, viz. in the compaction of Venus and Mercury, which compaction at death falls wholly into one thing, viz. into one power of Jupiter, that is, into the centre of the liberty; for here the desire to cold and heat goes out, all earthly will and desire of the properties dies, and there is no more any hunger after the earthly, or death's property.

Chapter XII
Of The Seventh Form In The Kingdom Of The Mother; How The Seventh Kingdom, Viz. The Kingdom Of The Sun, Is Again Opened And Made Alive; Set Forth In Parable, Or By Way Of Similitude Of Christ's Resurrection

1. We are not to think that when Christ died the natural death in the human property, that he died as to his creaturely soul, much less as to the Deity; also he did not disappear or die in the heavenly essentiality and in the heavenly tincture: This cannot be; only the will and dominion of self, viz. of the outward world, which domineered in man unto the own will and own powers of the selfish creature (wherein man was disobedient to God), he gave that wholly into the Father's hands, viz. into the end of nature, into the Father's great mystery; not that it should be dead, but that God's Spirit might alone be the life thereof, that the divine dominion might be in Christ's

person, that the Eternal Father might rule and reign with his Eternal Spirit in his image; and therefore God has determined to keep the last judgment by this Jesus.

2. Now the creature of Christ does it not alone, but God in his image through the creature in the dominion of his Eternal Spirit of all the three principles, which is the life and dominion of every being, in each thing according to its property.

3. And understand us right, when Christ died on the cross, the name Jesus did not also die, which destroyed death, and tinctured the expressed word, viz. the form of the Deity (or the formed word), viz. the soul with love: No, it cannot be, the eternity does not die, only the spoken word, which stands again in the desire of the speaking, viz. in the fiat, which changes itself in its own speaking, viz. in the self-desire, and brings its own sound into another form and source than the speaking word had spoken it, and set it forth with the verbum fiat into a form, signature, and will; as Lucifer with his royal throne, and Adam also did, when they both departed out of resignation into selfhood; the instrument would be master.

4. The outward working sensitive life wherein the anger of God was set on fire did wholly die away, not that it should be a nothing, but it fell into the nothing, viz. into God's will, into God's working and feeling, quite from the will of the outward world, which is evil and good, so that it might no longer live to the world, viz. to the astrum in the walm, the boiling or seething power of the four elements; but to the Eternal Father's nature in the walm of the pure divine element the life of the outward world died.

5. Thus the true human life fell immediately again into that place from whence Adam had brought it, viz. into paradise, upon which Christ said to the thief, "To-day thou shalt be with me in paradise;" it fell into Adam's death, whereby he died to paradise, and sprang up in Adam's death as a new creature out of the old, like as the branch springs from the corn: And this it did from the might and power of the speaking word, which of grace was entered with living essentiality into the disappeared heavenly essentiality of man, and had freely given itself into the centre of the soul-like nature, and also into the wrath of the anger and death in the flesh, and changed the anger into love, and tinctured the corrupt blood in the anger with the love.

6. The divine tincture tinctured the human; the divine sun entered into the human; the divine sun entered into Adam's night, viz. into

Adam's sleep; God's sun with the name Jesus entered with Adam's soul and humanity in Christ's person into death, understand into Adam's sleep.

7. When Christ died, then Adam died also to his self-hood in Christ's death; the name Jesus was in Christ the serpent-destroyer in Adam's humanity; Christ entered into the image of the first Adam, so that the first Adam in the humanity of Christ became the same Christ, and serpent-destroyer, indeed not in the same creature, but in the same soul's and body's property.

8. The first Adam fell into sleep, viz. into the impotence of the divine world, and died in the death of death; the second Adam entered into the death of death; and took the death of death captive in himself, viz. in the humanity of Adam: He was a death to death, and brought forth the life out of death into the eternal liberty: He arose in the divine omnipotence in the essence of the first Adam: God's Spirit in the speaking eternal word brought forth Adam out of death in Christ's humanity. Adam arose in Christ's humanity, and all the children of Adam, which are partakers of Christ's kingdom, arise in Christ; all in Christ's flesh and blood, soul and spirit, but every one in his creature which he has had here, and mortified in Christ's death.

9. Every one is a particular twig; but there is only one tree, which is Christ in Adam, and Adam in Christ, only one, not two; only one Christ in all Christians; so that I may say, "If I be dead in Christ to the world, I am the same Christ, viz. a branch on the same tree."

10. But seeing that I in the outward man do yet live in my self-hood, therefore I must also die with the outward man in Christ's death, and arise and live in him. Now therefore I live with the will of faith in the mind in Christ, and am a Christian in the will of the mind in the desire of faith, and receive Christ with his humanity into my will, and cast my will into his death; and thus my inward man is also dead in Christ's death, and lives no longer to self-hood; but I am resigned in him, and lie buried in his death: But seeing he is risen in God's will, I also live in his resurrection in him; but my earthliness in its selfish property lives to the earthly world, until it also dies quite to self-hood, and enters into the resignation and putrefaction, and then Christ will awaken it through my inward man, which now lives in him.

11. Like as he is risen from the dead, even so shall I, who shall die to the earthliness in him, viz. in my first father Adam, in the name

Jesus as a Christian in Christ; my twig, withered in sin on the tree, shall obtain strength and sap in the name Jesus to life. I shall and must spring forth afresh with my humanity in him as in my stem who is become a heart and power in my father Adam, and bring forth fruit to the praise of God.

12. My will-spirit, which now is in Christ's humanity, and lives in Christ's Spirit, that shall in Christ's power give sap to the dry tree, that it shall again arise at the last day in the sound of the trumpet of the divine breath in Christ's voice, which also is my voice in his breath, and spring afresh in the tree Christ, viz. in paradise: The paradise shall be in me; all whatever God has and is shall appear in me as a form and image of the divine world's being; all colours, powers, and virtues of his eternal wisdom shall be manifest in me, and on me, as on his likeness: I shall be the manifestation of the spiritual divine world, and an instrument of God's Spirit, wherein he makes melody with himself, with this voice, which I myself am, as with his signature: I shall be his instrument, and organ of his expressed word and voice; and not only I, but all my fellow-members in the glorious tuned instrument of God: We are all strings in his joyful consort; the spirit of his mouth strikes the tune and note on our strings.

13. And therefore God became man, that he might again repair his glorious instrument which he had made for his praise, which perished as to him, and would not sound according to the desire of his joy and love, and introduce again the true love-sound into the strings: He has introduced the voice which sounds in his presence again into us, viz. into his instrument, he is become that which I am, and has made me that which he is, so that I may say, that I am in my resignation in him his trumpet, and the sound of his instrument and divine voice, at which now I rejoice in all my fellow-strings and voices, which with me are tuned and set as an eternal work, to the praise and glory of God.

14. Thus know ye now my fellow-voices in the praise of God, that I sound with my string played upon in the spirit upon and in your note, and thus sing I to you; that whatever Jesus has done through the Christ, viz. through his and my humanity, the same he does yet to-day in me and in all my fellow-members. He died to my self-hood in his death, and I also die to my self-hood in his death: He is given up to his resignation in God his Father, and God his Father has raised him up with the spirit of his mouth in him, and set him forth for the

royal image according to the Holy Trinity, through and with whom God will judge all things in the place of this world.

15. Thus God also has awakened in him my spirit and soul through his spirit in the great name Jesus in Christ, so that I in my resignation in him need not to die, for he died in me and for me; his death, in that he is risen from death, is become my eternal life, so that now I live in his death, as one dying; and yet there is no more any death in him, but thus I die to myself and sin in him, seeing that my desire and will presses forth from my self-hood into it, so that I die daily to myself, till once I shall obtain the limit of my self-hood, and my self-hood with the earthly will and desire does wholly die to its selfishness; then shall my self-hood, and all whatever is in me which seeks and loves itself, fall into the death of Christ, viz. into the first mother, from whence God created me, and my self-hood shall become a nothing; and even then my self-hood lies in Christ's death in the resignation as an instrument of God, who then will make it his instrument as he pleases.

16. But seeing now my soul and spirit lives in his resurrection, and his voice (air or breath) is in me, according to the resignation in him, as St. Paul says, "Our conversation is in heaven, from whence we wait for the Saviour Jesus Christ;" therefore also his voice, which is in me in that I am or live no longer to my self-hood, but he alone is and lives in me, shall raise up my dead body, which I resign to him, and bring it into his first image, to which he created it.

17. Thus now I live in God, and my self-hood does not know it, for it lives not in God, but in itself (God is indeed in it, but it does not apprehend him), and hides the pearl which I am in Christ; not I, but he in his humanity in my creature in himself: And thus I speak and write of the great mystery of all beings, not that I have apprehended it in my self-hood, but he strikes my signature in my desire, which presses into him, as he pleases.

18. I am known to myself, but not in my self-hood, but in his mirror which of grace he has put into me, thereby to allure my self-hood to him, viz. into the resignation; and so likewise, dear brethren, it shall again be represented to you out of his glass, which he has set forth through my capacity in him, as his instrument.

19. Thus it goes also in the philosophic work; Sulphur, Mercury, and Sal are entered by the curse of God into their self-hood, viz. into a self-working and living; all does now work in the curse and anger of God according to the property of the first principle; if God had not

placed the sun as a nature-god of the outward visible world therein, which tinctures every working life, even everything which grows and moves, all would be in the dark death's impression, viz. in the abyss of hell.

20. Now if anything shall be freed from this self-hood, viz. from the wrathful death, and be again brought into the universal, viz. into the highest perfection, then it must die wholly to its self-hood, and enter into the stillness, viz. into the death of the resignation at nature's end: Mars must wholly lose the might of the fire and wrath, and Mercury also his poison-life; Saturn must be a death to himself, insomuch that the artist sees nothing but the great darkness, and even then the light appears in the resignation; for St. John says, "The light shineth in the darkness, and the darkness apprehended it not;" that is, in its self-hood, viz. in its own will and working it cannot apprehend it; but in the resignation the nothing, viz. the liberty of God shines in it.

21. For the nothing manifests itself in its lubet out of the liberty in the darkness of death; for the nothing will not be a nothing, and also cannot be a nothing, and likewise it cannot otherwise manifest itself, but according to the property of the free lubet, which is now fixed or steadfast, and in it also as a nothing, for there is no turba therein; the self-will and hunger is dead, and in the nothing, and the lubet of the eternal liberty is its life: Now seeing that the highest being has once moved itself, and come into a visible comprehensible essence, it does again figure or form that same essence, which departs from its self-hood, and enters into the nothing, into such a being or essence as it was before the times of the world: But seeing the verbum fiat stands yet to this day creating of the corporal essence, it does again make a fixed perfect essence; as the like is brought to pass in the philosophic work, where a new life arises out of death, as God does raise us up in himself in Christ, if we die to self-hood, and wholly resign up ourselves to him.

22. And thus when the expressed Mercury in the Sulphur of Saturn resigns its self-hood into Venus, then the verbum fiat changes it again into such an essence according to the lubet of the liberty; the death arises in a new body out of the darkness of death, in a white fair colour, but as an hidden lustre, wherein the colour is not rightly and distinctly known, till it dissolves itself, and the materia becomes desiring; then the sun arises in the centre, and Saturn in the property of Jupiter and Venus in all the seven forms (that is in the verbum fiat)

as a new creation, and the desire of all the seven forms tend to Sol's lustre, viz. to the white and red colour from the fire and light, which is the majestical colour, lustre, or glory.

23. Christ after his resurrection walked forty days in the mystery of all the three principles at once, in the property of the first Adam after his creation before his sleep, and before his Eve was formed, and appeared to his disciples in his property which he had here from the outward world, and did eat with them, and shewed them his assumed humanity, and that he had in no wise wholly put it off.

24. Even so let the artist understand us, that in the philosophic work the first matter does not wholly pass away or vanish, but it enters into the death of the life of its wrathful property, and dies in the curse of God, but rises again in its former being, which it had before the curse of God: The curse only is destroyed therein, and the first life does again rise up therein, and therefore it is fixed, and subsists in the fire, for it is dead to the dominion of the four elements, and lives in the fifth essence; not that it has that same life, but it stands still therein; yet the spirit of the new-born essence is a vegetative life with its growing therein; its lustre stands therein, it shews the first Adam in innocence, who stood likewise in such perfection.

25. And as Christ tinctured our corrupt humanity, in which Mercury was turned to poison, with the heavenly blood of the eternal divine virginity and essentiality, whereby the human self-hood died in the poison, and the resigned life did again arise; so the poisonful mercurial, martial, and saturnine will and desire die in the blood of Venus in the philosophic work, and both enter together into death, and arise both together in one love, in one will.

26. Therefore let the artist observe the tincture; it is more noble and precious for man's use in this valley of misery than the body which arises in the tincture; for the spirit is the life; the body is only a figure of the life, and the blood is a mansion of the spirit.

27. The artist must well observe this; in the blood of the young man, when his pearl gives itself to the three murtherers, that it also sheds its blood in and with the young man's, then the champion stands in hell, and disclaims the human self-hood: Then the white lion appears upon his crimson-coloured beast; even there lies the cure of sickness, and the death of death.

28. The body is dissolved in the blood of love in the death out of the earthly into an heavenly property. The tincture gives itself into the

new body; and afterwards, when the body rises in Sol's splendour, it also forsakes its will; it resigns itself wholly into the body's essence, and becomes its beauty, splendour, and colour, which the artist can never separate; for they are together in the fifth essence, viz. in the mystery of the verbum fiat, and belong to God's motion of the final day of separation; in this time to his own manifestation unto his honour, and deeds of wonder; but after this time to the crystalline world in the glassy sea before the ancient in the Apocalypse.

A Brief Summary of the Philosophic Work

29. Our meaning might seem very difficult to the reader, in that we go so far about and shew Christ all along therein; at which let no man wonder, we do not seek gold, or any temporal goods thereby, and drive man into vain curiosities; we speak only with the children whom God has chosen thereunto; for the time is born, where that which is lost shall be again found; yea not only the universal for the body of this world, but also for the soul.

30. The process is very short in both, and it is only of one property which is thus: The tree, understand the life, is divided into seven forms; now the curse of God is come into the seven forms, so that they are in strife and enmity, and one form annoys the other, and can never agree unless they all seven enter into death, and die to the self-will. Now this cannot be, unless a death comes into them, which breaks all their will, and be a death to them; as the deity in Christ was a death to the human self-hood, and the seven forms in the human life; thus it is here also: The human will was changed in Christ into the eternal sun, viz. into the resignation in God; so must all the forms in the philosophic work be changed into one, viz. into Sol: Seven must become one, and yet remain in seven, but in one desire, where each form desires the other in love, and then there is no more any strife and contest.

31. Therefore let the artist but consider how he may give death to the death with the pure life, and how he may awaken the dead and disappeared life, which is heavenly, and lies hidden and captivated in the curse, so that it may again receive the fire-soul; and if he does but bring it so far, it works of itself.

32. When the virgin again receives her bridegroom, who has been faithless, then he is prepared and fitted to the work; otherwise he is no way at all fitted; but all is in vain and to no purpose which he attempts. There is not any possibility for the heavenly image

according to God's likeness in man to be otherwise helped and restored after that the fire-soul had entered into its self-hood, unless the Spirit of God introduced itself into the disappeared image, viz. into the heavenly essentiality, and gave itself in with the image awakened in it into the soul's fire, viz. into the wrath of death, and be a death to death, viz. to the wrathful anger of God, that it might be drowned in the love, in the blood of the heavenly essentiality; and though there could be no parting nor dying, yet there was a dying of the wrath, so that the wrath was changed into a joy and love.

33. Thus the artist's work is exactly and throughout no otherwise: For man was created out of all beings, out of the heaven and earth; but when he became wholly earthly, and the curse seized on him, the curse also came over the earthly being, from whence man was made: Thus the heaven was shut up from man, and the heaven also was shut up in the earth, as metals, trees, and herbs, in the food of man, and whatever belonged to his ornament and delight.

34. The soul of the earth, viz. the property of the fire of the first principle is entered into its self-hood, viz. into God's anger; now the heaven is hidden in it; therefore the artist must in his work reduce the soul in the curse and the heaven again into one: He must introduce the soul again into heaven, or else there is no possibility: Now he cannot bring the soul in its iniquity into heaven, for it will not, and therefore he must bring the heaven into the soul, and wholly give in the heaven to the soul, that the soul may eat of heaven, whether she will or no; the heaven must be as death in the soul, so that the soul cannot get rid of it, how angry soever she be, and vehemently rages against it, till she be overcome in her wrath, and enters with the desire into heaven, viz. into the disappeared essence, and wills to murther it, as the Jews did Christ; and if she so enters into the heavenly essence, then the image of the heavenly essence falls into the jaws of the murtherer.

35. Thus when the heavenly essence gives its desire to the murtherer, the murtherer is dismayed at the dear love-life, and arises in the flagrat in the heavenly essentiality; thus the disappeared essence does again receive the fire flagrat into itself, and wholly unites itself with the fire-life; and so the fire must burn in love and meekness, and forego its right in the centre, as the light which shines from the fire; thus and no otherwise the heavenly essence obtains its life; and as a fire does thoroughly heat an iron that it appears as if it were mere fire, and it is so, but the iron does still retain its substance;

so the disappeared essence, viz. the heaven is manifest in the poisonful mercurial and martial fire-soul, and makes of seven wills only one, and yet seven remain, but the enmity ceases.

36. This is an universal, which also changes the enmity or malignity of all diseases in the human body into one will into unity ; so that the raging and raving, viz. the seven forms of life in their enmity become unanimous; and then the hunger of the disease ceases, and the process to the universal is as has been already mentioned. It is not my intention to mention a clear declaration thereof; it is clear enough; he that will not seek thereby a new man born in God, and apply himself diligently thereto, let him not meddle with my writings.

37. I have not written anything for such a seeker, and also he shall not be able to apprehend our meaning fundamentally, though he strives never so much about it, unless he enters into the resignation in Christ; there he may apprehend the spirit of the universal, otherwise all is to no purpose; and we faithfully warn the curious critic not to amuse himself, for he will not effect anything in this way, unless he himself enters thereinto, and then it will be shewn him without much seeking; for the way is child-like (plain and easy).

Chapter XIII
Of The Enmity Of The Spirit And Of The Body, And Of Their Cure And Remedy

1. Everything is in itself a senseless, and as a dead thing or being; it is only a manifestation of the spirit, which is in the body: The spirit is signed with the body; whatever the spirit is in itself in an incomprehensible imperceptible operation, the same is the body in the comprehensible and visible working. There is one form of the seven forms of nature superior and chief; the other hang to it, and give their signs also, according as each of them is strong in the essence; and as the forms stand in their order in each thing, so they sign the body of every thing and creature in its generation or kind : This is the manifestation of the divine wisdom in the expressed word of love and anger.

2. There is not anything but it has its soul in it according to its property, and the soul is a kernel to another body: Whatever lives and grows has its seed in it; God has comprehended all things in his word, and spoken them forth into a form, as the will had formed itself in the

desire, the expressed word is a platform of the speaking, and has again the speaking in it; this same speaking is a seed to another image according to the first, for both work, viz. the speaking, and the spoken word.

3. The speaking works in itself, viz. in the eternity, and the spoken also in itself, viz. in the time; the speaking is the master, and the spoken is the instrument; the speaking makes the nature of eternity, and the spoken makes the nature of time; each makes in its comprehension two properties, viz. light and darkness, wherein the element of all beings consists, which in the expressed word operates itself into four elements, but in the speaking word there is but one: The element in itself is neither hot nor cold, also neither dry nor moist; but it is a lubet, viz. a desiring will, wherein the divine wisdom makes the different and various colours; all according to the desire's property, in which there is neither number nor end: But in the four elements there is number and end; for with the expressing (in that they are become self-fulll) they have taken a beginning, and have formed themselves into a model or platform of a time, which runneth as a watch-work; it forms, frames, and destroys.

4. This watch-work consists of seven forms, or properties (as is before mentioned), which make in themselves a threefold spirit, viz. a vegetative, sensitive, and rational: The vegetative consists in the four elements; the sensitive in the seven forms of nature, and the reasoning power in the constellation; but the understanding proceeds only from God, for it rises out of the eternal nature; all life whatever, which has its limit in the expressed word, consists in Sal, Sulphur, and Mercury; for therein consist the seven properties of every life of this world; and also the spirit of vegetation, sensation, and reason.

5. Sulphur is the mother of all spirituality and corporality; Mercury manages the dominion therein; and Sal is the house of its habitation, which Mercury itself makes in Sulphur: Reason arises in the oil of the Sulphur, whereinto the constellation gives its desire, viz. the essence of its property, from whence immediately the senses and thoughts arise; but the understanding proceeds from the oil of the element, viz. in the free lubet in the speaking Mercury.

6. Now then, seeing it is very necessary for us poor children of Eve to know from whence the disease and enmity of our life arise, and what that is in us which makes us our own enemies,. and vex, perplex, and plague us in ourselves; much more necessary it is to

know the cure, whereby we may cure ourselves in our self-hood, and bring ourselves into the limit of rest.

7. This we will delineate and declare, if there be any one that has a mind to enter upon it, and truly prove and try it; and we will set forth from whence evil and good arise originally, and how they arise, and give occasion to the understanding searcher to seek: And we will shew how the will to evil and good arises, and how the evil is the death of the good, and on the contrary the good the death of the evil.

8. When we consider what the mercurial life is, then we find that it consists in Sulphur; for Sulphur is a dry hunger after matter, which makes an austere impression, and in its austere impression it has the fire, and also in its impression the oil, from whence the life burns. Now the impression makes coldness, and its compunction or attraction makes heat, so that now there is a cold fire and an hot fire in one thing; the cold makes in itself hardness and darkness, and the heat makes in itself the light, and yet there could be no light, if the oil in the Sulphur did not die in hot anguish, as the candle in the fire.

9. Now there is a twofold dying in Sulphur, from whence also a twofold life is generated; First, the impression or desire does draw in, contract, enclose, make hard, cold, thick; and the hardness, viz. the enclosed, causes a death in the enclosed being, and yet in that spirit there is no death, but a pricking, raging, and anxious cold fire-life, which is generated with the impression, and is the life of the darkness.

10. Secondly, in the same anguish, in the austere desire, the hot fire is generated, which consumes the substance, which the coldness, viz. the impression of the desire to nature makes: Thus there remains in the fire the contention betwixt the cold and heat; the cold will have its life according to its property, and in that it strives for life, it enkindles the heat in its impression, and immediately the heat deprives the cold of its might, and consumes the cold substance, and then also the fire-spirit cannot subsist; for unless it has substance it goes out, therefore it must continually, and without intermission, die in itself in the fiery anxious desire: So long as it has the cold's substance to live upon, its life arises, and yet it is nothing but a constant dying and consuming, and in its devouring is the greatest hunger after substance; this same hunger passes forth through and with the devouring out of the dying of the fire, and dwells in the nothing, yet it may not be a nothing, and also it cannot be a nothing, therefore it draws the fire again into itself; for its own desire is bent

towards its mother: But seeing it is once dead to the fire-source, it cannot die any more in the fire of the heat or cold, but it continually proceeds forth from the fire, and the fire draws it again continually into itself, and so it is the life of the fire; and this is the air, which in the fire is rightly called wind, by reason of the strength and force; and in that which is proceeded forth it is properly called air, by reason of its life of meekness.

11. And in the dying of the fire we are to understand the oil, whence the fire receives its shining light, in which the true life is understood; for that which proceeds forth in the fire-death with the desire to be delivered and freed from the fire-source, that is a desire of meekness, and takes its original in the first will to nature, in which the eternal nothing brings itself with its lubet into a desire.

12. This lubet brings forth itself through the cold and hot death (through both the dyings) again into the liberty, viz. into the Nothing; and so it is manifested in the austere impression through the fire, and brought into a principle, and yet it is not either of the fire or of the cold, but so is its manifestation.

13. But seeing the eternal lubet to nature introduces itself with nature into a desire; thereupon this desire cannot die either in the cold or heat, for it takes its origin neither in the heat or cold, but in the nothing; and so it is, after it proceeds from the dying in the fire, again desiring, namely of its own property, and impresses itself, for in the fire it has taken the impression.

14. Now it cannot conceive anything in its impression but an essence according to its desire, which is now water; understand according to the dark impression's property it is water, and according to the fire it is oil; and that which in the cold impression is wholly enclosed in the hardness, as a conception according to the wrath's property, is earth.

15. Thus the wrathful fiery desire draws continually the same air, water, and oil into itself, and devours it, and so the fire-wrath is changed in the air, and oil, and water, into a shining light; for the nothing desires nothing else but power and lustre, and so it makes itself manifest, and brings itself into essence: And the spirit which proceeds forth out of the fire burning in the oil, viz. in the light from the fire and light, gives reason and understanding; for it has originally taken its rise in the nothing, and was the desire to nature; and has brought itself through all the properties of nature, through heat and

cold, through the dying in the fire through the light, and dwells again in the nothing.

16. It is a prover and knower of all the properties, for it is generated through all, and proceeded forth from all; it is as a Nothing, and yet has all things, and passes through heat and cold, and yet none of them apprehend it; as we see that the life of the creature dwells in heat and cold, and yet the right life is neither hot nor cold.

17. Now therefore understand us right: This birth in the eternity is spiritual, but in the time it is material; for I cannot say of God that he is darkness and fire, much less air, water, or earth; but in his eternal desire he has so formed himself with the time in the place of this world into such an essence, which he formed in the speaking Mercury according to the properties of the will, and brought with the expressed word into such a formation according to the properties of the desire in the eternal nature, viz. in the verbum fiat.

18. Now the expressed word, viz. the eternal nature's property is understood in Sulphur, for therein is the sevenfold wheel of the birth, which in the spirit, viz. in the first conception to nature, is a constellation, and divides itself out of the constellation in its own peculiar birth into seven properties, and out of the seven properties into four elements.

19. This constellation is a chaos, wherein all things lie, but hidden; and it is the first body, but spiritual; and the sevenfold wheel is the first explication or working forth of the chaos, and makes the second body, viz. the reason; the second manifests the first, and it is also a spiritual body; the third body is elementary, a cabinet of both the first, and is a visible tangible body.

20. The first body, viz. the chaos, or the first constellation, seeing it is spiritual, is the word expressed out of the eternal conception; the same has again its speaking in itself, which is the mercurial wheel in the Sulphur with the seven forms, which speaks forth again from itself the four elements.

21. Thus the one proceeds forth from the other; the first before the chaos is the lubet of eternity in the abyss, which takes in itself a will to its own manifestation; this is all God; and the will conceives in itself a desire in the lubet; this is the chaos, or first astrum, wherein consists the eternal nature, which with the desire to nature introduces itself into seven forms, as is before mentioned, and so manifests the chaos, viz. the eternal hidden wisdom of God; and with the desire in the

mercurial wheel the element is formed, being a spiritual body of the mercurial life.

22. Now all this is twofold, viz. the desire makes in itself in its impression the darkness, wherein is the strong might of the enkindling of nature, and it is painful; and the free lubet to the desire makes in itself through the enkindling of the desire light and pleasing motion; the light is the power and lustre, and the element is its body, or essence; whereas yet it is only spiritual: Thus the fire-desire is a joyfulness in the free lubet, and in the darkness it is an aching painful source.

23. Out of this whole essence man was created to the image of God, and understand us right, he stood after and in the creation in the dominion of the element; the mercurial wheel in Sulphur stood in the light, and in the free lubet of eternity; but he departed further with his desire into the four elements, viz. into the centre of darkness, from whence heat and cold arise.

24. His desire in the beginning was bent into the liberty of God, viz. into the element, where he was resigned in God; and then God's love-will ruled him with the free lubet's property, but he departed out of the free lubet of God, out of the resignation into a self-will, which he forged in the centre to nature, from whence the pain and torture arise, viz. heat and cold, so also astringency, sour bitterness, and all the properties of the dark impression.

25. Even there he fell into the eternal death, viz. into the dying source, in which the mercurial life in the Sulphur rules in the poison, where one form in the mercurial sphere does envy, hate, annoy, and destroy the other, where there is meer anguish, aching, tormenting, and enmity; for the free lubet was quenched in him, wherein the holy element, viz. the divine body consists, and there arose in the same pure element the four elements of the outward source; there the image of God was cursed, which is nothing else but that God's love-will, which ruled in the image of his likeness, withdrew from man, and so man fell into the dominion of nature: And seeing the four elements have a temporal beginning and end, and must again enter into the end, therefore also the human body, which is now become wholly earthly in the four elements, must fall again into the four elements, and be destroyed therein: And therefore now we are to consider of his cure and restoration, how he may again be delivered from death, and be again introduced with the body into the pure element, and with the spirit into the dominion of God's will.

26. Now there is no other remedy but that he with the spirit which arises in the chaos, and was inspired by God's will-spirit into the created image, does again depart out of his self-hood, viz. out of his natural will, and resign himself up fully and freely into the first will, which in the beginning formed him into an image: He must wholly die to his self-hood in himself in the death of the dark impression (as far as he lives therein to his own will in the self-desire of the outward life of the four elements) and cast himself with total resignation into God's will, viz. into God's mercy, that he may no longer live and will to himself, but to God, viz. to the first will of God, which created him in its image, whereby God manifested himself in an image; and so he is with the first astrum, viz. with the chaos of the soul, again in the same comprehension wherein God created him to his image.

27. But seeing the self-hood, viz. the self-will, strives against this, and will in no wise die to its self-hood (understand the will of the outward world, which is from the outward stars and four elements), therefore God's food must be given to the inward will of the spirit to eat of, that it may live without need and hunger as to the outward being, that it may continually mortify and break the will of the earthly self-hood, till the earthliness, viz. the earthly body, does freely unloose or dissolve itself in death, and also enter again into the mother, from whence it was created, and forsake its self-hood, that the pure body of the element (in which the true life in God's will-spirit does again enkindle the soul in the resigned will 1) and the disappeared body from the pure element may become a mansion of the soul, viz. a paradisical budding or bloomy renovation in the eternal spring-time of paradise.

28. And that the own will of the soul might be able to do this, viz. that it might break itself off from its self-hood, and willingly enter into the death of its self-hood, and become a nothing in its self-hood, the free will of God, viz. the eternal lubet to the chaos of the soul, which is the eternal Mercury in the power of the majesty, is again entered into the disappeared image of God proceeded from the pure element, viz. into the virgin-like life, and draws the will of the soul to itself, and gives it again out of love and grace the heavenly corporality of the pure element for food, and the water in that element in the tincture of the fire and light, viz. of the eternal life, for drink: And it has incorporated itself in the humanity, and freely tenders itself to all souls with full desire: That soul which dies to its self-hood, and brings

its hunger again into God's mercy, may enjoy this food, whereby it again becomes the first creature in God's love.

29. Now we are to consider how the poor soul captivated in God's anger, being void of the heavenly food, lives in mere anguish, and distress, and restless pain; as the outward earthly body in its properties lives in its hunger in mere anguish, distress, and oppressing pain, unless the soul with the pure element does so overpower and keep it under, that it does not fully domineer in its own dominion of the outward astrum and four elements in the poisonful mercurial wheel, according to the dark impression, by reason of the influence of the element: If the universal does withstand it, then it may stand in quiet rest, but yet no longer than the inward penetrates the outward body, and tinctures it: There is in the four elements no perfection, till the body is changed again into the pure element; therefore it must enter again into that from whence the four elements arise.

30. Now in this time of the four elements there is mere pain and vexation; the soul amuses itself on the outward astrum, which forces into it, from whence its false imagination arises, and the body stirs up the poisonful mercurial wheel, from whence sickness and pains befall it; therefore the soul must be cured with the inward perfection, viz. by the speaking word, wherein it stands in God's hand, which alone is able to tincture the soul, and bring it into rest: The outward body must be tinctured and healed with the expressed Mercury; and if the outward Mercury does also stand in the curse as a poison-wheel, then he must be tinctured with his own light in his mother in the body or womb of Sulphur: Mercury's own will and hunger must be broken, that the envious odious hunger may become a love desire.

31. And now to know how this may be brought to pass, we must consider the generation in Sulphur, from whence joy and sorrow do arise; for the poisonful Mercury may not otherwise be resisted, and also nothing can resist it, but its own mother which brings it forth, in whose womb it is couched: As nothing can resist the cold but the heat only, and yet the heat is the cold's son; so also the poisonful Mercury must be resisted with its own child, which he himself generates in his mother's womb out of heat and cold out of himself.

32. As the love proceeding from the heart of the Father, which is his Son, withstands the anger of the Father, whereby the Father is merciful; so likewise it is in the expressed word or Mercury.

33. Now understand it thus: I do not mean that the cold poison of Mercury should be, or could be resisted with the enkindled heat; no, but if the cold poison be enkindled, then the remedy must be from the same likeness; but it must be first freed from the coldness, viz. from the enflamed cold wrath, and brought into meekness, and then it does also still and appease the hunger of the cold's desire in the disease of the body: For if enkindled heat be administered to the enkindled cold, then the cold is dismayed at the heat, and falls into a swound, viz. into death's property; and so the heat becomes in this death's property a poison-life, viz. an anxious sting; and the mercurial wheel runs into sadness, viz. into sickness, or a crazy dotage, wherein all joy is forgotten.

34. For if the life shall subsist in its own right, then the heat and cold must stand in equality, that so they may accord one with another, and no enmity or disaffection be at all in any of them; the one must not exceed or over-top the other, but they must stand in one will; for the enkindled cold desires no heat, but only likeness: Every hunger desires only likeness for its food, but if the hunger be too strongly enkindled in the cold, such a cure is not to be given it which is so enkindled; indeed it must be in as high a degree in the cold; but the violent force must be first taken away from it; so that it may be only as the mother which generates it, not according to the enkindled poison-source, but according to the mother's joy; and so the sickness, viz. the poison in the anguish, will be likewise changed into such a joy, and so the life receives again its first property.

35. The raw opposite body does not belong to the cure, but its oil, which must be mollified with its own love, understand with a meek essence, which also belongs to the same property; for the seven forms of nature are only one in the centre: Therefore that oil must be brought so far in the wheel, till it enters into its highest love-desire, and then it is rightly fit for cure; for there is nothing so evil but it has a good in it, and that very good resists its evil or poisonful malignity.

36. Thus also in the same sickness it may withstand the enkindled wrath in the body; for if the cold poison be enkindled in the body, then its good falls into faintness; and if it cannot obtain the likeness of its essence for its help, it remains in faintness; and then the enkindled wrath also does immediately consume itself, and falls also into faintness; and so the natural death is in both, and the moving life in the body ceases; but if it attains the likeness, then it gathers strength again, and the enkindled hunger of the disease must cease.

37. In like manner also we are to consider of the heat, which needs no cold property, but the likeness; yet it must be first freed from the wrath of the same likeness, and brought into its own highest joy and good, so that this likeness does not effectually operate either in heat or cold, but in its own love-desire, viz. in its best relish, and so it will bring the heat in the body into such a desire: All corruptions in the body proceed from the cold; if the brimstone be too vehemently enkindled by the heat, then the right and property of the cold dies, and enters into sorrow.

38. Mercury is the moving life in all, and his mother is Sulphur; now the life and death lie in Sulphur, viz. in the wrestling mercurial wheel. In the Sulphur there is fire, light, and darkness; the impression causes darkness, coldness, and hardness, and also great anguish: and from the impression of the attraction Mercury takes his rise, and he is the sting of the attraction, viz. the motion or disquietude, and arises in the great anguish of the impression, where coldness, viz. a dark cold fire, by reason of the hardness, arises in the impression; and in the sting of anguish, viz. in the disquietude, an hot fire arises.

39. Now Mercury is the wheel of motion, and a stirring up of the cold and heat; and in this placeit is only a painful aching source in heat and cold, viz. a cold and hot fiery poison-anguish, and forces forward as a wheel, and yet it is a cause of joy, and all life and motion; but if it shall be freed from the anguish, and introduced into the joy, then it must be brought forth through death.

40. Now every sickness and malady is a death's property; for Mercury has too much enkindled and enflamed himself either in heat or cold, whereby the essence or flesh, which he has attracted to himself in his desire, viz. in his mother in the Sulphur, is burnt, whereby the earthliness arises both in the water and flesh: Even as the matter of the earth and stones, viz. the grossness of the same, is nothing else but a burnt Sulphur, and water in Mercury is his property, where the salniter in the flagrat of the mercurial wheel, from whence the manifold salts arise, is burnt or too vehemently enflamed, from whence come the stink and evil taste.

41. Otherwise if the Mercury did so effectually operate therein in the oil of Sulphur, that he might be brought through the death of the impression from the heat and cold, then the earth would be again in paradise, and the joy-desire would again spring or bloom afresh through the anguish of the cold's impression: And this is the cause that God laid the curse upon the earth; for the mercurial wheel was

deprived of its good (viz. the love-desire, which arises in the eternal liberty, and manifests itself with this mercurial wheel through cold and heat, and proceeds forth through the fire, and makes a shining of the light) and the curse was brought thereinto, which is a withdrawing of the love-desire.

42. Now this Mercury, being a life in the Sulphur of its mother, stands in the curse, viz. in the anguish of heat and cold, and makes in his flagrat, or salnitral walm, continually salts, according to such property as he is in each place, and as he is enkindled in each body; these salts are only the taste in the seven properties.

43. Now if the Mercury be too vehemently enkindled in the cold, then he makes in the salnitral flagrat in his mother in the Sulphur a cold hard impressive salt, from whence melancholy, darkness, and sadness arise in the life of Sulphur; for observe what salt is in each thing, such a lustre of the fire, and such a vital shining from the fire is also therein; but if Mercury be enkindled in immoderate heat, he then burns up the cold essence, and makes raging pains and achings according to the impression, and according to the sting's property, from whence arises in the Sulphur great heat and inflammation; he dries up and consumes the water, so that the desire's hunger or sting has then no food to satisfy its wrathful hunger, upon which he rages and tears in the salt, as it is the poison's property so to do, from whence the painful distemper in the flesh arises.

44. But if he obtains the likeness again in the property as he stands in the centre of his mother, viz. in the Sulphur, understand as she has generated him in the beginning, viz. as he at first came forth to the natural life in both tinctures of man and woman, understand in the child where his life did enkindle, then he is freed from all anguish, and enters again into the likeness of the heat and cold; and though the strife arises in many even from the very womb, yet the combat is first raised up after the beginning of the life: In the life's beginning the life enters into its highest joy; for the gates of the three principles are opened in equal accord; but the strife soon begins about the conquest between the darkness and light.

45. But now we are to consider what is to be done to Mercury, if he be enkindled either in heat or cold, whereby he raises up sickness and pains: Now it were very good that men had the right cure; but alas! it will remain hidden and covered by reason of the curse of the earth, and the abominations and sins of men, because they awaken this poison in Mercury with their immoderate bestiality.

46. Yet the poor captive has need of deliverance; and though men have not the high universal, which reaches the centre, and brings the wheel of life into its first property, yet men must take from the mercurial walm of the earth its fruits thereunto, seeing the body is also become earthly: A man must accord (or assimilate) one likeness with another, one salt with another, according as the inflammation is in the salt of the body: For observe, in what property the brimstone is enkindled, either in heat or cold, in melancholy or falling sickness (whether the brimstone be burnt too in the body and putrified, or whether it be yet fresh and burning), even such an herb, such a brimstone belongs to the cure, lest the heat or cold be terrified in the salniter, where the salt arises, by a strange might which comes into it, and generates a mort salt, and sets open more and more the house of sadness: But it is not sufficient and powerful enough in its wild nature and property as it grows out of the walm of the earth; it is not able to master the root of the enkindled Mercury in the brimstone, but it does more vehemently enkindle it in such a source and property.

47. That which thou desirest should happen to the body, the same must first happen to that which shall cure the body: To the cure of a foul sickness there belongs a foul brimstone, and so to a cold or hot sickness the like is to be understood; for look in what degree of the fire or cold Mercury is enkindled, and in what form among the seven properties of nature; that is, what salt soever among the seven salts is enkindled, such a salt belongs to the cure: For sickness is nothing else but an hunger; now the hunger desires nothing else but its likeness; but now the property of that life, which in its beginning of its rise stood in joy, is the root; and the sickness is its immoderate enkindling, whereby the order or temperature is broken and divided: Thus the root desires in its hunger the likeness, but the inflammation has taken it away; now the inflammation is stronger than the root, therefore the hunger of the inflammation must be appeased, and that which itself is must be administered to it.

48. But as God cured us with his love, and restored to us the salvation of the soul, when we had enkindled the same in the poisonful Mercury of his anger; in like manner also this likeness must be first cured and circulated in the mercurial wheel, and freed from the heat and cold; indeed not taken away from them (this cannot be, and it were also unprofitable), but it must be brought into his highest joy, and then it will make such a property in the body in the Mercury of the brimstone and salt; for the root of life does again quicken itself

therein, and lifts up the first desire, so that now the hunger vanishes in the fall of the inflammation.

49. Now it behoves the physician to know how he may deal with the medicaments in the likeness, so that he does not enrage them, and bring them into another property; for in their property they are even as a man's life is: He must take care that they remain in their degree, as they are originally brought forth in their mother; for nothing can come higher than it is in the centre of its original according to the hiddenness; but if it shall come higher, then it must assume another property to itself; and so it is not in its own degree, and has not its proper virtue, but an improper one; which indeed may very well be, but it has lost its nature-right, wherein it stands in joy, and is not able to effect any proper operation in the assimulate of its own nature.

50. Therefore there is nothing better than to let everything remain in its innate genuine virtue; only its wrath must be changed into its own joy, that so its own virtue according to the good part may be advanced into its dominion, and then in the likeness it is powerful enough in all sicknesses without any other mixture: For the original in the life desires no other multiplicity, but only its likeness, that it may stand, live, and burn in its own power and property.

51. The power of the Most High has given to all things (to every one according to its property) a fixed perfection; for "all was very good," as Moses says, but with the curse the turba is introduced, so that the properties stand in the strife of Mercury; yet in each property, in every herb, or whatever is, in whatever grows or arises out of the walm of the four elements, there is a fixity hidden; for all things which are in the four elements are originally sprung forth out of the eternal element, in which there is no strife, neither heat nor cold, but all things were in equal weight of all the properties in a love-play, as it is so now in paradise; and the same paradise sprung forth in the beginning of this world before the curse through the earth: Thus it is also yet hidden in all things, and may be opened by understanding and art, so that the first virtue may overcome the enflamed malignity.

52. Though we men have not full power to do it in self-might, yet it may be done in God's permission, who has again turned his mercy towards us, and again opened paradise and its comprehension in man: Hath God given us power to become his children, and to rule over the world? Why then not over the curse of the earth? Let none hold it for impossible; there is required only a divine understanding

and knowledge thereunto, which shall blossom in the time of the lily, and not in Babel, for whom we also have not written.

Chapter XIV
Of The Wheel Of Sulphur, Mercury, And Salt; Of The Generation Of Good And Evil; Shewing How The One Is Changed Into The Other, And How One Manifests Its Property In The Other, And Yet Both Remain In The First Creation In The Wonder Of God To His Own Manifestation And Glory

1. This is an open gate of the foregoing description: Every one says, "Shew me the way to the manifestation of the good." Hear and observe well, dear reason; thou must thyself be the way, the understanding must be born in thee, otherwise I cannot shew it thee; thou must enter into it, so that the understanding of the work in its practic art, wherein I deal not, may be opened to thee; I write only in the spirit of contemplation; how the generation of good and evil is, and open the fountain: He shall draw the water whom God has appointed thereunto; I will here only describe the wheel of life as it is in itself.

2. When I speak of Sulphur, Mercury, and Salt, I speak of one only thing, be it either spiritual or corporeal; all created things are that one thing, but the properties in the generation of this only thing make a difference or give various gradual distinctions ; for when I name a man, or lion, bear, wolf, hare, or any other beast; yea also a root, herb, tree, or whatever may be named, it is the same only thing.

3. All whatever is corporeal is the same being; the herbs and trees, and also the animals, but each thing in its difference of the first beginning: According as the property in the verbum fiat has imprinted itself in each thing, so is that kind in its propagation, and all things stand in the seed and procreation; and there is not anything but has a fixity in it, be it either hidden or manifest, for all shall stand to the glory of God.

4. Whatever is risen from the eternal fixity, as angels and the souls of men, remains indestructible in its fixt being; but whatever is risen in the unfixt being, viz. with the motion of time, that does again enter into the first motion from whence it has taken its original, and is a map of its form which it had here, like a picture, or as an image in a

glass without life; for so it was from eternity before the times of this world, which the Most High has introduced into an image, into the comprehensible natural life in time, to behold the great wonders of his wisdom in a creaturely being, as we plainly see.

5. Now we are to consider the only mother, how the same is in her property, from whence the innumerable multiplicity arises, and has continually risen; and how she generates life and death, evil and good; and how all things may be brought into their first ens, viz. into the place where they originally arise, to which the death, or the dying, is the greatest mystery.

6. For nothing, which is departed out of its first order, as the mother brought it forth, can go back again, and enter with its assumed order into its root, unless it dies again with its assumed order in its mother; and even then it is again in the end, and in the place whence it was created, and so it stands again in the verbum fiat, viz. in the bound of its order in the expressed word, and may enter again into that which it was in the beginning before it was corporeal; and there it is good, for it stands again in that from whence it proceeded.

7. Now therefore we are to consider the beginnings of all things, for we cannot say that this world was made out of something, it was only and barely a desire out of the free lubet, that the abyss, viz. the highest good or being, viz. the eternal will, would behold itself in the lubet as in a glass; therefore the eternal will has conceived the lubet, and brought it into a desire, which has impressed itself, and figurised, and corporised itself both to a body and spirit according to the same impression's property, according as the impression has introduced itself into forms, whereby the possibilities or powers are risen in the impression as a nature.

8. This impression is the only mother of the manifestation of the mystery, and it is called nature and essence, for it manifests what has been from eternity in the eternal will; yet we are to conceive that there was in eternity a nature in the eternal will, as an eternal mind in the will; but it was only a spirit in the will, and the essence of its ability was not made manifest, but only in the looking-glass of the will, which is the eternal wisdom, wherein all things which are in this world were known in two centres, viz. according to the fire and light, and then according to the darkness and essence; all which came with the motion of the eternal will through the desire in the will into a manifest mystery, and so introduced itself into a manifest possibility.

9. This is now the essence expressed or made manifest out of eternity into a time, and consists in the fore-mentioned forms in Sulphur, Mercury, and Salt, where the one is not divided or parted asunder from the other: It is one eternal essence, and shapes itself into the properties of the desire according to the possibility of the manifestation; and we are to understand that one property is not, nor cannot be without the other; they are altogether the same only possibility: And now we will speak of their differences, viz. how this only possibility introduces itself into good and evil, viz. into still peace and constant unquietness.

10. We find seven especial properties in nature, whereby this only mother works all things, which are these, viz. First, the desire, which is astringent, cold, hard, and dark. Secondly, bitter, which is the sting of the astringent hard enclosure; this is the cause of all motion and life. Thirdly, the anguish, by reason of the raging in the impression, where the impressed hardness falls into a tearing anguish and pain by reason of the sting.

11. Fourthly, the fire, where the eternal will in this anxious desire introduces itself into an anxious darting flash or twinkling lightening, viz. into strength and devouring of the darkness, with which the hardness is again consumed, and introduced into a corporeal moving spirit.

12. Fifthly, the egress of the free will out of the darkness and out of the fire, and dwelling in itself, where the free will has received the lustre, so that it enlightens and shines as a light out of the fire, and the potent desire of the free will, which it has sharpened in the fire (in that it is dead in the fire to the essence of the darkness of the first form, and consumed) does now in the light's desire draw into itself the essence from the dying of the fire, according to its hunger, which is now water; and in the lustre it is a tincture from the fire and light, viz. a love-desire, or a beauty of colours; and here all colours arise; as we have fully set it down in our other books, but especially in the Threefold Life of Man.

13. Sixthly, the voice or sound, which in the first form is only a noise from the hardness, and is dead or mortified as to that hardness in the fire, and yet in the fifth form, in the love-desire, viz. in the pleasant property, it is again received as a clear sound out of the dying of the fire in the lustre of the light in the tincture, wherein all the five senses, viz. Hearing, Seeing, Feeling, Smelling, and Tasting, arise in the tincture of the light from the fire.

14. Seventhly, the menstruum, or the seed of all these forms which the desire impresses into a comprehensive body or essence wherein all lies; whatever the six forms are spiritually, that the seventh is essentially.

15. Thus these are the seven forms of the mother of all beings, from whence all whatever is in this world is generated; and moreover the Most High has, according to this mother,. introduced and created such properties as this mother is in her wrestling forms (understand, as she brings herself with the wrestling into properties) into a wheel, which is as a mind of the mother, from whence she continually creates and works; and these are the stars with the planetary orb according to the platform of the eternal astrum, which is only a spirit, and the eternal mind in the wisdom of God, viz. the eternal nature, from whence the eternal spirits are proceeded and entered into a creaturely being.

16. And moreover the Most High has introduced the property of this wheel in the motion, as a life into the four officers, which manage the dominion in the pregnant mother; and these are the four elements to which the wheel of the mind, viz. the astrum affords will and desire; so that this whole being is but one only thing, and yet is so proportioned or composed as a mind of a man: Even as he is in soul and body, so also is this only essence; for it was created out of this whole essence into an image according to eternity and time; out of eternity according to the soul, and out of time according to the outward essence, as a similitude and image of eternity and time, both according to the eternal will and mind and its essence, and also according to the mind of time and its essence: And therefore now we are rightly to consider of the sulphurean wheel of all essences, how the properties introduce themselves into good and evil, and again bring themselves out of good and evil.

17. The impression or desire, viz. the first form to nature, which is called, and is also the fiat, receives the desire's property according to the property of all the seven forms into itself, and impresses them, so that out of the nothing proceeds forth an essence according to the properties of the will: Now its own property, seeing it is only a desire, and impresses itself, is dark, and causes hardness, viz. a strong pulsation, which is a cause of the tone or sound, which becomes yet more hard in the fire, viz. in the fourth form, where then the grossness dies away, and it is received again in the fifth form, viz. in the love-desire; and again it proceeds forth in its own property in the love-

desire, and makes the sixth form, viz. the sound, voice, or tone out of the fire and water.

18. Now this tone or sound, which is called Mercury, arises in the first form, viz. in the impression, by reason of the will and attractive desire; for the attraction makes the motions and the compunction in the hardness, which we distinguish, and call the second form, but it is a son of the first, and in the first.

19. This second form or property is the raging, stinging, and bitter pain; for the first is astringent, and the second is drawing, viz. the desire into an essence; this same essence is the property of the first, and the attraction makes therein the second property, viz. a bitter stinging which the hardness cannot endure; for it would be still, and thereupon it does more vehemently impress itself to withhold the sting, and yet the sting does thereby only grow the greater: Now the hardness, viz. the astringency draws inwards, and the sting from the hardness upwards: Hence arises the first enmity and opposition; for the two forms, which yet are but one, make themselves their own enemies; and yet if this were not, there would not be any essence, neither body nor spirit, also no manifestation of the eternity of the abyss.

20. But now seeing the bitter sting cannot ascend, and the hardness also cannot hold or enclose it, they fall into a turning or breaking through like a wheel, which runs into itself as an horrible essence, where both properties are known only as one, and yet each remains in itself unaltered, and produce the third property between both, viz. the great anguish; out of which the will, understand the fixt will to nature, desires to go forth again into the liberty, viz. into the nothing, into the eternal rest; for here it has thus found itself, and manifested itself, and yet there is no separating or departing: and this anxious form is the mother of Sulphur, for the sting makes it painful, and the hardness impresses it, that it is as a dying source, and yet it is the true original to life.

21. It has two properties in itself, viz. according to the impression or desire it is dark and hard; and according to the desire of the will, which wills to be free from the anguish, and enters again into the liberty, it is spiritual and light; and the sting breaks in pieces its conceived essence which the astringent desire conceives in itself, so that its essence is hard and spalt, and wholly darting as a flash of lightning from the darkness, and from the desire of the light, understand to the liberty.

22. Now these three forms are in one essence as a raging spirit; and the desire impresses these properties, so that an essence is made according to their property, viz. according to the astringent dark desire, viz. according to the first original: There is an earthly essence, out of which in the beginning of the great motion the earth was made, and according to the bitter raging spirit there is the instigation in the essence, viz. a poison, and it also imprints or impresses itself in the essence, from whence the earthliness is so wholly loathsome and bitter; and the third form, viz. the anguish gives a fiery property thereinto; and yet here there cannot be as yet any essence, but it is only a spiritual essence, and the mother to the essence.

23. The fourth form in this essence is the fire, which as to one part takes its original out of the dark hard impression, viz. from the hardness, and from the raging sting in the anguish, which is the cold black fire, and the pain of the great anguish; and as to the other part it takes its original in the will's spirit to nature, which goes again out of this hard dark coldness into itself, viz. into the liberty without the nature of the austere motion, and enkindles the liberty, viz. the eternal lubet to the desire of nature, with its sharpness, which it has conceived in the impression, whereby it is a moving and stirring lustre: For the liberty is neither dark nor light; but by reason of the motion it is light, for its lubet brings itself into the desire to light, that it may be manifest in the light and lustre; and yet it cannot be otherwise brought to pass but through darkness, so that the light might be made known and manifest, and the eternal mind might find and manifest itself; for a will is only one thing and essence, but through the multiplicity its form is made manifest, that it is infinite, and a mere wonder, of which we speak with a babe's tongue, being only as a little spark out of these great infinite wonders.

24. Now understand us thus; the liberty is, and stands in the darkness (and inclining to the dark desire after the desire of the light), it attains with the eternal will the darkness; and the darkness reaches after the light of the liberty, and cannot attain it; for it encloses itself with the desire in itself, and makes itself darkness in itself; and out of both these, viz. out of the dark impression, and out of the desire of the light or liberty towards the impression, there is a twinkling or darting flash in the impression, viz. the original of the fire; for the liberty shines in the impression, but the impression in the anguish comprehends it into itself, and so it is now as a flash: But seeing the liberty is incomprehensible, and as a nothing, and moreover without

and before the impression, and abyssal, therefore the impression cannot conceive or hold it; but it gives itself into the liberty, and the liberty devours its dark property and essence, and rules with the assumed mobility in the darkness, unapprehensible to the darkness.

25. Thus understand us right: There is in the fire a devouring; the sharpness of the fire is from the austere impression of the coldness and bitterness, from the anguish; and the devouring is from the liberty, which makes out of the something again a nothing according to its property.

26. And understand us very exactly and well: The liberty will not be a nothing, for therefore the lubet of the liberty introduces itself into nature and essence, that it might be manifest in power, wonder, and being; it likewise assumes to itself through the sharpness in the cold and dark impression the properties, that it might manifest the power of the liberty: For it consumes the dark essence in the fire, and proceeds forth out of the fire, out of the anguish of the impression, with the spiritual properties in the light; as you see, that the outward light so shines forth out of the fire, and has not the source and pain of the fire in it, but only the property; the light manifests the properties of the darkness, and that only in itself; the darkness remains in itself dark, and the light continues in itself light.

27. The liberty (which is called God) is the cause of the light; and the impression of the desire is the cause of the darkness and painful source: Now herein understand two eternal beginnings, viz. two principles, one in the liberty in the light, the other in the impression in the pain and source of the darkness, each dwelling in itself.

28. And understand us farther concerning their opening essence and will, how nature is introduced into seven properties; for we speak not of a beginning, for there is none in eternity; but thus the eternal generation is from eternity to eternity in itself; and this same eternal generation has according to the property of eternity through its own desire and motion introduced itself with this visible world (as with a likeness of the eternal spirit into such a creaturely being which is a type or platform of the eternal being) into a time, of which we will speak afterwards, and shew what the creature is, namely a similitude of the operation of eternity, and how it has also this same working temporally in itself.

29. Now concerning the fire understand us thus: The fire is the principle of every life; to the darkness it gives essence and source, else

there would be no sensibility in the darkness, also no spirit, but mere hardness, a hard, sharp, bitter, galling sting, as it is really so in the eternal darkness; but so far as the hot fire may be obtained, the dark compunctive property stands in the aspiring covetous greediness like to a horrible madness, that it may be known what wisdom and folly is.

30. Now the fire gives also desire, source, and properties to the light, viz. to the liberty; yet know this, the liberty, viz. the nothing, has no essence in itself, but the impression of the austere desire makes the first essence, which the will-spirit of the liberty (which has manifested itself through the nature of the desire) receives into itself, and brings it forth through the fire, where the grossness, viz. the rawness, does then die in the fire.

31. Understand it thus: When the flash of fire reaches the dark essentiality, then it becomes a great flagrat, where the cold fire is dismayed, and does as it were die, falls into a swoon, and sinks down: And this flagrat is effected in the enkindling of the fire in the essence of the anguish, which has two properties in it; viz. the one goes downwards into the death's property, being a mortification of the cold fire, from whence the water arises, and according to the grossness the earth is risen; and the other part ascends in the will of the liberty, in the lubet, as a flagrat of joyfulness; and this same essence is also mortified in the flagrat in the fire, understand the cold fire's property, and gives also a water-source, understand such a property.

32. Now the flash, when it is enkindled by the liberty, and by the cold fire, makes in its rising a cross with the comprehension of all properties; for here arises the spirit in the essence, and it stands thus:

If thou hast here re understanding, thou needest ask no more; it is eternity and time, God in love and anger, moreover heaven and hell.

33. The lower part, which is thus marked, is the first principle, and is the eternal nature in the anger, viz. the kingdom of darkness dwelling in itself; and the upper part, with this figure is the salniter: The upper cross above the circle is the kingdom of glory, which proceeds forth in the flagrat of joy, in the will of the free lubet in itself out of the fire in the lustre of the light into the power of the liberty; and this spiritual water, which also arises in the flagrat of joy, is the corporality, or essentiality, in which the lustre from the fire and light makes a tincture, viz. a budding and growing, and a manifestation of colours from the fire and light.

34. And this form of separation between the living and the dead essentiality is the fifth form, and is called the love-desire; its original is from the liberty, which in the fire has introduced itself into a desire, viz. out of the lubet of the liberty into the fair and fiery elevation of joy, being a flame of love, which also imprints in its love-desire the property of that which it has conceived in the will of the eternal mind, which brings itself through the fire's sharpness again into itself, viz. into the first properties, which arise in the first impression, viz. from the motion and stirring; and the joyfulness arises out of the anguish: For this is joy, that the will to nature is delivered and freed from the dark anguish, for else there would be no knowledge of what joy was, if there was not a painful source; and in its love-desire it conceives the first properties in the first impression, which divide themselves in this desire into five forms; viz. from the fire-flash into seeing, for the water of love reaches the lustre of the tincture, wherein the sight consists; and from the hardness, viz. from the penetration of the sting in the hardness, into hearing, so that in this same nothing, viz. in the liberty, there is a sound, which the tincture catches, and brings it forth in the water of the desire: and from the raging sting into feeling, so that one property feels another; for if all properties were only one, there would be no seeing, hearing, or feeling, also no understanding: And from the assimilation, that one property arises in the other, but with another property, comes the taste; and from the egressive spirit of the properties (in that the egress of each property enters into the other) arises the smell.

35. Now these five forms do all of them together make in the love-desire, viz. in the fifth form, the sixth, that is, the sound or voice, as a manifestation of all the forms in the spirit's property, which the fiery light's desire encloses with the spiritual water as one only essence, which is now the fiery will's own essence, which has brought itself forth in the light, wherein it works and makes the seventh form, as an habitation of the sixth, from whence the essence and dominion of this world were generated, and introduced into a form according to the right of the eternal birth.

36. Now understand us right; we do not hereby understand a beginning of the Deity, but the manifestation of the Deity: The Deity is herein known and manifested in Trinity; the Deity is the eternal liberty without all nature, viz. the eternal abyss; but thus it brings itself into byss for its own manifestation, eternal wisdom, and deeds of wonder.

37. The Eternal Father is manifested in the fire, and the Son in the light of the fire, and the Holy Spirit in the power of the life and motion proceeding from the fire in the light of the kingdom of joy, being the egressive power in the love-flame; we speak only by parts of the universal as a creature.

38. The Deity is wholly everywhere all in all; but he is only called God according to the light of love, and according to the proceeding spirit of joy; but according to the dark impression he is called God's anger and the dark world; and according to the eternal fire-spirit he is called a consuming fire.

39. We give you only to understand the Being of all beings, whose original in itself is only one eternal essence; but with its own manifestation it comes into many beings, to its own honour and glory; and now we will shew you what the creature's life and dominion is in this all-essential Being.

40. Now therefore understand us right what we mean by these three words, Sulphur, Mercury, and Sal: In the eternity all is spirit; but when God moved himself with the eternal nature, wherein his own manifestation consists, he produced out of the spiritual essence a palpable and manifest essence, and introduced it into a creaturely being according to the eternal properties, which also consists of spirit and essence, according to the right or law of eternity.

41. And now I will speak of the outward kingdom, viz. of the third principle or beginning; for in this world there is also light and darkness in each other as in the eternity: God has given this world a sun, as a nature-god of the outward powers, but he rules therein as Lord; the outward kingdom is only his prepared work, which he rules and makes with the assimulate, as a master makes his work with an instrument.

42. Sulphur is in the outward world, viz. in the mystery of the great God's manifestation, the first mother of the creatures; for it arises out of darkness, fire, and light; it is on one part, according to the dark impression, astringent, bitter, and anxious; and on the other part, towards the Deity, as a similitude of the Deity, it is fire, light, and water, which in the fire separates itself into two forms, viz. according to the mortification into water, and according to the life into oil, in which the true life of all the creatures of the outward world consists.

43. Mercury is the wheel of motion in the Sulphur; he is on one part according to the dark impression the stinging rager, and the great

unquietness, and separates itself also in the fire in its mother, viz. in the Sulphur, into two properties, viz. into a twofold water; for in the mortification of the fire all is turned to water, understand into a living pleasant water according to the light, which produces silver in the brimstone, viz. in the seventh property of nature, which is the powerful body, and in the fire its water is quicksilver, and in the astringency, viz. in the anguish of the darkness, it is a rust or smoke; therefore if its outward water-body be cast into the fire, understand that body which it receives in Sulphur from the watery property, then it does evaporate, for in the fire every property separates itself again into the first essence, from whence it came originally, where all things were only a spirit.

44. And then secondly it separates itself according to the water of the dark impression into a poison-source, which yet cannot be understood to be a water, but only a corporeal essence of the spirit; for as the spirit's property is, so is also its water; and even so it is in the fire-flagrat.

45. Further understand us in the fiery flagrat concerning the salniter, from whence the manifold salts and powers arise; for all the properties of the spirit are become corporeal in the great motion of the essence of all essences, and entered into a visible and comprehensible being: This flagrat is effected in the enkindling of the fire; and in the mortification of the fire it impresses into itself from the water's original a water, according to the property of the flagrat, which yet is rather fire than water, but its mortal essence is water according to the property of the flagrat; it is the comprisal of all properties, it brings forth in its comprehension, viz. in the fiery flagrat all properties in itself, and apprehends the property of the light in its powers, and also the property of the dark impression in its powers, and makes all fiery; one part according to the coldness, and one part according to the heat; but the most part according to the endless Mercury, which is the life of all essences in evil and good, in light and darkness.

46. This salniter is the mother of all salts in vegetables and animals, viz. in herbs and trees and everything; he is in all things, which give a taste and smell, the first root according to each thing's property; in the good (which grow in the love-desire in the oil of brimstone) he is good, powerful, and pleasant; and in the evil he is evil in the anguish of brimstone; and in the darkness he is the eternal horror and despair, continually desiring in the flagrat to aspire above the gates in the fire, from whence arises the will of all devils, and of

all pride, to ascend above the humility of the love-desire; and in the fire is the trial of his essence, as we see how he clashes and consumes himself in the flash as a sudden thought.

47. For its essence arises not in the essence of eternity, also it cannot inherit it, but in the enkindling of the temporal fire, yet it is perceived in the eternal spirit by reason of the elevation of the joy; but according to the essence of mortification, viz. according to the salt of the fire it subsists in the fire: For this property arises out of the first desire, viz. in the essence of the first impression, which property the philosophers call Saturn, therefore the salt is manifold: All sharpness in the taste is salt, the good taste arises out of the oleous salt, and so also the smell, which is the egressive spirit in which the tincture appears as a lustre or fair complexion of colours.

48. Thus understand us right; the salniter in the fire-flagrat is the separation of the properties, where death and life separate themselves, viz. the life which enters with the love-desire into an essence and dominion; and then the life which in the flagrat of death, according to the property of the cold, sinks down in the mortification of the flagrat as an impotency, and gives weight; and according to the subtility it gives water, and according to the grossness of the austereness earth; and according to Sulphur and Mercury, sand and stones; and according to the subtility in Sulphur and Mercury, understand according to the water of the same, it makes flesh, and according to the anxious darkness a smoke or rust; but according to the oleous property, viz. according to the love-desire, a sweet spiritual essence; and according to the spirit a pleasant smell; and according to the moving of the fire and light the one element; and from the lustre in the fire-flagrat with aspect of the light the precious tincture, which tinctures all oily salts, from whence the pleasant taste and smell arise.

49. The salnitral flagrat is the sude in the essence, from whence the growth and pullulation arise, that there is a growing in the impression of the essence; the salt is the preservation, or upholding of the essence, so that a thing subsists in a body or comprehension; it holds the Sulphur and Mercury, else they would part from each other in the fire-flagrat.

50. All things consist of Sulphur, Mercury, and Salt: In the salnitral flagrat the element separates itself into four properties, viz. into Fire, Air, Water, and Earth, which in itself is none of these, but only a moving and gentle walming, not as the air, but as a moving of the will in the body, a cause of life in the essence; for as the eternal Spirit of

God proceeds from the Father, who is a spirit from the fire and light, and is the motion and life of the eternity; so likewise the air proceeds forth continually out of all the properties in the salnitral flagrat in the fire, from the anguish in Sulphur in the forcing mercurial wheel, as an impetuous aspiring motion; it is a son of all the properties, and also the life of the same; the fire of all the forms affords it, and also receives it again for its life; the water is its body, wherein it makes the seething in the salniter, and the earth is its power, wherein it enkindles its strength and fire-soul.

51. There is but one only element, and that unfolds itself in the salnitral flagrat into four parts, viz. with the enkindling it gives a consuming fire of the darkness, and its essence; and in the flagrat of the dying of the cold and the darkness it parts itself into essences, viz. according to the subtility into water, and according to the grossness into earth; and then according to the motion in the flagrat's walming into air, which does most resemble the element, but not wholly essentially; for the one element is neither hot nor cold, also not forcing or compulsive, but gently moving.

Of the Desire of the Properties

52. Every property keeps its own desire; for a property is nothing else but an hunger, and the hunger forms itself into such an essence as itself is, and in the salnitral sude it gives such a spirit into the four elements; for the original of the sude is in the element, from whence four elements proceed in this flagrat.

53. Each body stands in the inward motion in the element, and in the growth and life in the four elements; but every creature has not the true life of the element, but only the high spirits, as angels and souls of men, which stand in the first principle; in them the element is incitable: In the life of the third principle it stands still, and is as a hand of God, where he holds and governs the four elements as an exit, or instrument with which he works and builds.

54. Now every property of nature does in its hunger take its food out of the four elements; as the hunger is, so it takes a property out of the elements; for the four elements are the body of the properties, and each spirit eats of its own body.

55. First, there are the sulphurean properties according to the first and second impression, viz. according to the dark, astringent, and anxious impression; and then according to the love-impression in the light, viz. according to evil and good.

56. The dark hunger desires essence according to its property, viz. earthly things, all whatever resembles the earth; and the bitter hunger desires bitter raging, stinging, and pain; it receives into itself such an essence (as the poison-source) out of the elements: And the hunger of anguish desires anxious hunger, viz. the anguish in the brimstone; also the melancholy takes the desire to die, and continual sadness; and the fire-flash receives into it anger, aspiring, ambition, pride, a desiring to destroy all, and make it subject to it, a desire to domineer in and above all, to consume all, and to be peculiar; and it takes the bitterness from whence the flash arises to envy and hatred, and the astringency to covetousness, and the fire to anger and indignation.

57. Here is the true desire of God's anger and all devils, and of all whatever is against God and love; and this hunger draws such an essence into self; as it is to be known and searched out in the creatures, and also in the herbs.

58. Now the fire-flash is the end of the first desire, viz. of the dark nature, and in the fire the dying of the first hunger and will begins; for the fire consumes all grossness of the first forms, and casts them into death; and here is the separation of both wills, viz. the one which enters back again into the property of death, and is a will in the life of the dark desire; as the devils have done, who would domineer in the fire-flash in the salnitral sude over time and eternity; but they were driven back by the Spirit of God, and spewed forth out of the love-desire as an abomination: And thus also it happens here to the wicked soul of man, upon which the election follows. Here is the aim or scope of the election of grace, of which the Scripture speaks, that God knows his; and here the eternal lubet of God's liberty apprehends the will-spirit, which is arisen in the dark centre, and brings it through the dying in the fire into the element.

59. In the salnitral flagrat lies the possibility backwards and forwards; if the will of the desire goes back, then it is as to the kingdom of this world earthly, and as to the kingdom of the eternal world it is in God's anger, and cannot see God unless it be converted, and enters into the dying in the fire, and wholly dies to its selfness, and enters into the resignation of the eternal will in the salnitral flagrat into the element, viz. into the heavenly essentiality and corporality, so that the hunger may eat of the pure element; and then it has further no other desire; for it is in the fire dead to the austere dark hunger, which is evil; thus from the dying in the fire arises the

light, for here the liberty is enkindled, that it becomes also an hunger, and a desire; this is now a love-desire, a love-hunger.

60. In the outward world it is the light of the sun in the four elements; and it is the bestial love-desire, viz. after the sulphurean body and essence, from whence the copulation and multiplication arise, viz. the vegetative life; and from the Mercury in the salniter (in which the sensible life is) therein the astrum gives the reason in the animals from the properties of the salniter.

61. For the whole astrum is nothing else but a salniter in the verbum fiat in the motion of the Being of all beings in the fiery flagrat, comprehended in the properties of the salts, wherein all the powers of the element stand as an external birth, which continually boil in the four elements as a salnitral salt, and introduce their property in their desire in the four elements into the essence of bodies, as is to be seen in trees, herbs, grass, and all growing things.

62. Thus understand us farther concerning the second centre, which is manifest in the dying of the fire in the light, whereby the abyss of God's liberty introduces itself into the byss of nature, both with the inward world in the kingdom of heaven in the eternity; and then also with the outward kingdom in the time.

63. Now all this has also the properties of the desire, and takes its original from the first principle, viz. from the first centre, and there is yet no right dying in the fire; the dark essence only dies, and the will-spirit goes forth with the eternal will to nature again out of the fiery death in the light; it is only a transmutation of the spirit, so that an hunger arises out of the liberty, and this hunger is a love-desire; as to the soul of man it draws essence from the element of God, viz. in the divine salniter it takes the divine salts or powers into itself; and as to the outward world's desire it draws the oil out of the Sulphur into itself, in which oil the outward life burns; and so it is likewise in the vegetables and metals, and other things.

64. The sun makes the outward transmutation, and the divine light in the soul's property makes the inward; according as each thing stands in its degree, so does its hunger reach a property: those which are in the time receive a property from the time, and those in eternity likewise out of eternity: The hunger which proceeds from eternity eats of the eternity, and that which is of the time eats of the time. The true life of all creatures eats of the spiritual Mercury, viz. of the sixth form, where all salts are essentially; the spirit cats of the five senses, for they are the spirit's corporality; and the body, viz. the vegetable life, eats of

the essence of the Sulphur and Salt; for Christ says in like manner, "Man liveth not by bread only, but by every word which proceedeth out of the mouth of God."

65. Now the sixth form of nature is the expressed spiritual word; and the speaking word therein is the eternal word: In the first impression in the darkness it is the word of God's anger; and in the outward world it is the poisonful Mercury, viz. a cause of all life and stirring, of all tones and sounds; now every property eats of its likeness in its degree; the hunger of time eats of time, and the hunger of eternity eats of eternity, both the spirit of Mercury and the spirit of Sulphur; whereas yet there are not two spirits but only two properties; all whatever does only take its original in one principle, as the creatures of the outward world, they have only one region, but a twofold inclination from the good and evil; but whatever takes its original out of two principles, as man, he has also a twofold food and dominion, viz. from the dark centre, and from the outward centre; but if he dies to his self-hood, and brings his hunger into God's kingdom, then he may eat of the divine Mercury, viz. of the five divine senses with the soul, and of the element in the divine essence; and yet the outward man apprehends not in this life-time the divine essence corporeally, but only through the imagination, where the inward body penetrates the outward; as the sun shines through the water, and yet the water continues still water, for here lies our fall in Adam.

66. The element did wholly penetrate the four elements, and it was wholly one in man, but in the curse the element separated from the soul, so that the poor soul now lives only in the vessel of the four elements, unless it again enters in the death of its earthly will into the divine desire, and springs forth in the element.

67. Thus also the outward body is in the curse, and eats of the cursed earth's property, viz. only of the earthly salniter, where one hunger of the earthly properties continually opposes another; for the curse is a loathsome abominate in all salts, and from thence it comes that a constant contrariety arises in the outward body; for one hunger of the properties receives or catches from the other the abominate: Now to help the body that it may be freed from the abominate, it must take the assimulate of the lothing abominate, which is risen in the body as a sude or seething, and introduce it into the dying of the fire, and bring it out in the love-desire from the curse of the vanity; now this is no otherwise effected, but as the true life dies to the dark vanity.

68. The abominate of the outward life arises from a property of the salt which is contrary to the oil of the life: Thus the abominate does forthwith enkindle itself in the four elements, and begins to seethe in the salniter as a strange life: This strange life does at last darken and destroy the first true life, if it be not resisted; and it can have no better help than with the assimulate of the introduced abominate, which the life has taken into itself; therefore that must be done to the cure, which is to be done to the life, that it might be freed from the abominate.

69. The cure must be freed from the same abominate, which it has received in the four elements from the like false insinuation influence, or impression, it must be brought into the death of the four elements, and its spirit must also be tinctured in the fifth form with the Venus desire, viz. with a pleasant essence, that the spiritual Mercury may arise in Jupiter's property; understand, the cure must first die to its sickness in all the four elements; it must be introduced into the putrefaction of all the four elements; in the fire it dies to its earthliness, and in the putrefaction to the water's earthliness, and in the air's putrefaction to the abominate and earthliness of the air; and then it must be brought into Venus, and from Venus into Jupiter, and then the sun will arise in the love-desire, and with this the abominate in the body may be resisted.

70. All other cures, which are administered raw and undigested (as when one takes cold, and will resist heat, and so likewise heat to resist cold), are only an opposite fiery flagrat, whereby indeed the enkindled fire ceases from its powerful working, but the flagrat enters into death's anguish, and the root of the abominate becomes a poisonful Mercury unless the heat and cold are before tempered with Venus and Jupiter, and then indeed it is an appeasing of the abominate in the salnitral sude; but the root of the abominate remains still, unless the life be strong, and mightily brings forth its desire out of the abominate. This the physicians must well observe, that the raw herbs do not reach the root, where the abominate is arisen in the centre in the property of the life's form; they reach only the four elements, and give some easement, but the abominate remains still in the root as an hidden sickness.

71. The like is also to be understood concerning the astrum, which has its sude in the outward body as a peculiar body in the four elements; if the cure may be freed from the abominate of the four elements, then the astrum falls also into the good part, and introduces

its desire thereinto, and so the body is also freed from the abominate of the astrum; for the Scripture says, that " the whole creature longeth together with us to be freed from the vanity: "Now the curse of the earth, wherein the astrum injects its desire, is the vanity; and if it tastes a pure life in itself, then it also rejoices therein, and casts forth the abominate.

72. Every abominate of the oily life arises from the inward Mercury in the inward Sulphur; for sin also does hence take its original, that the poisonful Mercury (which is a cause of the life) does in the fire-flash in the original of the salniter, in retiring backwards, introduce itself again into self-hood, for even there is the original of the poison-life.

73. Every life which will be without spot, must die in the will-spirit to nature in the fire of the abominate to the first impression of the wrath, and must give itself forth, in the will-spirit to nature, as a resigned will through the mortification in the light of love: Let it be either heavenly or earthly it must hold that process, or else it comes not to the highest perfection in its degree; for man could not be helped unless the love-centre of the love-desire did enter again into the humanity, and bring forth the own life, viz. the human self, through the mortification into itself: This is an exact type or resemblance, that whatsoever will be freed from the abominate, viz. from the curse, the same must die to the four elements in the abominate, and bring forth its degree through the mortification of the fire in the light.

74. Thus likewise is the salnitral sude in the earth, from whence metals, good herbs and trees grow; each property is desirous of the assimulate; and if it can reach the assimulate in Sulphur, and Mercury in the love, then it brings forth itself higher than it is in its degree; as the eternal liberty with its lubet introduces the eternal nature through the mortification into desire, and thereby brings itself forth higher, viz. in power and majesty; the like is to be considered in all things; for all things arise out of one only being; the same is a mystery of all beings, and a manifestation of the abyss in byss.

75. All things are generated out of the grand mystery, and proceed out of one degree into another: Now whatever goes forwards in its degree, the same receives no abominate, let it be either in vegetables or animals; but whatever enters in itself into its self-hood, viz. into its own lubet, the same receives, in passing through the degrees, the abominate; for each form of nature out of the mystery receives of its

property in its hunger, and therein it is not annoyed or molested, for it is of their property.

76. But if the will enters back again into the birth of the other properties, then it receives the lust, and the lust makes an hunger, and the hunger receives strange essence into itself: Here now is the abominate and turba born; for this will is entered contrary to the course of nature into a strange essence, which is not of its property; this strange essence domineers now in the strange will, and overcomes the will; now the will must either cast it out, or else it will itself be cast out by the strange essence; and seeing this also cannot be, thereupon arises anger and enmity.

77. For the properties run to their centre of the first impression, and seek the strength and might of the fire, from whence arises the heat and cold in the body, and they are in one another as enemies, whereby the first mother is stirred up in her most wrathful malice and malignity according to the austere impression, and then begins the contest for the conquest, and that property which maintains and keeps its power and prevalence, casts the other into death's property, viz. into the devoration, into the house of misery.

Chapter XV
Concerning The Will Of The Great Mystery In Good And Evil, Shewing From Whence A Good And Evil Will Arises, And How One Introduces Itself Into The Other

1. Every property takes its original from the first, viz. from the first impression or desire to nature, viz. out of the grand mystery, and brings forth itself out of itself, as the air proceeds out of the fire, and all whatever proceeds forward in one will is uncontrollable, for it gives itself to no property; it dwells even from the first original only in itself, and goes forth in one will; and this is the true way of eternity, wherein there is no corruptibility if a thing remains in its own peculiar property, for the great mystery is from eternity: Now if the form of the same proceeds forth, and manifests itself out of itself, then this form stands with the root in the mystery of eternity; but if the form brings itself forth into another lust, so that two properties must dwell in one, then from thence arises the enmity and abominate; for there has been from eternity only the one element in motion, and the free lubet of eternity, which proceeded forth with its motion from the great mystery of eternity as a spirit, which spirit is God's.

2. But when the great mystery did once move itself, and introduced the free lubet into the desire of the essence, then in the desire the strife began; for there arose in the desire out of the element, which bears only one will, four elements, viz. manifold desires and wills, which rule in one only body, where now there is contrariety and strife; as heat against cold, fire against water, air against earth, each is the death and destruction of the other; so that the creature which stands in this dominion is nothing else but a continual dying and a strife; it is an enmity and contrary will in itself, and cannot be remedied unless it enters again into one will, which also cannot be brought to pass, unless the multiplicity of the wills be destroyed, and wholly die to the desire, from whence the four elements arise; so that the will does again become that which it was from eternity: Herein we men do know what we are in the dominion of the four elements, nothing else but a strife and a contrary will, a self-envying, a desire of the abominate, a lust of death.

3. For the lust which arises out of the desire must die; if the will (which proceeded out of the great mystery of eternity, which the Spirit of God breathed into the image of man, viz. into the likeness) will be freed from the abominate and contrary will, then the desire of the four elements must die, and the will must enter again into the one only element, it must again receive the right of eternity, and act and go forth in one element, in manner also as God created him, whom he himself has opposed, and brought himself into the dominion of the four elements, in which he has inherited death, and also the strife in the forms of life, from whence arises his sickness, loathing, and enmity: For all whatever lives in God's will, that is not risen in the self-will, or if it be risen therein, it is again dead to the own or selfish desire.

4. Every will which enters into its self-hood, and seeks the ground of its life's form, the same breaks itself off from the great mystery, and enters into a self-fullness, it will be its own or of its own selfish jurisdiction, and so it is contrary to the first mystery, for the same is alone all: And this child is accounted evil, for it strives in disobedience against its own mother which has brought it forth; but if the child does again introduce its will and desire into that, from whence it is generated and risen originally, then it is wholly one with the same, and cannot be annoyed by anything; for it enters into the nothing, viz. into the essence, from whence it proceeded.

5. Thus, O man! understand what thou art to do; behold thyself in thyself, what thou art, whether or no thou standest in the resignation of thy mother (out of which thou wert generated and created in the beginning), whether thou art inclined with the same will; if not, then know that thou art a rebellious, stubborn, disobedient child, and hast made thyself thine own enemy, in that thou art entered into self-desire and will, and hast made thyself thy own self-full possession, so that thou canst not dwell in the first mother, but in thyself: For thy will is entered into self-hood; and all that does vex, plague, and annoy thee, is only thy self-hood; thou makest thyself thy own enemy, and bringest thyself into self-destruction or death.

6. Now if thou wilt get again out of death, then thou must wholly forsake thy own self-desire, which has introduced itself into strange essence, and become in self-hood, and the self-desire, as a nothing, so that thou dost no longer will or desire to thyself, but wholly and fully introduce thy desire again with the resignation into the eternal, viz. into God's will, that the same will may be thy will and desire.

7. Without this there is nothing but misery and death, a continual dying and perishing; for hence arises the election of grace. If the human will (which is departed out of the unity of eternity, and entered into a self-fullness, viz. into a selfish lust and desire) does again break itself off from self-hood, and enter into the mortification of self-will, and introduce its desire again only into the first mother, then the first mother does again choose it to be its child, and makes it again one with the only will of eternity: But that will or person which continues in self-hood, he continues in the eternal dying, viz. in an eternal selfish enmity; and this also is only called sin, because that it is an enmity against God, in that the creature will be at its self-full command and government.

8. Thus in its self-hood, viz. in a dominion full of contention and strife, it cannot either will or do anything that is good; and as it does impose, awaken, and powerfully stir up to its self nothing else but the dying and death, so likewise it can do nothing else to its fellow-members; for hence also arises the falsehood or lyes, that the creature denies the union with or in the will of God, and sets his self-hood in the place; so that it goes forth from the unity into desires and self-lusts: If it did but truly know that all beings were its mothers, which brought it forth, and did not hold the mother's substance for its own, but for common, then the covetousness, envy, strife, and contrary will

and enmity would not arise; from which the anger, viz. the fire of destruction does arise.

9. All sins arise from self; for the self-hood forces itself with the desire into its self-fullness; it makes itself covetousness and envy, it draws in its own desire strange essence into itself, and makes the possessor of the strange essence also an enemy against itself, so that sin is wrought with sin, vileness with vileness, and all run confusedly in and among one another, as a mere abomination before the eternal mother.

10. In like manner also we are to consider of the regenerate will, which goes out of its selfishness or self-hood again into the resignation; the same becomes also an enemy and an abominate to self-hood; as sickness is an enemy to health, and on the contrary, health an enemy to sickness: Thus the resigned will, and also the self-will are a continual enmity, and an incessant lasting war and combat.

11. Self-will seeks only what serves to its self-hood; and the resigned will is not at all careful, but brings its desire only into its eternal mother, that it might be one with her: It will be a nothing, that the mother might be alone all in it. Self-will says to the resigned will, Thou art foolish, in that thou givest thyself to death, and yet mightest well live gloriously in me; but the resigned will says, Thou art my abomination, pain, and enmity, and bringest me out of eternity into a time only into perplexity and misery; thou plaguest me a while, and then thou givest my body to the earth, and the soul to hell.

12. True real resignation is the mortification of the abominate against God; he that wholly forsakes his self-hood, and gives himself up with mind and desire, senses and will, into God's mercy, into the dying of Jesus Christ, he is dead to the earthly world with the will, and is a twofold man; where the abominate works only in itself to death, bait the resigned will lives in Christ's death, and rises up continually in Christ's resurrection in God: And though the self-desire sins, which indeed can do nothing else but sin, yet the resigned will lives not in sin, for it is mortified to the desire of sin, and lives through Christ in God in the land of the living; but self-hood lives in the land of death, viz. in the continual dying, in the continual enmity against God.

13. The earthly man is the curse of God, and is an abominate before God's holiness; he can do nothing else but seek his selfhood, for he is in the wrath of God: And though he does some thing that is good, yet he does it not from his own self-will, but the will resigned in

God compels him that he must do what his self would not willingly do: And now if he does it, he does it as an instrument of the resigned will, not from his own desire, but from God's will, which guides the resigned will in the desire as an instrument.

14. Therefore now whoever will see the kingdom of God, and attain thereunto, he must educe or bring forth his soul out of self-hood, out of the earthly desire, as the physician brings forth the cure of the disease from the painful tormenting desire, and introduces it into a love-desire; and then the cure also brings forth the sickness in the body out of the painful desire, and sets it into a love-desire: Sickness becomes the servant of the physic; and so likewise the evil earthly will, when the soul's will is cured, is the resigned will's servant.

15. The elemental and siderial man must only be the instrument wherewith man's soul labours in the resigned will; for thereto God has also created it; but the soul has made and set up itself in Adam for lord and master, and is entered into his prison, and given its will thereinto; but if it will be acknowledged for God's child, then it must again die to the same, and be wholly mortified to the earthly self-hood and desire in God's will in Christ's death, and be wholly regenerated anew in God's will, and deprive the earthly will in self-hood of its power, and rule over it, and guide it in subjection and command, as a master does his instrument, and then self-hood loses the power and prevalence, and the lust of self-hood arises as a continual longing; self-hood does then continually long after the forms of its own life, viz. after self-glory, and after earthly abundance, also after envy and anger, whether it may be able to attain that abundance; and also after the cunning lyes of falsehood: These are the vital forms of the earthly self-hood.

16. But the resigned will does as a potent champion continually bruise the head of this serpent, and says, "Thou art arisen from the devil, and God's anger, I will have none of thee, thou art an abomination before God." And though the resigned will is sometimes captivated with false lust, when it overwhelms and overpowers it with the devil's desire and insinuation of its imagination, yet the resigned will does forthwith cry to the word of God, that God's will does again bring it out of the abomination of death.

17. The resigned will has no rest here in this cottage, but must always be in combat, for it is lodged in a false house: It is indeed in itself in God's hand; but, without itself it is in the jaws and throat of

the abyss of God's anger in the kingdom of devils, which continually pass up and down with it, and desire to try and tempt the soul, viz. the centre.

18. In like manner also the good angels stand by him in the resigned will, viz. in the divine desire, and defend him from the poisonful imagination of the devil; they keep off the fiery darts of the wicked one, as St. Peter says.

19. For all do work and desire in man, God's love and anger: He stands while he is in this tabernacle in the gate either to go out or in: Both eternal principles are stirring in him; to which the soul's will gives itself, of that it is received, and thereto it is chosen; he is drawn of both, and if the will of the soul remains in self-hood, then he is m the hand of God's anger.

20. But if he departs out of his self-hood, and forsakes his own damnation, and continually casts himself only into God's mercy, viz. into the suffering and death of Christ, and into his resurrection and restoration, and wills nothing of himself, but what God wills in him, and by him, then the will is dead to the life and desire of God's anger; for it has no own life, but lies in the death of self-hood and the desire of the devil; and the anger of God cannot reach him; for he is as a nothing, and yet is in God, and lives in the divine essence wholly, but not to himself, but to his first mother of eternity: He is again in the limit or place where he was before he was a creature, and in the will wherein God created him, and is an instrument in the voice of God, upon which only the will-spirit of God does strike, to its honour and deeds of wonder.

21. All self-fulll seeking and searching in self-hood is a vain thing; self-will apprehends nothing of God, for it is not in God, but without God in its self-hood; but the resigned will apprehends it; for it does not do it, but the spirit in whom it stands still, whose instrument it is, he manifests himself in the divine voice in it as much as he pleases: And though it may apprehend much in self-hood by searching and learning (which is not wholly to no purpose), yet its apprehension is only without in the expressed word, viz. in a form of the letter; and it understands nothing of the form of the expressed word, how the same is in its ground; for it is only born in the form from without, and not in the power of the universal pregnatress, whose ground has neither beginning, comprehension, or end.

22. Now that he is born from within out of the speaking voice of God in God's will-spirit, he goes in the byss and abyss everywhere

free, and is bound to no form; for he goes not in self-hood, but the eternal will guides him as its instrument, according as it pleases God: but he that is born only in the letter, he is born in the form of the expressed word, and goes on in self-hood, and is a self-full voice; for he seeks what he pleases, and contends about the form, and leaves the spirit which has made the form.

23. Such a doctor Babel is; it contends, wrangles, and rages about the form of the word, and continually introduces the self-full spirit and understanding in the form, and cries out, Here is the Church of Christ; and it is only a self-full voice, understanding nothing of the spirit of the form which is incomprehensible, and strikes upon its prepared instrument without limit and measure as it pleases. For conjecture, opinion, or the self-full own imagination, which arises in the expressed voice or literal outward word, is not God's word; but that which arises in God's Spirit in the wholly resigned will in divine power in the eternal speaking word, that takes its original out of God's voice, and makes the form in the heart, viz. a divine desire, whereby the soul's will is drawn into God.

24. He is a shepherd, and teacher of Christ, who enters in through the door of Christ, that is, who speaks and teaches by Christ's spirit; without this there is only the form, viz. the history that was once brought to pass, and that a man need only accept of it, and comfort himself therewith: but this will remains without, for it will be a child of an assumed grace, and not wholly die to its self-hood in the grace, and become a child of grace in the resigned will.

25. All whatever teaches of Christ's satisfaction, and comforting oneself with Christ's suffering, if it teaches not also the true ground how a man must wholly die to self-hood in the death, and give himself up in the resigned will wholly into the obedience of God, as a new child of a new will, the same is without, and not in the speaking voice of God, viz. in Christ's door.

26. No flattering or comforting avails anything, but to die to the false will and desire in Christ's death, and to arise in the wholly resigned will in Christ's resurrection in him, and continually mortify the earthly self-hood, and quench the evil which the earthly will introduces into the imagination, as an evil fire which would fain continually burn.

27. Comforting and setting the suffering of Christ in the forefront is not the true faith; no, no, it is only without, and not within: But a

converted will, which enters into sorrow for its earthly iniquity, and will have none of it any more; and yet finds that it is kept back by the self-full earthly lust, and with his converted will departs sincerely out of this abomination and false desire into God's mercy, and casts himself with great anxious earnest desire into Christ's obedience, suffering, and death, and in the converted will wholly dies to the earthly lust in Christ's death, which will not depart out of Christ's death, and continually cries Abba, loving Father! take thy dear Son's obedience for me; let me only in his death live in his obedience in thee; let me die in him, that I may be nothing in myself, but live and be in his will, in his humanity in thee; receive me, but wholly in his resurrection, and not in my unworthiness; but receive me in him; let me be dead in him, and give me his life, that I may be thy obedient son in him, that his suffering and death may be mine, that I may be before the same Christ in him who has deprived death of its might, viz. a branch or twig of his life.

28. Thus, and no otherwise, is the true Christian faith; it is not only a comforting, but an incessant desire; the desire obtains the suffering of Christ, which desire would continually fain be obedient, if it knew but how it should behave itself before him, which continually does fall down before him, and dives itself into the deepest humility before him; it suffers and does all things readily, only that it might but receive grace; it is willing to take the cross of Christ upon itself, and regards not all the scorn of all the world in its self-hood, but continually presses forward into Christ's love-desire: This desire does only grow out of Christ's death, and out of his resurrection in God, and brings forth fruit in patience which is hidden in God, of which the earthly man knows nothing, for it finds itself in its selfhood.

29. A true Christian is a continual champion, and walks wholly in the will and desire in Christ's person, as he hath walked up and down upon the earth. Christ, when he was upon the earth, desired to overcome death, and bring the human self-hood in true resignation into divine obedience: And this likewise a right Christian desires to do; he desires continually to die to the iniquity of death and wrath, and give himself up to obedience, and to arise and live in Christ's obedience in God.

30. Therefore, dear brethren, take heed of putting on Christ's purple mantle without a resigned will; the poor sinner without sorrow for his sins, and conversion of his will, does only take it in

scorn to Christ: Keep you from that doctrine which teaches of self-full abilities, and of the works of justification.

31. A true Christian is himself the great and anxious work which continually desires to work in God's will, and forces against the self-full lusts of self-hood, and wills continually so to do, and yet is many times hindered by self-hood: He breaks self-hood, as a vessel, wherein he lies captive, and buds forth continually in God's will-spirit, with his desire resigned in God (as a fair blossom springs out of the earth), and works in and with God, what God pleases.

32. Therefore let the true Christendom know, and deeply lay to heart, what is now told and spoken to her, viz. that she depart from the false conjecture or opinion of comforting, without conversion of the will; it is only an outward expressed form of the new-birth; a Christian must be one spirit with Christ, and have Christ's will and life in him; the form does not renew him, neither comforting, or giving good words does at all help or avail, but a mortifying of the evil inbred will, which is God's child, and born out of Christ's death, no other will attains Christ's inheritance; my much knowing doth not also do it; the herdsman in the field is as near to it as the doctor; no wit or subtle art in disputation about the way of God does help or avail anything thereto, it is only a let and hinderance; the true will enters into the love of God and his children; it seeks no form, but falls down before its creator, and desires the death of its false self-hood; it seeks the work of love towards all men; it will not flourish in the world's scorn, but in its God; its whole life is a mere repentance, and a continual sorrow for the evil which cleaves to it: It seeks no glory or applause to shew itself, but lives in humility: It acknowledges itself always as unworthy and simple; its true Christianity is always hidden in its self-hood. He says, "I am in my self-hood an unprofitable servant, and have not as yet begun to do or work repentance right." He is always in the beginning to work repentance, and would always fain reach the gates of the sweet grace; he labours for that purpose as a woman in travail labours to bring forth, and knows not how it fares with him; the Lord hides his face from him, that his working may be great towards him: He sows in anguish and tears, and knows not his fruit, for it is hidden in God; as a painful traveller goes a long way, aiming at his wished-for journey's end, so also he runs after the far mark of his rest, and finds it not; unless his pearl does appear to him in its beauty, and embraces him in its love: If it again departs from his self-hood, then arises sighing and sorrowing again with continual

desire; and one day calls another, the day the night, and the night the morning; and yet there is no place of rest in the earthly self-hood, but only in the fair solar lustre of his precious pearl; when the sun arises to him in the darkness, then the night departs, and all sorrow and anguish fly away.

33. Therefore, dear brethren, learn to take heed and beware of contention, where men contend about the literal form: A true Christian has nothing to contend for, for he dies to his reason's desire; he desires only God's knowledge in his love and grace, and lets all go which contends and strives about the form, for Christ's spirit must make the form in himself; the outward form is only a guide: God must become man, or else man becomes not God.

34. Therefore a Christian is the most simple or plainest man upon the earth, as Isaiah says, "Who is so simple as my servant?" All heathens desire self-hood, and tear and devour one another for the authority and honours: But a true Christian desires to die to them; he seeks not his own, but Christ's honour. All whatever contends about self-hood, viz. about the self-full honour and pleasure of this life, the same is heathenish, and far worse than heathenish; yea like the devil, who departed from God into self-fullness: Let it cover itself with Christ's mantle as much as ever it will, yet the man of false self-hood is lodged under it; if he will be a Christian, then he must quite die to self-hood, that the same may only hang to him from without as a garment of this world, wherein he is a stranger and pilgrim, and always consider and think that he is but a servant in his high office, and serves God therein as a servant, and not be his own lord and master.

35. All whatever does lord itself without God's call and appointment, the same is from the devil, and serves the devil in his own power and form: Defend and flatter thyself as much as thou wilt, it does not avail before God; thy own heart accuses thee that thou art a false branch; thy nobility and highness do not at all avail or help thee in the sight of God, if thou dost not thereby drive in God's order; thy office is not thine, but God's; if thou walkest falsely therein, then thy own judgement is upon thee, and condemns thee to death; thou art a servant; and though thou art a king, yet thou servest, and must enter with the poorest into the new birth, or else thou shalt not see God.

36. All self-fulll assumed or arrogated laws and authority, wherewith the poor are vexed and oppressed, do all come from self-

hood, whose original is in the expressed form, which has with the form introduced itself into a self-hood, and brought itself out quite from God: Whatever does not serve in a servant's office before God, the same is all false, let it be either high or low, learned or unlearned: We are altogether servants of the great God; nothing brings itself into a self-fullness, unless it be born in God's anger in the impression of nature: And though a Christian possesses an own-hood, which is not false, yet he is only but a servant therein, viz. a distributer for his Master, a steward and overseer of his Master's work: He deals for his Master therein, and not for his self-hood only; all whatever he plots and devises to bring into self-hood, and brings it, that he brings into the anxious cabinet of covetousness, envy, and self-full pleasure of the flesh, viz. into a vessel that is separated from God, viz. into the impression of nature, and steals from his Lord and Master who has set him up for a steward; he is a sacrilegious person, let him excuse himself, and pretend what he pleases.

37. A true Christian acknowledges himself for a servant of God, to whom it is given in charge to deal right with God's works. He is not his own, for he is also not at home in this earthly work of this tabernacle: Let him seek, search, plant and build, traffic and trade; and whatever else he does, he must always know that he does it to God, and shall give an account thereof, and that he is a stranger and servant in this work, and serves his Master; and not at all look upon the course of his forefathers who have walked therein in the pleasure of the earthly life; whoever does so is far from the kingdom of God, and can with no conscience and ground call himself or think himself to be a Christian; for he stands only in the form of Christianity, and not in the spirit of Christ; the form shall be destroyed, and cease with time, but the spirit remains steadfast for ever.

38. A true Christian is in the spirit a Christian, and in continual exercise to bring forth its own form, not only with words in sound and shew, but in the power of the work, as a visible palpable form, not weening, conjecturing, and giving good words out of the self-full self-hood, and yet remaining in self-hood; but a dying to self-hood, and a growing forth in the will of God in the love-self-hood as a servant of God in God's deeds of wonder; a helping to strike his instrument in God's will, and be a true sounding string in God's harmonious concert; a continual making word in God's voice, viz. in the verbum fiat, which makes and works in and with God what God makes, forms, and works, as an instrument of God.

39. Therefore, O thou dear Christendom, behold thyself, whether thou workest in the working word of God in his will, or whether thou standest only in the form of Christendom, and workest thy own self-fullness in falsehood: Thou wilt find, how thou art become an abomination before the Most High, and thy casting forth from the Most High out of this form (which thou in thy self-hood hast introduced into his expressed form) shall presently follow; and that because thou coverest thyself with the true form, and art a false child therein: Therefore thou art sought, and found with a false veil or covering in thy own form.

40. And as thou hast brought thyself into a false self-full form under the true form, so thou shalt also destroy thyself, whereto the heaven helps thee, which thou hast a long time served in obedience, and from this there is no withholding; thy work is found to be in the turba, which shall well satisfy and satiate itself in destroying, as thou hast built up thyself in thy apostate falsehood in thy own form under the name of the true form, and hast played the hypocrite before God with the shew and ostentation of holiness, and only served the earthly man: But the servant of the Lord shall be sought and found; the Lord feeds his lambs in his own form, and brings them into his pasture; all the haughty and wealthy of the world shall find by experience what judgment the Lord will bring upon the face of all the earth, and all wicked hope shall be destroyed; for the day of the harvest draws near: "A terror from the Lord shaketh the earth, and his voice soundeth in all the ends of the earth;" and the star of his wonders arises, no one hinders it, for it is concluded of in the counsel of the watchmen in the gates of the deep.

41. Therefore let every one seek and find himself; for the time of visitation is at hand, that he may be found in his love; for the turba has found all false lust in it, and the Most High worker of all essences manifests the turba; and then all false lust or imagination becomes manifest, and each thing enters into its eternal keeper, for all things are generated out of imagination: So also it shall receive its property in the imagination, and every imagination reaps its own work which it has wrought; for to that end all things have appeared, that the eternity might be manifest in a time: With deeds of wonder it brought itself into the form of time, and with deeds of wonder it carries itself forth again out of the time into its first place.

42. All things enter again into that from whence they proceeded; but they keep their own form and model, as they have introduced

themselves in the expressed word; and everything shall also be received of its likeness, and the end is always; and as all things generate themselves in the expressed word, so also they are signed in their inward form, which also signs the outward.

43. The self-full will makes a form according to its innate nature; but a form is made in the resigned will according to the platform or model of eternity, as it was known in the glass of God's eternal wisdom before the times of this world; so the eternal will figures and forms it into a model of its likeness to the honour and wonderful acts of God; for all whatever goes on in its self-hood, the same forms itself; but what resigns itself freely, that is formed of the free will: Now no self-full form with its own self-will can inherit the only Eternal Being; for where there are two wills in one, there is enmity.

44. Seeing then God is one only God, then all whatever will live in him must be like his will and word: As a concert of music must be tuned into one harmony, though there be many strings, and manifold voices and sounds therein; so must the true human harmony be tuned with all voices into a love melody, and that will-spirit which is not tuned unto the only concert in the divine voice, the same is cast forth out of this tune, and brought into its self-fulll tune, viz. into its true fellow-voices of its own likeness; for every likeness shall receive its own.

45. Has any been here an evil spirit? Then he shall be introduced into the root of his likeness; for every hunger receives its like into itself; now the whole manifestation of eternity with this time is nothing else but an hunger and generation; as the hunger is, so is also the essence of its satiating; for with the hunger the creature took its beginning, and with the hunger it enters into its eternal being.

46. In the hunger the spirit with the body is generated, and in the same hunger it goes into its eternal being, unless it breaks its first hunger, and brings itself into another by mortification, else all is at its end as soon as it is born; but death is the only means whereby the spirit may enter into another source and form: If it dies to its self-hood, and breaks its will in death, then a new twig springs forth out of the same, but not according to the first will, but according to the eternal will; for if a thing enters into its nothing, then it falls again to the creator, who makes that thing as it was known in the eternal will, before it was created to a creature; there it is in the right aim or limit of eternity, and has no turba, for it is in nature's end.

47. Whatever runs on in nature torments itself, but that which attains nature's end, the same is in rest without source, and yet works, but only in one desire: All whatever makes anguish and strife in nature, that makes mere joy in God; for the whole host of heaven is set and tuned into one harmony; each angelical kingdom into a peculiar instrument, but all mutually composed together into one music, viz. into the only love-voice of God.

Every string of this melody exalts and rejoices the other; and it is only a mere ravishing lovely and delightful hearing, tasting, feeling, smelling, and seeing: Whatever God is in himself, that the creature is also in its desire in him; a God-angel, and a God-man, God all in all, and without him nothing else. As it was before the times of this world in his eternal harmony or voice, so also it continues in the creaturely voice in him in his eternity; and this is the beginning and the end of all things.

Chapter XVI
Concerning The Eternal Signature And Heavenly Joy; Why All Things Were Brought Into Evil And Good

1. The creation of the whole creation is nothing else but a manifestation of the all-essential, unsearchable God; all whatever he is in his eternal unbeginning generation and dominion, of that is also the creation, but not in the omnipotence and power, but like an apple which grows upon the tree, which is not the tree itself, but grows from the power of the tree: Even so all things are sprung forth out of the divine desire, and created into an essence, where in the beginning there was no such essence present, but only that same mystery of the eternal generation, in which there has been an eternal perfection.

2. For God has not brought forth the creation, that he should be thereby perfect, but for his own manifestation, viz. for the great joy and glory; not that this joy first began with the creation, no, for it was from eternity in the great mystery, yet only as a spiritual melody and sport in itself.

3. The creation is the same sport out of himself, viz. a platform or instrument of the Eternal Spirit, with which he melodises: and it is even as a great harmony of manifold instruments which are all tuned into one harmony; for the eternal word, or divine sound or voice, which is a spirit, has introduced itself with the generation of the great

mystery into formings, viz. into an expressed word or sound: And as the joyful melody is in itself in the spirit of the eternal generation, so likewise is the instrument, viz. the expressed form in itself, which the living eternal voice guides, and strikes with his own eternal will-spirit, that it sounds and melodises; as an organ of diverse and various sounds or notes is moved with one only air, so that each note, yea every pipe has its peculiar tune, and yet there is but one manner of air or breath in all notes, which sounds in each note or pipe according as the instrument or organ is made.

4. Thus in the eternity there is only one spirit in the whole work of the divine manifestation, which is the manifestator in the expressed voice and also in the speaking voice of God, which is the life of the grand mystery, and of all that is generated from thence; he is the manifestator of all the works of God.

5. All the angelical kingdoms are as a prepared work, viz. a manifestation of the eternal sound of the voice of God, and are as a particularity out of the great mystery, and yet are only one in the divine eternal speaking word, sound, or voice of God; for one only spirit rules them; each angelical prince is a property out of the voice of God, and bears the great name of God; as we have a type and figure of it in the stars of the firmament, and in the kingdoms and dominions upon the earth among all generations, where every lord bears his high title, respective name and office: So likewise do the stars in the firmament, which are altogether one only dominion in power under them, where the great stars bear the name and the office of the forms in the mystery of the seven properties, and the other after them, as a particularity of houses or divisions, where every one is a peculiar harmony or operation, like a kingdom, and yet all proceeds in one harmony; like a clock-work, which is entirely composed in itself, and all the pieces work mutually together in one; and yet the great fixed stars keep their peculiar property in the essence of operation, especially the seven planets according to the seven properties of nature, as an under pregnatress of the eternal mystery, or as an instrument of the spirit out of the eternal mystery.

6. This birth of the astrum begets in the four elements, viz. in its body or essence, joy and sorrow, and all is very good in itself; only the alteration of the creature proceeds from the lustful imagination, whereby the creature elevates the wrath of the fire in the properties, and brings them forth out of the likeness of their accord: Nothing is evil which remains in the equal accord; for that which the worst

causes and makes with its coming forth out of the accord, that likewise the best makes in the equal accord; that which there makes sorrow, that makes also in the likeness joy; therefore no creature can blame its creator, as if he made it evil; all was very exceeding good; but with its own elevation and departure out of the likeness it becomes evil, and brings itself out of the form or property of the love and joy, into a painful tormenting form and property.

7. King Lucifer stood in the beginning of his creation in highest joyfulness, but he departed from the likeness, and put himself forth out of the accord or heavenly concert into the cold, dark, fiery generation, out of which the hot fiery generation arises; he forsook his order, and went out of the harmony, wherein God created him; he would be lord over all, and so he entered into the austere fire's domination, and is now an instrument in the austere fire's might, upon which also the all-essential spirit strikes and sounds upon his instrument, but it sounds only according to the wrathful fire's property: as the harmony, viz. the life's-form is in each thing, so is also the sound or tone of the eternal voice therein; in the holy it is holy, in the perverse it is perverse: All things must praise the Creator of all beings; the devils praise him in the might of wrath, and the angels and men praise him in the might of love.

8. The Being of all beings is but one only Being, but in its generation it separates itself into two principles, viz. into light and darkness, into joy and sorrow, into evil and good, into love and anger, into fire and light, and out of these two eternal beginnings or principles into the third beginning, viz. into the creation, to its own love-play and melody, according to the property of both eternal desires.

9. Thus each thing goes into its harmony, and is guided or driven by one only spirit, which is in each thing according to the property of the thing; and this is the clock or watch-work of the great mystery of eternity in each principle according to the property of the principle, and then according to the innate form of the composed instrument of the same creatures, even in all these beginnings or principles.

10. Death is the bound-mark of all whatever is temporal, whereby the evil may be destroyed; but that which arises out of the eternal beginnings, and in its harmony and life's-form enters into another figure, that departs out of God's harmony, out of the true order wherein God created it, and is cast out of the same harmony into its likeness, as a dissonant discording melody or sound in the great

excellent well-tuned harmony; for it is an opposite contrary thing, and bears another tone, sound, and will, and so it is introduced into its likeness; and therefore hell is given to the devil for his house and habitation, because he introduced his life's-form into the anger of God, and into the fiery wrath of the eternal nature, so that now he is the instrument in the eternal fire of God, and the anger-spirit strikes his instrument, and yet it must stand to the honour and admiration of God, and be the sport and play in the desire and property of the wrathful anger.

11. The anger and wrath of God are now his joy, not as if he feared, sorrowed, and lived in impotency; no, but in great strength and fiery might, as a potent king and lord, yet only in the same property of which he himself is, viz. in the first principle in the dark world.

12. The like also we are to know concerning the angelical world, viz. the second principle, where God's light and glorious beauty shine in every being or thing, and the divine voice or sound rises up in all creatures in great joyfulness; where the spirit proceeding from the divine voice makes a joyfulness, and an incessant continual love-desire in those creatures, and in all the divine angelical beings: As there is an anguish-source and trembling in the painful fire, so in like manner there is a trembling joyfulness in the light and love-fire, viz. a great elevation of the voice of God, which makes in the angels and in the like creatures, as the souls of men, a great manifestation of the divine joyfulness.

13. The voice or breath of God continually and eternally brings forth its joy through the creature, as through an instrument; the creature is the manifestation of the voice of God: What God is in the eternal generation of his eternal word out of the great mystery of the Father's property, that the creature is in the image as a joyful harmony, wherewith the Eternal Spirit plays or melodises.

14. All properties of the great eternal mystery of the pregnatress of all beings are manifest in the holy angelical and humane creatures; and we are not to think thereof, as if the creatures only stood still and rejoiced at the glory of God, and admired only in joy; not, but it is as the Eternal Spirit of God works from eternity to eternity in the great mystery of the divine generation, and continually manifests the infinite and numberless wisdom of God; even as the earth brings forth always fair blossoms, herbs, and trees, so also metals and all manner of beings, and puts them forth sometimes more sovereign, powerful,

and fair, than at other times; and as one arises in the essence, another falls down, and there is an incessant lasting enjoyment. and labour.

15. Thus likewise is the eternal generation of the holy mystery in great power and reprocreation or paradisical pullulation where one divine fruit of the great love-desire stands with another in the divine essence; and all is as a continual love-combat or wrestling delight; a blooming of fair colours, and a pleasant ravishing smell of the divine Mercury, according to the divine nature's property, a continual good taste of love from the divine desire.

16. Of all whatever this world is an earthly type and resemblance, that is in the divine kingdom in great perfection in the spiritual essence; not only spirit, as a will, or thought, but essence, corporeal essence, sap and power; but as incomprehensible in reference to the outward world: For this visible world was generated and created out of the same spiritual essence in which the pure element is; and also out of the dark essence in the mystery of the wrath (being the original of the eternal manifest essence from whence the properties arise) as an out-spoken breath out of the Being of all beings: Not that it was made of the eternal essence, but out of the breathing forth or expression of the eternal essence; out of love and anger, out of evil and good, as a peculiar generation of a peculiar principle in the hand of the Eternal Spirit.

17. Therefore all whatever is in this world is a type and figure of the angelical world: not that the evil, which is alike manifest with the good in this world, is also manifest in heaven; no, they are separated into two principles; in heaven all is good which is evil in hell; whatever is anguish and torment in hell, that is good and a joy in heaven; for there all stands in the light's source; and in hell all stands in the wrath in the dark source.

18. Hell, viz. the dark world has also its generation of fruits; and there is even such an essence and dominion in them as in heaven, but in nature and manner of the wrathful property; for the fiery property makes all evil in the darkness, and in the light it makes all things good; and in sum, all is wholly one in both eternal worlds; but light and darkness separates them, so that they stand as an eternal enmity opposite one to another, to the end that it may be known what is evil or good, joy or sorrow, love or anger: There is only a distinction between the love-desire of the light, and the anger-desire of the darkness.

19. In the original of the eternal nature, in the Father's property in the great mystery of all beings, it is wholly one: for the same only fire is even in the angelical world, but in another source, viz. a love-fire, which is a poison, and a fire of anger to the devils, and to hell; for the love-fire is a death, mortification, and an enmity of the anger-fire; it deprives the wrath of its might, and this the wrath wills not, and it also cannot be; for if there were no wrath, there would be no fire, and also no light: If the eternal wrath were not, the eternal joy also would not be; in the light the wrath is changed into joy; the wrathful fire's essence is mortified as to the darkness in the wrathful fire, and out of the same dying the light and love-fire arise; as the light burns forth from the candle, and yet in the candle the fire and light are but one thing.

20. Thus also the great mystery of all beings is in the eternity in itself only one thing, but in its explication and manifestation it goes from eternity to eternity into two essences, viz. into evil and good; what is evil to one thing, that is good to another. Hell is evil to the angels, for they were not created thereunto; but it is good to the hellish creatures: So also heaven is evil to the hellish creatures, for it is their poison and death, an eternal dying, and an eternal captivity.

21. Therefore there is an eternal enmity, and God is only called God according to the light of his love; he is indeed himself all, but according to the darkness he saith, "I am an angry jealous God, and a consuming fire."

22. Every creature must remain in its place wherein it was apprehended in its creation and formed into an image, and not depart out of that same harmony, or else it becomes an enemy of the Being of all beings.

23. And thus hell is even an enemy of the devil, for he is a strange guest therein, viz. a perjured fiend cast out of heaven: he will be lord in that wherein he was not created; the whole creation accuses him for a false perjured apostate spirit, which is departed from his order; yea even the nature in the wrath is his enemy though he be of the same property; yet he is a stranger, and will be lord, though he has lost his kingdom, and is only an inmate in the wrath of God; he that was too rich, is now become too poor; he had all when he stood in humility, and now he has nothing, and is moreover captivated in the gulf: this is his shame, that he is a king, and yet has fooled away his kingdom in pride; the royal creature remains, but the dominion is taken away; of a king he is become an executioner; what God's anger apprehends,

there he is a judge, viz. an officer of God's anger, yet he must do what his Lord and Master wills.

24. This reason most ignorantly gainsays, and says, "God is omnipotent, and omniscient, he has made it: Even he hath done with his work as he hath pleased, who will contend with the Most High?" Yes, dear reason, now thou thinkest thou hittest it right; but first learn the A B C in the great mystery: All whatever is risen out of the eternal will, viz. out of the great eternal mystery of all beings (as angels and the souls of men are), stands in equal weight in evil and good in the free will as God himself; that desire which powerfully and predominantly works in the creature, and quite overtops the other, of that property the creature is. As a candle puts forth out of itself a fire, and out of the fire the wind, which wind the fire draws again into itself, and yet gives it forth again; and when this spirit is gone forth from the fire and light, then it is free from the fire and light; what property it again receives, of that it is: The first mystery wherein the creature consists is the all-essential mystery, and the other in the forth-going spirit is its propriety, and a self-full will. Has not every angel its own peculiar spirit, which is generated out of its own mystery, which has its original out of eternity? Why will this spirit be a tempter of God, and tempt the mystery, which immediately captivates it in the wrath, as happened to Lucifer? It has the drawing to God's wrath and to God's love in it; why does not the spirit (which is generated out of both) which is the similitude of the Spirit of God, continue in its place in obedience, as a child before the mother in humility?

25. Thou sayst it cannot; It is not so: Every spirit stands in the place where it was created in equal weight, and has its free will; it is a spirit with the all-essential Eternal Spirit, and may take to itself a lubet in the all-essential Eternal Spirit as it wills, either in God's love or anger; whereinto it introduces its longing imagination, the essence and property of that it receives in the great mystery of all beings.

26. In God the birth is manifest in love and anger; why not also in the creature which is created out of God's essence and will, out of his voice and breath into an image? What property or note of the voice the creature awakes in itself, the same sounds in, and rules the creature: God's will to the creature was only one, viz. a general manifestation of the spirit, as each creature was apprehended in the property of the eternal mystery; yet, Lucifer was apprehended in the good angelical property, which plainly testifies that he was an angel

in heaven; but his own incorporised will-spirit forced itself into the wrathful mother, to awaken the same in it, and thereby to be a lord over every created being. Now the will-spirit is free, it is the eternal original, let it do what it will.

27. Therefore we are to know this, and it is no otherwise, that the will-spirit which takes its original out of love and anger, out of both eternal principles, has given itself into the wrath, whereby the wrath has powerfully got the upper hand and dominion, and put itself out of the equal harmony into a dissonance or discord, and so he must be driven into his likeness; this is his fall, and so it is also the fall of all evil men.

28. Now self-reason alledges the Scripture, where it is written, "Many are called, but few are chosen: "Also, "I have loved Jacob and hated Esau;" also, "Hath not a potter power to make of one lump of earth what he pleaseth?" I say the same also, "That many are called, but few are chosen;" for they will not; they give their free will into God's anger, where they are even apprehended, and so are chosen to be "children of wrath;" whereas they were all called in Adam into paradise, and in Christ into the regeneration; but they would not, the free will would not, it exalted itself into the wrath of God which apprehended it, and so they were not chosen children; for God's love chooses only its likeness, and so likewise God's anger; yet the gate of the regeneration stands open to the wicked, whom the anger of God has apprehended. Man has the death in him, whereby he may die to the evil; but the devil has not, for he was created to the highest perfection.

29. Thus it is also with Jacob and Esau: In Jacob the line of Christ got the upper hand in the wrestling wheel; and in Esau the fall of Adam; now Christ was therefore promised into the humanity, that he might heal the fall of Adam, and redeem Esau, which was captivated in the wrath, from the wrath; Jacob denotes Christ; and Esau Adam; now Christ is to redeem Adam from death and wrath, wherein he was captivated: But did Esau continue in sin? That I know not; the Scripture also does not declare it; the blessing belonged to Esau, that is, to Adam, but he fooled it away in the Fall, and so the blessing fell upon Jacob, that is upon Christ, who should bless Adam and Esau, so that the kingdom and blessing might be given of free grace again to Adam and Esau; though he was apprehended in the curse, yet the door of grace stood open in Jacob, that is, in Christ; therefore Jacob said afterward, that is Christ, when he was entered into Adam's soul

and flesh, "Come unto me all ye that are weary and heavy laden with your sins, and I will refresh you: "Also, "I am come to call the sinner to repentance;" not Jacob, who needs it not, but Esau, who needs it; and when he (viz. Esau) is come, then says Christ, "There is more joy in heaven for him, than for ninety-nine righteous ones, which need no repentance;" viz. for one Esau that repents there is more joy than for ninety-nine Jacobs, who in the centre of the life's original are apprehended in the line of Christ: There is more joy for one poor sinner, whom the anger has apprehended in the centre of God's wrath in the life's original, and chosen to condemnation, if he brings the sins of death again into the mortification or death of sin, than for ninety-nine righteous ones that need no repentance.

30. But who are the righteous, for we are all become sinners in Adam? Answer, They are those whom the line of Christ in the humanity apprehends in the life's rise or at the first point of opening of life in them, not that they cannot fall as Adam, but that they are apprehended in Christ's will-spirit in the wrestling wheel, where love and anger are counterpoised, and chosen to life; as happened to Jacob, so also to Isaac, and Abel: But this line should be the preacher and teacher of Cain, Ishmael, and Esau, and exhort them to repentance, and to turn out of the anger: And this line did give itself into the anger which was enkindled in Adam, Cain, Ishmael, and destroyed the devil's sting with love, that Cain, Ishmael, and Esau had an open gate to grace; if they would but turn and die in Jacob, that is, if they would enter into Christ's death, and die to sin in Abel, Isaac, and Jacob, and Christ, then they should be received into the election of grace.

31. Jacob took Esau's place in the blessing: Why did that come to pass? In Jacob was the promised seed of Abraham and Adam; from this line the blessing should come upon the sinful Adam and Esau; Jacob must be filled with God's blessing, that he might bless the first-born of angry Adam and Esau; for the blessing, that is, Christ must be born in our flesh and soul, that the seed of the woman might bruise the head of the serpent.

32. The anger must be drowned and appeased in the humanity; an offering did not do it, but this resigning into the wrath, that the love might drown the wrath. Jacob in Christ must drown Esau in the love-power in his blood, that Esau might also become a Jacob in Christ: But Esau was not willing to receive his brother Jacob, and contended

about the first birth; that is, Adam in sin will not, cannot receive or accept of Christ, he shall and must die to the sinful flesh and will.

33. Therefore Esau has ever fought against Jacob; for Jacob should drown him in Christ in his blood; this the evil Adam in Esau would not have, he would live in his self-hood, therefore he strove with the earthly Adam against Jacob; but when Jacob met him with his gifts, that is, when Christ came with his free love-gift into the humanity, then Esau fell upon his brother Jacob's neck and wept; for when Christ entered into the humanity, Adam wept in Esau, and repented him of his sins and evil intent, that he would kill Jacob: For when God's love in the humanity entered into God's anger, the angry Father bewailed our sins and misery, and Jacob with his humility drove forth mournful tears out of his brother Esau; that is, the love in the humanity brought forth the great compassion out of and through the angry Father; so that the angry Father in the midst of his enkindled wrath in the humanity did set open a gate of mercy for Adam and all his children; for his love broke the anger, which love put itself into death, and made an open gate for poor sinners in the death to his grace.

34. Now it is commanded the poor sinner, whom the anger has chosen to the condemnation of eternal death, that he enter into this same death, and die in Christ's death to sin, and then Christ drowns it in his blood, and chuses him again to be God's child.

35. Here is the calling: Christ calls us into his death, into his dying; this the sinner will not have: Here is now strife in the sinner between the seed of the woman and the seed of the serpent; which now overcomes, that conceives the child: Now the free will may reach to which it pleases; both gates stand open to him. Many who are in Christ's line are also brought through imagination and lust, as Adam was, into iniquity; they are indeed called, but they persevere not in the election, for the election is set upon him who departs from sin; he is elected that dies to sin in Christ's death, and rises in Christ's resurrection, who receives God in Christ, not only in the mouth, but in divine desire in the will and new-birth, as a new fiery generation: Knowledge apprehends it not, only the earnest desire and breaking of the sinful will, that apprehends it.

36. Thus there is no sufficient ground in the election of grace as reason holds it forth: Adam is chosen in Christ; but that many a twig withers on the tree, is not the tree's fault, for it withdraws its sap from

no twig, only the twig gives forth itself too eagerly with the desire; it runs on in self-will, viz. it is taken by the inflammation of the sun and the fire, before it can draw sap again in its mother, and refresh itself.

37. Thus also man perishes among the evil company in evil vain ways: God offers him his grace that he should repent; but evil company and the devil lead him in wicked ways, till he be even too hard captivated in the anger; and then it goes very hardly with him; he indeed was called, but he is evil; God chooses only children: Seeing he is evil, the choice passes over him; but if he again reforms and amends, the eternal choice or election does again receive him.

38. Thus says the Scripture, "Many are called;" but when the choice in Christ's suffering and death comes upon them, then they are not capable of the same, by reason of the self-full evil will which they had before embraced, and so they are not the elected, but evil children; and here it is then rightly said, "We have piped unto you, but you have not danced; we have mourned unto you, and ye have not lamented unto us: O Jerusalem, how often would I have gathered thy children together, as a hen gathereth her chickens under her wings, and thou wouldest not: "It is not said, "thou couldest not," but " thou wouldest not;" and while they remain in the iniquity of sin, they also cannot: God will not cast his pearl before swine; but to the children which draw near to him he gives the pearl and his bread.

39. Therefore whoever blames God, despises his mercy, which he has introduced into the humanity, and brings the judgement headlong upon his body and soul.

40. Thus I have truly warned the reader, and set before his eyes what the Lord of all beings has given me: He may behold himself in this looking-glass both within and without, and find what and who he is: Every reader shall find his profit therein, be he either good or evil: It is a very clear gate of the mystery of all beings. With glosses and self-wit none shall apprehend it in its own ground; but it may well embrace the real seeker, and create him much profit and joy, and even be helpful to him in all natural things, provided he applies himself right, and seeks it in the fear of God, seeing it is now a time of seeking; for a lily blossoms upon the mountains and valleys in all the ends of the earth: He that seeketh findeth. Amen.

Sermons

by Meister Eckhart

The Attractive Power of God
St John vi. 44. – "No one can come unto Me, except the Father which hath sent Me draw him."

Our Lord Jesus Christ hath in the Gospel spoken with His own blessed lips these words, which signify, "No man can come to Me unless My Father draw him." In another place He says, "I am in the Father and the Father in Me." Therefore whoever cometh to the Son cometh to the Father. Further, He saith, "I and the Father are One. Therefore whomsoever the Father draweth, the Son draweth likewise." St Augustine also saith, "The works of the Holy Trinity are inseparable from each other." Therefore the Father draweth to the Son, and the Son draweth to the Holy Ghost, and the Holy Ghost draweth to the Father and the Son; and each Person of the Trinity, when He draweth to the Two Others, draweth to Himself, because the Three are One. The Father draweth with the might of His power, the Son draweth with His unfathomable wisdom, the Holy Ghost draweth with His love. Thus we are drawn by the Sacred Trinity with the cords of Power, Wisdom and Love, when we are drawn from an evil thing to a good thing, and from a good thing to a better, and from a better thing to the best of all. Now the Father draws us from the evil of sin to the goodness of His grace with the might of His measureless power, and He needs all the resources of His strength in order to convert sinners, more than when He was about to make heaven and earth, which He made with His own power without help from any creature. But when He is about to convert a sinner, He always needs the sinner's help. "He converts thee not without thy help," as St Augustine says.

Therefore deadly sin is a breach of nature, a death of the soul, a disquiet of the heart, a weakening of power, a blindness of the sense, a sorrow of the spirit, a death of grace, a death of virtue, a death of good works, an aberration of the spirit, a fellowship with the devil, an expulsion of Christianity, a dungeon of hell, a banquet of hell, an eternity of hell. Therefore, if thou committest a deadly sin thou art guilty of all these and incurrest their consequences. Regarding the first point: Deadly sin is a breach of nature, for every man's nature is an image and likeness and mirror of the Trinity, of Godhead and of eternity. All these together are marred by a deadly sin; therefore, it is a breach of nature. Such sin is also the death of the soul, for death is to lose life. Now God is the life of the soul, and deadly sin separates from God; therefore it is a death of the soul. Deadly sin is also a disquiet of the heart, for everything rests nowhere except in its own proper place; and the proper resting-place of the soul is nowhere except in God as St Augustine saith, "Lord! Thou hast made us for Thyself, therefore we may not rest anywhere save in Thee." Deadly sin is also a weakening of the powers, for by his own power no one can throw off the load of sin nor restrain himself from committing sin. It is also a blindness of the sense, for it prevents a man recognizing how brief is the space of time that can be spent in the pleasure of voluptuousness, and how long are the pains of hell and the joys of heaven. Deadly sin is also a death of all grace, for whenever such a sin is committed, the soul is bereft of all grace. Similarly, it is the death of all virtue and good works, and an aberration of the spirit.

It is also a fellowship with the Devil, for everything hath fellowship with its like; and sin maketh the soul and Satan resemble each other. It is also an expulsion of Christianity, for it depriveth the sinner of all the profit that comes from Christianity. It is also a dungeon of hell, for if the soul remain in the purity in which God created her, neither angel nor devil may rob her of her freedom. But sin confines it in hell. Sin is also an eternity of hell, for eternity is in the will, and were it not in the will, it would not be in the consciousness.

Now, people say when they commit sin, that they do not intend to do so always; they intend to turn away from sin. That is just as though a man were to kill himself and suppose that he could make himself alive again by his own strength. That is, however, impossible; but to turn from sin by one's own power and come to God is still much more impossible. Therefore, whosoever is to turn from sin and come to God in His heavenly kingdom, must be drawn by the heavenly Father with the might of His divine power. The Father also draws the Son who comes to help us with His grace, by stimulating our free will to turn away from, and hate sin, which has drawn us aside from God, and from the immutable goodness of the Godhead. Then, if she is willing, He pours the gift of His grace into the soul, which renounces all her misery and sin, and all her works become living. Now, this grace springs from the centre of Godhead and the Father's heart, and flows perpetually, nor ever ceases, if the soul obeys His everlasting love. Therefore He saith in the prophets: "I have loved thee with an everlasting love, therefore with loving kindness have I drawn thee." Out of the overflow of His universal love He desires to draw all to Himself, and to His Only-begotten Son, and to the Holy Ghost in the joy of the heavenly kingdom. Now, we should know that before our Lord Jesus Christ was born, the Heavenly Father drew men with all His might for five thousand, two hundred years; and yet, as far as we know, brought not one into the heavenly kingdom. So, when the Son saw that the Father had thus strongly drawn men and even wearied Himself, and yet not succeeded, He said to the Father: "I will draw them with the cords of a man." It was as though He said, "I see well, Father, that Thou with all Thy might, canst not succeed, therefore will I myself draw them with the cords of a man."

Therefore the Son came down from heaven, and was incarnate of a Virgin, and took upon Him all our bodily weaknesses, except sin and folly, into which Adam had cast us; and out of all His words and works and limbs and nerves, He made a cord, and drew us so skillfully, and so heartily, that the bloody sweat poured from His sacred Body. And when He had drawn men without ceasing for three and thirty years, He saw the beginnings of a movement and the redemption of all things that would follow. Therefore He said, "And I, if I be lifted up on the Cross, will draw all men unto Me." Therefore

He was stretched upon the Cross, and laid aside all His glory, and whatever might hinder His drawing men.

Now, there are three natural means of attraction with which Christ on the Cross drew to Himself between the third and the ninth hour, more people than He had drawn before during the three and thirty years of His life. The first means by which He draws is affinity, that affinity which brings creatures of the same species together, and like to its like. With this cord of affinity he drew men to the Godhead, Whom He always resembles. In order that God may draw more to Himself, and forget His wrath, the Son saith, "Beloved Father, seeing that Thou wouldest not forgive sins because of all the former sacrifices offered, lo I, Thine Only begotten Son, Who resemble Thy Godhead in all things, in Whom Thou hast hidden all the riches of divine love, I come to the Cross, that I may be a living sacrifice before Thine eyes; that out of Thy fatherly compassion Thou mayest bend and look on Me, Thine only Son, and on My Blood flowing from My wounds, and slake the fiery sword with which in the angel's hands Thou hast barred the way to Paradise, that all who have repented and bewailed their sins through Me, may enter therein."

The second means of attraction which He used is Emptiness, as we see when we place one end of a hollow pipe in water, and draw up it by suction; the water runs up the stem to the mouth, because the emptiness of the pipe, from which the air has been drawn, draws the water to itself. So Our Lord Jesus Christ made Himself empty that He might wisely draw all things to Himself. Therefore He let all the blood that was in His Body flow out, and so attracted to Himself all the compassion and grace that was in His Father's heart, so completely and profitably as to suffice for the whole world. Accordingly, the Father said, "My compassion will I never forget," and further, "Now, My Son, be bold and strong that Thou mayest lead the people altogether into the land which I have promised, the land of heavenly joys, the land which floweth with the honey of My Godhead, and with the milk of Thy manhood."

The third means of attraction is this—that as we see the sun draw up the mists from the earth to heaven, so the heart of our Lord Jesus Christ waxed hot as a fiery furnace upon the Cross, so fiercely burned the flame of love which He felt towards the whole world. Thus, with the heat of His love, from which nothing could be hidden, so intense was it—He drew the whole world to Himself. Never did our Lord Jesus Christ display such great love as when He suffered the torture of the Cross when He gave His life for us, and washed our sins with His precious Blood. Therefore with the cords of Love, He drew us all to Himself upon the Cross that those who feel the drawing of His death and martyrdom might live with Him in everlasting felicity.

Now when the Holy Spirit saw that the Only Begotten Son of the Father had drawn so wisely that He had won to Himself all things in heaven and earth, He also felt impelled by His own love and kindness to draw. Therefore He said, "I will also draw with My cords and My net." So He made a net of the seven high attributes of the Father, of the seven graces of the Son, of His own seven gifts, and of the seven Christian virtues. Thus He assures us that we shall never perish, for we are so caught by His goodness that He expels from us all the evil works of the flesh, and produces in us His fruits, so that we gain the reward of everlasting life. May the Father of His love, and the Son of His grace, and the Holy Spirit with His fellowship, grant us to be worthy of the same. Amen.

The Nearness of the Kingdom
St Luke xxi, 31. – " Know that the Kingdom of God is near."

Our Lord saith that the Kingdom of God is near us. Yea, the Kingdom of God is within us as St Paul saith "our salvation is nearer than when we believed." Now we should know in what manner the Kingdom of God is near us. Therefore let us pay diligent attention to the meaning of the words. If I were a king, and did not know it, I should not really be a king. But, if I were fully convinced that I was a king, and all mankind coincided in my belief, and I knew that they shared my conviction, I should indeed be a king, and all the wealth of the king would be mine. But, if one of these three conditions were lacking, I should not really be a king.

In similar fashion our salvation depends upon our knowing and recognizing the Chief Good which is God Himself. I have a capacity in my soul for taking in God entirely. I am as sure as I live that nothing is so near to me as God. God is nearer to me than I am to myself; my existence depends on the nearness and presence of God. He is also near things of wood and stone, but they know it not. If a piece of wood became as aware of the nearness of God as an archangel is, the piece of wood would be as happy as an archangel. For this reason man is happier than the inanimate wood, because he knows and understands how God is near him. His happiness increases and diminishes in proportion to the increase and diminution in his knowledge of this. His happiness does not arise from this that God is near him, and in him, and that He possesses God; but from this, that he knows the nearness of God, and loves Him, and is aware that "the Kingdom of God is near." So, when I think on God's Kingdom, I am compelled to be silent because of its immensity, because God's Kingdom is none other than God Himself with all His riches. God's Kingdom is no small thing: we may survey in imagination all the worlds of God's creation, but they are not God's Kingdom. In whichever soul God's Kingdom appeareth, and which knoweth God's Kingdom, that soul needeth no human preaching or instruction; it is taught from within and assured of eternal life. Whoever knows and recognizes how near God's Kingdom is to him may say with Jacob, "God is in this place, and I knew it not."

God is equally near in all creatures. The wise man saith, "God hath spread out His net over all creatures, so that whosoever wishes to discover Him may find and recognize Him in each one." Another saith, "He knows God rightly who recognizes Him alike in all things." To serve God with fear is good; to serve Him out of love is better; but to fear and love Him together is best of all. To have a restful or peaceful life in God is good; to bear a life of pain in patience is better; but to have peace in the midst of pain is the best of all.

A man may go into the field and say his prayer and be aware of God, or, he may be in Church and be aware of God; but, if he is more aware of Him because he is in a quiet place, that is his own deficiency and not due to God, Who is alike present in all things and places, and is willing to give Himself everywhere so far as lies in Him. He knows God rightly who knows Him everywhere. St Bernard saith, "How is it that mine eye and not my foot sees heaven? Because mine eye is more like heaven than my foot is. So, if my soul is to know God, it must be God-like."

Now, how is the soul to arrive at this heavenly state that it recognizes God in itself, and knows that He is near? By copying the heavens, which can receive no impulse from without to mar their tranquility. Thus must the soul, which would know God, be rooted and grounded in Him so steadfastly, as to suffer no perturbation of fear or hope, or joy or sorrow, or love or hate, or anything which may disturb its peace.

The heavens are everywhere alike remote from earth, so should the soul be remote from all earthly things alike so as not to be nearer to one than another. It should keep the same attitude of aloofness in love and hate, in possession and renouncement, that is, it should be simultaneously dead, resigned and lifted up. The heavens are pure and clear without shadow of stain, out of space and out of time. Nothing corporeal is found there. Their revolutions are incredibly swift and independent of time, though time depends on them. Nothing hinders the soul so much in attaining to the knowledge of God as time and place. Therefore, if the soul is to know God, it must know Him outside time and place, since God is neither in this or that, but One and above them. If the soul is to see God, it must look at nothing in time; for while the soul is occupied with time or place or any image of the kind, it cannot recognize God. If it is to know Him, it must have no fellowship with nothingness. Only he knows God who recognizes that all creatures are nothingness. For, if one creature be set over against another, it may appear to be beautiful and somewhat, but if it be set over against God, it is nothing. I say moreover: If the soul is to know God it must forget itself and lose itself, for as long as it contemplates self, it cannot contemplate God. When it has lost itself and everything in God, it finds itself again in God when it attains to the knowledge of Him, and it finds also everything which it had abandoned complete in God. If I am to know the highest good, and the everlasting Godhead, truly, I must know them as they are in themselves apart from creation. If I am to know real existence, I must know it as it is in itself, not as it is parceled out in creatures.

The whole Being of God is contained in God alone. The whole of humanity is not contained in one man, for one man is not all men. But in God the soul knows all humanity, and all things at their highest level of existence, since it knows them in their essence. Suppose any one to be in a beautifully adorned house: he would know much more about it than one who had never entered therein, and yet wished to speak much about it. Thus, I am as sure, as I am of my own existence and God's, that, if the soul is to know God, it must know Him outside of time and place. Such a soul will know clearly how near God's kingdom is.

Schoolmen have often asked how it is possible for the soul to know God. It is not from severity that God demands much from men in order to obtain the knowledge of Himself: it is of His kindness that He wills the soul by effort to grow capacious of receiving much, and that He may give much. Let no man think that to attain this knowledge is too difficult, although it may sound so, and indeed the commencement of it, and the renouncement of all things, is difficult.

But when one attains to it, no life is easier nor more pleasant nor more lovable, since God is always endeavouring to dwell with man, and teach him in order to bring him to Himself. No man desires anything so eagerly as God desires to bring men to the knowledge of Himself. God is always ready, but we are very unready. God is near us, but we are far from Him. God is within, and we are without. God is friendly; we are estranged. The prophet saith, "God leadeth the righteous by a narrow path into a broad and wide place, that is into the true freedom of those who have become one spirit with God." May God help us all to follow Him that He may bring us to Himself. Amen.

The Angel's Greeting

St. Luke i. 28. – "Hail, thou that art highly favoured among women, the Lord is with thee."

Here there are three things to understand: the first, the modesty of the angel; the second, that he thought himself unworthy to accost the Mother of God; the third, that he not only addressed her, but the great multitude of souls who long after God.

I affirm that had the Virgin not first borne God spiritually He would never have been born from her in bodily fashion. A certain woman said to Christ, "Blessed is the womb that bear Thee." To which Christ answered, "Nay, rather blessed are they that hear the Word of God and keep it." It is more worthy of God that He be born spiritually of every pure and virgin soul, than that He be born of Mary. Hereby we should understand that humanity is, so to speak, the Son of God born from all eternity. The Father produced all creatures, and me among them, and I issued forth from Him with all creatures, and yet I abide in the Father. Just as the word which I now speak is conceived and spoken forth by me, and you all receive it, yet none the less it abides in me. Thus I and all creatures abide in the Father.

Hereto I adjoin a parable. There were a certain man and wife; the woman by accident lost an eye, and was sorely troubled thereat. Her husband then said to her, "Wife, why are you troubled? "She answered, "It is not the loss of my eye that troubles me, but the thought that you may love me less on account of that loss." He said, "I love you all the same." Not long after he put one of his own eyes out, and came to his wife and said, "Wife, that you may believe I love you, I have made myself like you: I, too, now, have only one eye." So men could hardly believe that God loved them till God put one of His eyes out, that is took upon Himself human nature, and was made man. Just as fire infuses its essence and clearness into the dry wood, so has God done with man. He has created the human soul and infused His glory into it, and yet in His own essence has remained unchangeable. If you ask me whether, seeing that my spiritual birth is out of time, whether I am an eternal son, I answer "Yes," and "No." In the everlasting foreknowledge of God, I slumbered like a word unspoken. He hath brought me forth His son in the image of His eternal fatherhood, that I also should be a father and bring forth Him. It is as if one stood before a high mountain, and cried, "Art thou there?" The echo comes back, "Art thou there?" If one cries, "Come out." the echo answers, "Come out."

Again: If I am in a higher place and say to some one, "Come up hither," that might be difficult for him. But if I say, "Sit down," that would be easy. Thus God dealeth with us. When man humbles himself, God cannot restrain His mercy; He must come down and pour His grace into the humble man, and He gives Himself most of all, and all at once, to the least of all. It is essential to God to give, for His essence is His goodness and His goodness is His love. Love is the root of all joy and sorrow. Slavish fear of God is to be put away. The right fear is the fear of losing God. If the earth flee downward from heaven, it finds heaven beneath it; if it flee upward, it comes again to heaven. The earth cannot flee from heaven: whether it flee up or down, the heaven rains its influence upon it, and stamps its impress upon it, and makes it fruitful, whether it be willing or not. Thus doth God with men: whoever thinketh to escape Him, flies into His bosom, for every corner is open to Him. God brings forth His Son in thee, whether thou likest it or not, whether thou sleepest or wakest; God worketh His own will. That man is unaware of it, is man's fault, for his taste is so spoilt by feeding on earthly things that he cannot relish God's love. If we had love to God, we should relish God, and all His works; we should receive all things from God, and work the same works as He worketh.

God created the soul after the image of His highest perfection. He issued forth from the treasure-house of the everlasting Fatherhood in which He had rested from all eternity. Then the Son opened the tent of His everlasting glory and came forth from His high place to fetch His Bride, whom the Father had espoused to Him from all Eternity, back to that heaven from which she came. Therefore He came forth rejoicing as a bridegroom and suffered the pangs of love. Then He returned to His secret chamber in the silence and stillness of the everlasting Fatherhood. As He came forth from the Highest, so He returned to the Highest with His Bride, and revealed to her the hidden treasures of His Godhead.

The first beginning is for the sake of the last end. God Himself doth not rest because He is the beginning, but because He is the end and goal of all creation. This end is concealed in the darkness of the everlasting Godhead, and is unknown, and never was known, and never will be known. God Himself remains unknown; the light of the everlasting Father shineth in darkness, and the darkness comprehended it not. May the truth of which we have spoken lead us to the truth. Amen.

True Hearing
Ecclesiasticus xxiv. 30. – "Whoso heareth Me shall not be confounded."
The everlasting and paternal wisdom saith, "Whoso heareth Me is not ashamed." If he is ashamed of anything he is ashamed of being ashamed. Whoso worketh in Me sineth not. Whoso confesseth Me and feareth Me, shall have eternal life. Whoso will hear the wisdom of the Father must dwell deep, and abide at home, and be at unity with himself. Three things hinder us from hearing the everlasting Word. The first is fleshliness, the second is distraction, the third is the illusion of time. If a man could get free of these, he would dwell in eternity, and in the spirit, and in solitude, and in the desert, and there would hear the everlasting Word. Our Lord saith, "No man can hear My word nor my teaching without renouncing himself." All that the Eternal Father teaches and reveals is His being, His nature, and His Godhead, which He manifests to us in His Son, and teaches us that we are also His Son.

All that God worketh and teacheth, He worketh in His Son. All His work is directed to this end that we also may be His Son. When God sees that we are indeed His son, He yearns after us, and in the depth of His Divine Being waves of longing break forth, to reveal to us the abyss of His Godhead, and the fullness of His essence; He hastens to identify Himself with us. Herein He hath joy and gladness in full measure. God loveth men not less than He loveth Himself. If thou really lovest thyself, thou lovest all men as thyself; as long as thou lovest any one less than thyself, thou dost not really love thyself. That man is right who loves all men as himself.

Some folk say: "I love my friends, who do me kindness, more than other people." Such love is imperfect and incomplete; it is like having your sails only half-filled with wind. When I love anyone as much as myself, I would just as soon that joy or sorrow, death or life were mine, as well as his. That would be the dictate of right reason.

St Paul felt such love when he said, "I would that I were cut off from God for my friends' sake." Now to be cut off from God is equivalent to suffering the pains of hell. Some ask whether St Paul was on the way to perfection or was perfect. I answer, he was perfect, or he would have spoken otherwise.

I wish further to elucidate this saying of St Paul that he was willing to be cut off from God. The highest act of renunciation for man is for God's sake to give up God, and that is what St Paul was willing to do; to give up all the blessings that he might receive from God. When for God's sake he gave up God, God still remained with him, since God's essence is Himself, not any impression or reception of Himself. He who does so is a true man to whom no grief may happen, any more than it happens to the Divine Being. There is a somewhat in the soul that is, as it were, a blood-relative of God. It is one, it has nothing in common with nothing, nor is it like nothingness, nothing. All that is created is nothing, all far from and foreign to the soul. Could I but find myself one instant in that sphere of pure existence, I should regard myself as little as a worm.

A question arises regarding the angels who dwell with us, serve us and protect us, whether their joys are equal to those of the angels in heaven, or whether they are diminished by the fact that they protect and serve us. No, they are certainly not; for the work of the angels is the will of God, and the will of God is the work of the angels; their service to us does not hinder their joy nor their working. If God told an angel to go to a tree and pluck caterpillars off it, the angel would be quite ready to do so, and it would be his happiness, if it were the will of God.

The man who abides in the will of God wills nothing else than what God is, and what He wills. If he were ill he would not wish to be well. If he really abides in God's will, all pain is to him a joy, all complication, simple: yea, even the pains of hell would be a joy to him. He is free and gone out from himself, and from all that he receives, he must be free. If my eye is to discern colour, it must itself be free from all colour. The eye with which I see God is the same with which God sees me. My eye and God's eye is one eye, and one sight, and one knowledge, and one love.

The man who abides in God's love must be dead to himself and all created things, and regard himself as a mere unit among a thousand million. Such a man must renounce himself and all the world. Supposing a man possessed all the world, and gave it back to God intact just as he received it, God would give him back, all the world and everlasting life to boot. And supposing there were another man who had nothing but a good will, and he thought in his heart, "Lord, were all this world mine, and two worlds more beside it, I would give them and myself also back to Thee as I received them from thee"; to that man God would give back as much as he had given away. And supposing a man had renounced himself for twenty years, if he took himself back for a moment, that man's renunciation would be as nothing. The man who has truly renounced himself and does not once cast a glance on what he has renounced, and thus remains immovable and unalterable, that man alone has really renounced self. May God and the Eternal Wisdom grant us to remain equally immovable and unalterable with Himself. Amen

The Self-Communication of God

St John xiv. 23. – "If a man love me, he will keep my words; and my Father will love him, and we will come unto him, and make our abode with him."

We read in the Gospels that Our Lord fed many people with five loaves and two fishes. Speaking parabolically, we may say that the first loaf was— that we should know ourselves, what we have been everlastingly to God, and what we now are to Him. The second— that we should pity our fellow Christian who is blinded; his loss should grieve us as much as our own. The third— that we should know our Lord Jesus Christ's life, and follow it to the utmost of our capacity. The fourth— that we should know the judgments of God. All that may be said of the pains of hell is true. St Dionysius saith, "To be separated from God is hell, and the sight of God's countenance is heaven." The fifth is— that we should know the Godhead which has flowed into the Father and filled Him with joy, and which has flowed into the Son and filled Him with wisdom, and the Two are essentially one. Therefore said Christ, "Where I am, there is My Father, and where My Father is, there am I" And They have flowed into the Holy

Ghost and filled Him with good will. Therefore said Christ, "I and My Father have one Spirit," and the Holy Ghost has flowed into the soul.

The soul has by nature two capacities. The one is intelligence, which may comprehend the Holy Trinity with all its works and be contained by It as water is by a vessel. When the vessel is full, it has enclosed all that is contained in it, and is united with that which it has enclosed, and of which it is full. Thus intelligence becomes one with that which it has understood and comprehended. It is united therewith by grace, as the Son is one with the Father.

The second capacity is Will. That is a nobler one, and its essential characteristic is to plunge into the Unknown which is God. There the Will lays hold of God in a mysterious manner, and the Unknown God imparts His impress to the Will. The Will draws thought and all the powers of the soul after it in its train, so that the soul becomes one with God by grace, as the Holy Ghost is one with the Father and with the Son by nature. In God it is more worthy to be loved, than it is in itself. Therefore St Augustine saith that the soul is greater by its love-giving power than by its life-giving power. If man might only abide in this union, and do all the works which have ever been done by creatures, he would be no other than God, if his higher powers so brought his lower powers under control, that he could only work God-like works. That however may not be, and man's highest faculty therefore contemplates God as best it can, and so influences his lower faculties that they can discern between Good and Evil.

Adam possessed that union with God which we have spoken of, and while he had it, his capacity contained the capacities of all creatures. The load-stone attracts the needle, and the needle receives the magnetic power, so that it can also attract other needles and draw them to the load-stone. But if one draws the first needle away, all the other needles come with it. Thus was it with Adam: when, in his highest capacity, he was separated from God all his capacities deteriorated. Thence came also discord and the clashing of oppugnant wills among the lower creation, and deterioration of their powers down to the lowest. It is necessary, therefore, for all the creatures which issued forth from God to co-operate earnestly with all their powers to form a Man who may again attain that union with God which Adam enjoyed before he fell, and who may again restore to the creatures their forfeited powers. This is fulfilled in Christ as He Himself said, "I, if I be lifted up, will draw all men unto Me." He means, if He is exalted in our knowledge, He will draw us unto

Himself. In Him human nature grew divine, and thanked God and loved Him with immeasurable love. This also befits God that he loves human nature with so great love. I counsel you, sisters and brothers, that you grow in knowledge, and thank God, while you are in time, that He brought you out of non-existence to existence, and united you with the Divine Nature. But if the Divine Nature be beyond your comprehension, believe simply on Christ;Â follow His holy example and remain steadfast. Convert Jews, heathen, heretics, bad Christians, and all who do not enjoy your knowledge of God, and are still astray.

Now rejoice, all ye powers of my soul, that you are so united with God that no one may separate you from Him. I cannot fully praise nor love Him therefore must I die, and cast myself into the divine void, till I rise from non-existence to existence. If I should remain entombed in flesh till the judgment day and suffer the pains of hell, that would be for me a small thing to bear for my beloved Lord Jesus Christ, if I had the certainty at last of not being separated from Him. While I am here, He is in me; after this life, I am in Him. All things are therefore possible to me, if I am united to Him Who can do all things. Previously I could not distinguish whether we were divine by nature or by grace. Then came Jesus and enlightened me so that I recognized in the Divine Nature Three Persons, and that the Father was the Bringer-Forth of all things, as St James says, "every perfect gift cometh down from the Father of lights."

The Father and the Son have one Will, and that Will is the Holy Ghost, Who gives Himself to the soul so that the Divine Nature permeates the powers of the soul so that it can only do God-like works. Just as a spring, which perpetually flows and waters the roots of the flowers, so that the flowers bloom and receive their colours from the water of the spring, so the Godhead imparts Itself to the capacities of the soul that it may grow in the likeness of God. The more that the soul receives of the Divine Nature, the more it grows like It, and the closer becomes its union with God. It may arrive at such an intimate union that God at last draws it to Himself altogether, so that there is no distinction left, in the soul's consciousness, between itself and God, though God still regards it as a creature. Wherefore let yourselves not be misled by the light of nature. The higher the degree of knowledge which the soul attains to in the light of grace, the darker seems to it the light of nature. If the soul would know the real truth it must examine itself, whether it has withdrawn from all things, whether it has lost itself, whether it loves God purely with His love and nothing of its own at the same time, so that it may not be separated from Him by anything, and whether God alone dwells in it. If it has lost itself, it is as when the Virgin Mary lost Christ. She sought Him for three days, and yet was sure that she would find Him. All the while Christ was in the highest class in the school of His Father, unconscious of His mother's seeking Him. Thus happens it to the noble soul which goes to God to school, and learns there what God is in His essence, and what He is in the Trinity, and what He is in man, and what is most acceptable to Him. St Augustine saith that the righteousness of God in the Godhead and in the Trinity and in all creatures is the source of the chief joy which is in heaven. God in human nature is a lamp of living light, and "the light shineth in darkness and the darkness comprehendeth it not." The darkness must ever more flee the light, as the night flees day. Thus the soul learns to know God's will. St Paul saith, "This is God's will, our sanctification." And this is our sanctification, to know what we were before time; what we are in time, and what we shall be after time. Thus the soul loses itself in these three, and recketh naught of the body, till it comes to it in the temple, and obeys it without murmuring. The Father is a revelation of the Godhead, the Son is an image and countenance of the Father, and the Holy Ghost is an effulgence of that countenance, and a mutual love between Them, and these properties They have always possessed in Themselves. The Three Persons have stooped out of pity down to human nature, and the Son became man, and was the most despised man on the earth, and suffered pain at the hands of the creatures whom He Himself created with the Father, through Whose will He became man. Thus was Christ till His death, and when He rose from the dead then was seen the most despised of all men united with the Godhead in the Person of Christ.

Sanctification
St Luke x. 42. – "One thing is needful."
I have read many writings both of heathen philosophers and inspired prophets, ancient and modern, and have sought earnestly to discover what is the best and highest quality whereby man may approach most nearly to union with God, and whereby he may most resemble the ideal of himself which existed in God, before God created men. And after having thoroughly searched these writings as far as my reason may penetrate, I find no higher quality than sanctification or separation from all creatures. Therefore said our Lord

to Martha, "One thing is necessary," as if to say, "whoso wishes to be untroubled and content, must have one thing, that is sanctification."

Various teachers have praised love greatly, as St Paul does, when he saith, "to whatever height I may attain, if I have not love, I am nothing." But I set sanctification even above love; in the first place because the best thing in love is that it compels me to love God. Now it is a greater thing that I compel God to come to me, than that I compel myself to go to God. Sanctification compels God to come to me, and I prove this as follows:

Everything settles in its own appropriate place; now God's proper place is that of oneness and holiness; these come from sanctification; therefore God must of necessity give Himself to a sanctified heart.

In the second place I set sanctification above love, because love compels me to suffer all things for the sake of God; sanctification compels me to be the recipient of nothing but God; now, it is a higher state to be the recipient of nothing but God than to suffer all things for God, because in suffering one must have some regard to the person who inflicts the suffering, but sanctification is independent of all creatures.

Many teachers also praise humility as a virtue. But I set sanctification above humility for the following reason. Although humility may exist without sanctification, perfect sanctification cannot exist without perfect humility. Perfect humility tends to the annihilation of self; sanctification also is so close to self-annihilation that nothing can come between them. Therefore perfect sanctification cannot exist without humility, and to have both of these virtues is better than to have only one of them.

The second reason why I set sanctification above humility is that humility stoops to be under all creatures, and in doing so goes out of itself. But sanctification remains self-contained. But to remain contained within oneself is nobler than to go out of oneself for any purpose whatever; therefore saith the Psalmist, "The King's daughter is all glorious within," that is, all her glory is from her inwardness. Perfect sanctification has no inclination nor going-out towards any creature; it wishes neither to be above or below, neither to be like nor unlike any creature, but only to be one. Whosoever wishes to be this or that wishes to be somewhat; but sanctification wishes to be nothing.

But some one may say: "All virtues must have existed in fullness in Our Lady, therefore perfect sanctification must have been in her. If sanctification is higher than humility, why did Our Lady speak of her humility, and not of her sanctification, when she said, "For He hath regarded the lowliness of His handmaiden?" To this I answer that God possesses both sanctification and humility, so far as we may attribute virtues to God. Now thou shouldest know that His humility brought God to stoop down to human nature, and our Lady knew that He wished for the same quality in her, and in that matter had regard to her humility alone. Therefore she made mention of her humility and not of her sanctification, in which she remained unmoved and unaffected. If she had said, "He hath regarded the sanctification of His handmaiden," her sanctification would have been disturbed, for, so to speak, would have been a going out of herself. Therefore the Psalmist said, "I will hear what the Lord God will say in me," as if to say, "If God will Speak to me, let Him come in, for I will not come out." And Boethius saith, "Men, why seek ye outside you what is inside you— salvation?"

I set also sanctification above pity, for pity is only going out of oneself to sympathize with one's fellow-creature's sorrows. From such an out-going sanctification is free and abides in itself, and does not let itself be troubled. To speak briefly: when I consider all the virtues I find none so entirely without flaw and so conducive to union with God as sanctification.

The philosopher Avicenna says, "The spirit which is truly sanctified attains to so lofty a degree that all which it sees is real, all which it desires is granted, and in all which it commands, it is obeyed." When the free spirit is stablished in true sanctification, it draws God to itself, and were it placed beyond the reach of contingencies, it would assume the properties of God. But God cannot part with those to anyone; all that He can do for the sanctified spirit is to impart Himself to it. The man who is wholly sanctified is so drawn towards the Eternal, that no transitory thing may move him, no corporeal thing affect him, no earthly thing attract him. This was the meaning of St Paul when he said, "I live; yet not I; Christ liveth in me."

Now the question arises what is sanctification, since it has so lofty a rank. Thou shouldest know that real sanctification consists in this that the spirit remain as immovable and unaffected by all impact of love or hate, joy or sorrow, honour or shame, as a huge mountain is unstirred by a gentle breeze. This immovable sanctification causes man to attain the nearest likeness to God that he is capable of. God's very essence consists of His immovable sanctity; thence springs His glory and unity and impassibility. If a man is to become as like God as a creature may, that must be by sanctification. It is this which draws men upward to glory, and from glory to unity, and from unity to impassibility, and effects a resemblance between God and men. The chief agent in this is grace, because grace draws men from the transitory and purifies them from the earthly. And thou shouldest know that to be empty of all creature's love is to be full of God, and to be full of creature-love is to be empty of God.

God has remained from everlasting in immovable sanctity, and still remains so. When He created heaven and earth and all creatures, His sanctity was as little affected thereby as though He had created nothing. I say further: God's sanctity is as little affected by men's good works and prayers, as though they had accomplished none, and He is by those means no more favourably inclined towards men than if they ceased praying and working. I say even more: when the Divine Son became man and suffered that affected the sanctity of God as little as though He had never become man at all.

Here some one may make the objection: "Are then all good works and prayers thrown away, since God is unmoved by them, and at the same time we are told to pray to Him for everything?" In answer to this I say that God from all eternity saw everything that would happen, and also when, and how He would make all creatures: He foresaw also all the prayers which would be offered, and which of them He would hear: He saw the earnest prayers which thou wilt offer tomorrow, but He will not listen to them tomorrow, because He heard them in eternity, before thou wast a man at all. If, however, thy prayer is half-hearted and not in earnest, God will not deny it now, seeing that He has denied it in eternity. Thus God remains always in His immovable sanctity, but sincere prayer and good works are not lost, for whoso doeth well, will be well rewarded.

When God appears to be angry or to do us a kindness, it is we who are altered, while He remains unchangeable, as the same sunshine is injurious to weak eyes and beneficial to strong ones, remaining in itself the same. Regarding this Isidorus in his book concerning the highest good says, "People ask what was God doing before He created heaven and earth, or whence came the new desire in God to create?" To this he answers, "No new desire arose in God, seeing that creation was everlastingly present in Him, and in His intelligence." Moses said to God, "When Pharaoh asks me who Thou art, what shall I answer?" God said, "Say, I AM hath sent me unto you," that is to say, "He Who is unchangeable hath sent me."

Perhaps some one may ask, "Was Christ then also unchangeable, when He said, 'My soul is troubled even unto death,' or Mary when she stood under the Cross and lamented?" Here, thou shouldest know that in every man are two kinds of men, the outer and the inner man. Every man, who loves God, only uses his outer senses so far as is absolutely necessary; he takes care that they do not drag him down to the level of the beasts, as they do some who might rather he termed beasts than men. The soul of the spiritual man whom God moves to love Him with all his powers concentrates all its forces on the inner man. Therefore He saith, "Thou shalt love the Lord thy God with all thy heart." Now, there are some who waste the powers of the soul for the use of the outer man; these are they who turn all their thoughts and desires towards transitory things, and know nothing of the inner life. But a good man sometimes deprives his outer man of all power that it may have a higher object, while sensualists deprive the inner man of all power to use it for the outer man.

The outer man may go through various experiences, while the inner man is quite free and immovable. Now both in Christ and in Our Lady there was an inner and an outer man; when they spoke of outward things, they did so with the outward man, while the inner man remained immovable.

It may be asked: "What is the object of this immovable sanctity?" I answer, "Nothing": that is, so far as God has His way with a man, for He has not His way with all men.

Although God is Almighty, He can only work in a heart when He finds readiness or makes it. He works differently in men than in stones. For this we may take the following illustration: if we bake in one oven three loaves of barley-bread, of rye-bread, and of wheat, we shall find the same heat of the oven affects them differently; when one is well-baked, another will be still raw, and another yet more raw. That is not due to the heat, but to the variety of the materials. Similarly God works in all hearts not alike but in proportion as He finds them prepared and susceptible. If the heart is to be ready for the highest, it must he vacant of all other things. If I wish to write on a white tablet, whatever else is written on the tablet, however noble its purport, is a hindrance to me. If I am to write, I must wipe the tablet clean of everything, and the tablet is most suitable for my purpose when it is blank. Similarly, if God is to write on my heart, everything else must come out of it till it is really sanctified. Only so can God work His highest will, and so the sanctified heart has no outward object at all.

The question arises: But what then does the sanctified heart pray for? I answer that when truly sanctified, it prays for nothing, for whosoever prays asks God to give him some good, or to take some evil from him. But the sanctified heart desires nothing, and contains nothing that it wishes to be freed from. Therefore it is free of all want except that it wants to be like God. St Dionysius commenting on the text, "Know ye not that all run, but one receiveth the prize?" says "this running is nothing else than a turning away from all creatures and being united to the Uncreated." When the soul gets to this point, it loses its own distinctiveness, and vanishes in God as the crimson of sunrise disappears in the sun. To this goal only pure sanctification can arrive.

St Augustine says. "the strong attraction of the soul to the Divine reduces everything to nothingness: on earth this attraction is manifested as sanctification. When this process has reached its culminating point, knowledge becomes ignorance, desire indifference and light darkness. The reason why God desires a sanctified heart more than any other is apparent when we ask the question, "What does God seek in all things?" The mouth of Wisdom says to us, "In all things I seek rest," and rest is to be found only in the sanctified heart; therein therefore God is more glad to dwell than in any other thing.

Thou shouldest also know that the more a man sets himself to be receptive of divine influence, the happier he is: who most sets himself so, is the happiest. Now no man can reach this condition of receptivity except by conformity with God, which comes from submission to God. This is what Saint Paul means when he says, "Put on the Lord Jesus Christ," that is "be conformed to Christ." Whosoever wishes to comprehend the lofty rank and benefit of sanctification must mark Christ's words to His disciples regarding His humanity, "It is profitable for you, that I go away, for, if I go not away, the Comforter will not come to you." As if to say, "Ye have so much desire towards my natural outward form, that ye cannot fully desire the Holy Spirit." Therefore put away forms and unite yourselves with formless Being, for God's spiritual comfort is only offered to those who despise earthly comfort.

Now, all thoughtful folk, mark me! no one can be truly happy, except he who abides in the strictest sanctification. No bodily and fleshly delight can ever take place with out spiritual loss, for the flesh lusteth against the spirit, and the spirit against the flesh. Therefore, the more a man fleeth from the created, the more the Creator hastens to him. And consider this: if the pleasure we take in the outward image of our Lord Jesus Christ diminishes our capacity for receiving the Holy Spirit, how much more must our unbridled desire for earthly comforts diminish it!

Therefore sanctification is the best of all things, for it cleanses the soul, and illuminates the conscience, and kindles the heart, and wakens the spirit, and girds up the loins, and glorifies virtue and separates us from creatures, and unites us with God. The quickest means to bring us to perfection is suffering; none enjoy everlasting blessedness more than those who share with Christ the bitterest pangs. Nothing is sharper than suffering, nothing is sweeter than to have suffered. The surest foundation in which this perfection may rest is humility; whatever here crawls in the deepest abjectness, that the Spirit lifts to the very heights of God, for love brings suffering and suffering brings love. Ways of living are many; one lives thus, and another thus; but whosoever will reach the highest life, let him in a few words hear the conclusion of the whole matter: keep thyself clear of all men, keep thyself from all imaginations that crowd upon the mind, free thyself from all that is contingent, entangling, and cumbersome and direct thy mind always to gazing upon God in thy heart with a steadfast look that never wavers: as for other spiritual exercises — fasting, watching and prayer — direct them all to this one end, and practice them so far as they may be helpful thereto, so wilt thou win to perfection. Here some one may ask, "Who can thus gaze always without wavering at a divine object?" I answer: "No one who now lives." This has only been said to thee that thou mightest know what the highest is, and that thou mightest have desires after it. But when thou losest sight of the Divine, thou shouldest feel as if bereft of thine eternal salvation, and shouldest long to recover it, and watch over thyself at all times, and direct thy aims and longing towards it. May God be blessed for ever. Amen.

Outward and Inward Morality
I Cor. xv. 10. — "The Grace of God."
Grace is from God, and works in the depth of the soul whose powers it employs. It is a light which issues forth to do service under the guidance of the Spirit. The Divine Light permeates the soul, and

lifts it above the turmoil of temporal things to rest in God. The soul cannot progress except with the light which God has given it as a nuptial gift; love works the likeness of God into the soul. The peace, freedom and blessedness of all souls consist in their abiding in God's will. Towards this union with God for which it is created the soul strives perpetually. Fire converts wood into its own likeness, and the stronger the wind blows, the greater grows the fire. Now by the fire understand love, and by the wind the Holy Spirit. The stronger the influence of the Holy Spirit, the brighter grows the fire of love; but not all at once, rather gradually as the soul grows. Light causes flowers and plants to grow and bear fruit; in animals it produces life, but in men blessedness. This comes from the grace of God, Who uplifts the soul, for if the soul is to grow God-like it must be lifted above itself.

To produce real moral freedom, God's grace and man's will must co-operate. As God is the Prime Mover of nature, so also He creates free impulses towards Himself and to all good things. Grace renders the will free that it may do everything with God's help, working with grace as with an instrument which belongs to it. So the will arrives at freedom through love, nay, becomes itself love, for love unites with God. All true morality, inward and outward, is comprehended in love, for love is the foundation of all the commandments.

All outward morality must be built upon this basis, not on self-interest. As long as man loves something else than God, or outside God, he is not free, because he has not love. Therefore there is no inner freedom which does not manifest itself in works of love. True freedom is the government of nature in and outside man through God; freedom is essential existence unaffected by creatures. But love often begins with fear; fear is the approach to love: fear is like the awl which draws the shoemaker's thread through the leather.

As for outward works they are ordained for this purpose that the outward man may be directed to God. But the inner work, the work of God in the soul is the chief matter; when a man finds this within himself, he can let go externals. No law is given to the righteous, because he fulfils the law inwardly, and bears it in himself, for the least thing done by God is better than all the work of creatures. But this is intended for those who are enlightened by God and the Holy Scriptures.

But here on earth man never attains to being unaffected by external things. There never was a Saint so great as to be immovable. I can never arrive at a state when discord shall be as pleasing to my ears as harmony. Some people wish to do without good works. I say, "This cannot be." As soon as the disciples received the Holy Ghost, they began to work. When Mary sat at the feet of our Lord that was her school time. But afterwards when Christ went to heaven, and she received the Holy Spirit, she began to serve and was a handmaid of the disciples. When saints become saints, they begin to work, and so gather to the refuge of everlasting safety.

How can a man abide in love, when he does not keep God's commands which issue forth from love? How can the inner man be born in God, when the outer man abides not in the following of Christ, in self-mortification and in suffering, for there is no being born of God, except through Christ. Love is the fulfilling of all commands; therefore however much man strives to reach this freedom, the body can never quite attain thereto, and must be ever in conflict. Seeing that good works are the witness of the Holy Ghost, man can never do without them. The aim of man is not outward holiness by works, but life in God, yet this last expresses itself in works of love.

Outward as well as inward morality helps to form the idea of true Christian freedom. We are right to lay stress on inwardness, but in this world there is no inwardness without an outward expression. If we regard the soul as the formative principle of the body, and God as the formative principle of the soul, we have a profounder principle of ethics than is found in Pantheism. The fundamental thought of this system is the real distinction between God and the world, together with their real inseparability, for only really distinct elements can interpenetrate each other.

The inner work is first of all the work of God's grace in the depth of the soul which subsequently distributes itself among the faculties of the soul, in that of Reason appearing as Belief, in that of Will as Love, and in that of Desire as Hope. When the Divine Light penetrates the soul, it is united with God as light with light. This is the light of faith. Faith bears the soul to heights unreachable by her natural senses and faculties.

As the peculiar faculty of the eye is to see form and colour, and of the ear to hear sweet tones and voices, so is aspiration peculiar to the soul. To relax from ceaseless aspiration is sin. This energy of aspiration directed to and grasping God, as far as is possible for the creature, is called Hope, which is also a divine virtue. Through this faculty the soul acquires such great confidence that she deems nothing in the Divine Nature beyond her reach.

The third faculty is the inward Will, which, always turned to God like a face, absorbs to itself love from God. According to the diversee directions in which redemptive Grace through the Holy Spirit is imparted to the different faculties of men, it finds corresponding expression as one of the Spirit's seven gifts. This impartation constitutes man's spiritual birth which brings him out of sin into a state of grace while natural birth makes him a sinner.

As God can only be seen by His own light, so He can only be loved by His own love. The merely natural man is incapable of this, because nature by itself is incapable of responding to the Divine Love and is confined within its own circle. Therefore it is necessary for Grace, which is a simple supernatural power, to elevate the natural faculties to union in God above the merely temporal objects of existence. The possibility of love to God is grounded in the relative likeness between man and God. If the soul is to reach its moral goal, i.e. Godlikeness, it must become inwardly like God through grace, and a spiritual birth which is the spring of true morality. The inner work that man has to do is the practical realization of Grace: without this, all outward work is ineffectual for salvation. Virtue is never mere virtue, it is either from God, or through God, or in God. All the soul's works which are to inherit an everlasting recompense must be carried on in God. They are rewarded by Him in proportion as they are carried on in Him, for the soul is an instrument of God whereby He carries on His work.

The essence of morality is inwardness, the intensity of will from which it springs, and the nobleness of the aim for which it is practiced. When a good work is done by a man, he is free of it, and through that freedom is liker and nearer to his Original than he was before.

The moral task of man is a process of spiritualization. All creatures are go-betweens, and we are placed in time that by diligence in spiritual business we may grow liker and nearer to God. The aim of man is beyond the temporal — in the serene region of the everlasting Present.

In this sense the New Birth of man is the focus towards which all creation strives, because man is the image of God after the likeness of which the world is created. All time strives towards eternity or the timeless Now, out of which it issued at creation. The merely temporal life in itself is a negation of real being, because it depends on itself and not on the deepest foundation of life; therefore also natural love is cramped finite and defective. It must through grace be lifted to the highest sphere of existence, and attain to freedom outside the narrow confines of the natural. Thereby love becomes real love, because only that is real which is comprehended and loved in its essence. Only by grace man comes from the temporal and transitory to be one with God. This lifting of manifoldness to unity is the supreme aim of ethics; by thus the divine birth is completed on the side of man.

This passage from nothingness to real being, this quitting of oneself is a birth accompanied by pain, for by it natural love is excluded. All grief except grief for sin comes from love of the world. In God is neither sorrow, nor grief, nor trouble. Wouldst thou be free from all grief and trouble, abide and walk in God, and to God alone. As long as love of the creature is in us, pain cannot cease.

This is the chief significance of the suffering of Christ for us, that we cast all our grief into the ocean of His suffering. If thou sufferest only regarding thyself, from whatever cause it may be, that suffering causes grief to thee, and is hard to bear. But if thou sufferest regarding God and Him alone, that suffering is not grievous, nor hard to bear, because God bears the load. The love of the Cross must swallow up our personal grief. Whoso does not suffer from love, for him sorrow is sorrow and grievous to bear; but whoso suffers from love he sorrows not, and his suffering is fruitful in God. Therefore is sorrow so noble; he who sorrows most is the noblest. Now no mortal's sorrow was like the sorrow which Christ bore; therefore he is far nobler than any man. Verily were there anything nobler than sorrow, God would have redeemed man thereby. Sorrow is the root of all virtue.

Through the higher love the whole life of man is to be elevated from temporal selfishness to the spring of all love, to God: man will again be master over nature by abiding in God and lifting her up to God.

The Cloud of Unknowing

Here beginneth a book of contemplation, the which is called the Cloud of Unknowing, in the which a soul is oned with God.

Here Beginneth the Prayer on the Prologue

God, unto whom all hearts be open, and unto whom all will speaketh, and unto whom no privy thing is hid. I beseech Thee so for to cleanse the intent of mine heart with the unspeakable gift of Thy grace, that I may perfectly love Thee, and worthily praise Thee. Amen.

Here Beginneth the Prologue

In the name of the Father and of the Son and of the Holy Ghost! I charge thee and I beseech thee, with as much power and virtue as the bond of charity is sufficient to suffer, whatsoever thou be that this book shalt have in possession, either by property, either by keeping, by bearing as messenger, or else by borrowing, that in as much as in thee is by will and advisement, neither thou read it, nor write it, nor speak it, nor yet suffer it be read, written, or spoken, of any or to any but if it be of such one, or to such one, that hath by thy supposing in a true will and by an whole intent purposed him to be a perfect follower of Christ not only in active living, but in the sovereignest point of contemplative living the which is possible by grace for to be come to in this present life of a perfect soul yet abiding in this deadly body; and thereto that doth that in him is, and by thy supposing hath done long time before, for to able him to contemplative living by the virtuous means of active living. For else it accordeth nothing to him. And over this I charge thee and I beseech thee by the authority of charity, that if any such shall read it, write it, or speak it, or else hear it be read or spoken, that thou charge him as I do thee, for to take him time to read it, speak it, write it, or hear it, all over. For peradventure there is some matter therein in the beginning or in the middle, the which is hanging, and not fully declared where it standeth: and if it be not there, it is soon after, or else in the end. Wherefore if a man saw one matter and not another, peradventure he might lightly be led into error; and therefore in eschewing of this error, both in thyself and in all other, I pray thee for charity do as I say thee.

Fleshly janglers, open praisers and blamers of themselves or of any other, tellers of trifles, ronners and tattlers of tales, and all manner of pinchers, cared I never that they saw this book. For mine intent was never to write such thing unto them, and therefore I would that they meddle not therewith; neither they, nor any of these curious, lettered, or unlearned men. Yea, although that they be full good men of active living, yet this matter accordeth nothing to them. But if it be to those men, the which although they stand in activity by outward form of living, nevertheless yet by inward stirring after the privy spirit of God, whose dooms be hid, they be full graciously disposed, not continually as it is proper to very contemplatives, but now and then to be perceivers in the highest point of this contemplative act; if such men might see it, they should by the grace of God be greatly comforted thereby.

This book is distinguished in seventy chapters and five. Of the which chapters, the last chapter of all teacheth some certain tokens by the which a soul may verily prove whether he be called of God to be a worker in this work or none.

Here Beginneth The First Chapter
Of four degrees of Christian men's living; and of the course of his calling that this book was made unto.

Ghostly friend in God, thou shalt well understand that I find, in my boisterous beholding, four degrees and forms of Christian men's living: and they be these, Common, Special, Singular, and Perfect.

Three of these may be begun and ended in this life; and the fourth may by grace be begun here, but it shall ever last without end in the bliss of Heaven. And right as thou seest how they be set here in order each one after other; first Common, then Special, after Singular, and last Perfect, right so me thinketh that in the same order and in the same course our Lord hath of His great mercy called thee and led thee unto Him by the desire of thine heart. For first thou wottest well that when thou wert living in the common degree of Christian men's living in company of thy worldly friends, it seemeth to me that the everlasting love of His Godhead, through the which He made thee and wrought thee when thou wert nought, and sithen bought thee with the price of His precious blood when thou wert lost in Adam, might not suffer thee to be so far from Him in form and degree of living. And therefore He kindled thy desire full graciously, and fastened by it a leash of longing, and led thee by it into a more special state and form of living, to be a servant among the special servants of His; where thou mightest learn to live more specially and more ghostly in His service than thou didst, or mightest do, in the common degree of living before. And what more?

Yet it seemeth that He would not leave thee thus lightly, for love of His heart, the which He hath evermore had unto thee since thou wert aught: but what did He? Seest thou nought how Mistily and how graciously He hath privily pulled thee to the third degree and manner of living, the which is called Singular? In the which solitary form and manner of living, thou mayest learn to lift up the foot of thy love; and step towards that state and degree of living that is perfect, and the last state of all.

Here Beginneth The Second Chapter
A short stirring to meekness, and to the work of this book.
Look up now, weak wretch, and see what thou art. What art thou, and what hast thou merited, thus to be called of our Lord? What weary wretched heart, and sleeping in sloth, is that, the which is not wakened with the draught of this love and the voice of this calling! Beware, thou wretch, in this while with thine enemy; and hold thee never the holier nor the better, for the worthiness of this calling and for the singular form of living that thou art in. But the more wretched and cursed, unless thou do that in thee is goodly, by grace and by counsel, to live after thy calling. And insomuch thou shouldest be more meek and loving to thy ghostly spouse, that He that is the

Almighty God, King of Kings and Lord of Lords, would meek Him so low unto thee, and amongst all the flock of His sheep so graciously would choose thee to be one of His specials, and sithen set thee in the place of pasture, where thou mayest be fed with the sweetness of His love, in earnest of thine heritage the Kingdom of Heaven.

Do on then, I pray thee, fast. Look now forwards and let be backwards; and see what thee faileth, and not what thou hast, for that is the readiest getting and keeping of meekness. All thy life now behoveth altogether to stand in desire, if thou shalt profit in degree of perfection. This desire behoveth altogether be wrought in thy will, by the hand of Almighty God and thy consent. But one thing I tell thee. He is a jealous lover and suffereth no fellowship, and Him list not work in thy will but if He be only with thee by Himself. He asketh none help, but only thyself. He wills, thou do but look on Him and let Him alone. And keep thou the windows and the door, for flies and enemies assailing. And if thou be willing to do this, thee needeth but meekly press upon him with prayer, and soon will He help thee. Press on then, let see how thou bearest thee. He is full ready, and doth but abideth thee. But what shalt thou do, and how shalt thou press?

Here Beginneth The Third Chapter
How the work of this book shall be wrought, and of the worthiness of it before all other works.

Lift up thine heart unto God with a meek stirring of love; and mean Himself, and none of His goods. And thereto, look the loath to think on aught but Himself. So that nought work in thy wit, nor in thy will, but only Himself. And do that in thee is to forget all the creatures that ever God made and the works of them; so that thy thought nor thy desire be not directed nor stretched to any of them, neither in general nor in special, but let them be, and take no heed to them. This is the work of the soul that most pleaseth God. All saints and angels have joy of this work, and hasten them to help it in all their might. All fiends be furious when thou thus dost, and try for to defeat it in all that they can. All men living in earth be wonderfully holpen of this work, thou wottest not how. Yea, the souls in purgatory be eased of their pain by virtue of this work. Thyself art cleansed and made virtuous by no work so much. And yet it is the lightest work of all, when a soul is helped with grace in sensible list, and soonest done. But else it is hard, and wonderful to thee for to do.

Let not, therefore, but travail therein till thou feel list. For at the first time when thou dost it, thou findest but a darkness; and as it were a cloud of unknowing, thou knowest not what, saving that thou feelest in thy will a naked intent unto God. This darkness and this cloud is, howsoever thou dost, betwixt thee and thy God, and letteth thee that thou mayest neither see Him clearly by light of understanding in thy reason, nor feel Him in sweetness of love in thine affection.

And therefore shape thee to bide in this darkness as long as thou mayest, evermore crying after Him that thou lovest. For if ever thou shalt feel Him or see Him, as it may be here, it behoveth always to be in this cloud in this darkness. And if thou wilt busily travail as I bid thee, I trust in His mercy that thou shalt come thereto.

Here Beginneth The Fourth Chapter
Of the shortness of this word, and how it may not be come to by curiosity of wit, nor by imagination.

But for this, that thou shalt not err in this working and ween that it be otherwise than it is, I shall tell thee a little more thereof, as me thinketh.

This work asketh no long time or it be once truly done, as some men ween; for it is the shortest work of all that man may imagine. It is never longer, nor shorter, than is an atom: the which atom, by the definition of true philosophers in the science of astronomy, is the least part of time. And it is so little that for the littleness of it, it is indivisible and nearly incomprehensible. This is that time of the which it is written: All time that is given to thee, it shall be asked of thee, how thou hast dispended it. And reasonable thing it is that thou give account of it: for it is neither longer nor shorter, but even according to one only stirring that is within the principal working might of thy soul, the which is thy will. For even so many willings or desirings, and no more nor no fewer, may be and are in one hour in thy will, as are atoms in one hour. And if thou wert reformed by grace to the first state of man's soul, as it was before sin, then thou shouldest evermore by help of that grace be lord of that stirring or of those stirrings. So that none went forby, but all they should stretch into the sovereign desirable, and into the highest willable thing: the which is God. For He is even meet to our soul by measuring of His Godhead; and our soul even meet unto Him by worthiness of our creation to His image and to His likeness. And He by Himself without more, and none but He, is sufficient to the full and much more to fulfil the will and the desire of our soul. And our soul by virtue of this reforming grace is made sufficient to the full to comprehend all Him by love, the which is incomprehensible to all created knowledgeable powers, as is angel, or man's soul; I mean, by their knowing, and not by their loving. And therefore I call them in this case knowledgeable powers. But yet all reasonable creatures, angel and man, have in them each one by himself, one principal working power, the which is called a knowledgeable power, and another principal working power, the which is called a loving power. Of the which two powers, to the first, the which is a knowledgeable power, God that is the maker of them is evermore incomprehensible; and to the second, the which is the loving power, in each one diverseely He is all comprehensible to the full. Insomuch that a loving soul alone in itself, by virtue of love should comprehend in itself Him that is sufficient to the full—and much more, without comparison—to fill all the souls and angels that ever may be. And this is the endless marvellous miracle of love; the working of which shall never take end, for ever shall He do it, and never shall He cease for to do it. See who by grace see may, for the feeling of this is endless bliss, and the contrary is endless pain.

And therefore whoso were reformed by grace thus to continue in keeping of the stirrings of his will, should never be in this life—as he may not be without these stirrings in nature—without some taste of the endless sweetness, and in the bliss of heaven without the full food. And therefore have no wonder though I stir thee to this work. For this is the work, as thou shalt hear afterward, in the which man should have continued if he never had sinned: and to the which working man was made, and all things for man, to help him and further him thereto, and by the which working a man shall be repaired again. And for the defailing of this working, a man falleth evermore deeper and deeper in sin, and further and further from God. And by keeping and continual working in this work only without more, a man evermore riseth higher and higher from sin, and nearer and nearer unto God.

And therefore take good heed unto time, how that thou dispendest it: for nothing is more precious than time. In one little time, as little as it is, may heaven be won and lost. A token it is that time is precious: for God, that is given of time, giveth never two times together, but each one after other. And this He doth, for He will not reverse the order or the ordinal course in the cause of His creation. For time is made for man, and not man for time. And therefore God, that is the ruler of nature, will not in His giving of time go before the stirring of nature in man's soul; the which is even according to one time only. So that man shall have none excusation against God in the Doom, and at the giving of account of dispending of time, saying, "Thou givest two times at once, and I have but one stirring at once."

But sorrowfully thou sayest now, "How shall I do? and sith this is thus that thou sayest, how shall I give account of each time severally; I that have unto this day, now of four and twenty years age, never took heed of time? If I would now amend it, thou wottest well, by very reason of thy words written before, it may not be after the course of nature, nor of common grace, that I should now heed or else make satisfaction, for any more times than for those that be for to come. Yea, and moreover well I wot by very proof, that of those that be to come I shall on no wise, for abundance of frailty and slowness of spirits, be able to observe one of an hundred. So that I am verily concluded in these reasons. Help me now for the love of Jesus!"

Right well hast thou said, for the love of Jesus. For in the love of Jesus; there shall be thine help. Love is such a power, that it maketh all thing common. Love therefore Jesus; and all thing that He hath, it is thine. He by His Godhead is maker and giver of time. He by His manhood is the very keeper of time. And He by His Godhead and His manhood together, is the truest Doomsman, and the asker of account of dispensing of time. Knit thee therefore to Him, by love and by belief, and then by virtue of that knot thou shalt be common perceiver with Him, and with all that by love so be knitted unto Him: that is to say, with our Lady Saint Mary that full was of all grace in keeping of time, with all the angels of heaven that never may lose time, and with all the saints in heaven and in earth, that by the grace of Jesus heed time full justly in virtue of love. Lo! here lieth comfort; construe thou clearly, and pick thee some profit. But of one thing I warn thee amongst all other. I cannot see who may truly challenge community thus with Jesus and His just Mother, His high angels and also with His saints; but if he be such an one, that doth that in him is with helping of grace in keeping of time. So that he be seen to be a profiter on his part, so little as is, unto the community; as each one of them doth on his.

And therefore take heed to this work, and to the marvellous manner of it within in thy soul. For if it be truly conceived, it is but a sudden stirring, and as it were unadvised, speedily springing unto God as a sparkle from the coal. And it is marvellous to number the stirrings that may be in one hour wrought in a soul that is disposed to this work. And yet in one stirring of all these, he may have suddenly and perfectly forgotten all created thing. But fast after each stirring, for corruption of the flesh, it falleth down again to some thought or to some done or undone deed. But what thereof? For fast after, it riseth again as suddenly as it did before.

And here may men shortly conceive the manner of this working, and clearly know that it is far from any fantasy, or any false imagination or quaint opinion: the which be brought in, not by such a devout and a meek blind stirring of love, but by a proud, curious, and an imaginative wit. Such a proud, curious wit behoveth always be borne down and stiffly trodden down under foot, if this work shall truly be conceived in purity of spirit. For whoso heareth this work either be read or spoken of, and weeneth that it may, or should, be come to by travail in their wits, and therefore they sit and seek in their wits how that it may be, and in this curiosity they travail their imagination peradventure against the course of nature, and they feign a manner of working the which is neither bodily nor ghostly—truly this man, whatsoever he be, is perilously deceived. Insomuch, that unless God of His great goodness shew His merciful miracle, and make him soon to leave work, and meek him to counsel of proved workers, he shall fall either into frenzies, or else into other great mischiefs of ghostly sins and devils' deceits; through the which he may lightly be lost, both life and soul, without any end. And therefore for God's love be wary in this work, and travail not in thy wits nor in thy imagination on nowise: for I tell thee truly, it may not be come to by travail in them, and therefore leave them and work not with them.

And ween not, for I call it a darkness or a cloud, that it be any cloud congealed of the humours that flee in the air, nor yet any darkness such as is in thine house on nights when the candle is out. For such a darkness and such a cloud mayest thou imagine with curiosity of wit, for to bear before thine eyes in the lightest day of summer: and also contrariwise in the darkest night of winter, thou mayest imagine a clear shining light. Let be such falsehood. I mean not thus. For when I say darkness, I mean a lacking of knowing: as all that thing that thou knowest not, or else that thou hast forgotten, it is dark to thee; for thou seest it not with thy ghostly eye. And for this reason it is not called a cloud of the air, but a cloud of unknowing, that is betwixt thee and thy God.

Here Beginneth The Fifth Chapter

That in the time of this word all the creatures that ever have been, be now, or ever shall be, and all the works of those same creatures, should be hid under the cloud of forgetting.

And if ever thou shalt come to this cloud and dwell and work therein as I bid thee, thee behoveth as this cloud of unknowing is above thee, betwixt thee and thy God, right so put a cloud of forgetting beneath thee; betwixt thee and all the creatures that ever be made. Thee thinketh, peradventure, that thou art full far from God because that this cloud of unknowing is betwixt thee and thy God: but surely, an it be well conceived, thou art well further from Him when thou hast no cloud of forgetting betwixt thee and all the creatures that ever be made. As oft as I say, all the creatures that ever be made, as oft I mean not only the creatures themselves, but also all the works and the conditions of the same creatures. I take out not one creature, whether they be bodily creatures or ghostly, nor yet any condition or work of any creature, whether they be good or evil: but shortly to say, all should be hid under the cloud of forgetting in this case.

For although it be full profitable sometime to think of certain conditions and deeds of some certain special creatures, nevertheless yet in this work it profiteth little or nought. For why? Memory or thinking of any creature that ever God made, or of any of their deeds either, it is a manner of ghostly light: for the eye of thy soul is opened on it and even fixed thereupon, as the eye of a shooter is upon the prick that he shooteth to. And one thing I tell thee, that all thing that thou thinketh upon, it is above thee for the time, and betwixt thee and thy God: and insomuch thou art the further from God, that aught is in thy mind but only God.

Yea! and, if it be courteous and seemly to say, in this work it profiteth little or nought to think of the kindness or the worthiness of God, nor on our Lady, nor on the saints or angels in heaven, nor yet on the joys in heaven: that is to say, with a special beholding to them, as thou wouldest by that beholding feed and increase thy purpose. I trow that on nowise it should help in this case and in this work. For although it be good to think upon the kindness of God, and to love Him and praise Him for it, yet it is far better to think upon the naked being of Him, and to love Him and praise Him for Himself

Here Beginneth The Sixth Chapter

A short conceit of the work of this book, treated by question.

But now thou askest me and sayest, "How shall I think on Himself, and what is He?" and to this I cannot answer thee but thus: "I wot not."

For thou hast brought me with thy question into that same darkness, and into that same cloud of unknowing, that I would thou wert in thyself. For of all other creatures and their works, yea, and of the works of God's self, may a man through grace have fullhead of knowing, and well he can think of them: but of God Himself can no man think. And therefore I would leave all that thing that I can think, and choose to my love that thing that I cannot think. For why; He may well be loved, but not thought. By love may He be gotten and holden; but by thought never. And therefore, although it be good sometime to think of the kindness and the worthiness of God in special, and although it be a light and a part of contemplation: nevertheless yet in this work it shall be cast down and covered with a cloud of forgetting. And thou shalt step above it stalwartly, but Mistily, with a devout and a pleasing stirring of love, and try for to pierce that darkness above thee. And smite upon that thick cloud of unknowing with a sharp dart of longing love; and go not thence for thing that befalleth.

Here Beginneth The Seventh Chapter

How a man shall have him in this work against all thoughts, and specially against all those that arise of his own curiosity, of cunning, and of natural wit.

And if any thought rise and will press continually above thee betwixt thee and that darkness, and ask thee saying, "What seekest thou, and what wouldest thou have?" say thou, that it is God that thou wouldest have. "Him I covet, Him I seek, and nought but Him."

And if he ask thee, "What is that God?" say thou, that it is God that made thee and bought thee, and that graciously hath called thee to thy degree. "And in Him," say, "thou hast no skill." And therefore say, "Go thou down again," and tread him fast down with a stirring of love, although he seem to thee right holy, and seem to thee as he would help thee to seek Him. For peradventure he will bring to thy mind diversee full fair and wonderful points of His kindness, and say that He is full sweet, and full loving, full gracious, and full merciful. And if thou wilt hear him, he coveteth no better; for at the last he will thus jangle ever more and more till he bring thee lower, to the mind of His Passion.

And there will he let thee see the wonderful kindness of God, and if thou hear him, he careth for nought better. For soon after he will let thee see thine old wretched living, and peradventure in seeing and thinking thereof he will bring to thy mind some place that thou hast dwelt in before this time. So that at the last, or ever thou wit, thou shalt be scattered thou wottest not where. The cause of this scattering is, that thou heardest him first wilfully, then answeredest him, receivedest him, and lettest him alone.

And yet, nevertheless, the thing that he said was both good and holy. Yea, and so holy, that what man or woman that weeneth to come to contemplation without many such sweet meditations of their own wretchedness, the passion, the kindness, and the great goodness, and the worthiness of God coming before, surely he shall err and fail of his purpose. And yet, nevertheless, it behoveth a man or a woman that hath long time been used in these meditations, nevertheless to leave them, and put them and hold them far down under the cloud of forgetting, if ever he shall pierce the cloud of unknowing betwixt him and his God. Therefore what time that thou purposest thee to this work, and feelest by grace that thou art called of God, lift then up thine heart unto God with a meek stirring of love; and mean God that made thee, and bought thee, and that graciously hath called thee to thy degree, and receive none other thought of God. And yet not all these, but if thou list; for it sufficeth enough, a naked intent direct unto God without any other cause than Himself.

And if thee list have this intent lapped and folden in one word, for thou shouldest have better hold thereupon, take thee but a little word of one syllable: for so it is better than of two, for ever the shorter it is the better it accordeth with the work of the Spirit. And such a word is this word God or this word *love*. Choose thee whether thou wilt, or another; as thee list, which that thee liketh best of one syllable. And fasten this word to thine heart, so that it never go thence for thing that befalleth.

This word shall be thy shield and thy spear, whether thou ridest on peace or on war. With this word, thou shalt beat on this cloud and this darkness above thee. With this word, thou shall smite down all manner of thought under the cloud of forgetting. Insomuch, that if any thought press upon thee to ask thee what thou wouldest have, answer them with no more words but with this one word. And if he proffer thee of his great clergy to expound thee that word and to tell thee the conditions of that word, say him: That thou wilt have it all whole, and not broken nor undone. And if thou wilt hold thee fast on this purpose, be thou sure, he will no while abide. And why? For that thou wilt not let him feed him on such sweet meditations of God touched before.

Here Beginneth The Eighth Chapter
A good declaring of certain doubts that may fall in this word treated by question, in destroying of a man's own curiosity, of cunning, and of natural wit, and in distinguishing of the degrees and the parts of active living and contemplative.

But now thou askest me, "What is he, this that thus presseth upon me in this work; and whether it is a good thing or an evil? And if it be an evil thing, then have I marvel," thou sayest, "why that he will increase a man's devotion so much. For sometimes me think that it is a passing comfort to listen after his tales. For he will sometime, me think, make me weep full heartily for pity of the Passion of Christ, sometime for my wretchedness, and for many other reasons, that me thinketh be full holy, and that done me much good. And therefore me thinketh that he should on nowise be evil; and if he be good, and with his sweet tales doth me so much good withal, then I have great marvel why that thou biddest me put him down and away so far under the cloud of forgetting?"

Now surely me thinketh that this is a well moved question, and therefore I think to answer thereto so feebly as I can. First when thou askest me what is he, this that presseth so fast upon thee in this work, proffering to help thee in this work; I say that it is a sharp and a clear beholding of thy natural wit, printed in thy reason within in thy soul. And where thou askest me thereof whether it be good or evil, I say that it behoveth always be good in its nature. For why, it is a beam of the likeness of God. But the use thereof may be both good and evil. Good, when it is opened by grace for to see thy wretchedness, the passion, the kindness, and the wonderful works of God in His creatures bodily and ghostly. And then it is no wonder though it increase thy devotion full much, as thou sayest. But then is the use evil, when it is swollen with pride and with curiosity of much clergy and letterly cunning as in clerks; and maketh them press for to be holden not meek scholars and masters of divinity or of devotion, but proud scholars of the devil and masters of vanity and of falsehood. And in other men or women whatso they be, religious or seculars, the use and the working of this natural wit is then evil, when it is swollen with proud and curious skills of worldly things, and fleshly conceits in coveting of worldly worships and having of riches and vain plesaunce and flatterings of others.

And where that thou askest me, why that thou shalt put it down under the cloud of forgetting, since it is so, that it is good in its nature, and thereto when it is well used it doth thee so much good and increaseth thy devotion so much. To this I answer and say—That thou shalt well understand that there be two manner of lives in Holy Church. The one is active life, and the other is contemplative life. Active is the lower, and contemplative is the higher. Active life hath two degrees, a higher and a lower: and also contemplative life hath two degrees, a lower and a higher. Also, these two lives be so coupled together that although they be diverse in some part, yet neither of them may be had fully without some part of the other. For why? That part that is the higher part of active life, that same part is the lower part of contemplative life. So that a man may not be fully active, but if he be in part contemplative; nor yet fully contemplative, as it may be here, but if he be in part active. The condition of active life is such, that it is both begun and ended in this life; but not so of contemplative life. For it is begun in this life, and shall last without end. For why? That part that Mary chose shall never be taken away. Active life is troubled and travailed about many things; but contemplative sitteth in peace with one thing.

The lower part of active life standeth in good and honest bodily works of mercy and of charity. The higher part of active life and the lower part of contemplative life lieth in goodly ghostly meditations, and busy beholding unto a man's own wretchedness with sorrow and contrition, unto the Passion of Christ and of His servants with pity and compassion, and unto the wonderful gifts, kindness, and works of God in all His creatures bodily and ghostly with thanking and praising. But the higher part of contemplation, as it may be had here, hangeth all wholly in this darkness and in this cloud of unknowing; with a loving stirring and a blind beholding unto the naked being of God Himself only.

In the lower part of active life a man is without himself and beneath himself. In the higher part of active life and the lower part of contemplative life, a man is within himself and even with himself. But in the higher part of contemplative life, a man is above himself and under his God. Above himself he is: for why, he purposeth him to win thither by grace, whither he may not come by nature. That is to say, to be knit to God in spirit, and in onehead of love and accordance of will. And right as it is impossible, to man's understanding, for a man to come to the higher part of active life, but if he cease for a time of the lower part; so it is that a man shall not come to the higher part of contemplative life, but if he cease for a time of the lower part. And as unlawful a thing as it is, and as much as it would let a man that sat in his meditations, to have regard then to his outward bodily works, the which he had done, or else should do, although they were never so holy works in themselves: surely as unlikely a thing it is, and as much would it let a man that should work in this darkness and in this cloud of unknowing with an affectuous stirring of love to God for Himself, for to let any thought or any meditation of God's wonderful gifts, kindness, and works in any of His creatures bodily or ghostly, rise upon him to press betwixt him and his God; although they be never so holy thoughts, nor so profound, nor so comfortable.

And for this reason it is that I bid thee put down such a sharp subtle thought, and cover him with a thick cloud of forgetting, be he never so holy nor promise he thee never so well for to help thee in thy purpose. For why, love may reach to God in this life, but not knowing. And all the whiles that the soul dwelleth in this deadly body, evermore is the sharpness of our understanding in beholding of all ghostly things, but most specially of God, mingled with some manner of fantasy; for the which our work should be unclean. And unless more wonder were, it should lead us into much error.

Here Beginneth The Ninth Chapter
That in the time of this work the remembrance of the holiest Creature that ever God made letteth more than it profiteth.
And therefore the sharp stirring of thine understanding, that will always press upon thee when thou settest thee to this work, behoveth always be borne down; and but thou bear him down, he will bear thee down. Insomuch, that when thou weenest best to abide in this darkness, and that nought is in thy mind but only God; an thou look truly thou shalt find thy mind not occupied in this darkness, but in a clear beholding of some thing beneath God. And if it thus be, surely then is that thing above thee for the time, and betwixt thee and thy God. And therefore purpose thee to put down such clear beholdings, be they never so holy nor so likely. For one thing I tell thee, it is more profitable to the health of thy soul, more worthy in itself, and more pleasing to God and to all the saints and angels in heaven—yea, and

more helpful to all thy friends, bodily and ghostly, quick and dead—such a blind stirring of love unto God for Himself, and such a privy pressing upon this cloud of unknowing, and better thee were for to have it and for to feel it in thine affection ghostly, than it is for to have the eyes of thy soul opened in contemplation or beholding of all the angels or saints in heaven, or in hearing of all the mirth and the melody that is amongst them in bliss.

And look thou have no wonder of this: for mightest thou once see it as clearly, as thou mayest by grace come to for to grope it and feel it in this life, thou wouldest think as I say. But be thou sure that clear sight shall never man have here in this life: but the feeling may men have through grace when God vouchsafeth. And therefore lift up thy love to that cloud: rather, if I shall say thee sooth, let God draw thy love up to that cloud and strive thou through help of His grace to forget all other thing.

For since a naked remembrance of any thing under God pressing against thy will and thy witting putteth thee farther from God than thou shouldest be if it were not, and letteth thee, and maketh thee inasmuch more unable to feel in experience the fruit of His love, what trowest thou then that a remembrance wittingly and wilfully drawn upon thee will hinder thee in thy purpose? And since a remembrance of any special saint or of any clean ghostly thing will hinder thee so much, what trowest thou then that the remembrance of any man living in this wretched life, or of any manner of bodily or worldly thing, will hinder thee and let thee in this work?

I say not that such a naked sudden thought of any good and clean ghostly thing under God pressing against thy will or thy witting, or else wilfully drawn upon thee with advisement in increasing of thy devotion, although it be letting to this manner of work—that it is therefore evil. Nay! God forbid that thou take it so. But I say, although it be good and holy, yet in this work it letteth more than it profiteth. I mean for the time. For why? Surely he that seeketh God perfectly, he will not rest him finally in the remembrance of any angel or saint that is in heaven.

Here Beginneth The Tenth Chapter
How a man shall know when his thought is no sin; and if it be sin, when it is deadly and when it is venial.

But it is not thus of the remembrance of any man or woman living in this life, or of any bodily or worldly thing whatsoever that it be. For why, a naked sudden thought of any of them, pressing against thy will and thy witting, although it be no sin imputed unto thee—for it is the pain of the original sin pressing against thy power, of the which sin thou art cleansed in thy baptism—nevertheless yet if this sudden stirring or thought be not smitten soon down, as fast for frailty thy fleshly heart is strained thereby: with some manner of liking, if it be a thing that pleaseth thee or hath pleased thee before, or else with some manner of grumbling, if it be a thing that thee think grieveth thee, or hath grieved thee before. The which fastening, although it may in fleshly living men and women that be in deadly sin before be deadly; nevertheless in thee and in all other that have in a true will forsaken the world, and are obliged unto any degree in devout living in Holy Church, what so it be, privy or open, and thereto that will be ruled not after their own will and their own wit, but after the will and the counsel of their sovereigns, what so they be, religious or seculars, such a liking or a grumbling fastened in the fleshly heart is but venial sin. The cause of this is the grounding and the rooting of your intent in God, made in the beginning of your living in that state that ye stand in, by the witness and the counsel of some discreet father.

But if it so be, that this liking or grumbling fastened in thy fleshly heart be suffered so long to abide unreproved, that then at the last it is fastened to the ghostly heart, that is to say the will, with a full consent: then, it is deadly sin. And this befalleth when thou or any of them that I speak of wilfully draw upon thee the remembrance of any man or woman living in this life, or of any bodily or worldly thing other: insomuch, that if it be a thing the which grieveth or hath grieved thee before, there riseth in thee an angry passion and an appetite of vengeance, the which is called Wrath. Or else a fell disdain and a manner of loathsomeness of their person, with despiteful and condemning thoughts, the which is called Envy. Or else a weariness and an unlistiness of any good occupation bodily or ghostly, the which is called Sloth.

And if it be a thing that pleaseth thee, or hath pleased thee before, there riseth in thee a passing delight for to think on that thing what so it be. Insomuch, that thou restest thee in that thought, and finally fastenest thine heart and thy will thereto, and feedest thy fleshly heart therewith: so that thee think for the time that thou covetest none other wealth, but to live ever in such a peace and rest with that thing that thou thinkest upon. If this thought that thou thus drawest upon thee, or else receivest when it is put unto thee, and that thou restest thee thus in with delight, be worthiness of nature or of knowing, of grace or of degree, of favour or of fairhead, then it is Pride. And if it be any manner of worldly good, riches or chattels, or what that man may have or be lord of, then it is Covetyse. If it be dainty meats and drinks, or any manner of delights that man may taste, then it is Gluttony. And if it be love or plesaunce, or any manner of fleshly dalliance, glosing or flattering of any man or woman living in this life, or of thyself either: then it is Lechery.

Here Beginneth The Eleventh Chapter
That a man should weigh each thought and each stirring after that it is, and always eschew recklessness in venial sin.

I say not this for that I trow that thou, or any other such as I speak of, be guilty and cumbered with any such sins; but for that I would that thou weighest each thought and each stirring after that it is, and for I would that thou travailedst busily to destroy the first stirring and thought of these things that thou mayest thus sin in. For one thing I tell thee; that who weigheth not, or setteth little by, the first thought — yea, although it be no sin unto him — that he, whosoever that he be, shall not eschew recklessness in venial sin. Venial sin shall no man utterly eschew in this deadly life. But recklessness in venial sin should always be eschewed of all the true disciples of perfection; and else I have no wonder though they soon sin deadly

Here Beginneth The Twelfth Chapter
That by Virtue of this word sin is not only destroyed, but also Virtues begotten.

And, therefore, if thou wilt stand and not fall, cease never in thine intent: but beat evermore on this cloud of unknowing that is betwixt thee and thy God with a sharp dart of longing love, and loathe for to think on aught under God, and go not thence for anything that befalleth. For this is only by itself that work that destroyeth the ground and the root of sin. Fast thou never so much, wake thou never so long, rise thou never so early, lie thou never so hard, wear thou never so sharp; yea, and if it were lawful to do — as it is not — put thou out thine eyes, cut thou out thy tongue of thy mouth, stop thou thine ears and thy nose never so fast, though thou shear away thy members, and do all the pain to thy body that thou mayest or canst think: all this would help thee right nought. Yet will stirring and rising of sin be in thee.

Yea, and what more? Weep thou never so much for sorrow of thy sins, or of the Passion of Christ, or have thou never so much mind of the joys of heaven, what may it do to thee? Surely much good, much help, much profit, and much grace will it get thee. But in comparison of this blind stirring of love, it is but a little that it doth, or may do, without this. This by itself is the best part of Mary without these other. They without it profit but little or nought. It destroyeth not only the ground and the root of sin as it may be here, but thereto it getteth virtues. For an it be truly conceived, all virtues shall truly be, and perfectly conceived, and feelingly comprehended, in it, without any mingling of the intent. And have a man never so many virtues without it, all they be mingled with some crooked intent, for the which they be imperfect.

For virtue is nought else but an ordained and a measured affection, plainly directed unto God for Himself. For why? He in Himself is the pure cause of all virtues: insomuch, that if any man be stirred to any one virtue by any other cause mingled with Him, yea, although that He be the chief, yet that virtue is then imperfect. As thus by example may be seen in one virtue or two instead of all the other; and well may these two virtues be meekness and charity. For whoso might get these two clearly, him needeth no more: for why, he hath all.

Here Beginneth The Thirteenth Chapter
What meekness is in itself, and when it is perfect and when it is imperfect.

Now let see first of the virtue of meekness; how that it is imperfect when it is caused of any other thing mingled with God although He be the chief; and how that it is perfect when it is caused of God by Himself. And first it is to wit, what meekness is in itself, if this matter shall clearly be seen and conceived; and thereafter may it more verily be conceived in truth of spirit what is the cause thereof.

Meekness in itself is nought else, but a true knowing and feeling of a man's self as he is. For surely whoso might verily see and feel himself as he is, he should verily be meek. Two things there be, the which be cause of this meekness; the which be these. One is the filth, the wretchedness, and the frailty of man, into the which he is fallen by sin; and the which always him behoveth to feel in some part the whiles he liveth in this life, be he never so holy. Another is the over abundant love and the worthiness of God in Himself; in beholding of the which all nature quaketh, all clerks be fools, and all saints and angels be blind. Insomuch, that were it not that through the wisdom of His Godhead He measured their beholding after their ableness in nature and in grace, I defail to say what should befall them.

This second cause is perfect; for why, it shall last without end. And the tother before is imperfect; for why, it shall not only fail at the end of this life, but full oft it may befall that a soul in this deadly body for abundance of grace in multiplying of his desire—as oft and as long as God vouchsafeth for to work it—shall have suddenly and perfectly lost and forgotten all witting and feeling of his being, not looking after whether he have been holy or wretched. But whether this fall oft or seldom to a soul that is thus disposed, I trow that it lasteth but a full short while: and in this time it is perfectly meeked, for it knoweth and feeleth no cause but the Chief. And ever when it knoweth and feeleth the tother cause, communing therewith, although this be the chief: yet it is imperfect meekness. Nevertheless yet it is good and notwithstanding must be had; and God forbid that thou take it in any other manner than I say.

Here Beginneth The Fourteenth Chapter

That without imperfect meekness coming before, it is impossible for a sinner to come to the perfect Virtue of meekness in this life.

For although I call it imperfect meekness, yet I had liefer have a true knowing and a feeling of myself as I am, and sooner I trow that it should get me the perfect cause and virtue of meekness by itself, than it should an all the saints and angels in heaven, and all the men and women of Holy Church living in earth, religious or seculars in all degrees, were set at once all together to do nought else but to pray to God for me to get me perfect meekness. Yea, and yet it is impossible a sinner to get, or to keep when it is gotten, the perfect virtue of meekness without it.

And therefore swink and sweat in all that thou canst and mayest, for to get thee a true knowing and a feeling of thyself as thou art; and then I trow that soon after that thou shalt have a true knowing and a feeling of God as He is. Not as He is in Himself, for that may no man do but Himself; nor yet as thou shalt do in bliss both body and soul together. But as it is possible, and as He vouchsafeth to be known and felt of a meek soul living in this deadly body.

And think not because I set two causes of meekness, one perfect and another imperfect, that I will therefore that thou leavest the travail about imperfect meekness, and set thee wholly to get thee perfect. Nay, surely; I trow thou shouldest never bring it so about. But herefore I do that I do: because I think to tell thee and let thee see the worthiness of this ghostly exercise before all other exercise bodily or ghostly that man can or may do by grace. How that a privy love pressed in cleanness of spirit upon this dark cloud of unknowing betwixt thee and thy God, truly and perfectly containeth in it the perfect virtue of meekness without any special or clear beholding of any thing under God. And because I would that thou knewest which were perfect meekness, and settest it as a token before the love of thine heart, and didst it for thee and for me. And because I would by this knowing make thee more meek.

For ofttimes it befalleth that lacking of knowing is cause of much pride as me thinketh. For peradventure an thou knewest not which were perfect meekness, thou shouldest ween when thou hadst a little knowing and a feeling of this that I call imperfect meekness, that thou hadst almost gotten perfect meekness: and so shouldest thou deceive thyself, and ween that thou wert full meek when thou wert all belapped in foul stinking pride. And therefore try for to travail about perfect meekness; for the condition of it is such, that whoso hath it, and the whiles he hath it, he shall not sin, nor yet much after.

Here Beginneth The Fifteenth Chapter

A short proof against their error that say, that there is no perfecter cause to be meeked under, than is the knowledge of a man's own wretchedness.

And trust steadfastly that there is such a perfect meekness as I speak of, and that it may be come to through grace in this life. And this I say in confusion of their error, that say that there is no perfecter cause of meekness than is that which is raised of the remembrance of our wretchedness and our before done sins.

I grant well, that to them that have been in accustomed sins, as I am myself and have been, it is the most needful and speedful cause, to be meeked under the remembrance of our wretchedness and our before done sins, ever till the time be that the great rust of sin be in great part rubbed away, our conscience and our counsel to witness. But to other that be, as it were, innocents, the which never sinned deadly with an abiding will and avisement, but through frailty and unknowing, and the which set them to be contemplatives—and to us both if our counsel and our conscience witness our lawful amendment in contrition and in confession, and in making satisfaction after the statute and the ordinance of all Holy Church, and thereto if we feel us stirred and called by grace to be contemplatives also—there is then another cause to be meeked under as far above this cause as is the living of our Lady Saint Mary above the living of the sinfullest penitent in Holy Church; or the living of Christ above the living of any other man in this life; or else the living of an angel in heaven, the which never felt—nor shall feel—frailty, is above the life of the frailest man that is here in this world.

For if it so were that there were no perfect cause to be meeked under, but in seeing and feeling of wretchedness, then would I wit of them that say so, what cause they be meeked under that never see nor feel—nor never shall be in them—wretchedness nor stirring of sin: as it is of our Lord Jesus Christ, our Lady Saint Mary, and all the saints and angels in heaven. To this perfection, and all other, our Lord Jesus Christ calleth us Himself in the gospel: where He biddeth that we should be perfect by grace as He Himself is by nature.

Here Beginneth The Sixteenth Chapter

That by Virtue of this work a sinner truly turned and called to contemplation cometh sooner to perfection than by any other work; and by it soonest may get of God forgiveness of sins.

Look that no man think it presumption, that he that is the wretchedest sinner of this life dare take upon him after the time be that he have lawfully amended him, and after that he have felt him stirred to that life that is called contemplative, by the assent of his counsel and his conscience for to profer a meek stirring of love to his God, privily pressing upon the cloud of unknowing betwixt him and his God. When our Lord said to Mary, in person of all sinners that be called to contemplative life, "Thy sins be forgiven thee," it was not for her great sorrow, nor for the remembering of her sins, nor yet for her meekness that she had in the beholding of her wretchedness only. But why then? Surely because she loved much.

Lo! here may men see what a privy pressing of love may purchase of our Lord, before all other works that man may think. And yet I grant well, that she had full much sorrow, and wept full sore for her sins, and full much she was meeked in remembrance of her wretchedness. And so should we do, that have been wretches and accustomed sinners; all our lifetime make hideous and wonderful sorrow for our sins, and full much be meeked in remembrance of our wretchedness.

But how? Surely as Mary did. She, although she might not feel the deep hearty sorrow of her sins—for why, all her lifetime she had them with her whereso she went, as it were in a burthen bounden together and laid up full privily in the hole of her heart, in manner never to be forgotten—nevertheless yet, it may be said and affirmed by Scripture, that she had a more hearty sorrow, a more doleful desire, and a more deep sighing, and more she languished, yea! almost to the death, for lacking of love, although she had full much love (and have no wonder thereof, for it is the condition of a true lover that ever the more he loveth, the more he longeth for to love), than she had for any remembrance of her sins.

And yet she wist well, and felt well in herself in a sad soothfastness, that she was a wretch most foul of all other, and that her sins had made a division betwixt her and her God that she loved so much: and also that they were in great part cause of her languishing sickness for lacking of love. But what thereof? Came she therefore down from the height of desire into the deepness of her sinful life, and searched in the foul stinking fen and dunghill of her sins; searching them up, by one and by one, with all the circumstances of them, and sorrowed and wept so upon them each one by itself? Nay, surely she did not so. And why? Because God let her wit by His grace within in her soul, that she should never so bring it about. For so might she sooner have raised in herself an ableness to have oft sinned, than to have purchased by that work any plain forgiveness of all her sins.

And therefore she hung up her love and her longing desire in this cloud of unknowing, and learned her to love a thing the which she might not see clearly in this life, by light of understanding in her reason, nor yet verily feel in sweetness of love in her affection. Insomuch, that she had ofttimes little special remembrance, whether that ever she had been a sinner or none. Yea, and full ofttimes I hope that she was so deeply disposed to the love of His Godhead that she had but right little special beholding unto the beauty of His precious and His blessed body, in the which He sat full lovely speaking and preaching before her; nor yet to anything else, bodily or ghostly. That this be sooth, it seemeth by the gospel.

Here Beginneth The Seventeenth Chapter

That a very contemplative list not meddle him with active life, nor of anything that is done or spoken about him, nor yet to answer to his blamers in excusing of himself.

In the gospel of Saint Luke it is written, that when our Lord was in the house of Martha her sister, all the time that Martha made her busy about the dighting of His meat, Mary her sister sat at His feet. And in hearing of His word she beheld not to the business of her sister, although her business was full good and full holy, for truly it is the first part of active life; nor yet to the preciousness of His blessed body, nor to the sweet voice and the words of His manhood, although it is better and holier, for it is the second part of active life and the first of contemplative life.

But to the sovereignest wisdom of His Godhead lapped in the dark words of His manhood, thither beheld she with all the love of her heart. For from thence she would not remove, for nothing that she saw nor heard spoken nor done about her; but sat full still in her body, with many a sweet privy and a listy love pressed upon that high cloud of unknowing betwixt her and her God. For one thing I tell thee, that there was never yet pure creature in this life, nor never yet shall be, so high ravished in contemplation and love of the Godhead, that there is not evermore a high and a wonderful cloud of unknowing betwixt him and his God. In this cloud it was that Mary was occupied with many a privy love pressed. And why? Because it was the best and the holiest part of contemplation that may be in this life, and from this part her list not remove for nothing. Insomuch, that when her sister Martha complained to our Lord of her, and bade Him bid her sister rise and help her and let her not so work and travail by herself, she sat full still and answered not with one word, nor shewed not as much as a grumbling gesture against her sister for any plaint that she could make. And no wonder: for why, she had another work to do that Martha wist not of. And therefore she had no leisure to listen to her, nor to answer her at her plaint.

Lo! friend, all these works, these words, and these gestures, that were shewed betwixt our Lord and these two sisters, be set in ensample of all actives and all contemplatives that have been since in Holy Church, and shall be to the day of doom. For by Mary is understood all contemplatives; for they should conform their living after hers. And by Martha, actives on the same manner; and for the same reason in likeness.

Here Beginneth The Eighteenth Chapter

How that yet unto this day all actives complain of contemplatives as Martha did of Mary. Of the which complaining ignorance is the cause.

And right as Martha complained then on Mary her sister, right so yet unto this day all actives complain of contemplatives. For an there be a man or a woman in any company of this world, what company soever it be, religious or seculars—I out☐take none—the which man or woman, whichever that it be, feeleth him stirred through grace and by counsel to forsake all outward business, and for to set him fully for to live contemplative life after their cunning and their conscience, their counsel according; as fast, their own brethren and their sisters, and all their next friends, with many other that know not their stirrings nor that manner of living that they set them to, with a great complaining spirit shall rise upon them, and say sharply unto them that it is nought that they do. And as fast they will reckon up many false tales, and many true also, of falling of men and women that have given them to such life before: and never a good tale of them that stood.

I grant that many fall and have fallen of them that have in likeness forsaken the world. And where they should have become God's servants and His contemplatives, because that they would not rule them by true ghostly counsel they have become the devil's servants and his contemplatives; and turned either to hypocrites or to heretics, or fallen into frenzies and many other mischiefs, in slander of Holy Church. Of the which I leave to speak at this time, for troubling of our matter. But nevertheless here after when God vouchsafeth and if need be, men may see some of the conditions and the cause of their failings. And therefore no more of them at this time; but forth of our matter.

Here Beginneth The Nineteenth Chapter

A short excusation of him that made this book teaching how all contemplatives should have all actives fully excused of their complaining words and deeds.

Some might think that I do little worship to Martha, that special saint, for I liken her words of complaining of her sister unto these worldly men's words, or theirs unto hers: and truly I mean no unworship to her nor to them. And God forbid that I should in this work say anything that might be taken in condemnation of any of the servants of God in any degree, and namely of His special saint. For me thinketh that she should be full well had excused of her plaint, taking regard to the time and the manner that she said it in. For that that she said, her unknowing was the cause. And no wonder though she knew not at that time how Mary was occupied; for I trow that before she had little heard of such perfection. And also that she said, it was but courteously and in few words: and therefore she should always be had excused.

And so me thinketh that these worldly living men and women of active life should also full well be had excused of their complaining words touched before, although they say rudely that they say; having beholding to their ignorance. For why? Right as Martha wist full little what Mary her sister did when she complained of her to our Lord; right so on the same manner these folk nowadays wot full little, or else nought, what these young disciples of God mean, when they set them from the business of this world, and draw them to be God's special servants in holiness and rightfulness of spirit. And if they wist truly, I daresay that they would neither do nor say as they say. And therefore me thinketh always that they should be had excused: for why, they know no better living than is that they live in themselves. And also when I think on mine innumerable defaults, the which I have made myself before this time in words and deeds for default of knowing, me thinketh then if I would be had excused of God for mine ignorant defaults, that I should charitably and piteously have other men's ignorant words and deeds always excused. And surely else, do I not to others as I would they did to me.

Here Beginneth The Twentieth Chapter
How Almighty God will goodly answer for all those that for the excusing of themselves list not leave their business about the love of Him.

And therefore me thinketh, that they that set them to be contemplatives should not only have active men excused of their complaining words, but also me thinketh that they should be so occupied in spirit that they should take little heed or none what men did or said about them. Thus did Mary, our example of all, when Martha her sister complained to our Lord: and if we will truly do thus our Lord will do now for us as He did then for Mary.

And how was that? Surely thus. Our lovely Lord Jesus Christ, unto whom no privy thing is hid, although He was required of Martha as doomsman for to bid Mary rise and help her to serve Him; nevertheless yet, for He perceived that Mary was fervently occupied in spirit about the love of His Godhead, therefore courteously and as it was seemly for Him to do by the way of reason, He answered for her, that for the excusing of herself list not leave the love of Him. And how answered He? Surely not only as doomsman, as He was of Martha appealed: but as an advocate lawfully defended her that Him loved, and said, "Martha, Martha!" Twice for speed He named her name; for He would that she heard Him and took heed to His words. "Thou art full busy," He said, "and troubled about many things." For they that be actives behove always to be busied and travailed about many diversee things, the which them falleth, first for to have to their own use, and sithen in deeds of mercy to their even-christian, as charity asketh. And this He said unto Martha, for He would let her wit that her business was good and profitable to the health of her soul. But for this, that she should not think that it were the best work of all that man might do, therefore He added and said: 'But one thing is necessary.'

And what is that one thing? Surely that God be loved and praised by Himself, above all other business bodily or ghostly that man may do. And for this, that Martha should not think that she might both love God and praise Him above all other business bodily or ghostly, and also thereto to be busy about the necessaries of this life: therefore to deliver her of doubt that she might not both serve God in bodily business and ghostly together perfectly — imperfectly she may, but not perfectly — He added and said, that Mary had chosen the best part; the which should never be taken from her. For why, that perfect stirring of love that beginneth here is even in number with that that shall last without end in the bliss of heaven, for all it is but one.

Here Beginneth The One And Twentieth Chapter
The true exposition of this gospel word, "Mary hath chosen the best part."

What meaneth this; Mary hath chosen the best? Wheresoever the best is set or named, it asketh before it these two things — a good, and a better; so that it be the best, and the third in number. But which be these three good things, of the which Mary chose the best? Three lives be they not, for Holy Church maketh remembrance but of two, active life and contemplative life; the which two lives be privily understood in the story of this gospel by these two sisters Martha and Mary — by Martha active, by Mary contemplative. Without one of these two lives may no man be safe, and where no more be but two, may no man choose the best.

But although there be but two lives, nevertheless yet in these two lives be three parts, each one better than other. The which three, each one by itself, be specially set in their places before in this writing. For as it is said before, the first part standeth in good and honest bodily works of mercy and of charity; and this is the first degree of active life, as it is said before. The second part of these two lives lieth in good ghostly meditations of a man's own wretchedness, the Passion of Christ, and of the joys of heaven. The first part is good, and this part is the better; for this is the second degree of active life and the first of contemplative life. In this part is contemplative life and active life coupled together in ghostly kinship, and made sisters at the ensample of Martha and Mary. Thus high may an active come to contemplation; and no higher, but if it be full seldom and by a special grace. Thus low may a contemplative come towards active life; and no lower, but if it be full seldom and in great need.

The third part of these two lives hangeth in this dark cloud of unknowing, with many a privy love pressed to God by Himself. The first part is good, the second is better, but the third is best of all. This is the "best part" of Mary. And therefore it is plainly to wit, that our Lord said not, Mary hath chosen the best life; for there be no more lives but two, and of two may no man choose the best. But of these two lives Mary hath chosen, He said, the best part; the which shall never be taken from her. The first part and the second, although they be both good and holy, yet they end with this life. For in the tother life shall be no need as now to use the works of mercy, nor to weep for our wretchedness, nor for the Passion of Christ. For then shall none be able to hunger nor thirst as now, nor die for cold, nor be sick, nor houseless, nor in prison; nor yet need burial, for then shall none be able to die. But the third part that Mary chose, choose who by grace is called to choose: or, if I soothlier shall say, whoso is chosen thereto of God. Let him lustily incline thereto, for that shall never be taken away: for if it begin here, it shall last without end.

And therefore let the voice of our Lord cry on these actives, as if He said thus now for us unto them, as He did then for Mary to Martha, "Martha, Martha!" — "Actives, actives! make you as busy as ye can in the first part and in the second, now in the one and now in the tother: and, if you list right well and feel you disposed, in both two bodily. And meddle you not of contemplatives. Ye wot not what them aileth: let them sit in their rest and in their play, with the third and the best part of Mary."

Here Beginneth The Two And Twentieth Chapter
Of the wonderful love that Christ had to man in person of all sinners truly turned and called to the grace of contemplation.

Sweet was that love betwixt our Lord and Mary. Much love had she to Him. Much more had He to her. For whoso would utterly behold all the behaviour that was betwixt Him and her, not as a trifler may tell, but as the story of the gospel will witness—the which on nowise may be false—he should find that she was so heartily set for to love Him, that nothing beneath Him might comfort her, nor yet hold her heart from Him. This is she, that same Mary, that when she sought Him at the sepulchre with weeping cheer would not be comforted of angels. For when they spake unto her so sweetly and so lovely and said, "Weep not, Mary; for why, our Lord whom thou seekest is risen, and thou shalt have Him, and see Him live full fair amongst His disciples in Galilee as He hight," she would not cease for them. For why? Her thought that whoso sought verily the King of Angels, them list not cease for angels.

And what more? Surely whoso will look verily in the story of the gospel, he shall find many wonderful points of perfect love written of her to our ensample, and as even according to the work of this writing, as if they had been set and written therefore; and surely so were they, take whoso take may. And if a man list for to see in the gospel written the wonderful and the special love that our Lord had to her, in person of all accustomed sinners truly turned and called to the grace of contemplation, he shall find that our Lord might not suffer any man or woman—yea, not her own sister—speak a word against her, but if He answered for her Himself. Yea, and what more? He blamed Symon Leprous in his own house, for that he thought against her. This was great love: this was passing love.

Here Beginneth The Three And Twentieth Chapter
How God will answer and purvey for them in spirit, that for business about His love list not answer nor purvey for themselves

And truly an we will lustily conform our love and our living, inasmuch as in us is, by grace and by counsel, unto the love and the living of Mary, no doubt but He shall answer on the same manner now for us ghostly each day, privily in the hearts of all those that either say or think against us. I say not but that evermore some men shall say or think somewhat against us, the whiles we live in the travail of this life, as they did against Mary. But I say, an we will give no more heed to their saying nor to their thinking, nor no more cease of our ghostly privy work for their words and their thoughts, than she did—I say, then, that our Lord shall answer them in spirit, if it shall be well with them that so say and so think, that they shall within few days have shame of their words and their thoughts.

And as He will answer for us thus in spirit, so will He stir other men in spirit to give us our needful things that belong to this life, as meat and clothes with all these other; if He see that we will not leave the work of His love for business about them. And this I say in confusion of their error, that say that it is not lawful for men to set them to serve God in contemplative life, but if they be secure before of their bodily necessaries. For they say, that God sendeth the cow, but not by the horn. And truly they say wrong of God, as they well know. For trust steadfastly, thou whatsoever that thou be, that truly turnest thee from the world unto God, that one of these two God shall send thee, without business of thyself: and that is either abundance of necessaries, or strength in body and patience in spirit to bear need. What then recketh it, which man have? for all come to one in very contemplatives. And whoso is in doubt of this, either the devil is in his breast and reeveth him of belief, or else he is not yet truly turned to God as he should be; make he it never so quaint, nor never so holy reasons shew there again, whatnot ever that he be.

And therefore thou, that settest thee to be contemplative as Mary was, choose thee rather to be meeked under the wonderful height and the worthiness of God, the which is perfect, than under thine own wretchedness, the which is imperfect: that is to say, look that thy special beholding be more to the worthiness of God than to thy wretchedness. For to them that be perfectly meeked, no thing shall defail; neither bodily thing, nor ghostly. For why? They have God, in whom is all plenty; and whoso hath Him—yea, as this book telleth—him needeth nought else in this life.

Here Beginneth The Four And Twentieth Chapter
What charity is in itself, and how it is truly and perfectly contained in the work of this book.

And as it is said of meekness, how that it is truly and perfectly comprehended in this little blind love pressed, when it is beating upon this dark cloud of unknowing, all other things put down and forgotten: so it is to be understood of all other virtues, and specially of charity.

For charity is nought else to bemean to thine understanding, but love of God for Himself above all creatures, and of man for God even as thyself. And that in this work God is loved for Himself, and above all creatures, it seemeth right well. For as it is said before, that the substance of this work is nought else but a naked intent directed unto God for Himself.

A naked intent I call it. For why, in this work a perfect Prentice asketh neither releasing of pain, nor increasing of meed, nor shortly to say, nought but Himself. Insomuch, that neither he recketh nor looketh after whether that he be in pain or in bliss, else that His will be fulfilled that he loveth. And thus it seemeth that in this work God is perfectly loved for Himself, and that above all creatures. For in this work, a perfect worker may not suffer the memory of the holiest creature that ever God made to commune with him.

And that in this work the second and the lower branch of charity unto thine even christian is verily and perfectly fulfilled, it seemeth by the proof. For why, in this work a perfect worker hath no special beholding unto any man by himself, whether that he be kin or stranger, friend or foe. For all men him thinks equally kin unto him, and no man stranger. All men him thinks be his friends, and none his foes. Insomuch, that him thinks all those that pain him and do him disease in this life, they be his full and his special friends: and him thinketh, that he is stirred to will them as much good, as he would to the homeliest friend that he hath.

Here Beginneth The Five And Twentieth Chapter

That in the time of this work a perfect soul hath no special beholding to any one man in this life.

I say not that in this work he shall have a special beholding to any man in this life, whether that he be friend or foe, kin or stranger; for that may not be if this work shall perfectly be done, as it is when all things under God be fully forgotten, as falleth for this work. But I say that he shall be made so virtuous and so charitable by the virtue of this work, that his will shall be afterwards, when he condescendeth to commune or to pray for his even christian — not from all this work, for that may not be without great sin, but from the height of this work, the which is speedful and needful to do some time as charity asketh — as specially then directed to his foe as to his friend, his stranger as his kin. Yea, and some time more to his foe than to his friend.

Nevertheless, in this work he hath no leisure to look after who is his friend or his foe, his kin or his stranger. I say not but he shall feel some time—yea, full oft—his affection more homely to one, two, or three, than to all these other: for that is lawful to be, for many causes as charity asketh. For such an homely affection felt Christ to John and unto Mary, and unto Peter before many others. But I say, that in the time of this work shall all be equally homely unto him; for he shall feel then no cause, but only God. So that all shall be loved plainly and nakedly for God, and as well as himself.

For as all men were lost in Adam and all men that with work will witness their will of salvation are saved or shall be by virtue of the Passion of only Christ: not in the same manner, but as it were in the same manner, a soul that is perfectly disposed to this work, and oned thus to God in spirit as the proof of this work witnesseth, doth that in it is to make all men as perfect in this work as itself is. For right as if a limb of our body feeleth sore, all the tother limbs be pained and diseased therefore, or if a limb fare well, all the remnant be gladded therewith—right so is it ghostly of all the limbs of Holy Church. For Christ is our head, and we be the limbs if we be in charity: and whoso will be a perfect disciple of our Lord's, him behoveth strain up his spirit in this work ghostly, for the salvation of all his brethren and sisters in nature, as our Lord did His body on the Cross. And how? Not only for His friends and His kin and His homely lovers, but generally for all mankind, without any special beholding more to one than to another. For all that will leave sin and ask mercy shall be saved through the virtue of His Passion. And as it is said of meekness and charity, so it is to be understood of all other virtues. For all they be truly comprehended in this little pressing of love, touched before.

Here Beginneth The Six And Twentieth Chapter
That without full special grace, or long use in common grace, the work of this book is right travailous; and in this work, which is the work of the soul helped by grace, and which is the work of only God.

And therefore travail fast awhile, and beat upon this high cloud of unknowing, and rest afterward. Nevertheless, a travail shall he have who so shall use him in this work; yea, surely! and that a full great travail, unless he have a more special grace, or else that he have of long time used him therein.

But I pray thee, wherein shall that travail be? Surely not in that devout stirring of love that is continually wrought in his will, not by himself, but by the hand of Almighty God: the which is evermore ready to work this work in each soul that is disposed thereto, and that doth that in him is, and hath done long time before, to enable him to this work.

But wherein then is this travail, I pray thee? Surely, this travail is all in treading down of the remembrance of all the creatures that ever God made, and in holding of them under the cloud of forgetting named before. In this is all the travail, for this is man's travail, with help of grace. And the tother above—that is to say, the stirring of love—that is the work of only God. And therefore do on thy work, and surely I promise thee He shall not fail in His.

Do on then fast; let see how thou bearest thee. Seest thou not how He standeth and abideth thee? For shame! Travail fast but awhile, and thou shalt soon be eased of the greatness and of the hardness of this travail. For although it be hard and strait in the beginning, when thou hast no devotion; nevertheless yet after, when thou hast devotion, it shall be made full restful and full light unto thee that before was full hard. And thou shalt have either little travail or none, for then will God work sometimes all by Himself. But not ever, nor yet no long time together, but when Him list and as Him list; and then wilt thou think it merry to let Him alone.

Then will He sometimes peradventure send out a beam of ghostly light, piercing this cloud of unknowing that is betwixt thee and Him; and shew thee some of His privity, the which man may not, nor cannot speak. Then shalt thou feel thine affection inflamed with the fire of His love, far more than I can tell thee, or may or will at this time. For of that work, that falleth to only God, dare I not take upon me to speak with my blabbering fleshly tongue: and shortly to say, although I durst I would do not. But of that work that falleth to man when he feeleth him stirred and helped by grace, list me well tell thee: for therein is the less peril of the two.

Here Beginneth The Seven And Twentieth Chapter
Who should work in the gracious work of this book.
First and foremost, I will tell thee who should work in this work, and when, and by what means: and what discretion thou shalt have in it. If thou asketh me who shall work thus, I answer thee—all that have forsaken the world in a true will, and thereto that give them not to active life, but to that life that is called contemplative life. All those

should work in this grace and in this work, whatsoever that they be; whether they have been accustomed sinners or none

Here Beginneth The Eight And Twentieth Chapter
That a man should not presume to work in this work before the time that he be lawfully cleansed in conscience of all his special deeds of sin.

But if thou asketh me when they should work in this work, then I answer thee and I say: that not ere they have cleansed their conscience of all their special deeds of sin done before, after the common ordinance of Holy Church.

For in this work, a soul drieth up in it all the root and the ground of sin that will always live in it after confession, be it never so busy. And, therefore, whoso will travail in this work, let him first cleanse his conscience; and afterward when he hath done that in him is lawfully, let him dispose him boldly but meekly thereto. And let him think, that he hath full long been holden therefrom. For this is that work in the which a soul should travail all his lifetime, though he had never sinned deadly. And the whiles that a soul is dwelling in this deadly flesh, it shall evermore see and feel this cumbrous cloud of unknowing betwixt him and God. And not only that, but in pain of the original sin it shall evermore see and feel that some of all the creatures that ever God made, or some of their works, will evermore press in remembrance betwixt it and God. And this is the right wisdom of God, that man, when he had sovereignty and lordship of all other creatures, because that he wilfully made him underling to the stirring of his subjects, leaving the bidding of God and his Maker; that right so after, when he would fulfil the bidding of God, he saw and felt all the creatures that should be beneath him, proudly press above him, betwixt him and his God.

Here Beginneth The Nine And Twentieth Chapter
That a man should bidingly travail in this work, and suffer the pain thereof, and judge no man.

And therefore, whoso coveteth to come to cleanness that he lost for sin, and to win to that well-being where all woe wanteth, him behoveth bidingly to travail in this work, and suffer the pain thereof, whatsoever that he be: whether he have been an accustomed sinner or none.

All men have travail in this work; both sinners, and innocents that never sinned greatly. But far greater travail have those that have been sinners than they that have been none; and that is great reason. Nevertheless, ofttimes it befalleth that some that have been horrible and accustomed sinners come sooner to the perfection of this work than those that have been none. And this is the merciful miracle of our Lord, that so specially giveth His grace, to the wondering of all this world. Now truly I hope that on Doomsday it shall be fair, when that God shall be seen clearly and all His gifts. Then shall some that now be despised and set at little or nought as common sinners, and peradventure some that now be horrible sinners, sit full seemly with saints in His sight: when some of those that seem now full holy and be worshipped of men as angels, and some of those yet peradventure, that never yet sinned deadly, shall sit full sorry amongst hell caves.

Hereby mayest thou see that no man should be judged of other here in this life, for good nor for evil that they do. Nevertheless deeds may lawfully be judged, but not the man, whether they be good or evil.

Here Beginneth The Thirtieth Chapter
Who should blame and condemn other men's defaults.
But I pray thee, of whom shall men's deeds be judged?
Surely of them that have power, and cure of their souls: either given openly by the statute and the ordinance of Holy Church, or else privily in spirit at the special stirring of the Holy Ghost in perfect charity. Each man beware, that he presume not to take upon him to blame and condemn other men's defaults, but if he feel verily that he be stirred of the Holy Ghost within in his work; for else may he full lightly err in his dooms. And therefore beware: judge thyself as thee list betwixt thee and thy God or thy ghostly father, and let other men alone.

Here Beginneth The One And Thirtieth Chapter
How a man should have him in beginning of this work against all thoughts and stirrings of sin.
And from the time that thou feelest that thou hast done that in thee is, lawfully to amend thee at the doom of Holy Church, then shalt thou set thee sharply to work in this work. And then if it so be that thy foredone special deeds will always press in thy remembrance betwixt thee and thy God, or any new thought or stirring of any sin

either, thou shalt stalwartly step above them with a fervent stirring of love, and tread them down under thy feet. And try to cover them with a thick cloud of forgetting, as they never had been done in this life of thee nor of other man either. And if they oft rise, oft put them down: and shortly to say, as oft as they rise, as oft put them down. And if thee think that the travail be great, thou mayest seek arts and wiles and privy subtleties of ghostly devices to put them away: the which subtleties be better learned of God by the proof than of any man in this life.

Here Beginneth The Two And Thirtieth Chapter
Of two ghostly devices that be helpful to a ghostly beginner in the work of this book.

Nevertheless, somewhat of this subtlety shall I tell thee as me think. Prove thou and do better, if thou better mayest. Do that in thee is, to let be as thou wist not that they press so fast upon thee betwixt thee and thy God. And try to look as it were over their shoulders, seeking another thing: the which thing is God, enclosed in a cloud of unknowing. And if thou do thus, I trow that within short time thou shalt be eased of thy travail. I trow that an this device be well and truly conceived, it is nought else but a longing desire unto God, to feel Him and see Him as it may be here: and such a desire is charity, and it obtaineth always to be eased.

Another device there is: prove thou if thou wilt. When thou feelest that thou mayest on nowise put them down, cower thou down under them as a caitiff and a coward overcome in battle, and think that it is but a folly to thee to strive any longer with them, and therefore thou yieldest thee to God in the hands of thine enemies. And feel then thyself as thou wert foredone for ever. Take good heed of this device I pray thee, for me think in the proof of this device thou shouldest melt all to water. And surely me think an this device be truly conceived it is nought else but a true knowing and a feeling of thyself as thou art, a wretch and a filthy, far worse than nought: the which knowing and feeling is meekness. And this meekness obtaineth to have God Himself mightily descending, to venge thee of thine enemies, for to take thee up, and cherishingly dry thine ghostly eyen; as the father doth the child that is in point to perish under the mouths of wild swine or wode biting bears.

Here Beginneth The Three And Thirtieth Chapter
That in this work a soul is cleansed both of his special sins and of the pain of them, and yet how there is no perfect rest in this life.

More devices tell I thee not at this time; for an thou have grace to feel the proof of these, I trow that thou shalt know better to learn me than I thee. For although it should be thus, truly yet me think that I am full far therefrom. And therefore I pray thee help me, and do thou for thee and for me.

Do on then, and travail fast awhile, I pray thee, and suffer meekly the pain if thou mayest not soon win to these arts. For truly it is thy purgatory, and then when thy pain is all passed and thy devices be given of God, and graciously gotten in custom; then it is no doubt to me that thou art cleansed not only of sin, but also of the pain of sin. I mean, of the pain of thy special foredone sins, and not of the pain of the original sin. For that pain shall always last on thee to thy death day, be thou never so busy. Nevertheless, it shall but little provoke thee, in comparison of this pain of thy special sins; and yet shalt thou not be without great travail. For out of this original sin will all day spring new and fresh stirrings of sin: the which thee behoveth all day to smite down, and be busy to shear away with a sharp double-edged dreadful sword of discretion. And hereby mayest thou see and learn, that there is no soothfast security, nor yet no true rest in this life.

Nevertheless, herefore shalt thou not go back, nor yet be overfeared of thy failing. For an it so be that thou mayest have grace to destroy the pain of thine foredone special deeds, in the manner before said—or better if thou better mayest—sure be thou, that the pain of the original sin, or else the new stirrings of sin that be to come, shall but right little be able to provoke thee.

Here Beginneth The Four And Thirtieth Chapter
That God giveth this grace freely without any means, and that it may not be come to with means.

And if thou askest me by what means thou shalt come to this work, I beseech Almighty God of His great grace and His great courtesy to teach thee Himself. For truly I do thee well to wit that I cannot tell thee, and that is no wonder. For why, that is the work of only God, specially wrought in what soul that Him liketh without any desert of the same soul. For without it no saint nor no angel can think to desire it. And I trow that our Lord as specially and as oft—yea! and more specially and more oft—will vouchsafe to work this work in them that have been accustomed sinners, than in some other, that never grieved Him greatly in comparison of them. And this will He do, for He will be seen all merciful and almighty; and for He will be seen to work as Him list, where Him list, and when Him list.

And yet He giveth not this grace, nor worketh not this work, in any soul that is unable thereto. And yet, there is no soul without this grace, able to have this grace: none, whether it be a sinner's soul or an innocent soul. For neither it is given for innocence, nor withholden for sin. Take good heed, that I say withholden, and not withdrawn. Beware of error here, I pray thee; for ever, the nearer men touch the truth, more wary men behoveth to be of error. I mean but well: if thou canst not conceive it, lay it by thy side till God come and teach thee. Do then so, and hurt thee not.

Beware of pride, for it blasphemeth God in His gifts, and boldeneth sinners. Wert thou verily meek, thou shouldest feel of this work as I say: that God giveth it freely without any desert. The condition of this work is such, that the presence thereof enableth a soul for to have it and for to feel it. And that ableness may no soul have without it. The ableness to this work is oned to the work's self without departing; so that whoso feeleth this work is able thereto, and none else. Insomuch, that without this work a soul is as it were dead, and cannot covet it nor desire it. Forasmuch as thou willest it and desirest it, so much hast thou of it, and no more nor no less: and yet is it no will, nor no desire, but a thing thou wottest never what, that stirreth thee to will and desire thou wottest never what. Reck thee never if thou wittest no more, I pray thee: but do forth ever more and more, so that thou be ever doing.

And if I shall shortlier say, let that thing do with thee and lead thee whereso it list. Let it be the worker, and you but the sufferer: do but look upon it, and let it alone. Meddle thee not therewith as thou wouldest help it, for dread lest thou spill all. Be thou but the tree, and let it be the wright: be thou but the house, and let it be the husbandman dwelling therein. Be blind in this time, and shear away covetise of knowing, for it will more let thee than help thee. It sufficeth enough unto thee, that thou feelest thee stirred likingly with a thing thou wottest never what, else that in this stirring thou hast no special thought of any thing under God; and that thine intent be nakedly directed unto God.

And if it be thus, trust then steadfastly that it is only God that stirreth thy will and thy desire plainly by Himself, without means either on His part or on thine. And be not feared, for the devil may not come so near. He may never come to stir a man's will, but occasionally and by means from afar, be he never so subtle a devil. For sufficiently and without means may no good angel stir thy will: nor, shortly to say, nothing but only God. So that thou mayest conceive here by these words somewhat (but much more clearly by the proof), that in this work men shall use no means: nor yet men may not come thereto with means. All good means hang upon it, and it on no means; nor no means may lead thereto.

Here Beginneth The Five And Thirtieth Chapter
Of three means in the which a contemplative Prentice should be occupied, in reading, thinking, and praying.
Nevertheless, means there be in the which a contemplative prentice should be occupied, the which be these—Lesson, Meditation, and Orison: or else to thine understanding they may be called—Reading, Thinking, and Praying. Of these three thou shalt find written in another book of another man's work, much better than I can tell thee; and therefore it needeth not here to tell thee of the qualities of them. But this may I tell thee: these three be so coupled together, that unto them that be beginners and profiters—but not to them that be perfect, yea, as it may be here—thinking may not goodly be gotten, without reading or hearing coming before. All is one in manner, reading and hearing: clerks reading on books, and lewd men reading on clerks when they hear them preach the word of God. Nor prayer may not goodly be gotten in beginners and profiters, without thinking coming before.

See by the proof. In this same course, God's word either written or spoken is likened to a mirror. Ghostly, the eyes of thy soul is thy reason; thy conscience is thy visage ghostly. And right as thou seest that if a foul spot be in thy bodily visage, the eyes of the same visage may not see that spot nor wit where it is, without a mirror or a teaching of another than itself; right so it is ghostly, without reading or hearing of God's word it is impossible to man's understanding that a soul that is blinded in custom of sin should see the foul spot in his conscience.

And so following, when a man seeth in a bodily or ghostly mirror, or wots by other men's teaching, whereabouts the foul spot is on his visage, either bodily or ghostly; then at first, and not before, he runneth to the well to wash him. If this spot be any special sin, then is this well Holy Church, and this water confession, with the circumstances. If it be but a blind root and a stirring of sin, then is this well merciful God, and this water prayer, with the circumstances. And thus mayest thou see that no thinking may goodly be gotten in beginners and profiters, without reading or hearing coming before: nor praying without thinking.

Here Beginneth The Six And Thirtieth Chapter
Of the meditations of them that continually travail in the work of this book.

But it is not so with them that continually work in the work of this book. For their meditations be but as they were sudden conceits and blind feelings of their own wretchedness, or of the goodness of God; without any means of reading or hearing coming before, and without any special beholding of any thing under God. These sudden conceits and these blind feelings be sooner learned of God than of man. I care not though thou haddest nowadays none other meditations of thine own wretchedness, nor of the goodness of God (I mean if thou feel thee thus stirred by grace and by counsel), but such as thou mayest have in this word *sin*, and in this word God: or in such other, which as thee list. Not breaking nor expounding these words with curiosity of wit, in beholding after the qualities of these words, as thou wouldest by that beholding increase thy devotion. I trow it should never be so in this case and in this work. But hold them all whole these words; and mean by sin, a lump, thou wottest never what, none other thing but thyself. Me think that in this blind beholding of sin, thus congealed in a lump, none other thing than thyself, it should be no need to bind a madder thing, than thou shouldest be in this time. And yet peradventure, whoso looked upon thee should think thee full soberly disposed in thy body, without any changing of countenance; but sitting or going or lying, or leaning or standing or kneeling, whether thou wert, in a full sober restfulness.

Here Beginneth The Seven And Thirtieth Chapter
Of the special prayers of them that be continual workers in the word of this book

And right as the meditations of them that continually work in this grace and in this work rise suddenly without any means, right so do their prayers. I mean of their special prayers, not of those prayers that be ordained of Holy Church. For they that be true workers in this work, they worship no prayer so much: and therefore they do them, in the form and in the statute that they be ordained of holy fathers before us. But their special prayers rise evermore suddenly unto God, without any means or any premeditation in special coming before, or going therewith.

And if they be in words, as they be but seldom, then be they but in full few words: yea, and in ever the fewer the better. Yea, and if it be but a little word of one syllable, me think it better than of two: and more, too, according to the work of the spirit, since it so is that a ghostly worker in this work should evermore be in the highest and the sovereignest point of the spirit. That this be sooth, see by ensample in the course of nature. A man or a woman, afraid with any sudden chance of fire or of man's death or what else that it be, suddenly in the height of his spirit, he is driven upon haste and upon need for to cry or for to pray after help. Yea, how? Surely, not in many words, nor yet in one word of two syllables. And why is that? For him thinketh it over long tarrying for to declare the need and the work of his spirit. And therefore he bursteth up hideously with a great spirit, and cryeth a little word, but of one syllable: as is this word "fire," or this word "out!"

And right as this little word "fire" stirreth rather and pierceth more hastily the ears of the hearers, so doth a little word of one syllable when it is not only spoken or thought, but privily meant in the deepness of spirit; the which is the height, for in ghostliness all is one, height and deepness, length and breadth. And rather it pierceth the ears of Almighty God than doth any long psalter unmindfully mumbled in the teeth. And herefore it is written, that short prayer pierceth heaven.

Here Beginneth The Eight And Thirtieth Chapter
How and why that short prayer pierceth heaven
And why pierceth it heaven, this little short prayer of one little syllable? Surely because it is prayed with a full spirit, in the height and in the deepness, in the length and in the breadth of his spirit that prayeth it. In the height it is, for it is with all the might of the spirit. In the deepness it is, for in this little syllable be contained all the wits of the spirit. In the length it is, for might it ever feel as it feeleth, ever

would it cry as it cryeth. In the breadth it is, for it willeth the same to all other that it willeth to itself.

In this time it is that a soul hath comprehended after the lesson of Saint Paul with all saints—not fully, but in manner and in part, as it is according unto this work—which is the length and the breadth, the height and the deepness of everlasting and all□lovely, almighty, and all□witting God. The everlastingness of God is His length. His love is His breadth. His might is His height. And His wisdom is His deepness. No wonder though a soul that is thus nigh conformed by grace to the image and the likeness of God his maker, be soon heard of God! Yea, though it be a full sinful soul, the which is to God as it were an enemy; an he might through grace come for to cry such a little syllable in the height and the deepness, the length and the breadth of his spirit, yet he should for the hideous noise of his cry be always heard and helped of God.

See by ensample. He that is thy deadly enemy, an thou hear him so afraid that he cry in the height of his spirit this little word "fire," or this word "out"; yet without any beholding to him for he is thine enemy, but for pure pity in thine heart stirred and raised with the dolefulness of this cry, thou risest up—yea, though it be about midwinter's night—and helpest him to slack his fire, or for to still him and rest him in his distress. Oh, Lord! since a man may be made so merciful in grace, to have so much mercy and so much pity of his enemy, notwithstanding his enmity, what pity and what mercy shall God have then of a ghostly cry in soul, made and wrought in the height and the deepness, the length and the breadth of his spirit; the which hath all by nature that man hath by grace? And much more, surely without comparison, much more mercy will He have; since it is, that that thing that is so had by nature is nearer to an eternal thing than that which is had by grace.

Here Beginneth The Nine And Thirtieth Chapter
How a perfect worker shall pray, and what prayer is in itself; and if a man shall pray in words, which words accord them most to the property of prayer.

And therefore it is, to pray in the height and the deepness, the length and the breadth of our spirit. And that not in many words, but in a little word of one syllable.

And what shall this word be? Surely such a word as is best according unto the property of prayer. And what word is that? Let us first see what prayer is properly in itself, and thereafter we may clearlier know what word will best accord to the property of prayer.

Prayer in itself properly is not else, but a devout intent direct unto God, for getting of good and removing of evil. And then, since it so is that all evil be comprehended in sin, either by cause or by being, let us therefore when we will intentively pray for removing of evil either say, or think, or mean, nought else nor no more words, but this little word "sin." And if we will intentively pray for getting of good, let us cry, either with word or with thought or with desire, nought else nor no more words, but this word "God." For why, in God be all good, both by cause and by being. Have no marvel why I set these words forby all other. For if I could find any shorter words, so fully comprehending in them all good and all evil, as these two words do, or if I had been learned of God to take any other words either, I would then have taken them and left these; and so I counsel that thou do.

Study thou not for no words, for so shouldest thou never come to thy purpose nor to this work, for it is never got by study, but all only by grace. And therefore take thou none other words to pray in, although I set these here, but such as thou art stirred of God for to take. Nevertheless, if God stir thee to take these, I counsel not that thou leave them; I mean if thou shalt pray in words, and else not. For why, they be full short words. But although the shortness of prayer be greatly commended here, nevertheless the oftness of prayer is never the rather refrained. For as it is said before, it is prayed in the length of the spirit; so that it should never cease, till the time were that it had fully gotten that that it longed after. Ensample of this have we in a man or a woman afraid in the manner beforesaid. For we see well, that they cease never crying on this little word "out," or this little word "fire," ere the time be that they have in great part gotten help of their grief.

Here Beginneth The Fortieth Chapter
That in the time of this work a soul hath no special beholding to any vice in itself nor to any virtue in itself.

Do thou, on the same manner, fill thy spirit with the ghostly bemeaning of this word "sin," and without any special beholding unto any kind of sin, whether it be venial or deadly: Pride, Wrath, or Envy, Covetyse, Sloth, Gluttony, or Lechery. What recks it in contemplatives, what sin that it be, or how muckle a sin that it be? For all sins them thinketh—I mean for the time of this work—alike great in themselves, when the least sin departeth them from God, and letteth them of their ghostly peace.

And feel sin a lump, thou wottest never what, but none other thing than thyself. And cry then ghostly ever upon one: a Sin, sin, sin! Out, out, out!" This ghostly cry is better learned of God by the proof, than of any man by word. For it is best when it is in pure spirit, without special thought or any pronouncing of word; unless it be any seldom time, when for abundance of spirit it bursteth up into word, so that the body and the soul be both filled with sorrow and cumbering of sin.

On the same manner shalt thou do with this little word "God." Fill thy spirit with the ghostly bemeaning of it without any special beholding to any of His works—whether they be good, better, or best of all—bodily or ghostly, or to any virtue that may be wrought in man's soul by any grace; not looking after whether it be meekness or charity, patience or abstinence, hope, faith, or soberness, chastity or wilful poverty. What recks this in contemplatives? For all virtues they find and feel in God; for in Him is all thing, both by cause and by being. For they think that an they had God they had all good, and therefore they covet nothing with special beholding, but only good God. Do thou on the same manner as far forth as thou mayest by grace: and mean God all, and all God, so that nought work in thy wit and in thy will, but only God.

And because that ever the whiles thou livest in this wretched life, thee behoveth always feel in some part this foul stinking lump of sin, as it were oned and congealed with the substance of thy being, therefore shalt thou changeably mean these two words—sin and God. With this general knowing, that an thou haddest God, then shouldest thou lack sin: and mightest thou lack sin, then shouldest thou have God.

Here Beginneth The One And Fortieth Chapter
That in all other works beneath this, men should keep discretion; but in this none.

And furthermore, if thou ask me what discretion thou shalt have in this work, then I answer thee and say, right none! For in all thine other doings thou shalt have discretion, as in eating and in drinking, and in sleeping and in keeping of thy body from outrageous cold or heat, and in long praying or reading, or in communing in speech with

Essential Writings of Christian Mysticism

thine even-christian. In all these shalt thou keep discretion, that they be neither too much nor too little. But in this work shalt thou hold no measure: for I would that thou shouldest never cease of this work the whiles thou livest.

I say not that thou shalt continue ever therein alike fresh, for that may not be. For sometime sickness and other unordained dispositions in body and in soul, with many other needfulness to nature, will let thee full much, and ofttimes draw thee down from the height of this working. But I say that thou shouldest evermore have it either in earnest or in game; that is to say, either in work or in will. And therefore for God's love be wary with sickness as much as thou mayest goodly, so that thou be not the cause of thy feebleness, as far as thou mayest. For I tell thee truly, that this work asketh a full great restfulness, and a full whole and clean disposition, as well in body as in soul.

And therefore for God's love govern thee discreetly in body and in soul, and get thee thine health as much as thou mayest. And if sickness come against thy power, have patience and abide meekly God's mercy: and all is then good enough. For I tell thee truly, that ofttimes patience in sickness and in other diversee tribulations pleaseth God much more than any liking devotion that thou mayest have in thy health.

Here Beginneth The Two And Fortieth Chapter
That by indiscretion in this, men shall keep discretion in all other things; and surely else never

But peradventure thou askest me, how thou shalt govern thee discreetly in meat and in sleep, and in all these other. And hereto I think to answer thee right shortly: "Get that thou get mayest." Do this work evermore without ceasing and without discretion, and thou shalt well ken begin and cease in all other works with a great discretion. For I may not trow that a soul continuing in this work night and day without discretion, should err in any of these outward doings; and else, me think that he should always err.

And therefore, an I might get a waking and a busy beholding to this ghostly work within in my soul, I would then have a heedlessness in eating and in drinking, in sleeping and in speaking, and in all mine outward doings. For surely I trow I should rather come to discretion in them by such a heedlessness, than by any busy beholding to the same things, as I would by that beholding set a mark and a measure by them. Truly I should never bring it so about, for ought that I could do or say. Say what men say will, and let the proof witness. And therefore lift up thine heart with a blind stirring of love; and mean now sin, and now God. God wouldest thou have, and sin wouldest thou lack. God wanteth thee; and sin art thou sure of. Now good God help thee, for now hast thou need!

Here Beginneth The Three And Fortieth Chapter

That all witting and feeling of a man's own being must needs be lost if the perfection of this word shall verily be felt in any soul in this life.

Look that nought work in thy wit nor in thy will but only God. And try for to fell all witting and feeling of ought under God, and tread all down full far under the cloud of forgetting. And thou shalt understand, that thou shalt not only in this work forget all other creatures than thyself, or their deeds or thine, but also thou shalt in this work forget both thyself and also thy deeds for God, as well as all other creatures and their deeds. For it is the condition of a perfect lover, not only to love that thing that he loveth more than himself; but also in a manner for to hate himself for that thing that he loveth.

Thus shalt thou do with thyself: thou shalt loathe and be weary with all that thing that worketh in thy wit and in thy will unless it be only God. For why, surely else, whatsoever that it be, it is betwixt thee and thy God. And no wonder though thou loathe and hate for to think on thyself, when thou shalt always feel sin, a foul stinking lump thou wottest never what, betwixt thee and thy God: the which lump is none other thing than thyself. For thou shalt think it oned and congealed with the substance of thy being: yea, as it were without departing.

And therefore break down all witting and feeling of all manner of creatures; but most busily of thyself. For on the witting and the feeling of thyself hangeth witting and feeling of all other creatures; for in regard of it, all other creatures be lightly forgotten. For, an thou wilt busily set thee to the proof, thou shalt find when thou hast forgotten all other creatures and all their works—yea, and thereto all thine own works—that there shall live yet after, betwixt thee and thy God, a naked witting and a feeling of thine own being: the which witting and feeling behoveth always be destroyed, ere the time be that thou feel soothfastly the perfection of this work.

Here Beginneth The Four And Fortieth Chapter
How a soul shall dispose it on its own part, for to destroy all witting and feeling of its own being.

But now thou askest me, how thou mayest destroy this naked witting and feeling of thine own being. For peradventure thou thinkest that an it were destroyed, all other lettings were destroyed: and if thou thinkest thus, thou thinkest right truly. But to this I answer thee and I say, that without a full special grace full freely given of God, and thereto a full according ableness to receive this grace on thy part, this naked witting and feeling of thy being may on nowise be destroyed. And this ableness is nought else but a strong and a deep ghostly sorrow.

But in this sorrow needeth thee to have discretion, on this manner: thou shalt be wary in the time of this sorrow, that thou neither too rudely strain thy body nor thy spirit, but sit full still, as it were in a sleeping device, all forsobbed and forsunken in sorrow. This is true sorrow; this is perfect sorrow; and well were him that might win to this sorrow. All men have matter of sorrow: but most specially he feeleth matter of sorrow, that wotteth and feeleth that he is. All other sorrows be unto this in comparison but as it were game to earnest. For he may make sorrow earnestly, that wotteth and feeleth not only what he is, but that he is. And whoso felt never this sorrow, he may make sorrow: for why, he felt yet never perfect sorrow. This sorrow, when it is had, cleanseth the soul, not only of sin, but also of pain that it hath deserved for sin; and thereto it maketh a soul able to receive that joy, the which reeveth from a man all witting and feeling of his being.

This sorrow, if it be truly conceived, is full of holy desire: and else might never man in this life abide it nor bear it. For were it not that a soul were somewhat fed with a manner of comfort of his right working, else should he not be able to bear the pain that he hath of the witting and feeling of his being. For as oft as he would have a true witting and a feeling of his God in purity of spirit, as it may be here, and sithen feeleth that he may not—for he findeth evermore his witting and his feeling as it were occupied and filled with a foul stinking lump of himself, the which behoveth always be hated and be despised and forsaken, if he shall be God's perfect disciple learned of Himself in the mount of perfection—so oft, he goeth nigh mad for sorrow. Insomuch, that he weepeth and waileth, striveth, curseth, and banneth; and shortly to say, him thinketh that he beareth so heavy a burthen of himself that he careth never what betides him, so that God were pleased. And yet in all this sorrow he desireth not to unbe: for that were devil's madness and despite unto God. But him listeth right well to be; and he intendeth full heartily thanking to God, for the worthiness and the gift of his being, for all that he desire unceasingly for to lack the witting and the feeling of his being.

This sorrow and this desire behoveth every soul have and feel in itself, either in this manner or in another; as God vouchsafeth for to learn to His ghostly disciples after His well willing and their according ableness in body and in soul, in degree and disposition, ere the time be that they may perfectly be oned unto God in perfect charity — such as may be had here — if God vouchsafeth.

Here Beginneth The Five And Fortieth Chapter
A good declaring of some certain deceits that may befall in this work.

But one thing I tell thee, that in this work may a young disciple that hath not yet been well used and proved in ghostly working, full lightly be deceived; and, but he be soon wary, and have grace to leave off and meek him to counsel, peradventure be destroyed in his bodily powers and fall into fantasy in his ghostly wits. And all this is along of pride, and of fleshliness and curiosity of wit.

And on this manner may this deceit befall. A young man or a woman new set to the school of devotion heareth this sorrow and this desire be read and spoken: how that a man shall lift up his heart unto God, and unceasingly desire for to feel the love of his God. And as fast in a curiosity of wit they conceive these words not ghostly as they be meant, but fleshly and bodily; and travail their fleshly hearts outrageously in their breasts. And what for lacking of grace and pride and curiosity in themselves, they strain their veins and their bodily powers so beastly and so rudely, that within short time they fall either into frenzies, weariness, and a manner of unlisty feebleness in body and in soul, the which maketh them to wend out of themselves and seek some false and some vain fleshly and bodily comfort without, as it were for recreation of body and of spirit: or else, if they fall not in this, else they merit for ghostly blindness, and for fleshly chafing of their nature in their bodily breasts in the time of this feigned beastly and not ghostly working, for to have their breasts either enflamed with an unkindly heat of nature caused of misruling of their bodies or of this feigned working, or else they conceive a false heat wrought by the Fiend, their ghostly enemy, caused of their pride and of their fleshliness and their curiosity of wit. And yet peradventure they ween it be the fire of love, gotten and kindled by the grace and the goodness of the Holy Ghost. Truly, of this deceit, and of the branches thereof, spring many mischiefs: much hypocrisy, much heresy, and much error. For as fast after such a false feeling cometh a false knowing in the Fiend's school, right as after a true feeling cometh a true knowing in God's school. For I tell thee truly, that the devil hath his contemplatives as God hath His.

This deceit of false feeling, and of false knowing following thereon, hath diversee and wonderful variations, after the diversity of states and the subtle conditions of them that be deceived: as hath the true feeling and knowing of them that be saved. But I set no more deceits here but those with the which I trow thou shalt be assailed if ever thou purpose thee to work in this work. For what should it profit to thee to wit how these great clerks, and men and women of other degrees than thou art, be deceived? Surely right nought; and therefore I tell thee no more but those that fall unto thee if thou travail in this work. And therefore I tell thee this, for thou shalt be wary therewith in thy working, if thou be assailed therewith.

Here Beginneth The Six And Fortieth Chapter
A good teaching how a man shall flee these deceits, and work more with a listiness of spirit, than with any boisterousness of body

And therefore for God's love be wary in this work, and strain not thine heart in thy breast over rudely nor out of measure; but work more with a list than with any worthless strength. For ever the more Mistily, the more meekly and ghostly: and ever the more rudely, the more bodily and beastly. And therefore be wary, for surely what beastly heart that presumeth for to touch the high mount of this work, it shall be beaten away with stones. Stones be hard and dry in their kind, and they hurt full sore where they hit. And surely such rude strainings be full hard fastened in fleshliness of bodily feeling, and full dry from any witting of grace; and they hurt full sore the silly soul, and make it fester in fantasy feigned of fiends. And therefore be wary with this beastly rudeness, and learn thee to love listily, with a soft and a demure behaviour as well in body as in soul; and abide courteously and meekly the will of our Lord, and snatch not overhastily, as it were a greedy greyhound, hunger thee never so sore. And, gamingly be it said, I counsel that thou do that in thee is, refraining the rude and the great stirring of thy spirit, right as thou on nowise wouldest let Him wit how fain thou wouldest see Him, and have Him or feel Him.

This is childishly and playingly spoken, thee think peradventure. But I trow whoso had grace to do and feel as I say, he should feel good gamesome play with Him, as the father doth with the child, kissing and clipping, that well were him so.

Here Beginneth The Seven And Fortieth Chapter

A slight teaching of this work in purity of spirit; declaring how that on one manner a soul should shed his desire unto God, and on ye contrary unto man.

Look thou have no wonder why that I speak thus childishly, and as it were follily and lacking natural discretion; for I do it for certain reasons, and as me thinketh that I have been stirred many days, both to feel thus and think thus and say thus, as well to some other of my special friends in God, as I am now unto thee.

And one reason is this, why that I bid thee hide from God the desire of thine heart. For I hope it should more clearly come to His knowing, for thy profit and in fulfilling of thy desire, by such an hiding, than it should by any other manner of shewing that I trow thou couldest yet shew. And another reason is, for I would by such a hid shewing bring thee out of the boisterousness of bodily feeling into the purity and deepness of ghostly feeling; and so furthermore at the last to help thee to knit the ghostly knot of burning love betwixt thee and thy God, in ghostly onehead and according of will.

Thou wottest well this, that God is a Spirit; and whoso should be oned unto Him, it behoveth to be in soothfastness and deepness of spirit, full far from any feigned bodily thing. Sooth it is that all thing is known of God, and nothing may be hid from His witting, neither bodily thing nor ghostly. But more openly is that thing known and shewed unto Him, the which is hid in deepness of spirit, sith it so is that He is a Spirit, than is anything that is mingled with any manner of bodilyness. For all bodily thing is farther from God by the course of nature than any ghostly thing. By this reason it seemeth, that the whiles our desire is mingled with any matter of bodilyness, as it is when we stress and strain us in spirit and in body together, so long it is farther from God than it should be, an it were done more devoutly and more listily in soberness and in purity and in deepness of spirit.

And here mayest thou see somewhat and in part the reason why that I bid thee so childishly cover and hide the stirring of thy desire from God. And yet I bid thee not plainly hide it; for that were the bidding of a fool, for to bid thee plainly do that which on nowise may be done. But I bid thee do that in thee is to hide it. And why bid I thus? Surely because I would that thou cast it into deepness of spirit, far from any rude mingling of any bodilyness, the which would make it less ghostly and farther from God inasmuch: and because I wot well that ever the more that thy spirit hath of ghostliness, the less it hath of bodilyness and the nearer it is to God, and the better it pleaseth Him and the more clearly it may be seen of Him. Not that His sight may be any time or in any thing more clear than in another, for it is evermore unchangeable: but because it is more like unto Him, when it is in purity of spirit, for He is a Spirit.

Another reason there is, why that I bid thee do that in thee is to let Him not wit: for thou and I and many such as we be, we be so able to conceive a thing bodily the which is said ghostly, that peradventure an I had bidden thee shew unto God the stirring of thine heart, thou shouldest have made a bodily shewing unto Him, either in gesture or in voice, or in word, or in some other rude bodily straining, as it is when thou shalt shew a thing that is hid in thine heart to a bodily man: and insomuch thy work should have been impure. For on one manner shall a thing be shewed to man, and on another manner unto God.

Here Beginneth The Eight And Fortieth Chapter

How God will be served both with body and with soul, and reward men in both; and how men shall know when all those sounds and sweetness that fall into the body in time of prayer be both good and evil

I say not this because I will that thou desist any time, if thou be stirred for to pray with thy mouth, or for to burst out for abundance of devotion in thy spirit for to speak unto God as unto man, and say some good word as thou feelest thee stirred: as be these, "Good Jesus! Fair Jesus! Sweet Jesus!" and all such other. Nay, God forbid thou take it thus! For truly I mean not thus, and God forbid that I should depart that which God hath coupled, the body and the spirit. For God will be served with body and with soul both together, as seemly is, and will reward man his meed in bliss, both in body and in soul. And in earnest of that meed, sometimes He will enflame the body of devout servants of His here in this life: not once or twice, but peradventure right oft and as Him liketh, with full wonderful sweetness and comforts. Of the which, some be not coming from without into the body by the windows of our wits, but from within; rising and springing of abundance of ghostly gladness, and of true devotion in the spirit. Such a comfort and such a sweetness shall not be had suspect: and shortly to say, I trow that he that feeleth it may not have it suspect.

But all other comforts, sounds and gladness and sweetness, that come from without suddenly and thou wottest never whence, I pray thee have them suspect. For they may be both good and evil; wrought by a good angel if they be good, and by an evil angel if they be evil. And this may on nowise be evil, if their deceits of curiosity of wit, and of unordained straining of the fleshly heart be removed as I learn thee, or better if thou better mayest. And why is that? Surely for the cause of this comfort; that is to say, the devout stirring of love, the which dwelleth in pure spirit. It is wrought of the hand of Almighty God without means, and therefore it behoveth always be far from any fantasy, or any false opinion that may befall to man in this life.

And of the tother comforts and sounds and sweetness, how thou shouldest wit whether they be good or evil I think not to tell thee at this time: and that is because me think that it needeth not. For why, thou mayest find it written in another place of another man's work, a thousandfold better than I can say or write: and so mayest thou this that I set here, far better than it is here. But what thereof? Therefore shall I not let, nor it shall not noye me, to fulfil the desire and the stirring of thine heart; the which thou hast shewed thee to have unto me before this time in thy words, and now in thy deeds.

But this may I say thee of those sounds and of those sweetnesses, that come in by the windows of thy wits, the which may be both good and evil. Use thee continually in this blind and devout and this Misty stirring of love that I tell thee: and then I have no doubt, that it shall not well be able to tell thee of them. And if thou yet be in part astonished of them at the first time, and that is because that they be uncouth, yet this shall it do thee: it shall bind thine heart so fast, that thou shalt on nowise give full great credence to them, ere the time be that thou be either certified of them within wonderfully by the Spirit of God, or else without by counsel of some discreet father.

Here Beginneth The Nine And Fortieth Chapter

The substance of all perfection is nought else but a good will; and how that all sounds and comfort and sweetness that may befall in this life be to it but as it were accidents.

And therefore I pray thee, lean listily to this meek stirring of love in thine heart, and follow thereafter: for it will be thy guide in this life and bring thee to bliss in the tother. It is the substance of all good living, and without it no good work may be begun nor ended. It is nought else but a good and an according will unto God, and a manner of well☐pleasedness and a gladness that thou feelest in thy will of all that He doth.

Such a good will is the substance of all perfection. All sweetness and comforts, bodily or ghostly, be to this but as it were accidents, be they never so holy; and they do but hang on this good will. Accidents I call them, for they may be had and lacked without breaking asunder of it. I mean in this life, but it is not so in the bliss of heaven; for there shall they be oned with the substance without departing, as shall the body in the which they work with the soul. So that the substance of them here is but a good ghostly will. And surely I trow that he that feeleth the perfection of this will, as it may be had here, there may no sweetness nor no comfort fall to any man in this life, that he is not as fain and as glad to lack it at God's will, as to feel it and have it.

Here Beginneth The Fiftieth Chapter
Which is chaste love; and how in some creatures such sensible comforts be but seldom, and in some right oft.

And hereby mayest thou see that we should direct all our beholding unto this meek stirring of love in our will. And in all other sweetness and comforts, bodily or ghostly, be they never so liking nor so holy, if it be courteous and seemly to say, we should have a manner of recklessness. If they come, welcome them: but lean not too much on them for fear of feebleness, for it will take full much of thy powers to bide any long time in such sweet feelings and weepings. And peradventure thou mayest be stirred for to love God for them, and that shalt thou feel by this: if thou grumble overmuch when they be away. And if it be thus, thy love is not yet neither chaste nor perfect. For a love that is chaste and perfect, though it suffer that the body be fed and comforted in the presence of such sweet feelings and weepings, nevertheless yet it is not grumbling, but full well pleased for to lack them at God's will. And yet it is not commonly without such comforts in some creatures, and in some other creatures such sweetness and comforts be but seldom.

And all this is after the disposition and the ordinance of God, all after the profit and the needfulness of diversee creatures. For some creatures be so weak and so tender in spirit, that unless they were somewhat comforted by feeling of such sweetness, they might on nowise abide nor bear the diversity of temptations and tribulations that they suffer and be travailed with in this life of their bodily and ghostly enemies. And some there be that they be so weak in body that they may do no great penance to cleanse them with. And these creatures will our Lord cleanse full graciously in spirit by such sweet feelings and weepings. And also on the tother part there be some creatures so strong in spirit, that they can pick them comfort enough within in their souls, in offering up of this reverent and this meek stirring of love and accordance of will, that them needeth not much to be fed with such sweet comforts in bodily feelings. Which of these be holier or more dear with God, one than another, God wots and I not.

Here Beginneth The One And Fiftieth Chapter
That men should have great wariness so that they understand not bodily a thing that is meant ghostly; and specially it is good to be wary in understanding of this word "in," and of this word "up."

And therefore lean meekly to this blind stirring of love in thine heart. I mean not in thy bodily heart, but in thy ghostly heart, the which is thy will. And be well wary that thou conceive not bodily that that is said ghostly. For truly I tell thee, that bodily and fleshly conceits of them that have curious and imaginative wits be cause of much error.

Ensample of this mayest thou see, by that that I bid thee hide thy desire from God in that that in thee is. For peradventure an I had bidden thee shew thy desire unto God, thou shouldest have conceived it more bodily than thou dost now, when I bid thee hide it. For thou wottest well, that all that thing that is wilfully hidden, it is cast into the deepness of spirit. And thus me thinketh that it needeth greatly to have much wariness in understanding of words that be spoken to ghostly intent, so that thou conceive them not bodily but ghostly, as they be meant: and specially it is good to be wary with this word in, and this word up. For in misconceiving of these two words hangeth much error, and much deceit in them that purpose them to be ghostly workers, as me thinketh. Somewhat wot I by the proof, and somewhat by hearsay; and of these deceits list me tell thee a little as me thinketh.

A young disciple in God's school new turned from the world, the same weeneth that for a little time that he hath given him to penance and to prayer, taken by counsel in confession, that he be therefore able to take upon him ghostly working of the which he heareth men speak or read about him, or peradventure readeth himself. And therefore when they read or hear spoken of ghostly working—and specially of this word, "how a man shall draw all his wit within himself," or "how he shall climb above himself"—as fast for blindness in soul, and for fleshliness and curiosity of natural wit, they misunderstand these words, and ween, because they find in them a natural covetyse to hid things, that they be therefore called to that work by grace. Insomuch, that if counsel will not accord that they shall work in this work, as soon they feel a manner of grumbling against their counsel, and think—yea and peradventure say to such other as they be—that they can find no man that can wit what they mean fully. And therefore as fast, for boldness and presumption of their curious wit, they leave meek prayer and penance over soon; and set them, they ween, to a full ghostly work within in their soul. The which work, an it be truly conceived, is neither bodily working nor ghostly working; and shortly to say, it is a working against nature, and the devil is the chief worker thereof. And it is the readiest way to death of body and of soul, for it is madness and no wisdom, and leadeth a man even to madness. And yet they ween not thus: for they purpose them in this work to think on nought but on God.

Here Beginneth The Two And Fiftieth Chapter
How these young presumptuous disciples misunderstand this word "in," and of the deceits that follow thereon.
And on this manner is this madness wrought that I speak of. They read and hear well said that they should leave outward working with their wits, and work inwards: and because that they know not which is inward working, therefore they work wrong. For they turn their bodily wits inwards to their body against the course of nature; and strain them, as they would see inwards with their bodily eyes and hear inwards with their ears, and so forth of all their wits, smelling, tasting, and feeling inwards. And thus they reverse them against the course of nature, and with this curiosity they travail their imagination so indiscreetly, that at the last they turn their brain in their heads, and then as fast the devil hath power for to feign some false light or sounds, sweet smells in their noses, wonderful tastes in their mouths; and many quaint heats and burnings in their bodily breasts or in their bowels, in their backs and in their reins and in their members.

And yet in this fantasy them think that they have a restful remembrance of their God without any letting of vain thoughts; and surely so have they in manner, for they be so filled in falsehood that vanity may not provoke them. And why? Because he, that same fiend that should minister vain thoughts to them an they were in good way—he, that same, is the chief worker of this work. And wit thou right well, that him list not to let himself. The remembrance of God will he not put from them, for fear that he should be had in suspect.

Here Beginneth The Three And Fiftieth Chapter
Of diverse unseemly practices that follow them that lack the work of this book.

Many wonderful practices follow them that be deceived in this false work, or in any species thereof, beyond that doth them that be God's true disciples: for they be evermore full seemly in all their practices, bodily or ghostly. But it is not so of these other. For whoso would or might behold unto them where they sit in this time, an it so were that their eyelids were open, he should see them stare as they were mad, and leeringly look as if they saw the devil. Surely it is good they be wary, for truly the fiend is not far. Some set their eyes in their heads as they were sturdy sheep beaten in the head, and as they should die anon. Some hang their heads on one side as if a worm were in their ears. Some pipe when they should speak, as if there were no spirit in their bodies: and this is the proper condition of an hypocrite. Some cry and whine in their throats, so be they greedy and hasty to say that they think: and this is the condition of heretics, and of them that with presumption and with curiosity of wit will always maintain error.

Many unordained and unseemly practices follow on this error, whoso might perceive all. Nevertheless some there be that be so curious that they can refrain them in great part when they come before men. But might these men be seen in place where they be homely, then I trow they should not be hid. And nevertheless yet I trow that whoso would straitly gainsay their opinion, that they should soon see them burst out in some point; and yet them think that all that ever they do, it is for the love of God and for to maintain the truth. Now truly I hope that unless God shew His merciful miracle to make them soon leave off, they shall love God so long on this manner, that they shall go staring mad to the devil. I say not that the devil hath so perfect a servant in this life, that is deceived and infect with all these fantasies that I set here: and nevertheless yet it may be that one, yea, and many one, be infect with them all. But I say that he hath no perfect hypocrite nor heretic in earth that he is not guilty in some that I have said, or peradventure shall say if God vouchsafeth.

For some men are so cumbered in nice curious customs in bodily bearing, that when they shall ought hear, they writhe their heads on one side quaintly, and up with the chin: they gape with their mouths as they should hear with their mouth and not with their ears. Some when they should speak point with their fingers, either on their fingers, or on their own breasts, or on theirs that they speak to. Some can neither sit still, stand still, nor lie still, unless they be either wagging with their feet or else somewhat doing with their hands. Some row with their arms in time of their speaking, as them needed for to swim over a great water. Some be evermore smiling and laughing at every other word that they speak, as they were giggling girls and nice japing jugglers lacking behaviour. Seemly cheer were full fair, with sober and demure bearing of body and mirth in manner.

I say not that all these unseemly practices be great sins in themselves, nor yet all those that do them be great sinners themselves. But I say if that these unseemly and unordained practices be governors of that man that doth them, insomuch that he may not leave them when he will, then I say that they be tokens of pride and curiosity of wit, and of unordained shewing and covetyse of knowing. And specially they be very tokens of unstableness of heart and unrestfulness of mind, and specially of the lacking of the work of this book. And this is the only reason why that I set so many of these deceits here in this writing; for why, that a ghostly worker shall prove his work by them.

Here Beginneth The Four And Fiftieth Chapter
How that by Virtue of this word a man is governed full wisely, and made full seemly as well in body as in soul.

Whoso had this work, it should govern them full seemly, as well in body as in soul: and make them full favourable unto each man or woman that looked upon them. Insomuch, that the worst favoured man or woman that liveth in this life, an they might come by grace to work in this work, their favour should suddenly and graciously be changed: that each good man that them saw, should be fain and joyful to have them in company, and full much they should think that they were pleased in spirit and holpen by grace unto God in their presence.

And therefore get this gift whoso by grace get may: for whoso hath it verily, he shall well con govern himself by the virtue thereof, and all that longeth unto him. He should well give discretion, if need were, of all natures and all dispositions. He should well con make himself like unto all that with him communed, whether they were accustomed sinners or none, without sin in himself: in wondering of all that him saw, and in drawing of others by help of grace to the work of that same spirit that he worketh in himself.

His cheer and his words should be full of ghostly wisdom, full of fire, and of fruit spoken in sober soothfastness without any falsehood, far from any feigning or piping of hypocrites. For some there be that with all their might, inner and outer, imagineth in their speaking how they may stuff them and underprop them on each side from falling, with many meek piping words and gestures of devotion: more looking after for to seem holy in sight of men, than for to be so in the sight of God and His angels. For why, these folk will more weigh, and more sorrow make for an unordained gesture or unseemly or unfitting word spoken before men, than they will for a thousand vain thoughts and stinking stirrings of sin wilfully drawn upon them, or recklessly used in the sight of God and the saints and the angels in heaven. Ah, Lord God! where there be any pride within, there such meek piping words be so plenteous without. I grant well, that it is fitting and seemly to them that be meek within, for to shew meek and seemly words and gestures without, according to that meekness that is within in the heart. But I say not that they shall then be shewed in broken nor in piping voices, against the plain disposition of their nature that speak them. For why, if they be true, then be they spoken in soothfastness, and in wholeness of voice and of their spirit that speak them. And if he that hath a plain and an open boisterous voice by nature speak them poorly and pipingly—I mean but if he be sick in his body, or else that it be betwixt him and his God or his confessor—then it is a very token of hypocrisy. I mean either young hypocrisy or old.

And what shall I more say of these venomous deceits? Truly I trow, unless they have grace to leave off such piping hypocrisy, that betwixt that privy pride in their hearts within and such meek words without, the silly soul may full soon sink into sorrow.

Here Beginneth The Five And Fiftieth Chapter

How they be deceived that follow the fervour of spirit in condemning of some without discretion.

Some men the fiend will deceive on this manner. Full wonderfully he will enflame their brains to maintain God's law, and to destroy sin in all other men. He will never tempt them with a thing that is openly evil; he maketh them like busy prelates watching over all the degrees of Christian men's living, as an abbot over his monks. ALL men will they reprove of their defaults, right as they had cure of their souls: and yet they think that they do not else for God, unless they tell them their defaults that they see. And they say that they be stirred thereto by the fire of charity, and of God's love in their hearts: and truly they lie, for it is with the fire of hell, welling in their brains and in their imagination.

That this is sooth, it seemeth by this that followeth. The devil is a spirit, and of his own nature he hath no body, more than hath an angel. But yet nevertheless what time that he or an angel shall take any body by leave of God, to make any ministration to any man in this life; according as the work is that he shall minister, thereafter in likeness is the quality of his body in some part. Ensample of this we have in Holy Writ. As oft as any angel was sent in body in the Old Testament and in the New also, evermore it was shewed, either by his name or by some instrument or quality of his body, what his matter or his message was in spirit. On the same manner it fareth of the fiend. For when he appeareth in body, he figureth in some quality of his body what his servants be in spirit. Ensample of this may be seen in one instead of all these other. For as I have conceived by some disciples of necromancy, the which have it in science for to make advocation of wicked spirits, and by some unto whom the fiend hath appeared in bodily likeness; that in what bodily likeness the fiend appeareth, evermore he hath but one nostril, and that is great and wide, and he will gladly cast it up that a man may see in thereat to his brain up in his head. The which brain is nought else but the fire of hell, for the fiend may have none other brain; and if he might make a man look in thereto, he wants no better. For at that looking, he should lose his wits for ever. But a perfect prentice of necromancy knoweth this well enough, and can well ordain therefore, so that he provoke him not.

Therefore it is that I say, and have said, that evermore when the devil taketh any body, he figureth in some quality of his body what his servants be in spirit. For he enflameth so the imagination of his contemplatives with the fire of hell, that suddenly without discretion they shoot out their curious conceits, and without any advisement they will take upon them to blame other men's defaults over soon: and this is because they have but one nostril ghostly. For that division that is in a man's nose bodily, and the which departeth the one nostril from the tother, betokeneth that a man should have discretion ghostly; and can dissever the good from the evil, and the evil from the worse, and the good from the better, ere that he gave any full doom of anything that he heard or saw done or spoken about him. And by a man's brain is ghostly understood imagination; for by nature it dwelleth and worketh in the head.

Here Beginneth The Six And Fiftieth Chapter

Some there be, that although they be not deceived with this error as it is set here, yet for pride and curiosity of natural wit and letterly cunning leave the common doctrine and the counsel of Holy Church. And these with all their favourers lean over much to their own knowing: and for they were never grounded in meek blind feeling and virtuous living, therefore they merit to have a false feeling, feigned and wrought by the ghostly enemy. Insomuch, that at the last they burst up and blaspheme all the saints, sacraments, statutes, and ordinances of Holy Church. Fleshly living men of the world, the which think the statutes of Holy Church over hard to be amended by, they lean to these heretics full soon and full lightly, and stalwartly maintain them, and all because them think that they lead them a softer way than is ordained of Holy Church.

Now truly I trow, that who that will not go the strait way to heaven, that they shall go the soft way to hell. Each man prove by himself, for I trow that all such heretics, and all their favourers, an they might clearly be seen as they shall on the last day, should be seen full soon cumbered in great and horrible sins of the world in their foul flesh, privily, without their open presumption in maintaining of error: so that they be full properly called Antichrist's disciples. For it is said of them, that for all their false fairness openly, yet they should be full foul lechers privily.

Here Beginneth The Seven And Fiftieth Chapter

How these young presumptuous disciples misunderstand this other word "up"; and of the deceits that follow thereon.

No more of these at this time now: but forth of our matter, how that these young presumptuous ghostly disciples misunderstand this other word up.

For if it so be, that they either read, or hear read or spoken, how that men should lift up their hearts unto God, as fast they stare in the stars as if they would be above the moon, and hearken when they shall hear any angel sing out of heaven. These men will sometime with the curiosity of their imagination pierce the planets, and make an hole in the firmament to look in thereat. These men will make a God as them list, and clothe Him full richly in clothes, and set Him in a throne far more curiously than ever was He depicted in this earth. These men will make angels in bodily likeness, and set them about each one with diversee minstrelsy, far more curious than ever was any seen or heard in this life. Some of these men the devil will deceive full wonderfully. For he will send a manner of dew, angels' food they ween it be, as it were coming out of the air, and softly and sweetly falling in their mouths; and therefore they have it in custom to sit gaping as they would catch flies. Now truly all this is but deceit, seem it never so holy; for they have in this time full empty souls of any true devotion. Much vanity and falsehood is in their hearts, caused of their curious working. Insomuch, that ofttimes the devil feigneth quaint sounds in their ears, quaint lights and shining in their eyes, and wonderful smells in their noses: and all is but falsehood. And yet ween they not so, for them think that they have ensample of Saint Martin of this upward looking and working, that saw by revelation God clad in his mantle amongst His angels, and of Saint Stephen that saw our Lord stand in heaven, and of many other; and of Christ, that ascended bodily to heaven, seen of His disciples. And therefore they say that we should have our eyes up thither. I grant well that in our bodily observance we should lift up our eyes and our hands if we be stirred in spirit. But I say that the work of our spirit shall not be direct neither upwards nor downwards, nor on one side nor on other, nor forward nor backward, as it is of a bodily thing. For why, our work should be ghostly not bodily, nor on a bodily manner wrought.

Here Beginneth The Eight And Fiftieth Chapter

That a man shall not take ensample of Saint Martin and of Saint Stephen, for to strain his imagination bodily upwards in the time of his prayer.

For that that they say of Saint Martin and of Saint Stephen, although they saw such things with their bodily eyes, it was shewed but in miracle and in certifying of thing that was ghostly. For wit they right well that Saint Martin's mantle came never on Christ's own body substantially, for no need that He had thereto to keep Him from cold: but by miracle and in likeness for all us that be able to be saved, that be oned to the body of Christ ghostly. And whoso clotheth a poor man and doth any other good deed for God's love bodily or ghostly to any that hath need, sure be they they do it unto Christ ghostly: and they shall be rewarded as substantially therefore as they had done it to Christ's own body. Thus saith Himself in the gospel. And yet thought He it not enough, but if He affirmed it after by miracle; and for this cause He shewed Him unto Saint Martin by revelation. All the revelations that ever saw any man here in bodily likeness in this life, they have ghostly bemeanings. And I trow that if they unto whom they were shewed had been so ghostly, or could have conceived their bemeanings ghostly, that then they had never been shewed bodily. And therefore let us pick off the rough bark, and feed us off the sweet kernel.

But how? Not as these heretics do, the which be well likened to madmen having this custom, that ever when they have drunken of a fair cup, cast it to the wall and break it. Thus should not we do if we will well do. For we should not so feed us of the fruit, that we should despise the tree; nor so drink, that we should break the cup when we have drunken. The tree and the cup I call this visible miracle, and all seemly bodily observances, that is according and not letting the work of the spirit. The fruit and the drink I call the ghostly bemeaning of these visible miracles, and of these seemly bodily observances: as is lifting up of our eyes and our hands unto heaven. If they be done by stirring of the spirit, then be they well done; and else be they hypocrisy, and then be they false. If they be true and contain in them ghostly fruit, why should they then be despised? For men will kiss the cup for wine is therein.

And what thereof, though our Lord when He ascended to heaven bodily took His way upwards into the clouds, seen of His mother and His disciples with their bodily eyes? Should we therefore in our ghostly work ever stare upwards with our bodily eyes, to look after Him if we may see Him sit bodily in heaven, or else stand, as Saint Stephen did? Nay, surely He shewed Him not unto Saint Stephen bodily in heaven, because that He would give us ensample that we should in our ghostly work look bodily up into heaven if we might see Him as Saint Stephen did, either standing, or sitting, or else lying. For howso His body is in heaven—standing, sitting, or lying—wots no man. And it needeth not more to be witted, but that His body is oned with the soul, without departing. The body and the soul, the which is the manhood, is oned with the Godhead without departing also. Of His sitting, His standing, His lying, needeth it not to wit; but that He is there as Him list, and hath Him in body as most seemly is unto Him for to be. For if He shew Him lying, or standing, or sitting, by revelation bodily to any creature in this life, it is done for some ghostly bemeaning: and not for no manner of bodily bearing that He hath in heaven. See by ensample. By standing is understood a readiness of helping. And therefore it is said commonly of one friend to another, when he is in bodily battle: "Bear thee well, fellow, and fight fast, and give not up the battle over lightly; for I shall stand by thee." He meaneth not only bodily standing; for peradventure this battle is on horse and not on foot, and peradventure it is in going and not standing. But he meaneth when he saith that he shall stand by him, that he shall be ready to help him. For this reason it was that our Lord shewed Him bodily in heaven to Saint Stephen, when he was in his martyrdom: and not to give us ensample to look up to heaven. As He had said thus to Saint Stephen in person of all those that suffer persecution for His love: "Lo, Stephen! as verily as I open this bodily firmament, the which is called heaven, and let thee see My bodily standing, trust fast that as verily stand I beside thee ghostly by the might of My Godhead. And I am ready to help thee, and therefore stand thou stiffly in the faith and suffer boldly the fell buffets of those hard stones: for I shall crown thee in bliss for thy meed, and not only thee, but all those that suffer persecution for Me on any manner." And thus mayest thou see that these bodily shewings were done by ghostly bemeanings.

Here Beginneth The Nine And Fiftieth Chapter
That a man shall not take ensample at the bodily ascension of Christ, for to strain his imagination upwards bodily in the time of prayer: and that time, place, and body, these three should be forgotten in all ghostly working.

And if thou say aught touching the ascension of our Lord, for that was done bodily, and for a bodily bemeaning as well as for a ghostly, for both He ascended very God and very man: to this will I answer thee, that He had been dead, and was clad with undeadliness, and so shall we be at the Day of Doom. And then we shall be made so subtle in body and in soul together, that we shall be then as swiftly where us list bodily as we be now in our thought ghostly; whether it be up or down, on one side or on other, behind or before, all I hope shall then be alike good, as clerks say. But now thou mayest not come to heaven bodily, but ghostly. And yet it shall be so ghostly, that it shall not be on bodily manner; neither upwards nor downwards, nor on one side nor on other, behind nor before.

And wit well that all those that set them to be ghostly workers, and specially in the work of this book, that although they read "lift up" or "go in," although all that the work of this book be called a stirring, nevertheless yet them behoveth to have a full busy beholding, that this stirring stretch neither up bodily, nor in bodily, nor yet that it be any such stirring as is from one place to another. And although that it be sometime called a rest, nevertheless yet they shall not think that it is any such rest as is any abiding in a place without removing therefrom. For the perfection of this work is so pure and so ghostly in itself, that an it be well and truly conceived, it shall be seen far removed from any stirring and from any place.

And it should by some reason rather be called a sudden changing, than any stirring of place. For time, place, and body: these three should be forgotten in all ghostly working. And therefore be wary in this work, that thou take none ensample at the bodily ascension of Christ for to strain thine imagination in the time of thy prayer bodily upwards, as thou wouldest climb above the moon. For it should on nowise be so, ghostly. But if thou shouldest ascend into heaven bodily, as Christ did, then thou mightest take ensample at it: but that may none do but God, as Himself witnesseth, saying: "There is no man that may ascend unto heaven but only He that descended from heaven, and became man for the love of man." And if it were possible, as it on nowise may be, yet it should be for abundance of ghostly working only by the might of the spirit, full far from any bodily stressing or straining of our imagination bodily, either up, or in, on one side, or on other. And therefore let be such falsehood: it should not be so.

Here Beginneth The Sixtieth Chapter

That the high and the next way to heaven is run by desires, and not by paces of feet.

But now peradventure thou sayest, that how should it then be? For thee thinkest that thou hast very evidence that heaven is upwards; for Christ ascended the air bodily upwards, and sent the Holy Ghost as He promised coming from above bodily, seen of all His disciples; and this is our belief. And therefore thee thinkest since thou hast thus very evidence, why shalt thou not direct thy mind upward bodily in the time of thy prayer?

And to this will I answer thee so feebly as I can, and say: since it so was, that Christ should ascend bodily and thereafter send the Holy Ghost bodily, then it was more seemly that it was upwards and from above than either downwards and from beneath, behind, or before, on one side or on other. But else than for this seemliness, Him needed never the more to have went upwards than downwards; I mean for nearness of the way. For heaven ghostly is as nigh down as up, and up as down: behind as before, before as behind, on one side as other. Insomuch, that whoso had a true desire for to be at heaven, then that same time he were in heaven ghostly. For the high and the next way thither is run by desires, and not by paces of feet. And therefore saith Saint Paul of himself and many other thus; although our bodies be presently here in earth, nevertheless yet our living is in heaven. He meant their love and their desire, the which is ghostly their life. And surely as verily is a soul there where it loveth, as in the body that Doeth by it and to the which it giveth life. And therefore if we will go to heaven ghostly, it needeth not to strain our spirit neither up nor down, nor on one side nor on other.

Here Beginneth The One And Sixtieth Chapter
That all bodily thing is subject unto ghostly thing, and is ruled thereafter by the course of nature and not contrariwise.

Nevertheless it is needful to lift up our eyes and our hands bodily, as it were unto yon bodily heaven, in the which the elements be fastened. I mean if we be stirred of the work of our spirit, and else not. For all bodily thing is subject unto ghostly thing, and is ruled thereafter, and not contrariwise.

Ensample hereof may be seen by the ascension of our Lord: for when the time appointed was come, that Him liked to wend to His Father bodily in His manhood, the which was never nor never may be absent in His Godhead, then mightily by the virtue of the Spirit God, the manhood with the body followed in onehead of person. The visibility of this was most seemly, and most according, to be upward.

This same subjection of the body to the spirit may be in manner verily conceived in the proof of this ghostly work of this book, by them that work therein. For what time that a soul disposeth him effectually to this work, then as fast suddenly, unwitting himself that worketh, the body that peradventure before ere he began was somewhat bent downwards, on one side or on other for ease of the flesh, by virtue of the spirit shall set it upright: following in manner and in likeness bodily the work of the spirit that is made ghostly. And thus it is most seemly to be.

And for this seemliness it is, that a man—the which is the seemliest creature in body that ever God made—is not made crooked to the earthwards, as be an other beasts, but upright to heavenwards. For why? That it should figure in likeness bodily the work of the soul ghostly; the which falleth to be upright ghostly, and not crooked ghostly. Take heed that I say upright ghostly, and not bodily. For how should a soul, the which in his nature hath no manner thing of bodilyness, be strained upright bodily? Nay, it may not be.

And therefore be wary that thou conceive not bodily that which is meant ghostly, although it be spoken in bodily words, as be these, up or down, in or out, behind or before, on one side or on other. For although that a thing be never so ghostly in itself, nevertheless yet if it shall be spoken of, since it so is that speech is a bodily work wrought with the tongue, the which is an instrument of the body, it behoveth always be spoken in bodily words. But what thereof? Shall it therefore be taken and conceived bodily? Nay, but ghostly, as it be meant.

Here Beginneth The Two And Sixtieth Chapter
How a man may wit when his ghostly work is beneath him or without him, and when it is even with him or within him, and when it is above him and under his God.

And for this, that thou shalt be able better to wit how they shall be conceived ghostly, these words that be spoken bodily, therefore I think to declare to thee the ghostly bemeaning of some words that fall to ghostly working. So that thou mayest wit clearly without error when thy ghostly work is beneath thee and without thee, and when it is within thee and even with thee, and when it is above thee and under thy God.

All manner of bodily thing is without thy soul and beneath it in nature, yea! the sun and the moon and all the stars, although they be above thy body, nevertheless yet they be beneath thy soul.

All angels and all souls, although they be confirmed and adorned with grace and with virtues, for the which they be above thee in cleanness, nevertheless, yet they be but even with thee in nature.

Within in thyself in nature be the powers of thy soul: the which be these three principal, Memory, Reason, and Will; and secondary, Imagination and Sensuality.

Above thyself in nature is no manner of thing but only God.

Evermore where thou findest written thyself in ghostliness, then it is understood thy soul, and not thy body. And then all after that thing is on the which the powers of thy soul work, thereafter shall the worthiness and the condition of thy work be deemed; whether it be beneath thee, within thee, or above thee.

Here Beginneth The Three And Sixtieth Chapter
Of the powers of a soul in general, and how Memory in special is a principal power, comprehending in it all the other powers and all those things in the which they work.

Memory is such a power in itself, that properly to speak and in manner, it worketh not itself. But Reason and Will, they be two working powers, and so is Imagination and Sensuality also. And all these four powers and their works, Memory containeth and comprehendeth in itself. And otherwise it is not said that the Memory worketh, unless such a comprehension be a work.

And therefore it is that I call the powers of a soul, some principal, and some secondary. Not because a soul is divisible, for that may not be: but because all those things in the which they work be divisible, and some principal, as be all ghostly things, and some secondary, as be all bodily things. The two principal working powers, Reason and Will, work purely in themselves in all ghostly things, without help of the other two secondary powers. Imagination and Sensuality work beastly in all bodily things, whether they be present or absent, in the body and with the bodily wits. But by them, without help of Reason and of Will, may a soul never come to for to know the virtue and the conditions of bodily creatures, nor the cause of their beings and their makings.

And for this cause is Reason and Will called principal powers, for they work in pure spirit without any manner of bodilyness: and Imagination and Sensuality secondary, for they work in the body with bodily instruments, the which be our five wits. Memory is called a principal power, for it containeth in it ghostly not only all the other powers, but thereto all those things in the which they work. See by the proof.

Here Beginneth The Four And Sixtieth Chapter
Of the other two principal powers Reason and Will; and of the work of them before sin and after.

Reason is a power through the which we depart the evil from the good, the evil from the worse, the good from the better, the worse from the worst, the better from the best. Before ere man sinned, might Reason have done all this by nature. But now it is so blinded with the original sin, that it may not con work this work, unless it be illumined by grace. And both the self Reason, and the thing that it worketh in, be comprehended and contained in the Memory.

Will is a power through the which we choose good, after that it be determined with Reason; and through the which we love good, we desire good, and rest us with full liking and consent endlessly in God. Before ere man sinned, might not Will be deceived in his choosing, in his loving, nor in none of his works. For why, it had then by nature to savour each thing as it was; but now it may not do so, unless it be anointed with grace. For ofttimes because of infection of the original sin, it savoureth a thing for good that is full evil, and that hath but the likeness of good. And both the Will and the thing that is willed, the Memory containeth and comprehendeth in it.

Here Beginneth The Five And Sixtieth Chapter
Of the first secondary power, Imagination by name; and of the works and the obedience of it unto Reason, before Sin and after.

Imagination is a power through the which we portray all images of absent and present things, and both it and the thing that it worketh in be contained in the Memory. Before ere man sinned, was Imagination so obedient unto the Reason, to the which it is as it were servant, that it ministered never to it any unordained image of any bodily creature, or any fantasy of any ghostly creature: but now it is not so. For unless it be refrained by the light of grace in the Reason, else it will never cease, sleeping or waking, for to portray diversee unordained images of bodily creatures; or else some fantasy, the which is nought else but a bodily conceit of a ghostly thing, or else a ghostly conceit of a bodily thing. And this is evermore feigned and false, and next unto error.

This inobedience of the Imagination may clearly be conceived in them that be newlings turned from the world unto devotion, in the time of their prayer. For before the time be, that the Imagination be in great part refrained by the light of grace in the Reason, as it is in continual meditation of ghostly things—as be their own wretchedness, the passion and the kindness of our Lord God, with many such other—they may in nowise put away the wonderful and the diversee thoughts, fantasies, and images, the which be ministered and printed in their mind by the light of the curiosity of Imagination. And all this inobedience is the pain of the original sin.

Here Beginneth The Six And Sixtieth Chapter

Sensuality is a power of our soul, recking and reigning in the bodily wits, through the which we have bodily knowing and feeling of all bodily creatures, whether they be pleasing or unpleasing. And it hath two parts: one through the which it beholdeth to the needfulness of our body, another through the which it serveth to the lusts of the bodily wits. For this same power is it, that grumbleth when the body lacketh the needful things unto it, and that in the taking of the need stirreth us to take more than needeth in feeding and furthering of our lusts: that grumbleth in lacking of pleasing creatures, and lustily is delighted in their presence: that grumbleth in presence of misliking creatures, and is lustily pleased in their absence. Both this power and the thing that it worketh in be contained in the Memory.

Before ere man sinned was the Sensuality so obedient unto the Will, unto the which it is as it were servant, that it ministered never unto it any unordained liking or grumbling in any bodily creature, or any ghostly feigning of liking or misliking made by any ghostly enemy in the bodily wits. But now it is not so: for unless it be ruled by grace in the Will, for to suffer meekly and in measure the pain of the original sin, the which it feeleth in absence of needful comforts and in presence of speedful discomforts, and thereto also for to restrain it from lust in presence of needful comforts, and from lusty plesaunce in the absence of speedful discomforts: else will it wretchedly and wantonly welter, as a swine in the mire, in the wealths of this world and the foul flesh so much that all our living shall be more beastly and fleshly, than either manly or ghostly.

Here Beginneth The Seven And Sixtieth Chapter

That whoso knoweth not the powers of a soul and the manner of her working, may lightly be deceived in understanding of ghostly words and of ghostly working; and how a soul is made a God in grace.

Lo, ghostly friend! to such wretchedness as thou here mayest see be we fallen for sin: and therefore what wonder is it, though we be blindly and lightly deceived in understanding of ghostly words and of ghostly working, and specially those the which know not yet the powers of their souls and the manners of their working?

For ever when the Memory is occupied with any bodily thing be it taken to never so good an end, yet thou art beneath thyself in this working, and without any soul. And ever when thou feelest thy Memory occupied with the subtle conditions of the powers of thy soul and their workings in ghostly things, as be vices or virtues, of thyself, or of any creature that is ghostly and even with thee in nature, to that end that thou mightest by this work learn to know thyself in furthering of perfection: then thou art within thyself, and even with thyself. But ever when thou feelest thy Memory occupied with no manner of thing that is bodily or ghostly, but only with the self substance of God, as it is and may be, in the proof of the work of this book: then thou art above thyself and beneath thy God.

Above thyself thou art: for why, thou attainest to come thither by grace, whither thou mayest not come by nature. That is to say, to be oned to God, in spirit, and in love, and in accordance of will. Beneath thy God thou art: for why, although it may be said in manner, that in this time God and thou be not two but one in spirit—insomuch that thou or another, for such onehead that feeleth the perfection of this work, may soothfastly by witness of Scripture be called a God—nevertheless yet thou art beneath Him. For why, He is God by nature without beginning; and thou, that sometime wert nought in substance, and thereto after when thou wert by His might and His love made ought, wilfully with sin madest thyself worse than nought, only by His mercy without thy desert are made a God in grace, oned with Him in spirit without departing, both here and in bliss of heaven without any end. So that, although thou be all one with Him in grace, yet thou art full far beneath Him in nature.

Lo, ghostly friend! hereby mayest thou see somewhat in part, that whoso knoweth not the powers of their own soul, and the manner of their working, may full lightly be deceived in understanding of words that be written to ghostly intent. And therefore mayest thou see somewhat the cause why that I durst not plainly bid thee shew thy desire unto God, but I bade thee childishly do that in thee is to hide it and cover it. And this I do for fear lest thou shouldest conceive bodily that that is meant ghostly.

Here Beginneth The Eight And Sixtieth Chapter
That nowhere bodily, is everywhere ghostly; and how our outer man calleth the word of this book nought.

And on the same manner, where another man would bid thee gather thy powers and thy wits wholly within thyself, and worship God there—although he say full well and full truly, yea! and no man trulier, an he be well conceived—yet for fear of deceit and bodily conceiving of his words, me list not bid thee do so. But thus will I bid thee. Look on nowise that thou be within thyself. And shortly, without thyself will I not that thou be, nor yet above, nor behind, nor on one side, nor on other.

"Where then," sayest thou, "shall I be? Nowhere, by thy tale!" Now truly thou sayest well; for there would I have thee. For why, nowhere bodily, is everywhere ghostly. Look then busily that thy ghostly work be nowhere bodily; and then wheresoever that that thing is, on the which thou wilfully workest in thy mind in substance, surely there art thou in spirit, as verily as thy body is in that place that thou art bodily. And although thy bodily wits can find there nothing to feed them on, for them think it nought that thou dost, yea! do on then this nought, and do it for God's love. And let not therefore, but travail busily in that nought with a waking desire to will to have God that no man may know. For I tell thee truly, that I had rather be so nowhere bodily, wrestling with that blind nought, than to be so great a lord that I might when I would be everywhere bodily, merrily playing with all this ought as a lord with his own.

Let be this everywhere and this ought, in comparison or this nowhere and this nought. Reck thee never if thy wits cannot reason of this nought; for surely, I love it much the better. It is so worthy a thing in itself, that they cannot reason thereupon. This nought may better be felt than seen: for it is full blind and full dark to them that have but little while looked thereupon. Nevertheless, if I shall soothlier say, a soul is more blinded in feeling of it for abundance of ghostly light, than for any darkness or wanting of bodily light. What is he that calleth it nought? Surely it is our outer man, and not our inner. Our inner man calleth it All; for of it he is well learned to know the reason of all things bodily or ghostly, without any special beholding to any one thing by itself.

Here Beginneth The Nine And Sixtieth Chapter
How that a man's affection is marvelously changed in ghostly feeling of this nought, when it is nowhere wrought.

Wonderfully is a man's affection varied in ghostly feeling of this nought when it is nowhere wrought. For at the first time that a soul looketh thereupon, it shall find all the special deeds of sin that ever he did since he was born, bodily or ghostly, privily or darkly painted thereupon. And howsoever that he turneth it about, evermore they will appear before his eyes; until the time be, that with much hard travail, many sore sighings, and many bitter weepings, he have in great part washed them away. Sometime in this travail him think that it is to look thereupon as on hell; for him think that he despaireth to win to perfection of ghostly rest out of that pairs Thus far inwards come many, but for greatness of pain that they feel and for lacking of comfort, they go back in beholding of bodily things: seeking fleshly comforts without, for lacking of ghostly they have not yet deserved, as they should if they had abided.

For he that abideth feeleth sometime some comfort, and hath some hope of perfection; for he feeleth and seeth that many of his fordone special sins be in great part by help of grace rubbed away. Nevertheless yet ever among he feeleth pain, but he thinketh that it shall have an end, for it waxeth ever less and less. And therefore he calleth it nought else but purgatory. Sometime he can find no special sin written thereupon, but yet him think that sin is a lump, he wot never what, none other thing than himself; and then it may be called the base and the pain of the original sin. Sometime him think that it is paradise or heaven, for diversee wonderful sweetness and comforts, joys and blessed virtues that he findeth therein. Sometime him think it God, for peace and rest that he findeth therein.

Yea! think what he think will; for evermore he shall find it a cloud of unknowing, that is betwixt him and his God.

Here Beginneth The Seventieth Chapter
That right as by the defailing of our bodily wits we begin more readily to come to knowing of ghostly things, so by the defailing of our ghostly wits we begin most readily to come to the knowledge of God, such as is possible by grace to be had here.

And therefore travail fast in this nought, and this nowhere, and leave thine outward bodily wits and all that they work in: for I tell thee truly, that this work may not be conceived by them.

For by thine eyes thou mayest not conceive of anything, unless it be by the length and the breadth, the smallness and the greatness, the roundness and the squareness, the farness and the nearness, and the colour of it. And by thine ears, nought but noise or some manner of sound. By thine nose, nought but either stench or savour. And by thy taste, nought but either sour or sweet, salt or fresh, bitter or liking. And by thy feeling, nought but either hot or cold, hard or tender, soft or sharp. And truly, neither hath God nor ghostly things none of these qualities nor quantities. And therefore leave thine outward wits, and work not with them, neither within nor without: for all those that set them to be ghostly workers within, and ween that they should either hear, smell, or see, taste or feel, ghostly things, either within them or without, surely they be deceived, and work wrong against the course of nature.

For by nature they be ordained, that with them men should have knowing of all outward bodily things, and on nowise by them come to the knowing of ghostly things. I mean by their works. By their failings we may, as thus: when we read or hear speak of some certain things, and thereto conceive that our outward wits cannot tell us by no quality what those things be, then we may be verily certified that those things be ghostly things, and not bodily things.

On this same manner ghostly it fareth within our ghostly wits, when we travail about the knowing of God Himself. For have a man never so much ghostly understanding in knowing of all made ghostly things, yet may he never by the work of his understanding come to the knowing of an unmade ghostly thing: the which is nought but God. But by the failing it may: for why, that thing that it faileth in is nothing else but only God. And therefore it was that Saint Denis said, the most goodly knowing of God is that, the which is known by unknowing. And truly, whoso will look in Denis' books, he shall find that his words will clearly affirm all that I have said or shall say, from the beginning of this treatise to the end. On otherwise than thus, list me not cite him, nor none other doctor, for me at this time. For sometime, men thought it meekness to say nought of their own heads, unless they affirmed it by Scripture and doctors' words: and now it is turned into curiosity, and shewing of cunning. To thee it needeth not, and therefore I do it not. For whoso hath ears, let him hear, and whoso is stirred for to trow, let him trow: for else, shall they not.

Here Beginneth The One And Seventieth Chapter
That some may not come to feel the perfection of this work but in time of ravishing, and some may have it when they will, in the common state of man's soul.

Some think this matter so hard and so fearful, that they say it may not be come to without much strong travail coming before, nor conceived but seldom, and that but in the time of ravishing. And to these men will I answer as feebly as I can, and say, that it is all at the ordinance and the disposition of God, after their ableness in soul that this grace of contemplation and of ghostly working is given to.

For some there be that without much and long ghostly exercise may not come thereto, and yet it shall be but full seldom, and in special calling of our Lord that they shall feel the perfection of this work: the which calling is called ravishing. And some there be that be so subtle in grace and in spirit, and so homely with God in this grace of contemplation, that they may have it when they will in the common state of man's soul: as it is in sitting, going, standing, or kneeling. And yet in this time they have full deliberation of all their wits bodily or ghostly, and may use them if they desire: not without some letting (but without great letting). Ensample of the first we have by Moses, and of this other by Aaron the priest of the Temple: for why, this grace of contemplation is figured by the Ark of the Testament in the old law, and the workers in this grace be figured by them that most meddled them about this Ark, as the story will witness. And well is this grace and this work likened unto that Ark. For right as in that Ark were contained all the jewels and the relics of the Temple, right so in this little love put upon this cloud be contained all the virtues of man's soul, the which is the ghostly Temple of God.

Moses ere he might come to see this Ark and for to wit how it should be made, with great long travail he clomb up to the top of the mountain, and dwelled there, and wrought in a cloud six days: abiding unto the seventh day that our Lord would vouchsafe for to shew unto him the manner of this Ark-making. By Moses's long travail and his late shewing, be understood those that may not come to the perfection of this ghostly work without long travail coming before: and yet but full seldom, and when God will vouchsafe to shew it.

But that that Moses might not come to see but seldom, and that not without great long travail, Aaron had in his power because of his office, for to see it in the Temple within the Veil as oft as him liked for to enter. And by this Aaron is understood all those the which I spake of above, the which by their ghostly cunning, by help of grace, may assign unto them the perfection of this work as them liketh.

Here Beginneth The Two And Seventieth Chapter
That a worker in this work should not deem nor think of another worker as he feeleth in himself.

Lo! hereby mayest thou see that he that may not come for to see and feel the perfection of this work but by long travail, and yet is it but seldom, may lightly be deceived if he speak, think, and deem other men as he feeleth in himself, that they may not come to it but seldom, and that not without great travail. And on the same manner may he be deceived that may have it when he will, if he deem all other thereafter; saying that they may have it when they will. Let be this: nay, surely he may not think thus. For peradventure, when it liketh unto God, that those that may not at the first time have it but seldom, and that not without great travail, sithen after they shall have it when they will, as oft as them liketh. Ensample of this we have of Moses, that first but seldom, and not without great travail, in the mount might not see the manner of the Ark: and sithen after, as oft as by him liked, saw it in the Veil.

Here Beginneth The Three And Seventieth Chapter
How that after the likeness of Moses, of Bezaleel, and of Aaron meddling them about the Ark of the Testament, we profit on three manners in this grace of contemplation, for this grace is figured in that Ark.

Three men there were that most principally meddled them with this Ark of the Old Testament: Moses, Bezaleel, Aaron. Moses learned in the mount of our Lord how it should be made. Bezaleel wrought it and made it in the Veil after the ensample that was shewed in the mountain. And Aaron had it in keeping in the Temple, to feel it and see it as oft as him liked.

At the likeness of these three, we profit on three manners in this grace of contemplation. Sometime we profit only by grace, and then we be likened unto Moses, that for all the climbing and the travail that he had into the mount might not come to see it but seldom: and yet was that sight only by the shewing of our Lord when Him liked to shew it, and not for any desert of his travail. Sometime we profit in this grace by our own ghostly cunning, helped with grace, and then be we likened to Bezaleel, the which might not see the Ark ere the time that he had made it by his own travail, helped with the ensample that was shewed unto Moses in the mount. And sometime we profit in this grace by other men's teaching, and then be we likened to Aaron, the which had it in keeping and in custom to see and feel the Ark when him pleased, that Bezaleel had wrought and made ready before to his hands.

Lo! ghostly friend, in this work, though it be childishly and lewdly spoken, I bear, though I be a wretch unworthy to teach any creature, the office of Bezaleel: making and declaring in manner to thine hands the manner of this ghostly Ark. But far better and more worthily than I do, thou mayest work if thou wilt be Aaron: that is to say, continually working therein for thee and for me. Do then so I pray thee, for the love of God Almighty. And since we be both called of God to work in this work, I beseech thee for God's love fulfil in thy part what lacketh of mine.

Here Beginneth The Four And Seventieth Chapter

How that the matter of this book is never more read or spoken, nor heard read or spoken, of a soul disposed thereto without feeling of a very accordance to the effect of the same work: and of rehearsing of the same charge that is written in the prologue.

And if thee think that this manner of working be not according to thy disposition in body and in soul, thou mayest leave it and take another, safely with good ghostly counsel without blame. And then I beseech thee that thou wilt have me excused, for truly I would have profited unto thee in this writing at my simple cunning; and that was mine intent. And therefore read over twice or thrice; and ever the ofter the better, and the more thou shalt conceive thereof. Insomuch, peradventure, that some sentence that was full hard to thee at the first or the second reading, soon after thou shalt think it easy.

Yea! and it seemeth impossible to mine understanding, that any soul that is disposed to this work should read it or speak it, or else hear it read or spoken, but if that same soul should feel for that time a very accordance to the effect of this work. And then if thee think it doth thee good, thank God heartily, and for God's love pray for me.

Do then so. And I pray thee for God's love that thou let none see this book, unless it be such one that thee think is like to the book; after that thou findest written in the book before, where it telleth what men and when they should work in this work. And if thou shalt let any such men see it, then I pray thee that thou bid them take them time to look it all over. For peradventure there is some matter therein in the beginning, or in the midst, the which is hanging and not fully declared there as it standeth. But if it be not there, it is soon after, or else in the end. And thus if a man saw one part and not another, peradventure he should lightly be led into error: and therefore I pray thee to work as I say thee. And if thee think that there be any matter therein that thou wouldest have more opened than it is, let me wit which it is, and thy conceit thereupon; and at my simple cunning it shall be amended if I can.

Fleshly janglers, flatterers and blamers, ronkers and ronners, and all manner of pinchers, cared I never that they saw this book: for mine intent was never to write such thing to them. And therefore I would not that they heard it, neither they nor none of these curious lettered nor unlearned men: yea! although they be full good men in active living, for it accordeth not to them.

Here Beginneth The Five And Seventieth Chapter
Of some certain tokens by the which a man may prove whether he be called of God to work in this work

All those that read or hear the matter of this book be read or spoken, and in this reading or hearing think it a good and liking thing, be never the rather called of God to work in this work, only for this liking stirring that they feel in the time of this reading. For peradventure this stirring cometh more of a natural curiosity of wit, than of any calling of grace.

But, if they will prove whence this stirring cometh, they may prove thus, if them liketh. First let them look if they have done that in them is before, abling them thereto in cleansing of their conscience at the doom of Holy Church, their counsel according. If it be thus, it is well inasmuch: but if they will wit more near, let them look if it be evermore pressing in their remembrance more customably than is any other of ghostly exercise. And if them think that there is no manner of thing that they do, bodily or ghostly, that is sufficiently done with witness of their conscience, unless this privy little love pressed be in manner ghostly the chief of all their work: and if they thus feel, then it is a token that they be called of God to this work, and surely else not.

I say not that it shall ever last and dwell in all their minds continually, that be called to work in this work. Nay, so is it not. For from a young ghostly prentice in this work, the actual feeling thereof is ofttimes withdrawn for diverse reasons. Sometime, for he shall not take over presumptuously thereupon, and ween that it be in great part in his own power to have it when him list, and as him list. And such a weening were pride. And evermore when the feeling of grace is withdrawn, pride is the cause: not ever pride that is, but pride that should be, were it not that this feeling of grace were withdrawn. And thus ween ofttimes some young fools, that God is their enemy; when He is their full friend.

Sometimes it is withdrawn for their carelessness; and when it is thus, they feel soon after a full bitter pain that beateth them full sore. Sometimes our Lord will delay it by an artful device, for He will by such a delaying make it grow, and be had more in dainty when it is new found and felt again that long had been lost. And this is one of the readiest and sovereignest tokens that a soul may have to wit by, whether he be called or not to work in this work, if he feel after such a delaying and a long lacking of this work, that when it cometh suddenly as it doth, unpurchased with any means, that he hath then a greater fervour of desire and greater love longing to work in this work, than ever he had any before. Insomuch, that ofttimes I trow, he hath more joy of the finding thereof than ever he had sorrow of the losing.

And if it be thus, surely it is a very token without error, that he is called of God to work in this work, whatsoever that he be or hath been.

For not what thou art, nor what thou hast been, beholdeth God with His merciful eyes; but that thou wouldest be. And Saint Gregory to witness, that all holy desires grow by delays: and if they wane by delays, then were they never holy desires. For he that feeleth ever less joy and less, in new findings and sudden presentations of his old purposed desires, although they may be called natural desires to the good, nevertheless holy desires were they never. Of this holy desire speaketh Saint Austin and saith, that all the life of a good Christian man is nought else but holy desire.

Farewell, ghostly friend, in God's blessing and mine! And I beseech Almighty God, that true peace, holy counsel, and ghostly comfort in God with abundance of grace, evermore be with thee and all God's lovers in earth. Amen.

Here endeth the Cloud of Unknowing.

www.ingramcontent.com/pod-product-compliance
Lightning Source LLC
Chambersburg PA
CBHW071302110426
42743CB00042B/1139